Worship as Meaning

How, in this Christian age of belief, can we draw sense from the ritual acts of Christians assembled in worship? Convinced that people shape their meanings from the meanings available to them, Graham Hughes inquires into liturgical constructions of meaning within the larger cultural context of late twentieth-century meaning theory. Major theories of meaning are examined in terms of their contribution or hindrance to this meaning-making: analytic philosophy, phenomenology, structuralism and deconstruction. Drawing particularly upon the work of Charles Peirce, Hughes turns to semiotic theory to analyse the construction, transmission and apprehension of meaning within an actual worship service. Finally the book analyses the ways in which various worshipping styles of western Christianity undertake this meaning-making. Taking account of late modern values and precepts, this groundbreaking book will appeal to teachers and students of theology, to clergy, and to thoughtful lay Christians.

GRAHAM HUGHES is Lecturer Emeritus in Liturgical Studies at United Theological College, Sydney and Academic Associate at the School of Theology, Charles Sturt University. He is the author of *The Place of Prayer* (1998), *Beyond our Dreaming* (1996), *Leading in Prayer* (1992) and *Hebrews and Hermeneutics* (1981).

Cambridge Studies in Christian Doctrine

Edited by
Professor COLIN GUNTON, *King's College London*
Professor DANIEL W. HARDY, *University of Cambridge*

Cambridge Studies in Christian Doctrine is an important series which aims to engage critically with the traditional doctrines of Christianity, and at the same time to locate and make sense of them within a secular context. Without losing sight of the authority of scripture and the traditions of the church, the books in this series subject pertinent dogmas and credal statements to careful scrutiny, analysing them in light of the insights of both church and society, and thereby practising theology in the fullest sense of the word.

Titles published in the series

Titles forthcoming in the series

Worship as Meaning
A Liturgical Theology for Late Modernity

GRAHAM HUGHES

CAMBRIDGE
UNIVERSITY PRESS

PUBLISHED BY THE PRESS SYNDICATE OF THE UNIVERSITY OF CAMBRIDGE
The Pitt Building, Trumpington Street, Cambridge CB2 1RP, United Kingdom

CAMBRIDGE UNIVERSITY PRESS
The Edinburgh Building, Cambridge, CB2 2RU , UK
40 West 20th Street, New York, NY 10011–4211, USA
477 Williamstown Road, Port Melbourne, VIC 3207, Australia
Ruiz de Alarcón 13, 28014 Madrid, Spain
Dock House, The Waterfront, Cape Town 8001, South Africa

http://www.cambridge.org

First published 2003

Printed in the United Kingdom at the University Press, Cambridge

Typefaces Lexicon No. 2 9/13 pt. and Lexicon No. 1   *System* LᴬTEX 2ε   [TB]

A catalogue record for this book is available from the British Library

Library of Congress Cataloguing in Publication data

Hughes, Graham, 1937–
Worship as Meaning: a Liturgical Theology for Late Modernity / Graham Hughes.
    p.   cm. – (Cambridge Studies in Christian Doctrine; 10)
Includes bibliographical references and index.
ISBN 0 521 82851 1 (hardback) – ISBN 0 521 53557 3 (paperback)
1. Liturgics.   2. Meaning (Philosophy) – Religious aspects – Christianity.   I. Title.
II. Series.
BV178.H 84 2003
264′.001 – dc21   2003040950

ISBN 0 521 82851 1 hardback
ISBN 0 521 53557 3 paperback

For Donika,
who was there at the beginning as at the end.

Contents

Introduction

Like many books, this one began in a classroom. The project began (though I did not know it then) in my classes in liturgical gesture now many years ago. Each week students would be required to demonstrate to the class their ideas about movement, proxemics, posture and gesture for some specified point in the liturgy. Because in Protestantism we have no 'race-memory' of these kinds of things – even less a *General Instruction* – the suggested offerings frequently seemed to me idiosyncratic and, more pertinently, obscure as to their intended signification. But on those occasions on which I ventured such an opinion, the dialogue almost inevitably drove itself into the corral: 'Well, that's your opinion and I disagree.' The problem seemed to be that, whereas in spoken (or written) language there is a relatively high degree of precision about the received meanings of linguistic units ('You mean "perspicacious", not "perspicuous"'), our other forms of human signification are much less 'rule-governed' – almost to the point, in some cases, of there seeming to be a lack of *any* clear syntax or semantics. The task at this earliest stage, then, was to give an account of meanings for those significations in worship other than the linguistic ones, which account might allow a higher degree of conversation about the nature of the signs and their signification.

Rather obviously (though this is said more quickly in retrospect than at the time) the direction in which to look was, or is, the still emergent discipline of semiotics. And indeed, as the middle part of this book shows, that proved to be a rich and productive seam.

Being now launched into the question of meaning in worship, however, I began to see (no wondrous discovery, either, though somehow these things take longer than they might) that meanings are not made in a vacuum. In other words, I began to see that the entire constellation of

[1]

significations called a service of worship could only be meaningful for worshippers, individually and collectively, to the extent that these meanings were capable of being joined to, or set in relationship with, what, since Edmund Husserl, we have learned to call the worshippers' 'lifeworld'.

This consideration thus led to a prolonged meditation on the condition of 'modernity' which, I take it, Christians from western, industrialized societies inhabit as fish proverbially live in the sea. There are various ways of characterizing modernity, some of which I explore in greater detail in the body of the book. Max Weber, however, has given us the term 'the disenchantment of the world' as a means of encompassing these: western, technological society is a way of being in the world which has detached that world from any enveloping skein of religious reference.[1] 'Disenchantment' means two things: first, that the world is no longer seen religiously; and, second, that the fundamental mechanisms of society – legislature, judiciary, economy, medicine and education – once held within that encompassing web of meaning have, in their detachment from it, become discreet 'disciplines', each functioning in its own right and without perceived obligation to a larger social enterprise.[2] Of course, classical modernity is now widely assumed to have given way to postmodernity. While much did clearly change following the crucial decade of the 1960s, much remains unchanged too, including religious disenchantment.

It is hardly a secret that at the beginning of its twenty-first century institutional Christianity finds it increasingly difficult to portray itself as a viable source of meaning for people in such societies. It is hard not to suppose that 'the disenchantment of the world', now far advanced, is a major contributing factor in this. Of the multiple options available to people,[3] theism is less and less seen as efficacious. Admittedly, the case is mixed. There are people, still, who find in the mythic and ritual forms of

1. See, particularly, e.g., Weber's essays, 'Science as a Vocation' and 'Religious Rejections of the World and their Directions' in (H. H. Gerth and C. W. Mills, eds.) *From Max Weber: essays in sociology* (London: Routledge and Kegan Paul, 1974), 139, 155, 350–1, 357; or again, Max Weber, *Economy and Society: an outline of interpretive sociology* (Berkeley: University of California Press, 1978), 506. Charles Taylor, *Sources of the Self: the making of the modern identity* (Cambridge University Press, 1989), 500, says that Weber appropriated the term 'disenchantment' from Schiller.

2. See Jürgen Habermas, *The Philosophical Discourse of Modernity* (Cambridge, MA: The MIT Press, 1995), 83; or Habermas, 'Modernity: an unfinished project' in (Maurizio Passerin D'Entrèves and Seyla Benhabib, eds.) *Habermas and the Unfinished Project of Modernity* (Cambridge: Polity Press, 1996), 45; see also Daniel W. Hardy, *God's Ways with the World: thinking and practicing Christian faith* (Edinburgh: T. & T. Clark, 1996), esp. 133, 135, 256–7.

3. 'Availability' is a more or less technical term coined by Charles Taylor on which I draw in the body of this work. Taylor uses it to describe the force that an idea or practice has for the members of a given society, as a way of enabling people to 'make sense' of themselves and their world; Charles Taylor, *Sources*, particularly 313–14. See further, below, page 43.

Christianity a frame of reference which is both meaningful and meaning-giving. When the Pope travels to another country, for example, tens or hundreds of thousands of people can still be drawn together. Protestant fundamentalism seems also able to offer a religious form of meaning for a significant minority. Around these convinced believers, however, there are a great many others who attend church from a sense of obligation or habit, but who come away wondering what it all meant or was supposed to mean. There are others who, in moments of bereavement or catastrophe, dimly glimpse the point of religious reference, but find the point more elusive in ordinary circumstances. And both these groups (who are perhaps not exclusive of each other) are surrounded by an even larger populace in all the industrialized countries who may once have attended worship, or were taken by their parents when they were young, but for whom it is now, as they themselves will say, 'meaningless'.[4]

Academic theology, in its various disciplines, has scarcely been able to isolate itself from the now near-global dimensions of disenchantment. Systematic theologians especially – charged as they are with formulating faith in contemporary idioms – have, by and large, been concerned with questions of theistic meaning in the age of modernity for at least a century and a half. Biblical scholarship, in its dedication to the hermeneutical questions entailed in finding for our time meaning in ancient texts, has similarly grasped the nettle of modernity, and, more recently, post-modernity. Liturgical scholars have tended to be more historicist in their approach,[5] though, as I am reminded in conversation, 'most liturgists, except those hopelessly lost in a kind of romantic dream, are engaged in the project of persuading and inviting to participation.'[6] Engagement with contemporary intellectual method in liturgical studies has mostly taken the form of ritual studies and the study of symbols.[7] In the most recent period a new development seems to have emerged, bringing to the study of worship sociological, hermeneutical, philosophical and ethnographical points of view.[8] There is also a small but vibrant literature on the semiotics

---

4. See Langdon Gilkey, *Naming the Whirlwind: the renewal of God-Language* (Indianapolis: The Bobbs-Merrill Company, 1969), 13–20, 260–6, on *meaning* as more fundamental than questions of *validity* (truth or falsity); then see e.g., *ibid.*, 417, 420, 425, on the relationship of meaning and validity.

5. So, for example, Hardy, *God's Ways with the World*, 5.

6. Gordon Lathrop in a private communication.   7. See below, ch. 4, nn. 5 and 83.

8. I am thinking, for example, of Joyce Ann Zimmerman, *Liturgy as Language of Faith: a liturgical methodology in the mode of Paul Ricoeur's textual hermeneutics* (Lanham: University Press of America, 1988); Kieran Flanagan, *Sociology and Liturgy: re-presentations of the holy* (Houndmills, Basingstoke: The Macmillan Press, 1991); Bridget Nichols, *Liturgical Hermeneutics: interpreting liturgical rites in performance* (Frankfurt: Peter Lang, 1994); Catherine Pickstock, *After Writing: on*

of worship, on which I comment in my own text, though in less detail than it deserves.[9] I have not, however, found another work which attempts to relate worship to the theoretical discussion of meaning through the twentieth century, which is what I felt I needed to do.

Soon after beginning, I saw that to have chosen 'meaning' as the field of inquiry was to take the largest, most cumbersome, least sharply honed instrument available. There are many other words in English which might have offered greater precision. 'Denotation' and 'connotation', for example, is a pair which appealed to some theorists earlier in the twentieth century. 'Sense' and 'reference' is an even older pair. 'Signification' is a conceptualization on which I have heavily depended, along with its more or less adjacent neighbour, 'significance'. 'Intention' and 'intentionality' also offer themselves. 'Meaning', by contrast, is a kind of catch-all grab-bag word that we throw around all of these. 'Meaning' can range from the entries in dictionaries to 'the meaning of life'. Not only is the subject matter elusive; it is well-nigh inexhaustible. There have been times in my study for the book in which it has seemed to me that the human quest for meaning is not much different from, and not much less slight in scale than, the quest for God. I am indeed inclined to think the two quests or questions are not so far removed from one another.

Yet it does seem to me that this *is* the word, in all its breadth and complexity, which we want – for the reason that the subject matter in which we are interested, worship, itself contains this great range of senses and references.[10] Sometimes the question a worshipper asks is with respect to our most sharply defined sort of meaning: that of the preacher's words or concerning the arcane language of the prayers. On other occasions it will be more equivocal: why does the priest move to this place in the sanctuary for this part of the liturgy? And on yet other occasions the question of meaning will be as large as the worshipper's life – what would it mean for her to try to live in the way suggested. At some points what is at stake perhaps has more to do with what we might call 'disposition' or 'ambience' or 'feeling' – for example the effects of the architecture,

the liturgical consummation of philosophy (Oxford: Blackwells Publishers Ltd., 1998); and Martin D. Stringer, *On the Perception of Worship: the ethnography of worship in four Christian congregations in Manchester* (Birmingham University Press, 1999).

9. See below, pp. 129–34.

10. Taylor, *Sources*, 18, similarly remarks on the useful complexity of 'meaning': 'Finding a sense to life depends on framing meaningful expressions which are adequate. There is thus something particularly appropriate to our condition in the polysemy of the word "meaning": lives can have or lack it when they have or lack a point; while it also applies to language and other forms of expression . . . The problem of the meaning of life is therefore on our agenda.'

or the way in which the space is lit, or the style and arrangement of the furnishings. The music will always have been of central importance. And hardly less significant will have been the style, the manner, the bearing of the leader(s) – whether this communicated distance, officialdom, ritual propriety or pastoral warmth; or perhaps, at an opposite extreme, informality and conviviality. In the end, each of these things will have contributed directly to the meaning – and the 'meaningfulness' or otherwise – of the event. Enveloping all of these – that is, on its largest and most daunting scale – is the question whether 'God', as represented in the Judaeo–Christian tradition, can 'mean' anything for people living in our thoroughly secularized age. All these angles are held within the question of 'the meaning of worship'.

In my own search for illumination I began with the theories of meaning which were (just) still being explored in Anglo-American analytic philosophy. This was to some extent because the term 'theory of meaning' had been especially associated with this style of philosophy. It was quickly apparent to me that any theory of meaning for worship would have to be funded differently. I mentioned just now, for example, the great range in *kinds* of meaning transacted in a worship service. Much, perhaps the preponderance, of such meaning is transmitted not in linguistic signifiers as such, but in what has been called the 'the grain of the voice' – not just *what* is said but *the manner of its being said*.[11] But of this, analytic philosophy could have no comprehension; it methodically excluded all meanings other than semantic and syntactical ones. Nor do meaning theories conceived in this style have a sense of what has been called 'the creation of... a public space' – a shared perspective from which speaker and hearer are able to 'survey the world together';[12] whereas one of the most critical aspects of the meaning of a worship service is that it is constructed collaboratively – by those who are the sign-producers (those who have been its planners and who now bring it into effect) and the sign-recipients (those who must 'make sense' of the signs in the comprehensive way I have already suggested).

For these and associated reasons I turned to what are loosely called (by English speakers!) 'Continental' styles of philosophy. These used to be grounded either in Husserl's phenomenological 'constitution' of

---

11. Roland Barthes, 'The Grain of the Voice' in *Image Music Text* (London: Fontana Press, 1977), 179–89.
12. See Charles Taylor, 'Theories of Meaning' in *Human Agency and Language: philosophical papers 1* (Cambridge University Press, 1985), 259.

meaning by a perceiving subject, or in Saussure's structuralist and semi-otic analyses of language. The one lives on, though massively and critically adjusted, in 'construction of meaning' theorists such as Paul Ricoeur and Maurice Merleau-Ponty and, more recently, with these writers' disciples. The other legacy has passed to the so-called post-structuralists or decon-structionists, of whom I suppose Jacques Derrida is still the most widely known.

Notwithstanding major differences between these 'late-modern' the-orists of meaning or signification there are certain similarities: Derrida's 'difference' has affinities with Ricoeur's 'distanciation' and with Merleau-Ponty's 'gap' or 'dehiscence'.[13] No one, that is, is able now to endorse the notion of 'pure' meanings – self-evident independently of any context and stripped of all material signification. On the other hand those standing in the phenomenological tradition do still argue that one can speak of the production of meaning, albeit through what Ricoeur calls 'the round-about route' – 'through the mediate comprehension of human signs.'[14] I have generally followed this way.

In the middle part of my book, I join to these middle and late twentieth-century theorists the writings of a thinker of the late nineteenth and early twentieth centuries, grievously overlooked in his own day but now widely recognized as perhaps the foremost thinker produced in the United States, Charles Sanders Peirce.[15] In the company of much more erudite students of his work, I have come to think that Peirce perhaps offers the best chance we have at this time of theorizing our construction and transaction of meaning.

By the 1970s all the major theoretical frames within which twentieth-century theorization of meaning had been undertaken – analytic philos-ophy, phenomenology, structuralism and formalism – had pretty much fallen into desuetude. Further, in the widely influential deconstructionist postmodernity which ensued, the question of meaning was itself deemed virtually to be meaningless. One of my convictions – a kind of axiom for

13. Leonard Lawlor, *Imagination and Chance: the difference between the thought of Ricoeur and Derrida* (Albany: State University of New York Press, 1992); and M. C. Dillon (ed.), *Ecart & Différence: Merleau-Ponty and Derrida on seeing and writing* (Atlantic Highlands, NJ: Humanities Press International, 1997).

14. See for example, Paul Ricoeur, *The Conflict of Interpretations* (Evanston: Northwestern University Press, 1974), 112, 155, or 266.

15. See the 'Open Letter to President Bill Clinton Concerning the Fate of the Peirce Papers', *Transactions of the Charles S. Peirce Society* 33 (1997), 836, signed by twenty eminent German philosophers who, among other things, say: 'Peirce is considered by many scholars and scientists as the most important, versatile and profound American philosopher.'

which I find it difficult to given further substantiation – is that people for the most part shape their meanings from the stocks of meaning available to them.[16] It also seems to me that, though there may *seem* to be a 'great gulf fixed' between academic formulations and such forms of thought as occur naturally to people in everyday life as 'making sense', in fact powerful lines of continuity can be traced between them – even when such connections are submerged or not apparent. Especially in a postmodern age, but before that, too, the most abstruse theorizations are immediately present to people in the forms of the built spaces they move through every day, in the technologies of mass communication, in the effects of globalized economies, and doubtless in other carriers of public meaning.[17] If my suppositions are correct, both these large cultural circumstances – our dependence on cultural norms and the immediacy to people of postmodernist precepts – will, in their combination, have contributed to an ongoing sense of difficulty experienced by people in personal and public life in 'making sense of anything'.[18] One does have this impression. Paradoxically, I have found it equally impossible to rid myself of the conviction that people do succeed in meaning things every day, as they also constantly seek to apprehend the meanings of others. Some theorists thus have the candour to admit that the business of meaning goes on even when our most powerful intellects are unable to say how that happens.[19] More directly, notwithstanding the deleterious condition of institutional Christianity from which I began these remarks, there continue to be priests and leaders (on one side) and worshippers (on the other) who greatly desire to know how to let these ancient mythic forms on which – for whatever reasons – we have come to depend as our sources of meaning, be meaning*ful*. The work which follows has been directed and empowered by this simple need on my own part. I think this is the only reasonable explanation for a classroom assignment becoming the virtually all-consuming obsession of a decade.

The great sweep of the word 'meaning', in its application to worship, has given to the work something of an hourglass shape, wide at either end, narrow in the middle. Led by my conviction about people shaping their meanings from the meanings available to them, the work attempts in Part I to set liturgical constructions of meaning within the larger cultural

---

16. So Michael Polanyi and Harry Prosch, *Meaning* (University of Chicago Press, 1975), 66: 'Man [*sic*] lives in the meanings he is able to discern. He extends himself into that which he finds coherent and is at home there.'
17. See further, below, p. 45.   18. See below, ch. 1, n. 9, and pp. 50–1.
19. See below, ch. 1, n. 8.

context of late twentieth-century meaning-theory. This, then, is one of the wide ends of the work. In the middle part, drawing upon Charles Peirce's semiotic theories, I attempt to say how meaning is constructed, transmitted and apprehended actually within a worship service. But – again because the meanings of worship cannot be sealed from the meanings available to people in their lifeworld generally – the last part opens out once more to consider the question of theistic meaning for people deeply ensconced in, and shaped by, the axioms of disenchantment.

No such undertaking will escape an equivocation between description and prescription. My supposition that we can only make meanings from meanings available to us has meant that I have tried to be descriptive – descriptive, that is, of our time and of our cultural dispositions. I have tried to understand what makes sense to us and why it does so, but, of course, I can scarcely conceal from myself (let alone anyone else) that in all this there is little that is strictly objective. At every point I have been making hefty judgements – about how we *should* or how we *could* make meaning, not least theistic meanings, in such an age.

Perhaps the simplest thing, then, is to come back to the quasi-confession; to own that it has from the beginning been my own quest, my own question. I have wanted to know as well as I could how, in this age of Christian belief, we might 'make sense' of – i.e., draw sense from – the ritual acts of Christians assembled in worship. That the chronicle of this personal quest has become a book perused by others strikes me as a happy accident – a 'surplus' Paul Ricoeur might have called it.

Part I

The making of meaning

1
_____

Meaning in worship

Meaningful worship

A worshipper attends a worship service. Perhaps the event is for her deeply meaningful. Or conceivably she will leave doubtful as to its point and purpose. Someone, a priest or minister or possibly a team of people, had planned and administered the service of worship presumably with the intention of undertaking some meaningful thing in the world.

What sort of meaning is this which some people construct and in which other people participate which we call a liturgical event? Or, to put the question in a slightly different way, what would a theory of meaning look like which could guide or facilitate the achievement of this kind of meaning? Or, to have yet a third shot at it, is it possible to give some account of the ways in which the meanings of worship are organized and transmitted by those who lead and are appropriated by those who participate in a worship service?

In many respects this question in its multiple versions is my quarry in all that follows. The subject matter, meaning, will lead us soon enough into various kinds of abstraction. But we are also to speak about an urgent practical assignment undertaken weekly (at least) by those who lead public Christian worship, and about a lived experience on the part of those who participate. (If this seems at this early stage to suggest an essential bifurcation between leaders and participants, let me indicate in advance my steady insistence that these are symbiotic engagements.) I propose therefore to begin by constructing a typical scenario in which something of 'the meaning of worship' is played out. Of course, two or three hundred such conjectural scenes could be regarded as typical somewhere within the geographical and denominational spread of western Christianity; but the scene I shall draw is, I think, as recognizable as any.

My hypothetical worshipper approaches a building which in various ways indicates itself as a place where Christians gather to worship, a church. Already there will be certain signs which speak in a preliminary but reasonably reliable way of continuities with practices which are familiar to my subject, but there will also be some features quite particular to the place. In order to sharpen both these dimensions I will hypothesize that she is in an unfamiliar setting – in a town not her own and approaching a church which she has not previously attended. Still, already the design and proportions of the building speak: first, about the continuities which knit the opinions of those who initially constructed the building and of those whose worship it now accommodates into the broad bands of agreement that make these 'Christian' or 'Catholic'. But the building will speak, also and secondly, of the differences, the particular assumptions and convictions of the people to whose worship she has come. Some of these indicators of familiarity and of strangeness will impact themselves upon my subject.

She enters the vestibule and passes into the main worship space. Already, whether or not she construes the matter in this way, questions of 'meaning' are up and running. What sense is to be made of this space and its dispositions? What is she to make of its physical dimensions: its height or otherwise, and its shapes and proportions? For example what meanings are to be drawn from the relationship – distance or proximity – between the area specified for the people who are the congregation and the spaces dedicated to those who lead? What is suggested by the colours used, and the lighting? What of the building's warmth or its coldness? What are the objects within it, what are they intended to mean both in themselves and in their disposition to each other? What do the sounds mean: here the hushed tones of preparation strike her almost physically in their contrast to the buzz of conversation with which she is familiar in her own place of worship. So then what is to be made of other aspects of the demeanour of those already assembled – their posture, their interaction or lack of it, and so on? And, finally, what does the bearing and general appearance (particularly the dress!)[1] of those who seem to be designated leaders indicate about

1. See Flanagan, *Sociology and Liturgy*, 97–105, on the significance of human dress generally and of liturgical dress specifically.

their understanding of what is to happen within the next few minutes as the worship commences?[2]

All these are still preliminary (though not misleading) indicators of what the act of worship means, at least in the understanding of this community of people among whom my subject finds herself. And, as I said a little earlier, all these significations (many of which are constituted for her by their similarities with and differences from that with which she is familiar) generate lively questions of meaning for the visitor. But, with the commencement of the service proper, a good many other factors will be drawn into this question-and-construction of meaning: the linguistic elements, both the words used and the manner of their utterance; the gestures and facial expressions of the leader(s); the proxemics (where people place themselves in relation to others); the coherence of the events or their disconnectedness; and, perhaps more powerfully than all of these, the music – its choice and its execution – will each and in conjunction importantly become bearers of meaning (or conceivably ciphers without meaning) for the person whose experience we are trying to touch. By the time of the final blessing and dismissal, our worshipper will have heard, seen, touched, tasted and smelt a plenitude of thickly woven sense impressions, the totality of which she will judge either to have been 'meaningful' or otherwise.

Of course, to put it like this is to point towards yet another level of meaning or meaningfulness, one which lies somewhere within all these significations but which also goes beyond them. That is, the action within which she has been participant for the previous hour or so will find its most far-reaching degree of 'meaningfulness' in terms of its capacity to interpret to her, or for her, some dimension of her ordinary lived experience. It will be meaningful for her if it has helped to 'make sense' of otherwise discordant elements of her experience; it will have accomplished this if it has enabled her to 'comprehend' our human condition generally and her own circumstances particularly; if it has helped her to 'see' things more clearly or to 'make connections' which otherwise had eluded her. Eventually we shall want to say that one of the connections which is critically in view, if the action as a whole is to be deemed 'Christian', will be a connectedness between herself in her particularity and the tradition within which Christianity is carried. But for the moment we may leave

2. See Herbert Muck, 'Die Rezeption einer Dorfliturgie' in (Rainer Volp, ed.) *Zeichen: Semiotik in Theologie und Gottesdienst* (Munich and Mainz: Chr. Kaiser and Matthias Grünewald, 1982), 266–91, where such details are analysed from a semiotic point of view.

these considerations out of view and stay simply with those conditions which permitted the event to be, for this worshipper, a meaningful one (or, as I have noted, meant that it was meaningless).

All this has been to describe the process from the point of view of a worshipper, a person who has been the recipient of this series of significations called a worship service. ('Recipient' here is not to be taken in any sense as passive; I shall want to insist that 'sign-reception' is a role as actively constructive as 'sign-production'.) That is, on the other side of this concentrated work of 'making sense', there had been an equal engagement in the construction of meaning on the part of those who were the planners and leaders of the worship. Just as my hypothetical worshipper could have been represented in many different ways, so the assumptions and intentions of those who are leaders of worship cover a broad spectrum. At some point, perhaps towards one end of such a span, there will be leaders whose chief confidence for the event's being meaningful is vested in the familiarity and durability of the liturgical forms – the words, the actions, the vestments, the rubrics. Such leaders see their role as subordinate in some sense to the ritual prescriptions, as the facilitator or enactor of these. But other leaders will presume a great deal more personal intervention, taking it for granted that their words, their style, their formulations will be the means which persuade, convince or convert. Most leaders, I suppose, fall somewhere between the two, allowing to the familiar forms an importance of signification and yet assuming that they, the leaders, also have the capacity to render those forms meaningful or otherwise.[3] In all this – that is, given the diversity of supposed sources of meaning in worship and the variety of ways in which such meanings will be realized – the constant factor is that people are attempting to offer a meaningful account of the world, of God, of our human condition. (Not quite out of view, and therefore important as a sort of counter possibility, I suppose we should not overlook a cynicism in which the performance is undertaken without conviction – the extreme form of what Max Weber called 'routinization'.[4] The possibility always haunts, but most practitioners I have known do still believe and hope that their work 'means something'.)

The activities on both sides of this construction of meaning are presumably sufficiently recognizable to be scarcely in dispute. The much more

[3]. Gordon Lathrop, for example (*Holy Things: a liturgical theology* (Minneapolis: Fortress Press, 1993)), can say: 'The *liturgy* is a sanctuary of meaning for us' (p. 217); but he also says (p. 204), 'This book . . . has attempted . . . to discuss how . . . traditional symbolic actions and words *might be taught* as meaningful' (my emphases).

[4]. Weber, *Economy and Society*, e.g., 246–54, 489, 492, 530.

elusive question, announced at the outset, is whether, or how, we may give some *account* of this human undertaking. There appear to be many different reasons which conspire to make this difficult.

Perhaps the first complication already lies in the breadth and mobility of the notion itself: meaning. I take it that it has not escaped my reader that I have already slipped between the notions 'meaning' and 'meaningfulness'. But this easy commutation conceals the fact that they are not exactly the same things: the second is a quantitative notion, something is or was more or less meaningful. The first idea is a qualitative one: which meanings? Whose meanings?[5] We can practically assume that the meanings intended (by the leaders, shall we say, or by the designers of the liturgy) will not coincide identically with the meanings apprehended by the worshipper. In one sense all that accords with standard semiotic or communication theory. But the liturgical theologians Lawrence Hoffman, Margaret Mary Kelliher and others have given a sharpened particularity to this in their distinctions (Hoffman's taxonomy) between private, official, public and normative meanings.[6] Meaning, it turns out, is a very slippery commodity.[7]

Second, and still in a very general way, while human beings constantly, endlessly and (in some respects!) unthinkingly go about the business of making and exchanging meaning, the achievement of a coherent and theoretical explication of this process appears to be extraordinarily elusive.[8]

---

5. On 'meaning' and 'meaningfulness' see further, below, pp. 170–1.

6. Lawrence A. Hoffman, 'How Ritual Means: ritual circumcision in rabbinic culture and today', *Studia Liturgica* 23 (1993), 78–97 (esp. pp. 79–82). See also Margaret Mary Kelliher, 'Liturgical Theology: a task and a method', *Worship* 62 (1988), esp. pp. 6–7; also the same author's essays 'Liturgy: an ecclesial act of meaning', *Worship* 59 (1985), 482–97, and 'Hermeneutics in the Study of Liturgical Performance', *Worship* 67 (1993), 292–318. David Power, 'People at Liturgy' in (Paul Brand, Edward Schillebeeckx and Anto Weiler eds.) *Twenty Years of Concilium – retrospect and prospect* (*Concilium* 170) (New York and Edinburgh: The Seabury Press and T. & T. Clark Ltd., 1983), 9–10, speaks of 'three kinds of meaning that one may distinguish in the actual celebration of liturgy.' Finally, see Stringer, *Perception of Worship*, 67, 69–72, 125, who similarly distinguishes between 'official' and 'unofficial' discourses, and between 'official teaching' and 'popular belief' (pp. 172, 177).

7. All this is still in terms of how the English language works. Things become yet more complicated when one starts to look into the way(s) in which 'meaning' works even in other closely related European languages. See John R. Searle, 'Meaning, Communication and Representation' in (Richard E. Grandy and Richard Warner, eds.) *Philosophical Grounds of Rationality: intentions, categories, ends* (Oxford: Clarendon Press, 1986), 209.

8. Nearly every writer on theories of meaning notes this curious discrepancy between our ability, on the one hand, to partake in meaningful intercourse and, on the other, to explain this ability. See for example: L. Jonathon Cohen, *The Diversity of Meaning* (London: Methuen and Co., Ltd., 1962), 24; Donald Davidson, 'Truth and Meaning', *Synthese* 17 (1967), 308; Mark Platts, *Ways of Meaning: an introduction to a philosophy of language* (London, Routledge and Kegan Paul, 1979), 1–2; Gilbert Ryle, 'The Theory of Meaning' in (C. A. Mace, ed.) *British Philosophy in the Mid-Century: a Cambridge symposium* (London: Allen and Unwin, 1957; second edition 1966), 239; Gerhard Sauter, *The Question of Meaning: a theological and philosophical orientation* (Grand

Then, third, beyond the realm of theoretical discourse, we are constantly reminded on every side that our western, industrialized culture is one in which, or for which, meaning has become a global problem, i.e., one affecting people's perspectives or attitudes to life at all levels of society.[9] In every bookstore popular treatments of 'the search for meaning' abound.[10]

A more particular version of this (i.e., with respect to a theory of meaning for worship) rests in the cultural circumstances in which institutional Christianity now finds itself in such societies (to which arena my discussion is confined). I shall want to urge the point that, immersed as they are in this culture, and as its products, believing Christians cannot suppose themselves immune from the corrosion of theistic meanings deeply embodied in that culture, for which condition I have already invoked Weber's term 'disenchantment'. The circumstance, now publicly apparent for at least a century and a half and doubtless underway for something closer to four centuries, seems only to become more exacerbated with time, a growing popular quest for 'spirituality' notwithstanding.

In this next section I want to confine myself to the multi-stranded history of meaning-theory in academic or theoretical discourse through the century just now closed. In the light of this I will return to the question of meaning in worship. In the subsequent chapter I turn to the broader cultural and societal aspects of meaning.

'Theory of meaning' at the end of the twentieth century

Any rehearsal of the history of 'theories of meaning' in the western world through the twentieth century, in such limited compass as I can here give it, will suffer distortion by compression and omission. That said, to

Rapids: William B. Eerdmans, 1995), 75, n. 5; and Taylor, *Human Agency*, 248. Earl R. MacCormac, *A Cognitive Theory of Metaphor* (Cambridge, MA: The MIT Press, 1985), 23, makes the same point about metaphors.

9. Fredric Jameson, *Postmodernism: or the cultural logic of late capitalism* (London: Verso, 1991); 53–4; or see Mark C. Taylor, 'Postmodern Times' in (Michael Griffith and James Tulip, eds.) *Proceedings of the Religion, Literature and Arts Conference, 1995* (Sydney: The RLA Project, 1995), 77: 'In the absence of an overarching [spiritual, social and political] framework, questions of meaning and motivation become unanswerable and the problem of legitimation becomes irresolvable.' See also Sauter, *The Question of Meaning*, 6–10, where he shows that in the German language at some point in the nineteenth century the sense of the word *Sinn* ('meaning') moved from being a reference to lexicalizations (the meanings one looks up in dictionaries) to 'a category of reality'.

10. The citation of examples is surely redundant; I refer here for convenience to the title of a popular series of radio broadcasts given by the Australian Broadcasting Commission conducted by Caroline Jones.

characterize that discussion as having operated for the first six or seven decades of the century within three relatively well-defined theatres – for the most part in surprising isolation from each other – until all of them collapsed from exhaustion, whereupon the void was filled by two newer aspiring claimants, would not, I think, be wholly inaccurate. By any account, the decade of the 1960s stands as a watershed in intellectual method. There would also be widespread agreement that the three dominant approaches to meaning prior to the 1960s were: first, the so-called 'English language' or 'Anglo-Saxon' style, generally described as 'analytic' and said to be 'objectivist' or 'empirical' in its general orientation; second, the 'phenomenological' method deriving from Edmund Husserl and thus standing within the heritage of German idealism; and, third, 'structuralism', taking its departure from Ferdinand de Saussure's revolutionary method of linguistics and having certain affinities (though not a lot of direct commerce) with the 'formalist' or 'explanatory' tendencies operating in the Anglo-American world.

The situation created by their demise is widely described as 'postmodernity'; though by the century's end it had become notoriously difficult to say exactly what that meant or wherein it consists. To say, as I am inclined to do, that the postmodern period is characterized by two styles of thought – the deconstructive programme most usually associated with Jacques Derrida, and the newly emergent (but in fact very ancient) field of study calling itself semiotics, the study of signs and signification – will thus be more contentious.

My motivation in attempting to sketch, however briefly, the course of these movements through the twentieth century is (to reiterate) my conviction that people make meaning, can only make meaning, from the meanings which are 'available' to them. Accordingly, the meanings we can find for ourselves at the dawn of the new millennium are tied directly back to those mighty disputations in which, in one way or another, we have participated, and their outcomes; and – since I also assert that the meanings of worship cannot be insulated from the meanings available to us in the world at large, even when the academic clashes seem distantly stratospheric – neither are the effects of these struggles absent from the construction of meaningful liturgy.[11]

---

11. So Rainer Volp, *Liturgik: die Kunst Gott zu feiern*, 2 volumes (Gütersloh: Verlagshaus Mohn, 1991–3), 43: 'The meaning of a service of worship waxes and wanes to the degree that its asseverations engage with those of the specific time and place; they integrate and transform them or they distance themselves from them.'

Analytic philosophy

According to one of its foremost exponents, the question which its founders placed at the centre of analytic philosophy was: how does language 'hook on' to the world.[12] The sentence usefully gives us three points of reference: analytic philosophy saw itself as taking an *objective world* in total seriousness; it conceived meaning entirely in terms of *linguistic meanings*; and it saw as its task the *explication* of how these two things related.

First, then, the 'objectification of the world' was self-evidently a general and central part of modern consciousness almost from its beginning,[13] reaching its apogee by the mid-twentieth century with those stages or aspects of the analytic approach known as 'logical positivism' and the 'verificationist' theories of meaning.[14] We can pick up the thread, however, already at the beginning of the century in Gottlob Frege's famous essay on sense and reference (first published in 1892), often seen as the *point de départ* for analytic theory.[15] Frege's opening sentences already flag the issue pinpointed by Putnam, namely the nature of the relationship between words and things. Hence his famous and influential distinction between the *sense* of a word and its *reference*. Frege says that its sense is that aspect of a word which allows a competent speaker of the language to recognize it as a sign. We might say that a word's sense is that dimension of its meaning which is catalogued in dictionaries, the kind of meaning we are seeking when we ask: what does such-and-such word *mean*? Its reference, on the other hand, is that dimension of its capacity for meaning which allows it to pick out one item from another in an objective world: '"Air" means this gaseous substance which keeps us alive.' As we shall see in a moment, Frege noted that a word's sense can move about disarmingly. On the other hand it is its power of reference, that is its capacity for attachment to an extra-linguistic reality, which alone allows us to decide questions of truth and falsity: 'We are therefore justified in not being satisfied with the sense of a sentence, and in inquiring also as to its reference...Why...? Because, and to the extent that, we are concerned with its truth value...It

12. Hilary Putnam, *Realism with a Human Face* (Cambridge, MA: Harvard University Press, 1990), 43, 105. An almost identical sentence is given by John Deely, *Basics of Semiotics* (Bloomington: Indiana University Press, 1990), 18.
13. See Taylor, *Sources*, 160–1; or Habermas, *Philosophical Discourse*, 311.
14. Putnam, *Human Face*, 105–6.
15. G. Frege, 'On Sense and Reference', *Philosophical Studies* (P. T. Geach and M. Black, eds.) (Oxford: Basil Blackwell, 1960), 56–78 (originally published as 'Über Sinn und Bedeutung', *Zeitschrift für Philosophie und philosophische Kritik* 100 (1892), 25–50).

is the *striving for truth* that drives us always to advance from the sense to the reference.'[16]

The objectivity of the world as that against which truth or falsity is decided, and thus where linguistic meanings are to be tested, becomes the touchstone for analytic philosophy, beginning with the Vienna Circle of the 1920s, and then in its translation to an English-language setting through the migration of members of the circle to the United States in the 1930s, and through Bertrand Russell's influence at Cambridge University. It is encapsulated, for example, in Moritz Schlick's sentence (a leading member of the Vienna Circle): 'data have no owner,'[17] and in the notion of 'meaning as verification'.[18] In some strong sense, the preoccupation (with the relation between 'language' and 'meaning') is emblematized in the 'truth-condition' theories of meaning pioneered by Alfred Tarski[19] and carried forward in an English-language setting by Donald Davidson.[20]

Turning to the second item specified in Putnam's sentence, language as the seat of meaning, it is of utmost importance to recall that Frege came to questions of meaning primarily as a mathematician or logician.[21] This fact predetermined that linguistic meanings would be seen – by all means, in continuity with the long tradition of western philosophy – as ideal entities. *Meaning*, it is supposed, *transcends space, time and local usage.*

---

16. 'On Sense and Reference', 63 (my emphases). On the great difficulties of translating Frege's terms into precise English equivalents, see the two essays by Eugeniusz Grodzinski: 'Some Remarks on Joan Weiner's *Frege in Perspective*', *Semiotica* 99 3/4 (1993), 348–51, and 'The Defectiveness of Gottlob Frege's Basic Logical–Semantic Terminology', *Semiotica* 103 3/4 (1995), 291–308 (on 'Bedeutung' and 'bedeuten' particularly, see pp. 302–3).

17. Moritz Schlick, 'Meaning and Verification' in (Herbert Feigle and Wilfred Sellars, eds.) *Readings in Philosophical Analysis* (New York: Appleton-Century-Crofts, 1949), 168.

18. Classically, A. J. Ayer in his *Language, Truth and Logic* (London: Penguin Books, 1990), 16: 'We say that a sentence is factually significant to any given person if, and only if, he [*sic*] knows how to verify the proposition which it purports to express – that is, if he knows what observations would lead him, under certain conditions, to accept the proposition as being true, or reject it as being false.'

19. Alfred Tarski, 'The Semantic Conception of Truth and the Foundations of Semantics' in (Herbert Feigle and Wilfred Sellars, eds.) *Readings in Philosophical Analysis* (New York: Appleton-Century-Crofts, 1949), 52–84.

20. Donald Davidson, 'Truth and Meaning' (see n. 8 above). Taylor, *Human Agency*, 252–3, singles out truth conditional theories of meaning as particularly representative of Anglo-Saxon styles of philosophy. The two-part essay of Michael Dummett, 'What is a Theory of Meaning?', now in (Gareth Evans and John McDowell, eds.) *Truth and Meaning: essays in semantics* (Oxford: Clarendon Press, 1976), is generally said to have exposed the deep flaws in theories of meaning predicated on truth conditions.

21. See the Preface written by Newton Garver for the English translation of Jacques Derrida's *Speech and Phenomena and other essays on Husserl's theory of signs* (Evanston: Northwestern University Press, 1973), p. *xiii*. Garver's brief introductory essay is one of the most succinct and accessible treatments I have come across of the issues here being discussed.

A mathematical formulation or logical proposition does not change in changing circumstances. Similarly the meaning of a word, a sentence or an intellectual concept must remain identifiable across time and space; it cannot mean one thing today and another tomorrow. One cannot – Humpty-Dumpty like – make words mean anything one wants them to. One thus catches a hint of impatience in Frege's recognition that linguistic units of natural languages do *not* in fact behave as they should! They can slip in and out of meanings. Strictly this is an aberrance. Meaning needs to be stable and words should remain so too.[22] The assumptions, first, that meanings are conceptual – we might say metaphysical – entities not subject to the vagaries of spatio-temporal existence, and, second, that language does nevertheless name real entities in the world, is the conundrum with which meaning-theory for the entire length of this tradition will find itself entangled.

   This brings us, then, to the third item in Putnam's sentence: the question of how language 'hooks on' to the world. Given that meanings are ideal things and given that they must refer to a material world, analytic philosophy was committed to what Putnam calls in other places, 'A God's Eye View of the Universe'.[23] This is the conviction that the universe consists in a fixed number of extra-linguistic entities, which, even if they are not known and named in human languages, nevertheless *could*, in principle, be so named.[24] The task of philosophy thus becomes that of achieving as 'true' an account of the world as human language can manage; that is, to arrange the best possible 'fit' between the meanings carried in words, sentences or descriptions and extra-linguistic reality. In the end – these things are invariably seen after the event – the system could only collapse under the weight it placed on itself (one can only speak of it as a 'God's Eye View' when one realizes its impossibility). The problem is not just in the obvious impossibility of achieving a 'God's Eye View'. It is that the language through which, or in which, we encounter the world has as much to do with shaping the reality so encountered as whatever 'objectivity' that reality may carry in itself. Moritz Schlick had

---

22. Frege, 'On Sense and Reference', 58: 'The regular connexion between a sign, its sense, and its reference is of such a kind that to the sign there corresponds a definite sense and to that in turn a definite reference . . . To be sure exceptions to this regular behaviour occur. To every expression belonging to a complete totality of signs, there should certainly correspond a definite sense; but natural languages often do not satisfy this condition'.
23. Putnam, *Human Face*, e.g., 11, 50; also in his *Reason, Truth and History* (Cambridge University Press, 1981), e.g., 48–9.
24. See Putnam's essay 'Truth and Convention' in *Human Face*, 96–104.

perhaps caught half the truth in his insistence on 'ownerless data'. But another writer from within the analytic tradition completed the truth with his equal insistence that 'Language is the knife with which we cut our facts.'[25]

It becomes clear that the analytic theories of meaning both struggled with and remained ensconced within the ancient dualism of ideality and materiality, given such massive impetus for the modern period by Descartes's splitting of reality into *res cogitans* and *res extensa*. One observer thinks that 'the last timbers of this intellectual scaffolding' were already being dismantled from the middle of the nineteenth century, and that the 'objectivist' tendencies of positivism (the analytical method) were only hastily reinstated in order to meet the cultural anxieties unleashed in the catastrophic First and Second World Wars.[26] However one views this historical thesis, it is clear that by, or from, the 1960s this way of attempting to account for meaning had reached its termination.

Such was the (from our perspective, astonishing) degree of separation between English-language philosophers and those styles they chose to regard as 'Continental', that the circumstance that the latter consisted in two quite different approaches was mostly unnoticed. The two were: the phenomenological legacy of Edmund Husserl, and structuralism deriving from Ferdinand de Saussure. Coincidentally or otherwise, Frege, Husserl and Saussure were all relatively contemporaneous.

Phenomenology

If the self-appointed task of the positivists had been to deliver certainty for an age of cultural and political upheaval,[27] this was, strikingly enough, identically the agenda assumed by Husserl and his 'phenomenological' project. For Husserl, the most anxious-making aspect of modern thought was its rupture of intellectual method into endlessly fissiparous disciplines: the newly emergent sciences. Philosophy – the subject matter of which is 'pure', not 'applied' like the sciences – seemed to him to be in the greatest conceivable danger. He believed this to be the product precisely of the 'objectivist' tendencies of modernity, its predilection for impartiality or distanciation, a style of thinking he termed 'naturalistic': 'All

---

25. Friedrich Waismann, 'Verifiability' in (G. H. R. Parkinson, ed.) *The Theory of Meaning* (London: Oxford University Press, 1968), 58.
26. Stephen Toulmin, *Cosmopolis: the hidden agenda of modernity* (University of Chicago Press, 1990), 143–60.
27. Toulmin, *ibid.*

natural science is naive in regard to its point of departure. The nature that it will investigate is for it simply there...It is the aim of natural science to know these unquestioned data in an objectively valid, strictly scientific manner.'[28]

Husserl believed that such 'science' was illegitimately so-called; the true science would attend to things, not in terms of their natural appearance (which, we learn, is always deceptive), but in terms of their true 'essence'. It was to this end that he developed his theory of 'reduction' or 'suspension' or 'epoché'. This is a kind of radicalization of the Cartesian doubt:[29] one must suspend one's natural *intuitions* of the world in order to become conscious of one's *apprehensions* – otherwise expressed, to attend to the fact that what one encounters are not things, objectively present, but rather the *phenomena* (appearances) which present themselves in one's mind. Hence, his 'phenomenological' approach.[30]

Exactly opposite, then, to the decision of the analytic philosophers to turn towards the objective world as the place against which truth, and hence meaning, is to be tested, Husserl saw such a world as consisting only of constantly changing forms. He thus sought an irrefragable basis for truth and meaning, the only basis of philosophy as the true science, in the subjective world of one's innermost apprehensions of reality. Diametrically opposite to an understanding of a world in which 'data have no owner', Husserl saw the only *truly trustworthy* datum as that given by 'the infinite field of absolute mental processes'.[31] For Husserl, then, the world is not so much 'out there' as it is 'constituted' by my own interaction with it:

28. Edmund Husserl, 'Philosophy as Rigorous Science' in (Quentin Laura, ed.) *Phenomenology and the Crisis of Philosophy* (New York: Harper Torchbooks, 1965), 85. See, similarly, his *Cartesian Meditations: an introduction to phenomenology* (Dordrecht: Kluwer Academic Publishers, 1993), 117/84. (It is conventional to cite Husserl's original pagination for the *Cartesian Meditations*; I will observe this convention but I will also give the page numbers in Dorion Cairns' English translation following the slash).

29. *Cartesian Meditations*, 56/16.

30. See for example the summary statement in *Ideas Pertaining to a Pure Phenomenology: first book* (Dordrecht: Kluwer Academic Publishers, 1982), 114: 'Let us make this clear to ourselves in detail. In the natural attitude we simply *effect* all the acts by virtue of which the world is there for us. We live naively in perceiving and experiencing . . . In the phenomenological attitude . . . we *prevent the effecting* of all such cogitative positings, i.e., we "parenthesize" the positings effected . . . Instead of living *in* them, instead of effecting *them*, we effect acts of *reflection* directed to them; and we seize upon them themselves as the *absolute* being which they are. We are now living completely in such acts of the second degree, acts the datum of which is the infinite field of absolute mental processes – the fundamental *field of phenomenology*' (his emphases).

31. The reference is to the passage cited in the previous note; see also Derrida, *Writing and Difference*, 158.

Anything belonging to the world, any spatiotemporal being, exists for me – that is to say, is accepted by me – in that I experience it, perceive it, remember it, think of it somehow, judge about it, value it, desire it, or the like ... I can enter no world other than the one which gets its sense and acceptance or status in and from me, myself.[32]

Not the least interesting aspect – for us – of this 'constitution' of reality is that it is, for Husserl, an act of 'meaning':

Each *cogito*, each conscious process, we may ... say, *'means' something or other* and bears in itself, in this manner peculiar to the *meant*, its particular *cogitatum* ... The house-perception means a house – more precisely, as this individual house – and means it in the fashion peculiar to perception; a house-memory means a house in the fashion peculiar to memory; a house-fantasy, in the fashion peculiar to fantasy.[33]

In short: 'every *cogito* is indeed ... a meaning of its meant [*Meinung seines Gemeinten*].'[34]

Husserl's phenomenology was always vulnerable to the accusation of solipsism – the 'disconcerting glide from the "for me" into the "from me"'.[35] He was himself already sensitive to this and his latter works are dedicated to the attempt (generally judged to be less than successful) to ward off the charge. Through the early and middle parts of the twentieth century his disciples were for the most part engaged in saying how Husserl's insights into the actively constitutive nature of human meaning-making could relate to a world *actually extant* beyond the subject's constitution of it. The significant names in this respect are: Heidegger, in turning phenomenology towards the question of Being;[36] Roman Ingarden, in deriving from phenomenology a theory of literary reading;[37] Merleau-Ponty in his preoccupation with 'the phenomenology of perception';[38]

---

32. *Cartesian Meditations*, 60/21.   33. *Ibid.*, 71/33 (his emphases).   34. *Ibid.*, 84/46.

35. Paul Ricoeur, *Husserl: an analysis of his phenomenology* (Evanston, IL: Northwestern University Press, 1967), 89; similarly, *ibid.*, 10.

36. See John Caputo, *Radical Hermeneutics: repetition, deconstruction and the hermeneutic project* (Bloomington: Indiana University Press, 1987), 38, 52–8.

37. Roman Ingarden, *The Literary Work of Art: an investigation on the borderlines of ontology, logic and theory of literature* (Evanston, IL: Northwestern University Press, 1973) and *The Cognition of the Literary Work of Art* (Evanston, IL: Northwestern University Press, 1973).

38. E.g., Maurice Merleau-Ponty, *Phenomenology of Perception* (London: Routledge, 1962); but one should take cognizance of James Edie's introductory note to Merleau-Ponty's *The Primacy of Perception*, to the effect that *Phenomenology of Perception* was never intended other than as the presentation of a thesis for a much more wide-ranging application of phenomenology 'on imagination, language, culture, reason, and on aesthetic, ethical, political, and even religious experience' (Introduction to Maurice Merleau-Ponty, *The Primacy of Perception: and other essays on phenomenological psychology, the philosophy of art, history and politics* (Evanston, IL: Northwestern University Press, 1964), p. xv; see also, *ibid.*, p. 25).

Alfred Schutz's phenomenological sociology;[39] Emmanuel Levinas' studies on alterity;[40] and Paul Ricoeur with his interest in 'the long and more sure way of reflection upon the dynamics of the great cultural symbols'.[41] The several mid-century 'existentialists' (for example, Gabriel Marcel, Jean-Paul Sartre) also derive from Husserl's phenomenology.[42]

It has been Jacques Derrida's deconstructive critique, however, which has perhaps exposed the deepest flaw, or troubled inconsistency, in Husserl's work. Strikingly – in view of their virtually opposite approaches to the matter of meaning – this turns out to be the same fault-line as that which underlay the analytic project, namely, a conflict between the supposed ideality of mental events and the materiality of the world on which such cognitive processes must fasten. Derrida shows that the distinctions which Husserl wishes to draw between what he, Husserl, calls 'expression' and 'indication' will not stand.[43] 'Expression', for Husserl, consists in 'pure meaning' known immediately to the thinking subject (i.e., without the intervention of material signifiers). 'Indication', by contrast, is such meaning when mixed with the material elements – vocalization or writing – on which human discourse depends. Derrida shows in his characteristic way that this separation of the ideal from the material, and the protection or privileging of the one from or over the other, is impossible: 'Just as expression is not added like a "stratum" to the presence of a pre-expressive sense, so, in the same way, the inside of expression does not accidentally happen to be affected by the outside of indication. Their intertwining (*Verflechtung*) is primordial.'[44] We are bound to agree with the critique, I think.[45] We must now accept that human beings are irresolvably

39. Alfred Schutz, *On Phenomenology and Social Relations: selected writings* (Helmut R. Wagner, ed.) (University of Chicago Press, 1970).

40. Emmanuel Levinas, *Totality and Infinity: an essay on exteriority* (Pittsburgh: Duquesne University Press, 1969).

41. E.g., Ricoeur, *Conflict of Interpretations*, 290.

42. A concise overview of Husserl's phenomenology and that of his major interpreters will be found in Joseph J. Kockelmans (ed.), *Phenomenology: the philosophy of Edmund Husserl and its interpreters* (Garden City, NY: Doubleday and Company, Inc., 1967).

43. The work to which Derrida is directing his critique is Husserl's *Logical Investigations* (New York: Humanities Press, 1970).

44. Derrida, *Speech and Phenomena*, 86–7.

45. The issues are, admittedly, complicated. I agree with Derrida in terms of the 'entwinement' of physicality and expressivity, yet I stop before the word 'primordial'. What does this mean? Further on in my text I will urge – in dependence on Julia Kristeva's notion of the *chora*, the 'place' or 'space' whence comes language and thought – that one *can* speak meaningfully of some form of prelinguistic awareness. But Kristeva, too, would say that by the time we can speak of 'consciousness', 'thought', or 'language' we have the interweaving of both for which Derrida is arguing. Pickstock, *After Writing*, 106–7, criticizes Derrida's analysis of Husserl; her own treatment in terms of 'the necrophilia of modernity' is at least as elusive, however.

both *thinking* and *physical* beings. There cannot be human thought which is not, *ipso facto*, embodied thought, i.e., if we can put it so, physical thought! We cannot think outside of this human, which is to say embodied, form of existence. As Derrida says, quoting Husserl against himself, we are *verflochten*: that is, we are creatures which are *knit*; an intertwining of spirituality and physicality; a body in which memories, hopes, aches both physical and emotional, appetites, unnamed dreads and impossible aspirations, rationality and superstition, imagination, self-interest and social dependence are inextricably interwoven. None is separable from the rest. Physicality is the condition of our intellectuality.

Structuralism

The third identifiable intellectual force through the earlier part of the twentieth century derived from Saussure's radical break as a linguist from the historical or philological models currently regnant in his discipline.[46] Saussure's new ('scientific'!) method of linguistic studies involved a series of distinctions or oppositions: for example between the function of a word or other linguistic unit as signifying something (its status as signifier) and that which it signifies (the signified); between language as a system of signs passively available to a speaker (language as *langue*) and the act of forming a particular utterance (*parole*); between the evolution of any particular language over time (its diachronicity) and its present state as a system of signs available to a contemporary speaker (its synchronicity).[47] Saussure also insisted that individual signifiers in this system which is a language stand to their signified meanings in a purely arbitrary way; that the conjunction is sanctioned by customary usage not by some 'natural' affiliation. He also insisted that what allows each signifier to do its work of signification is its recognisable difference from every other signifier (a principle which in structuralism came to be called binary opposition: any given signifier is what all other signifiers are not).[48]

In so far as structuralism addressed itself to the processes of signification, it offered itself as a theory of meaning. In a moment I shall

---

46. F. de Saussure, *Course in General Linguistics* (London: Duckworth, 1983), ch. 1.

47. See Paul Ricoeur, *Rule of Metaphor: multidisciplinary studies of the creation of meaning in language* (University of Toronto Press, 1977), 103, 121–3, on 'the great dichotomies that dominate the *Cours*'.

48. See a useful introduction in Jonathan Culler, *Saussure* (London: Fontana Press, 1976), ch. 2. Fredric Jameson combines with his survey a more critical analysis (Fredric Jameson, *The Prison-House of Language: a critical account of structuralism and Russian formalism* (Princeton University Press, 1972), ch. 1).

summon witnesses who show that structuralism's entrenchment within the idealist/materialist paradigm of modernity entails for it a virtually insurmountable liability as an account of meaning. The encumbrance will appear more and more problematical as we proceed to a comparison with other theories of semiosis or signification. Yet we should not pass so quickly to that that we miss something important. Paul Ricoeur, in his indefatigable search for the nature of textuality, was finally critical of structuralism: simply to '*explain* the text in terms of its internal relations, its structure' is to treat it 'as a worldless and authorless object.'[49] Nevertheless and at the same time, one can hardly not notice that a text (or, we may say, any human signification) is a structured reality. Ricoeur sees this in terms of what he calls the 'distanciation' of a text – its separation from the subjectivity of its utterer or author and from the momentary event of its utterance.[50] From this (limited) point of view, the structural or explanatory analysis 'is not only possible but legitimate'.[51]

That said, 'the great dichotomies that dominate the *Course in General Linguistics*' (see note 47 above) mean that the gap between sensible reality and conceptual reality haunts this account of meaning as relentlessly as it has the others we have inspected. Fredric Jameson, for example, writes of Saussure: '[P]hilosophically, we are faced with a rather peculiar identification between change and matter, on the one hand, and meaning and the a-temporal, on the other.'[52] He also wonders, in a widely cited sentence, as to 'what degree the object of [Saussure's] study is the thought pattern of the linguist himself, rather than that of language'.[53] Derrida, predictably, has the same accusation: 'The semiological or, more specifically, linguistic "science" cannot therefore hold on to the difference between signifier and signified . . . without the difference between sensible [i.e., the materiality of signifiers] and intelligible [the ideality of the signified].'[54] Semiotically, this will result in what Augusto Ponzio has subsequently called 'the postal system' of semiotic exchange: 'something which passes from point A to point B as though we were dealing with a parcel despatched by one post office and received by another':[55]

49. Paul Ricoeur, *Hermeneutics and the Human Sciences* (Cambridge University Press, 1981), 152 (my emphasis).
50. *Ibid.*, 134.   51. *Ibid.*, 153.
52. Jameson, *The Prison-House of Language*, 16.   53. *Ibid.*, 39.
54. Jacques Derrida, *Of Grammatology* (Baltimore: Johns Hopkins University Press, 1974), 13. See, *ibid.*, 27–73, for Derrida's extended critique of Saussure.
55. Augusto Ponzio, *Man as a Sign: essays on the philosophy of language* (Berlin and New York: Mouton de Gruyter, 1990), 114.

> Using the theory of value of the School of Lausanne as a model,
> Saussure reduced linguistic value to exchange-value. The value of a
> sign is given by its position within a sign system just as the value of a
> commodity is determined in 'pure economics' by its relationship to the
> other commodities on the market. Saussure said *nothing about linguistic
> production.*[56]

Ponzio's point becomes clearer when we set this in juxtaposition with the
triadically conceived, 'interpretation' semiotic theory of C. S. Peirce (as I
shall do in an introductory way in a moment).

Postmodernity: deconstruction

The decade of the 1960s is said to be the watershed period in which the assumptions of modernity yielded to the forces of so-called postmodernity.[57]
It is certainly at about this time that each of the intellectual styles on which
I have so briefly touched ceased to attract significant interest. I have said
that, despite their very different starting points and methods, those efforts to theorize meaning display curiously consistent features: namely,
the assumption of a dualistic idealist/materialist framework of thought;
and an obsession with the achievement of indisputable solutions to questions, or, what is the same thing, finally definitive theories. By the 1960s,
either from internal exhaustion or external attack, they effectively ceased
as vehicles for thought. None of them had produced a theory of meaning.
In fact, thenceforth, the notion of theory itself – i.e., as some kind of master plan of things – suffered a serious loss of favour, although the verbal
idea, 'to theorize' as an ongoing process, remained or remains firmly in
place.

Postmodernity is often seen as roughly synonymous with poststruc-
turalism or the deconstructionist programme of which Jacques Derrida is
usually regarded as the chief architect. John Deely, himself a protagonist
for a very different view of postmodernity, thus writes:

> As a fashionable term . . . 'postmodern' has come to be frequently used
> as a label for the results of a so-called 'deconstruction' consisting in a
> kind of literary/sophistic attempt to eviscerate rational discourse in
> philosophy through a forced control of signifiers, made rather to
> dismantle rather than to constitute some text taken precisely as
> severed from any vestige of authorial intention.[58]

---

56. *Ibid.*, 186 (my emphases).   57. E.g., Toulmin, *Cosmopolis*, 160–1.
58. John Deely, *New Beginnings: Early Modern Philosophy and Postmodern Thought* (University of
Toronto Press, 1994), 10.

By all means, one has to move carefully in attributing any definitive view to Derrida or to deconstruction. Deconstruction, in its suspicion of all definitive positions, attempts to occupy no position of its own.[59] On the one hand, therefore, it cannot be said – this, over against views which are frequently attributed to him[60] – that Derrida has no room for meaning or truth. Against his striking vision of structuralism leaving a text as an uninhabited city, for instance, he opposes 'the living energy of meaning'.[61] Or again, it is of the interchange between reader and writer that one can ask: 'Does not meaning present itself as such at the point at which the other is found?'[62] On the other hand, Derrida's relentless pursuit is directed towards every form of ideality – immediacy of thought to itself, of language to thought, or of one's knowledge of oneself, to take only his most prominent examples. It is thus hardly surprising that 'meaning', which has so readily and for so long worked in closest conjunction with these kinds of ideal 'presence', should also be profoundly the object of his suspicion. Hence, if, on one side, meaning can be 'a living energy', if, like every other disputant, Derrida can protest, 'if words have a meaning . . .',[63] yet, on the other side, meaning can also be seen as the 'ideal content' of communication.[64] From this point of view, meaning must be practically identical with Saussure's 'signified' (the ideal content to which a signifier points) or to Husserl's 'expression', 'intention', or 'meaning'. Such meanings as may be accessible to us, then, can only be present in, or as, endless chains of signifiers; or, to invoke another of Derrida's terms, it is only ever 'disseminated'. Accordingly, not only is meaning as such, and its quest, highly to be distrusted,[65] but, a posteriori, there can be no theorizing of meaning, no charting of a direct route which would tell us where and how meaning is to be found: '[D]econstruction is not a theory that defines meaning in order to tell you how to find it. As a critical undoing of the hierarchical oppositions on which theories depend, it demonstrates the difficulties of any theory that would define meaning in a univocal way:

59. *Of Grammatology*, 24: 'Operating necessarily from the inside, borrowing all the strategic and economic resources of subversion from the old structure, borrowing them structurally, that is to say without being able to isolate their elements and atoms, the enterprise of deconstruction always in a certain way falls prey to its own work.'

60. See, in Derrida's defence, Kevin Hart, *The Trespass of the Sign: deconstruction, theology and philosophy* (Cambridge University Press, 1989), 144; or Christopher Norris, *Deconstruction: theory and practice* (London: Routledge, 1991), 143, 156.

61. *Writing and Difference*, 5.   62. *Ibid.*, 11.   63. *Of Grammatology*, 134.

64. *Margins of Philosophy* (New York: Harvester Wheatsheaf, 1982), 314.

65. This accounts for Ricoeur's uncharacteristically sharp retort to Derrida that he '[has] no theory of meaning'; Lawlor, *Imagination and Chance*, 136, 138.

as what an author intends, what conventions determine, what a reader experiences';[66] and, '[Derrida wishes to] make apparent the problem that both determines and subverts every theory of meaning.'[67] Far from working towards a framework for comprehending meaning, then, the deconstructive gesture has, generally speaking, been to abandon any such quest as meaningless.[68]

Postmodernity: the semiotic approach

Postmodernity is hardly an undifferentiated whole, however. Besides the common identification of it with deconstructive approaches, there are other claimants to the title. I cited John Deely as acknowledging the usual perception; but this in fact is precisely by way of mounting an alternative contention. Deely belongs to the still relatively esoteric but rapidly expanding circle of scholars who see in the 'doctrine of signs' – semiotics – the way towards a new (postmodern) century.[69] As an intellectual discipline, semiotics has itself been split between an approach deriving from Saussure's structural linguistics and an approach formulated by the American, Charles Sanders Peirce, working at roughly the same time as Saussure. Whereas Saussurean semiotics (often distinguished from the Peircean model by the term 'semiology') remains anchored in the dualistic structures everywhere apparent in modern thought, Peircean semiotics sees all signification as irreducibly triadic, building the role or function of interpretation directly into the sign's production of meaning (here I must content myself with an introductory sketch; I will deal with Peirce's semiotic in detail at a later point). In thus 'incorporat[ing] the human user *into* the sign',[70] Peirce's semiotic theory both builds a bridge back beyond the Cartesian bifurcation (reality is either objective or subjective) to the mature thought of the late Middle Ages (of which Peirce was an accomplished

66. Jonathan Culler, *On Deconstruction: theory and criticism after structuralism* (London: Routledge, 1983), 131.
67. *Ibid.*, 97.
68. So, Peter Dews, *The Limits of Disenchantment: essays on contemporary European philosophy* (London: Verso, 1995), 2: 'The dominant paradigm of hostility to meaning in recent European philosophy has undoubtedly been deconstruction.'
69. The term 'doctrine of signs' as an umbrella term for his semiotic theory is taken up by C. S. Peirce from John Locke; see Peirce's *Collected Papers* (hereafter *CP*) 2.227. (In all my references to the *Collected Papers* of Charles Sanders Peirce I shall use the standard form of reference, which is to cite in parentheses in the text body the volume number in arabic and then the paragraph number of that volume.)
70. John K. Sheriff, *The Fate of Meaning: Charles Peirce, structuralism and literature* (Princeton University Press, 1989), 49 (my emphasis). Sheriff gives a very convincing account of the superiority of Peircean semiotics, over structuralism and Derridean post-structuralism, in its ability to account for the meaning of literary texts.

student) and equally points a way forward to a post-Cartesian (i.e., post-modern) world. Though she does not invoke the term ('postmodern'), this is unquestionably what is in Susan Petrilli's mind in speaking of 'the semi-otics of interpretation' as providing us with 'adequate instruments for a critical interpretation of today's world',[71] whence she continues in great detail to bring Peirce's semiotic into relation with postmodern issues such as 'the self and alterity', 'the body as the locus of signification', 'prelinguis-tic meanings', and so on. Deely is more explicit in his claim for semiotic as a postmodern option. Characterizing the entire period of Cartesian dual-ism as a 'four-hundred-year-time-out' from the tasks ordinarily accruing to philosophy,[72] he sees Peirce's triadic 'doctrine of signs' as breaking the deadlock between idealism and realism.[73] On the basis of his achievement of 'an entirely new categorial scheme capable of accounting for the com-penetration . . . [of] the nature of things and . . . the working of thought,'[74] Deely places Peirce 'at the interface of modernity with postmodernity, the last of the moderns and first of the postmoderns.'[75] As will become appar-ent, I too incline to the view that a triadic conception of semiosis offers our best chance of understanding the mysterious process which is the con-struction among us of this which we call meaning.

Dimensions of a theory of meaning for worship

I return to my imaginary worshipper. What elements will be required in any account which might elucidate the processes which enabled the event in which she participated *to mean something*? Further, are we able to say *whose* meanings or *which* meanings she apprehended; which is an-other way of asking: can we say whether she *correctly* apprehended the meanings being proposed? Are there any control mechanisms regulating the meaning-exchange process between leaders and participants? Finally, what are the restraints or responsibilities accruing to those who have pro-posed the meanings of the liturgy, those who planned it and brought it to expression?

71. Susan Petrilli, 'About and Beyond Peirce', *Semiotica* 124 3/4 (1999), 314.
72. Deely, *New Beginnings*, 246.
73. *Ibid.*, 101; see also the same author's *Basics of Semiotics*, 5, 17, 76.
74. *New Beginnings*, 246. See the entire chapter of *New Beginnings*, 'Transition to the Future: the way of signs', 245–8.
75. *Ibid.*, 20. See, similarly, Deely's essay, 'Looking Back on *A Theory of Semiotics*' in (Rocco Capozzi, ed.) *Reading Eco: an anthology* (Bloomington: Indiana University Press, 1997), 84, 86. On the matter of Peirce and postmodernity, note should also be taken of T. L. Short's essay, 'What's the Use?', *Semiotica* 122 1/2 (1998), 1–68, but esp. pp. 2–8.

Since leaving her, I have reviewed in as broad scope as space allowed the various approaches to theory of meaning which have been pursued in the twentieth-century western world. I said that none of the styles undertaken under the aegis of classical modernity – i.e., attempts to fit our thought to the world and the world to thought in terms of a subjective and objective polarization – were able to produce a viable or working theory of meaning. On the other hand, the survey was not without its usefulness. Even though no self-sustaining theory emerges from any of them, yet each has posted an important reference point in our search: that meaning must engage with an extra-linguistic, extra-subjective *world*, for example (analytic philosophy); that it is simultaneously an act of *human construction* (phenomenology); and that every event of signification consists in an analysable *structure* (structuralism). Of the postmodern options, deconstruction shows that all our meanings are *mediate, materially contingent*; while semiotic theory of the Peircean style points us towards some real possibility of meaning exchange in *the mediation of our signs*.

But now, in this concluding section of the chapter, the question (of meaning) is directed back to these theoretical cogitations from within the liturgy: what makes sense, and how does it make sense, when one is a participant of worship? I cannot say that the connections between the theoretical analyses of meaning and such questions as now arise from within the liturgy are, at this stage, open or direct – yielding, as it were, one-to-one points of comparison. For the moment they remain crooked, indirect. But, because the worlds in which the believer lives (simultaneously: the worlds of late modernity *and* of theistic belief) are not separated but interfold and interfuse, it is my hope that these points of connection will become clearer as the investigation proceeds.

In what ensues I will list three criteria for, or dimensions of, meaning in worship: the event has to *make sense* in some degree or another (i.e., some level of rationality is demanded); the meanings have to be *multisensory*, transmitted and apprehended as much along nonverbal as verbal channels of signification; and they have to be *theologically competent* (make sense in terms of a theistic reading of the world).

Reasonableness

It is hard to suppose that meaning and rationality are not each deeply implicated in the other. Certainly, each term of the equation leads in the blink of an eye into thickets of disputation and conceptual abstruseness. Yet a cluster of English-language expressions reinforces this intuitive connection between what 'makes sense' and that which is 'meaningful'. To 'catch someone's meaning' is to 'figure out' what they are saying to us. A point of view has to be 'open to reason' if it is to mean something. There has to be about such utterance a plausibility, intelligibility, logicality. It has to carry within it a certain recognizable 'force' which is able to convince or persuade.[76] Conversely, if a point of view is skewed, illogical, makes no sense, we regard it as being without meaning, one to which we need attach no importance. 'Making sense' and 'being meaningful', if not synonymous, must be closely adjacent.

I cannot see how this does not equally apply to any schema for 'meaning in worship'. Negatively, it is when a liturgical event fails to 'make any sense' – when the worshipper has been unable to 'see any point in it' – that the event will be deemed to have been 'meaningless'. And, oppositely, when the parts (of the liturgy) have formed some sort of whole, and when the event in its integrity has made some connection with the person's larger life, then it will seem to have been 'meaningful', it will have 'made sense'.[77]

At the same time we cannot be unaware of the complications of any such collocation (rationality and worship), given the tendencies of twentieth-century (occidental) thought. The voluminous study by Max Weber of the rise of western rationality is, essentially, an account of primitive (magic, mystical) awareness being overtaken by rationalizing tendencies. Religious readings of the world are already, Weber thinks, attempts to make it meaningful.[78] But *precisely* 'this metaphysical need for a meaningful cosmos'[79] sets in train a process which eventually makes redundant the religious impulse out of which it sprang. This, in its extreme, totalizing form known to us in the west through most of the twentieth century, is the 'disenchantment of the world', which makes for so many inhabitants of such societies the notion of worshipping God as elusive and problematical as it is.[80]

All this notwithstanding, my brief overview of intellectual history in the twentieth century suggests that at the end of the century the landscape

---

76. E.g., Stephen Toulmin, *The Uses of Argument* (Cambridge University Press, 1964), 30–35.
77. Kelliher, 'Liturgy: an ecclesial act of meaning', 484.
78. See, e.g., Weber's essays 'The Social Psychology of the World Religions' and 'Religious Rejections of the World and their Directions' in (H. H. Gerth and C. W. Mills, eds.) *From Max Weber: essays in sociology* (London: Routledge and Kegan Paul, 1974), particularly pp. 275, 281, 352f., 355.
79. Weber, 'Social Psychology of World Religions', 281.
80. Weber, *Economy and Society*, 506.

does not appear as minacious as it did at its beginning (approximately when Weber was writing). We have seen that classical modernity reached some degree of exhaustion by the 1960s. The consequent revisions have included an extensive review of rationality: what it is, what it can do and what are its limits. The classical period had required the relegation 'to the junk heap of "appearance"'[81] of all modalities other than those empirically verifiable, and all statements not conformable to the law of non-contradiction. But, since that decade, the coercive power of rationality – already concealed within it but suppressed precisely by its coercive tendencies[82] – has begun to appear more clearly. We have understood better Weber's grim prognostication: 'the cloak [of the modern economic order] [would] become an iron cage'.[83]

True, reason is indispensable for human commerce: for understanding ourselves, each other, our human condition: 'To declare war upon reason is to alienate all who care for truth and to hold the door open for the imposter and the zealot.'[84] Notwithstanding, in the latter parts of the century we came to see that this same power for comprehension is, when allowed the totalizing power which it claims for itself, a deceptive[85] and dangerous[86] agency.

81. Putnam, *Human Face*, 162.
82. So Weber, 'Social Psychology of World Religions' in (Gerth and Mills, eds.) *From Max Weber*, 281: 'The various great ways of leading a rational and methodical life have been characterized by irrational presuppositions, which have been accepted simply as "given" and which have been incorporated into such ways of life.'
83. Max Weber, *The Protestant Ethic and the Spirit of Capitalism* (London: Routledge, 1992), 181.
84. H. J. Paton, *The Modern Predicament* (London: George Allen and Unwin, 1955), 58, cited by Frederick Ferré, *Logic, Language and God* (London: Eyre and Spottiswoode, 1962), 92.
85. Nietzsche's way of making the point is often cited: 'Just as it is certain that one leaf is never quite like another, so it is certain that the concept leaf is constructed by an arbitrary dropping of individual differences, through a forgetting of what differentiates; and this awakens the idea that there is something in nature beside leaves which would be "leaf", that is to say an original form, according to which all leaves are woven, drawn, circumscribed, coloured, curled, painted, but by clumsy hands, so that no example emerges correctly and reliably as a true copy of the original form. The overlooking of the individual gives us the form, whereas nature knows no forms and no concepts, and also no species, but only an X, which is inaccessible and indefinable to us.' See Dews, *The Limits of Disenchantment*, 28.
86. So John McGowan, *Postmodernism and its Critics* (Ithaca, NY: Cornell University Press, 1991), 20–1: 'The suppression of women and of minority groups within the society and of non-European races wherever they were encountered must be read as the outcome of the West's obsession with identity, singleness and purity, with its belief that only unified, homogenous entities (be they selves or states) can act effectively . . . Only by abandoning this traditional form of reason and by accepting the fact of heterogeneity could a different politics, a different understanding of how societies are constituted and what they could strive to achieve, be reached.'
   Caputo, *Radical Hermeneutics*, 228–33, similarly has an extended meditation on what he calls 'institutional reason', i.e., the rationalizing coercion used – often in concert – by universities, governments, military establishments and other institutionalized centres of power (including churches) to underwrite their collective will-to-power.

It is this new intellectual and cultural circumstance which has opened the field for forms of reason much more supple than the rationalism which ruled prior to the 1960s, a reasonableness which, in place of Weber's 'iron cage', offers a living space for 'the poet, the lover, the statesman, the moralist, or the religious believer.'[87] Charles Taylor, for example, writing of this new kind of rationality, urges that its role is 'to establish, not that some position is correct absolutely, but rather that some position is superior to some other'.[88] He calls this style of reasoning the 'Best Account' principle: '[T]he ultimate basis for accepting any ... [theory] is precisely that [it] makes better sense ... than do [its] rivals.'[89]

One clear manifestation of this new assessment of reason is the recovery (or rather a taking up for the first time, since for most of the twentieth century his ideas scarcely gained a significant audience) of the semiotic philosophy of C. S. Peirce of which I have already made brief mention. Peirce's semiotic in fact arose from his lifelong obsession with logic. Peirce was convinced that all human progress comes from correct reasoning. On the other hand, already in the latter part of the nineteenth century, it was clear to him that much human reasonableness does not fit the narrow canons of traditional logical processes; indeed the established moves of deduction and induction yield no real information beyond that already implicit in their premises. One aspect of Peirce's conviction about the intrinsic reasonableness of the human enterprise was his belief that even the forming of hypotheses – which even now the majority of philosophers of science see as standing outside the strictly logical process of *testing* hypotheses[90] – has about it (given the vast number of *possible* hypotheses which could be formulated) an inherently reasonable (though not canonically logical) process. He was thus led to supplement the two recognized moves of deduction and induction with a third kind of logic which he called 'abduction' or 'retroduction'.[91] Abduction is a process of reasoning which can be

87. Michael A. Arbib and Mary B. Hesse, *The Construction of Reality* (Cambridge University Press, 1986), 179.

88. Taylor, *Sources*, 72.   89. *Ibid.*, 32; see also pp. 57–8, 69, 73–5, 341.

90. See especially K. T. Fann, *Peirce's Theory of Abduction* (The Hague: Martinus Nijhoff, 1970), 1–5. My account of Peirce's theory of abduction is heavily dependent on Fann's book.

91. Peirce describes abduction so (CP 2.96): 'An originary Argument, or *Abduction*, is an argument which presents facts in its Premiss which present a similarity to the fact stated in the Conclusion, but which could perfectly well be true without the latter being so, much more without its being recognized; so that we are not led to assert the Conclusion positively but are only inclined toward admitting it as representing a fact of which the facts of the Premiss constitute an Icon.'

At another place he can sketch the relationship between deduction, induction and abduction as follows (CP 2.623):

compared with an 'informed guess'[92] or by 'a backwards movement from the consequent to the antecedent.'[93] It is thus the reasoning of a disciplined imagination, the reasoning of possibilities rather than certainties: 'The abductive imagination establishes a connection between the datum or result and an interpretant which is not its exact equivalent, it risks a relation which is not economical, in which there is an investment without a counterpart.'[94] Abduction is the order of inference particularly associated by Peirce with the kind of signification he called 'iconicity'[95] – a form of signification, I shall subsequently argue, especially applicable to the semiotics of worship. From this point of view we may (reasonably!) be encouraged to hold that even if their references are not finally demonstrable (in the way we have supposed to be 'scientific') yet such significations do not stand outside the bounds of the reasonable.[96] But, to reiterate, this is a point of view which was more readily available to us at the end of the twentieth century than it was at its beginning.[97]

Multisensory signification

One of the points made in Hilary Putnam's compact sentence about analytic philosophy 'hooking on' to the world (page 18, above) was philosophy's *central preoccupation with language*. This was hardly confined to

Deduction:	Rule [major premise]	All the beans from this bag are white.
	Case [minor premise]	These beans are from this bag.
∴	Result [conclusion]	These beans are white.
Induction:	Case	These beans are from this bag.
	Result	These beans are white.
∴	Rule	All the beans from this bag are white.
Hypothesis	[i.e., Abduction]: Rule	All the beans from this bag are white.
	Result	These beans are white.
∴	Case	These beans are from this bag.

And at yet another place (*CP* 5.189) he formulates the process of abduction so:

The surprising fact C is observed,
But if A were true, C would be a matter of course,
Hence, there is reason to suspect that A is true.

92. Fann, *Peirce's Theory of Abduction*, 35–8.
93. Ponzio, *Man as a Sign*, 267; see similarly Sandra Schillemans, 'Umberto Eco and William of Baskerville', *Semiotica* 92 3/4 (1992), 264–5.
94. Ponzio, *Man as a Sign*.
95. Petrilli, 'About and Beyond Peirce', 336–7; also her 'Dialogism and Interpretation in the Study of Signs', *Semiotica* 97 1/2 (1993), 113–14, and 'Towards Interpretation Semiotics' in (Rocco Capozzi, ed.) *Reading Eco: an anthology* (Bloomington: Indiana University Press, 1997), 132, 134–5.
96. See for example Lúcia Santaella Braga, 'Difficulties and Strategies in Applying Peirce's Semiotics', *Semiotica* 97 3/4 (1993), 403, where she speaks of a 'keen contemporary interest in the logic of uncertainty, imprecision and problem solving . . . in the cognitive sciences'.
97. The question of the rationality of the signs of worship, drawing on Peirce's abductive theories, is taken up again at the end of ch. 6, below.

English-language theories, however. It is conspicuously true of Husserl's phenomenology. And, of course, Saussure's work was a linguistic theory.[98] Even Derrida's deconstruction of these authors' works remains more or less oriented to language – 'writing and difference', 'grammatology', 'speech and phenomena'. At stake is the deep cleft we have everywhere encountered between intellectuality and materiality. The singular point of Derrida's sustained critique of the logocentrism or phonocentrism of classical theories of meaning – their resolute but untenable preference for orality over writing – lies in their instinctive wish to rid meaning (which is to say, linguistic meaning) of every last degree of materiality.

The strong predilection for language (leaving aside for the moment the question of orality vs. graphic forms of language; we shall see that a deep irony attaches to this) is everywhere apparent in the most self-conscious of the twentieth-century theorists of meaning, the analytic philosophers. According to any ordinary use of the English language, words for meaning cover *many different kinds* of human meaning-making. I adverted to not a few of them in my opening account of a visitor to a worship service. In the most tokenistic way, they range from the sense and reference which we met with Frege, to semiotic signification ('when the organ begins it means they are going to process'), to encompassing ideas such as 'what did it all mean?' and 'the meaning of life'. In the flourishing days of theory of meaning it was not at all uncommon for writers to offer a kind of lip-service to this breadth but then, immediately (arbitrarily, we may say), to discount every kind of meaning other than the linguistic variety.[99]

Of course, language has a role to play in liturgy – though not so much as one might imagine, at any rate in comparison with our more usual

---

98. Phenomenology was taken into avenues other than linguistic ones by Husserl's immediate followers; and Saussure is credited with being the originator of European semiotics – i.e., of *all* forms of human signification. But these possibilities were still awaiting their development from within the two originating forms of thought. Taylor, *Human Agency*, 215–16, advances some of the reasons for twentieth-century philosophy's obsession with language.

99. See, for example, William P. Alston, *Philosophy of Language* (Englewood Cliffs, NJ: Prentice-Hall Inc., 1964), 10–11; John Lyons, *Semantics* (Cambridge University Press, 1977), vol. I, p. 3; C. K. Ogden and I. A. Richards, *The Meaning of Meaning: a study of the influence of language upon thought and the science of symbolism* (London: Routledge and Kegan Paul, 1923; second edition, Ark Paperbacks, 1985), 186–7. In his book *The Body in the Mind: the bodily basis of meaning, imagination and reason* (The University of Chicago Press, 1987), 176, Mark Johnson complains, as I do here, about what he considers to be an arbitrary restriction of the meaning of 'meaning'. See also Charles Taylor, *Philosophy and the Human Sciences: philosophical papers 2* (Cambridge University Press, 1985), 21ff.

A more recent and disconcerting example – disconcerting, first, because his book has been about the meanings of worship and, second, because the qualification is offered just nine pages before the *end* of his book – comes in Stringer's *On the Perception of Worship*, 211.

forms of interchange. But, even in those places in which language does feature (prayers, the hymns, songs or chants, the readings and sermon), some far-reaching qualifications apply. First, the importance of the language of worship almost never rests in *written* forms – it is much more regularly spoken or sung. Secondly, the subject matter of such language will inevitably be more nearly poetic or imagistic than prosaic (I do not exclude the sermon from this judgement).[100]

First, then, the oral or melismatic quality of liturgical language. Of course, modern congregations do heavily depend on hymn books, overhead projections or printed orders of service. The point is: such texts are not written in order to be read (silently) but specifically to be vocalized. But that means that the *sound of the voice* becomes directly a dimension of the meanings which such language is to carry. To catch at the ancient division again (though I am saying that the elements have to be fused into a single manifestation) the *tone and quality of the enunciation* (its physicality) have as much to do with the meanings transmitted as the *semantic values* (its cognitive content) wherein it consists.[101]

Allow me to return to my hypothetical worshipper, but bring her forward to that section of the liturgy which is called The Reading of the Scriptures. To ask whether and to what extent the event which was the reading of the lesson was meaningful for those present, an answer will organize itself under these several different but mutually constitutive heads: (i) the bearing or manner or disposition of the person of the reader with respect to her or his vocation as a reader in public of the church's holy scriptures – that is, whether the act of reading signals for him or her a gravity or a joy or simply a dutiful conventionality;[102] (ii) the several skills of public oration – clarity of diction, force, suitability of expression, and so on – which

100. On the language of preaching see particularly Walter Brueggemann, *Finally Comes the Poet: daring speech for proclamation* (Minneapolis: Fortress Press, 1989); and on the poetic quality of liturgical language generally, see Patrick W. Collins, *More Than Meets the Eye: ritual and parish liturgy* (New York: Paulist Press, 1983), 101–7, or Don E. Saliers, *Worship as Theology: foretaste of divine glory* (Nashville: Abingdon Press, 1994), 211–13: 'Christian liturgy is symbolic, parabolic and metaphoric' (p. 212).

101. Joyce Zimmerman accordingly asks, 'If we are to worship, is this the way it should *sound*?' (*Liturgy as Language of Faith*, 2–3, my emphasis). Borrowing from Daniel Stevick, she goes on to distinguish a 'first level' type of articulation – 'the language of prayer, doxology, worship . . . formed in encounter, confrontation, recognition . . . full of the awed sense of the other: the "you"' (p. 4) – from a 'second level' type which 'derives from reflection, from discursive statement[s] of meaning' (p. 3); see Zimmerman's longer discussion (pp. 2–9).

102. See Robert W. Hovda, *Strong, Loving and Wise: presiding in liturgy* (Collegeville: The Liturgical Press, 1976), 65. So also Ray Lonergan, *A Well Trained Tongue: a workbook for lectors* (Chicago: Liturgy Training Publications, 1982), 9: 'Before your voice is heard as a lector, you are seen . . . Your movement [to the lectern] . . . says that you care about what you are going to do and so others should care.' See further, below, pp. 193, 195.

I will call here simply the 'musicality' of the reading;[103] (iii) signs as to the person's having prepared the work or otherwise; (iv) an intelligence as to the literary dynamics within the text and the rendering of these intelligent for a hearer; and, (v) admittedly and not least, the fusion of these into a meaningful whole by the sense (the semantic and syntactic structures) of the passage which is being read aloud. When *all* these dimensions of the event which is called the Reading of Scripture cohere in a deeply satisfying way, a worshipper will perhaps be heard to say afterwards how 'meaningful' was the reading. It is within such a frame of reference that I am wanting to say that the 'meaning' of the event consisted as much in the performance of the act as in the markings on the page – even if we agree that the one could not have come into being without the other.[104]

Herein lies a deep irony, with reference back to the classical theories of meaning. Assuming Derrida's point about those theorists' valorization of phonocentrism, then, one may say, the dimensions of meaning production and meaning transmission which I have just analysed in the action of the lector could have found no recognition in those theories. On one hand, their anti-materialism drove them to give their preference to *orality*; yet the *voice's musicality* precisely as a *dimension of meaning* nowhere features, and could hardly feature in their deliberations,[105] not at any rate prior to J. L. Austin's theory of illocutionary force.[106] On the other hand, much earlier in the century, Ernst Cassirer had exactly caught the point I am making: '[T]he sensuous character of expression and the logical factor of signification cannot be separated in the actual reality of language.'[107]

Language here has been for us a kind of test case or leading example. I said the issues raised by the language of worship open out into a larger theatre of operations, so that, if we see that precisely the linguistic elements

---

103. In my treatment of the semiotics of worship in chs. 3 and 6 below, I take up Julia Kristeva's notions of 'musicality' and 'materiality' in the production of signs; below, pp. 106–7, 186–90.

104. See particularly Nichols, *Liturgical Hermeneutics*, 9, whose work proceeds from '[the] . . . general conviction that liturgy is text *and* performance and that it is impossible to reflect on one without also taking account of the other' (her emphasis). On the recent interest, in liturgical studies, in the 'performance' of liturgy, see below, ch. 4, n. 20, and ch. 7, n. 13.

105. On the inability of the classical theories to acknowledge the musical (vocalic) dimension of language, see Derrida, *Of Grammatology*, 195–200, and Paul de Man, *Allegories of Reading: figural language in Rousseau, Nietzsche, Rilke and Proust* (New Haven, CT: Yale University Press, 1979), 88–90.

106. J. L. Austin, *How to Do Things with Words* (Oxford University Press, 1962), e.g., 98–9. On the signifying power *within the voice*, see particularly Barthes, 'The Grain of the Voice', esp. p. 188: 'The "grain" *is* the body in the voice as it sings, the hand as it writes, the limb as it performs' (my emphasis).

107. Ernst Cassirer, *The Philosophy of Symbolic Forms* (New Haven, CT: Yale University Press, 1957) (published in German in 1929), vol. III, p. 111.

depend on this fusion of sensuality and logicality, then we shall not be hindered from seeing that all the other vehicles of meaning function similarly. I said in my opening remarks that the visitor, by the time she comes to leave, will have been exposed to a thickly woven plenitude of sense impressions; she will have heard, seen, touched, tasted and smelt a dense texture of significations which she will judge to have been meaningful or otherwise. An exegesis of that sentence now says that the face, the hands, the voice, the manner of walking, the sitting and standing, in short the demeanour generally, of the presiding minister will have been instrumental in constructing meanings of one kind rather than another.[108] The music, the lighting and then every other sensory dimension of the event called the liturgy will signify in some way or another.

A second qualification of the language used in worship, I said, is its essentially poetic character.[109] This, too, is in the nature of the case. For, while worship must be anchored in the substantial world of decisions and dissension, mortgages and motherhood, its business is to set all these things in an other than ordinary, or predictable, or conventional light. In a conception of which I will make extensive use, the liturgy wishes to bring us to the 'frontier', or 'boundary', of our known world. Or, in a different but similar conceptualization taken from Paul Ricoeur, there is a 'world before the liturgy' just as there is 'a world in front of . . . text[s]'.[110] The liturgy wishes to 'orient' its participants in a particular way.[111] Obviously, as I shall say in greater detail in the next section, this orientation has to do with God, or Transcendence, that which is Wholly Other. This is why I noted above that even the prose passages of liturgy such as the sermon cannot be prosaic. The language of worship is inevitably poetic. Putnam noted

---

108. See Romano Guardini as cited by Mark Searle: 'the priest of the late nineteenth century who said, "We must organize the procession better; we must see to it that the singing and praying are done better" [should have rather] asked himself quite a different question: how can the act of walking become a religious act, a retinue for the Lord progressing through his land, so that an epiphany may take place?'; Mark Searle, 'Liturgy as Metaphor', *Worship* 55 (1981), 115.

And though I shall draw more extensively on his work when we come explicitly to the semiotics of worship, a preliminary reference to the work of A. Ronald Sequeira is due here. See particularly his essay 'Gottesdiest als menschliche Ausdruckshandlung' in (H. B. Meyer, et al., eds.) *Gottesdienst der Kirche: Gestalt des Gottesdienst* (Regensburg: Verlag Friedrich Pustet, second edition 1990), vol. III, pp. 7–39.

109. See Volp, *Liturgik*, 103–4.

110. Ricoeur, *Human Sciences,* 141, and frequently in his writings of this period. The idea is brought across into liturgical studies by Nichols, *Liturgical Hermeneutics*, e.g., 23, 49, 90. Nichols speaks frequently of the liturgy 'proposing the Kingdom' (see further below, ch. 5, n. 63).

111. Ricoeur, *Human Sciences*, 161: 'The text seeks to place us in its meaning, that is – according to another acceptation of the word *sens* – in the same direction.'

that the theorists of meaning (again I am thinking here chiefly of the analytic theorists) set themselves to explain how language could hook on to
the world. Given the formidable task, as we now see it, of saying how an
ideal meaning can relate to a material world, it must be apparent that the
theorists and the theories were incapable of stretching their frames of reference so far. One of the striking and depressing features of their work for
anyone visiting it from our time, in fact, is the sheer banality of the examples over which they laboured so prodigiously: 'Kennst du das Land, wo die
Zitronen blühen? (Do you know the land where the lemon trees bloom?)'
and 'Sam smokes habitually.'[112] As one of their number observed, the challenge of poetry, the problem of saying how a line like e. e. cummings' 'the
sweet small clumsy feet of april came into the ragged meadow of my soul'
can 'hook on' to the world was virtually insurmountable.[113] But such, in a
manner of speaking, are the meanings of worship.

Theistic reference

The reference to a 'world before the liturgy' leads me directly to a third
dimension of a putative theory of meaning for worship. I take this dimension to be by far the most demanding aspect (on the theory itself, that is).
There will be requirement of it to give an account of the ways in which
some sense of 'the divine', 'that which is quite Other', can be generated
from within this assemblage of significations which is a worship service.
I said earlier that the revisions which have been brought to rationality in
the latter part of the century have cleared away some roadblocks; a philosopher once secure in that tradition can now write of 'regain[ing] our sense of
mystery'.[114] Yet this is still vastly removed from an overtly religious reading of the world. At this point our considerations seem to pull apart not
just from the classical meaning theories we have traversed but from the
most widespread assumptions of our late modernity.

112. J. R. Searle, 'What is a Speech Event?' in (J. R. Searle, ed.) *The Philosophy of Language*
(Oxford University Press), 46, and John R. Searle, *Speech Acts: an essay in the philosophy of
language* (Cambridge University Press, 1969), 22. The examples are chosen at random, but they
illustrate the fact that the cases taken by analytic theorists of meaning never did pass beyond
the most basic sentence forms.
113. Alston, *Philosophy of Language*, 96. See similarly Ricoeur, *The Rule of Metaphor*, 209, where
he cites Marcus B. Hester as saying that Wittgenstein constructed a theory of ordinary
language alone, to the exclusion of poetic language.
114. Putnam, *Human Face*, 118. Perhaps yet more remarkable is that so convinced a
traditionalist as Jürgen Habermas can acknowledge that only some kind of 'contact with the
extraordinary [*das Außeralltägliche*]' can ultimately renew the sources of meaning; see Dews,
Limits of Disenchantment, 210.

For, on the one hand, so fundamental is the notion of a divine Other to an act of worship that without it the event under consideration can scarcely be brought beneath that description of it. It could perhaps be seen as a gathering of believers for their mutual encouragement, or in order to study their Scriptures, or to plan their mission, but, in the absence of prayer *to* the deity, and the drawing of approbation and sustenance *from* the deity, it is hard to see how the word 'worship' can apply.[115] Catherine Bell says of ritual practice generally, '[T]he schemes established by ritualization are impressed upon participants as deriving from a reality beyond the activities of the group.'[116] For rituals which are worship this means: the facilitation of access to the group's God, and the disclosure of that deity's character in such a way that an appropriate response is elicited. Any attempt to give an account of the 'meaning' or 'meanings' generated within such an assembly must be capable of comprehending this dimension.

On the other hand, meaning, as I am developing that notion, is a human construction, which means that it is inevitably, invariably culturally embedded. Into this construction of a world which makes the best sense it can (Taylor's 'Best Account'!) are incorporated, on the one hand, the great 'master narratives' of the person's dominant culture,[117] and, on the other, personal recollections, learned habits, social values, responses to given geographical and environmental conditions, and so on: a host of circumstances impossible to codify or catalogue.[118] I want to take up the question of our secular cultural setting in greater detail in the next chapter. But a delineation of meaning in terms of a person's embodied, cumulative responses to his or her 'lifeworld'[119] means that such cultural–religious influences as I touch on here can by no means remain out of view. If my convictions (i) about our cultural context supplying at least the bulk of the raw materials for our meaning-making processes, and (ii) about the severity of

---

115. See, for example, Ninian Smart, *The Concept of Worship* (London: Macmillan Press Ltd., 1972), 10: 'the language of worship begins with the vocative. In worship one *addresses* the focus of worship' (my emphasis).

116. Catherine Bell, 'Ritual, Change and Changing Rituals', *Worship* 63 (1989), 35.

117. See Fredric Jameson's Foreword to Jean-François Lyotard, *The Postmodern Condition: a report on knowledge* (Minneapolis: University of Minnesota Press, 1984), p. x; see Lyotard's text, pp. 37, 51, or 60 for his reference to 'the grand narrative' which informs a culture.

118. See Taylor, *Human Agency*, 48, on what he calls 'imports': such recollections as lead a person to experience a situation as 'humiliating, or shameful, or outrageous, or dismaying, or exhilarating, or wonderful; and so on.'

119. 'Lifeworld' is a term deriving from the late period of Husserl's work; it was coined by him to describe the totality of a person's phenomenological experience of the world. See his *The Crisis of European Sciences and Transcendental Phenomenology* (Evanston, IL: Northwestern University Press, 1970), e.g., 48ff., 103ff.

the conflict between, on the one hand, a cultural system which 'can only fashion its criteria out of itself'[120] and, on the other, the traditional values of theism – the clash, that is, between the meanings proposed in the liturgy and the meanings proposed by the world to which the worshipper returns – have any substance, then any theory of meaning for worship is charged with the task of effecting *some* kind of reconciliation between these divergent meaning systems.

This is not, I think, the place to say what such a schema might look like. I turn to all that in Part III. It perhaps suffices to say that it will hover uncertainly on the borderline between a theological response to modern secularism and a religious phenomenology of signs – that is, an account of how a particular system of significations is able to encourage a religious sensibility. Before that, however, I turn to the cultural and societal setting in which worship undertakes to offer its meanings.

---

120. Habermas, *The Philosophical Discourse of Modernity*, 41.

2

Meaning and modernity

No one makes meanings in a vacuum. Meanings which are available to one generation are no longer so in the next, and *vice versa*.[1] One might regard these simply as 'fashions', except that that suggests some sort of superficial change on a perduring base. The availability of meanings, contrariwise, has to do with the basic materials from which people fabricate an habitable world ('lifeworld'). Generally speaking, the axioms and viewpoints from which people fashion these 'webs of significance'[2] are less than apparent to them. They have opinions. But why and how they reached these opinions is – again, generally speaking – unapparent. The forces, historical and cultural, which formed their opinions are deeply concealed; such dicta seem 'simply obvious'.[3] In brief: meaning is made as emergent events are configured in relation to the meanings already available – though not overtly so – in any given cultural system. These considerations apply no less to the ways in which people engage with the meanings being proposed in the liturgy (the world before the liturgy).

1. I have already drawn attention to Charles Taylor's use of the notion 'availability' to describe the force or attraction which attaches to an idea in a particular cultural moment as offering a way of making sense of the human condition. See *Sources*, esp. pp. 313–14, but also pp. 106 and 112: 'For a given age and civilization, a particular reading seems to impose itself; it seems to common sense the only conceivable one.'
2. Clifford Geertz, *The Interpretation of Cultures* (New York: Basic Books, 1973), 5. On the metaphor 'web' as appropriated by semioticians, see Deely, *Basics of Semiotics*, 14–15.
3. So, Edward T. Hall, *The Silent Language* (Garden City: Doubleday, 1959), 53: 'Culture hides much more than it reveals, and strangely enough what it hides, it hides most effectively from its own participants.' Note might also be taken of Polanyi's 'fiduciary frameworks' (Michael Polanyi, *Personal Knowledge: towards a post critical philosophy* (University of Chicago Press, 1958), 264–8).

Postmodernity?

In so far as one can generalize about such enveloping structures as the cultural patterns of industrialized societies, the end of the twentieth century presented itself as a period of great mobility (i.e., instability) with respect to the availability of meanings. I have made the point that at some period soon after the middle of the century the major intellectual methods – whose roots were fixed in an era antedating the twentieth century by two or three centuries, the period we are accustomed to call 'modern' – collapsed under the weight they were being asked to bear. But the shifts in available meanings in the 1960s were not just intellectual. The emergence of a new ecological sensitivity was one such change. A similar shift of values saw the reversal of a 'progressivism' which had sanctioned, in the name of 'development' or 'modernization', the wholesale demolition of buildings and artifacts from earlier times. Or again, it made new demands for 'holism' or 'cross-disciplinary studies' rather than 'analytical' styles of discourse within self-contained fields.[4] This change of temper, both in intellectual approach and popular judgement, has, of course, become familiar to us under the description 'postmodernity' or 'postmodernism'.

On the other hand there were, through the latter decades of the twentieth century, sufficient lines of continuity with the paradigm of modernity to render questionable for many commentators the 'periodization' notion presumed in the 'post-' prefix. 'Postmodernity' is thus contested from a number of aspects: first, whether the cultural 'break' implied by the term[5] can be justified empirically[6] or conceptually;[7] accordingly, what the

---

4. Toulmin, *Cosmopolis*, e.g., 160–7, 181–2, 208, lists such changes under the notion of a new 'humanizing' tendency. Irmengard Rauch, 'Openness, Eco and the End of Another Millennium' in (Rocco Capozzi, ed.) *Reading Eco: an anthology* (Bloomington: Indiana University Press, 1997), 138, asks (citing Richard Tarnas): '[W]hy is there evident now such a widespread collective impetus in the Western mind to articulate a holistic and participatory world view, visible in virtually every field?'

5. Jameson, *Postmodernism*, 1: 'The case for [postmodernism's] existence depends on the hypothesis of some radical break or *coupure*, generally traced back to the end of the 1950s or the early 1960s.' See also Toulmin, *Cosmopolis*, 3: 'We are now at the end of an era . . . the era of Modernity itself.'

6. Margaret A. Rose, *The Post-modern and the Post-industrial: a critical analysis* (Cambridge University Press, 1991) shows in case after case that the indicators of postmodernity cited by one critic or group of critics is seen by others as characteristic of modernity, or that the feature in question can be found at a time generally agreed to antedate the rise of postmodernity.

7. Paul Ricoeur, *Lectures on Ideology and Utopia* (New York: Columbia University Press, 1986), 152: 'Is a complete break understandable without some kind of intellectual miracle, a sense of someone emerging from the dark?' or, *ibid.*, 157: 'I wonder whether a notion of a radical break can be thought.'

term 'postmodern' means;[8] whether modernity and post-modernity are not rather to be seen as different styles or methods running concurrently through the greater part of the century;[9] and, not least, whether we are talking about postmodernity or postmodernism (and then the degree to which *this* distinction applies to genuinely distinguishable periods).[10] For our purposes, the much more important question (than trying to determine what the age is best called) might be: *which meanings are available to us at the beginning of the twenty-first century?* In all this, one thing appears likely: that any strong distinction between the kinds of meanings disputed by intellectual theorists (such as I sketched in the previous chapter) and the affectivities according to which people make their everyday judgements about what is meaningful (if the distinction ever did apply) has tended to collapse. Readers of tabloid newspapers might not get to see the academic journals nor be able to articulate the influences of postmodernity on them. But the ideas inhabit the one no less than the other. The globalization of economies, technologies of mass communication, the public manifestation of postmodern ideas in built space, and doubtless any number of less obvious but no less influential carriers of meaning, mean that there is no clear cut-off point between an arcane exposition of such ideas and their influence at all levels of people's meaning-making.[11]

It must be entirely apparent that things do not make the same sense, or the same things do not now make sense, as they did in the middle of the twentieth century. Perhaps, as John McGowan puts it, the epicentre of change lies in the abandonment of the dream of purity.[12] The purity in question took various forms. We have surveyed some of them. Analytic philosophers worked for the day (deferred in reality to some utopian future but still held as achievable in principle) when language

---

8. Rose, in her concluding remarks, observes that the extensive range of ways in which the term has come to be used had made it necessary (in 1991) for any author employing the term ('postmodern') to specify his or her particular usage (see *Post-modern and Post-industrial*, 169).

9. So Charles Jencks' idea of 'double coding' especially in architecture: 'modern' styles standing side by side with some other 'postmodern' style. See Rose, *Post-modern and Post-industrial*, ch. 4.

10. McGowan, *Postmodernism*, 2, distinguishes 'modernity' as that condition applying in western societies 'during the past two to three hundred years' from 'modern*ism*' as designating 'the artistic movement which stretches from, roughly, 1890 to 1945.' The distinction seems helpful to me and I will follow it wherever I can.

11. So Jameson, *Postmodernism*, 38–9, or 53: 'These are not merely theoretical issues; they have urgent practical political consequences'; or de Man, *Allegories of Reading*, 15: 'It turns out that in these innocent-looking didactic exercises we are in fact playing for very sizeable stakes.'

12. McGowan, *Postmodernism*, 3–12.

would fit the world without remainder, a 'God's Eye View' of the universe. Husserlian phenomenology sought its 'eidetic reduction'. Structuralism worked to expose the deep structures hidden within or beneath all reality.[13] Every theory assumed the rhetoric of the final word, somehow oblivious to the fact that all such previous 'last' words had been overtaken before their ink was dry. Other aspirations to purity were encapsulated in the modernist slogan 'art for art's sake'[14] or in the Romantic separation out of artistic 'genius'.[15] For the notion of 'purity' we could equally write in Derrida's 'presence': '[T]he dream of a full and immediate presence closing history, the transparence and indivision of a parousia, the suppression of contradiction and difference.'[16] The supposition of ideal meanings refined of material signification broke under the weight put on it. In a wider application of the same tendency, we have learned in these last decades that *there are no purities* (accessible to human beings, anyway) – of thought, of essence, of truth, of meaning. It is not to say, I will want to insist, that we do not need, depend upon, such *working reference points*, but the achievement of them in an unalloyed purity is a dream we relinquished at some point on our way through the century.[17]

The abandonment of the dream of purity (finality) carried with it epoch-making changes in how people at every level of society view themselves and their condition in the world. For example, the notion of 'progress', automatically assumed in high modernity, was bound for massive reassessment. Several streams had fed the conviction: optimism in European liberal humanism; espousal of Darwinian evolutionary theories; confidence in scientific method(s) and their dazzling technological achievements; and, not least, for those living in the so-called 'new world', the expectation that life would be kinder to future generations than their

13. So Jameson, *The Prison-House of Language*, 109: 'the separation of these mental processes from reality [in structuralism] encourages an explicit search for the permanent structures of the mind itself, the organizational categories and forms through which the mind is able to experience the world, or to organize a meaning in what is essentially in itself meaningless.'
14. McGowan, *Postmodernism*, 8–9. And see Merleau-Ponty, *Primacy of Perception*, 180, on modernism: 'Cézanne knows already what cubism will repeat: that the external form, the envelope, is secondary and derived . . . that this shell of space must be shattered . . . and what is there to paint, then? Cubes, spheres, and cones . . . ? Pure forms which have the solidity of what could be defined by an internal law of construction.'
15. Hans-Georg Gadamer, *Truth and Method* (London: Sheed and Ward, 1975), 51ff.; or David Tracy, *The Analogical Imagination: Christian theology and the culture of pluralism* (London: SCM Press, 1981), 111, 125.
16. Derrida, *Of Grammatology*, 115.
17. For example, Putnam writes of the analytic project: 'a great dream is given up – the dream of a description of physical reality as it is apart from observers, a description which is objective in the sense of being "from no particular point of view"'; *Human Face*, 11.

pioneering predecessors. Of course, Marxist societies had shared similar utopian dreams. To cancel the dream of perfection, then, has entailed the evacuation of this form, or source, of meaning in the so-called postmodern period. Generally, people no longer assume automatically that 'things can only get better'.

Another casualty of the adulteration of purities was the presumption of a self-contained 'self': an autonomous consciousness or 'soul'. Patently, the idea runs back to antiquity. But it was built as a cornerstone into Cartesian modernity in Descartes's radical distinction between consciousness (*res cogitans*) and physicality (*res extensa*), the two constituent elements of human existence which, in principle, can have nothing to do with each other![18] As with the ideality of meanings, so the idea of consciousness as a transcendent power, not identifiable with any specific anatomical location and not reducible to physical responses to stimuli, seems so intuitively right that only in the latter parts of the twentieth century was it shown to be impossible.[19] It has been exposed to critique, however, not just from the identifiably 'deconstructionist' philosophers but from practically every quarter. So, already in 1969 Paul Ricoeur (in some sense as a phenomenologist) was attacking 'that illusion which bears the hallowed name of self-consciousness.'[20] Naturally Derrida ranges his deconstructive weapon against this particular instance of 'presence'.[21] But Jürgen Habermas, so ideologically opposed to every form of deconstruction, similarly wishes to base what he sees as the 'unfinished project of modernity'[22] in other than 'the paradigm of consciousness' or its associated 'philosophy of the subject'.[23] And last but by no means least, the conception has been

---

18. A helpful (and entertaining) introduction to Descartes's views on consciousness is given in Daniel C. Dennett, *Consciousness Explained* (London: Allen Lane/Penguin Books, 1991); see, e.g., pp. 33ff., and 101ff.

19. To my knowledge, the last theorist to contend for this view was Sir John Eccles in 1977; see Dennett, *Consciousness Explained*, 29, or Arbib and Hesse, *The Construction of Reality*, 73–4.

20. Ricoeur, *Conflict of Interpretations*, 148; see similarly, *ibid.*, 99, 243. The book was published in French in 1969.

21. E.g., *Margins of Philosophy*, 14–15, 65, or *Writing and Difference*, 177–8.

22. See Habermas, 'Modernity: an unfinished project', *passim*.

23. The citations are from Thomas McCarthy's Introduction to Jürgen Habermas, *The Philosophical Discourse of Modernity*, p. x. Habermas wishes to stay within the Enlightenment (i.e., 'modern') commitment to rationality, but to ground this in a social and collaborative process which he calls 'communicative action' rather than in individual consciousness. This theme appears frequently in *Philosophical Discourse* (e.g., p. 40) but it receives exhaustively detailed treatment in the two-volumed *Theory of Communicative Action* (Boston: Beacon Press, 1984, and Cambridge: Polity Press, 1987). See vol. II, pp. 11–14, for a compressed statement of Habermas' thesis; see also the essay 'Comments on John Searle: "Meaning, Communication and Representation"' in (Ernest Lepore and Robert van Gulick, eds.) *John Searle and his Critics* (Oxford: Basil Blackwell, 1991), 17–29, esp. p. 25.

dismantled by ongoing findings in neurophysiological research.[24] At the end of the century, the 'self', the virtually sacrosanct citadel of modernity, must be seen to be a social construction, a multiplicity inhabited by differences as much as by identity, in Ricoeur's language, 'a task precisely because it is not a given'.[25] In more pessimistic vein, Jameson writes of 'the "death" of the subject itself – the end of the autonomous bourgeois monad or ego or individual – and the accompanying stress . . . on the decentering of that formerly centered subject or psyche'.[26]

As with the mind/brain antinomy, so the postmodern period has witnessed the demise of dualism – in any and all of its applications – as an acceptable intellectual method. Stephen Toulmin holds the *res cogitans/res extensa* bifurcation to be 'the chief girder in [the] framework of modernity, to which all the other parts were connected'. He goes on to list 'a dozen further dichotomies' which follow from this one.[27] Among them are some we have already encountered: mental vs. material; mind vs. brain; signifier vs. signified; subject vs. object; facts vs. values; fixed laws of nature vs. human spontaneity; rationality vs. emotivity; history vs. fiction; depth vs. surface; or the real vs. artificiality. A moment's thought shows that the division of any given subject area into polar opposites is – in its own way – a bid for purity: for example, the purity of consciousness uncontaminated by its linkage with physiological processes, or of meaning without material signification. The new approach, by contrast, sees that some dimension of the one is inevitably present in the other. For example, in the history/fiction split (truth vs. untruth) – some late howls of protest notwithstanding[28] – Paul Ricoeur and others have secured the insight that *each* of these two great categories of human narrativity derives from and depends upon the other – even if we need to know, and can usually tell, which is which.[29] Derrida's work, of course, has been dedicated practically wholly to the exposure of these structured alternatives and the demonstration of their unsustainability. To take up as another example, then – the last of my list of

24. Dennett, *Consciousness Explained*, *passim*.
25. Ricoeur, *Conflict of Interpretations*, 327, or see *ibid.*, p. 329: 'the positing of the self is not a given, it is a task; it is not *gegeben* but *aufgegeben*.'
26. Jameson, *Postmodernism*, 15 (emphasis removed).
27. Toulmin, *Cosmopolis*, 108. Not all the items in my list of dualisms are mentioned by Toulmin.
28. See John R. Searle, *Expression and Meaning: studies in the theory of speech acts* (Cambridge University Press, 1979), 58–75.
29. Paul Ricoeur, *Time and Narrative*, 3 volumes (Chicago University Press, 1984–8). See summary statements of the point of view about the proximities of history and fiction at vol. I, pp. 81–2, and vol. II, pp. 3, 82.

'pairs', the real vs. the artificial – Derrida's analysis of Austin's distinction between 'conventional' (serious) and 'parasitical' (non-serious) speech acts showed not that the latter is derived from the (definitive) former, as Austin had supposed, but that it is a mutual dependency.[30] As one commentator puts it: 'Something can [signify] only if it is iterable, only if it can be repeated in various serious and non-serious contexts, cited and parodied. Imitation is not an accident that befalls an original but its condition of possibility.'[31] Going on from there, then, Jameson extrapolates as one of the defining marks of postmodernity 'a transformation of the "real" into so many pseudoevents'.[32] This abdication from clear alternatives (read: polar opposites) certainly empowers the suspicion, even among those who have themselves abandoned a modern preoccupation with certainty, that relativism is inherent in postmodern thought.[33] We will certainly need to return to the question if we are to speak of meaning in the postmodern era, but that such can be constructed on the basis of paired antitheses now seems to belong to a past age.

Such changes as I have listed here are not by any means the only surprises awaiting a mid-twentieth-century citizen were she or he to step into our available meanings. The ones I have touched on are some of those which encourage the notion of 'break' in the cultural paradigm. Other mind-boggling differences encountered by a mid-century visitor, however, have to be seen more nearly as *continuations* – as extensions or perhaps an intensification – of tendencies already entrenched in the modern paradigm. These differences, then, *counter* the proposal of 'post-' modernity, if the prefix is supposed to carry a 'periodizing' implication. They suggest that, duly taking into consideration the bewildering changes between the earlier part of the twentieth century and our own time, there is still reason to see ourselves living within modernity, what is then better called 'late modernity'.[34]

Among these, I suppose the most breathtaking must be the technological competencies which, even for those of us who live with them, still induce momentary incredulity. Medical science, gene technology and electronic communications are such instances. Our question is: how do these

---

30. Derrida, *Margins*, 321–7.

31. Culler, *On Deconstruction*, 120. On this, see also Norris, *Deconstruction*, 108ff., 143–4.

32. Jameson, *Postmodernism*, 48. Jameson's remark has subsequently been more than vindicated in the proliferation of 'reality' television programmes.

33. See, for example, Putnam, *Reason, Truth and History*, 119–24, or *Human Face*, 123–4. See also Taylor, 'Foucault on Freedom and Truth' in *Human Sciences*, 153–84, esp. pp. 177–8.

34. The term now finds wide usage; my own awareness of it derives from Charles Jencks; see Rose, *Post-modern and Post-industrial*, e.g., 116, 125ff.

dimensions of our 'lifeworld' – continuous with, yet different from, the versions known by our parents – affect the work of making meaning? One answer is: they are likely to make it difficult, confused, confusing. On the one hand, I said earlier, an important dimension of postmodern consciousness is its disbelief in inevitable progress. At the same time, or on the other hand, every time we go to the doctor there will be a new prescription drug or surgical procedure available. Children, to shift the focus, mostly know better than their parents how to operate computers. Grandparents simply smile. But contradictions in the values engendered by, and the sense of alienation in the face of, technological advance is not new – though its dimensions may well be. This has been the classic experience of high modernity. Only the speed, and the competencies demanded, have altered.[35]

Another aspect of life at the turn of the twenty-first century affecting every last individual not just of so-called developed nations but, because of its global reach, every person in the world, is the now globalized system of money. Jameson is one of the writers who attaches periodizing significance to the 'post-' prefix. As the subtitle of his book on postmodernism makes clear ('the cultural logic of late capitalism'), he ties this periodization closely to industrial and economic stages of development in the west: the ages of steam power, of electric and internal combustion engines, and now electronic communicative devices. To these three periods are tied 'three fundamental moments in capitalism': market capitalism, imperialization and, currently, multinational capital.[36] Holding in abeyance for the moment this industrial/economic approach to the

---

35. One of the sharpest clashes in the literature on postmodernity is over whether the age is fundamentally humanizing and benevolent, or, oppositely, yet more estranging and meaningless than had been modernity. Stephen Toulmin thinks the great cultural shift of the 1960s represented the recovery of a humanism which had begun with Erasmus, Montaigne and Rabelais but was derailed – by the horrendous political events of the early seventeenth century – into the familiar (Cartesian) quest for certainty (*Cosmopolis*, 22–8, 186–7; for a similar viewpoint, see Deely, *New Beginnings*, 122–3, 143, 180). By contrast, Jameson, in company with Baudrillard and others, reads the postmodern age greatly more pessimistically: '[R]eference and reality disappear altogether, and even meaning – the signified – is problematized. We are left with that pure and random play of signifiers that we call postmodernism, which no longer produces monumental works of the modernist type but ceaselessly reshuffles the fragments of preexistent texts, the building blocks of older cultural and social production, in some new and heightened bricolage: metabooks which cannibalize other books, metatexts which collate bits of other texts – such is the logic of postmodernism in general' (*Postmodernism*, 96; the passage is typical of Jameson's outlook; see similar passages, e.g., on pp. 167–8, or 245).
    On the objectifying, alienating effects of modernity see, e.g., Taylor, *Sources*, 144–58, 383, or 500–2.
36. Jameson, *Postmodernism*, 35.

postmodern condition, he follows another path (well worn in the literature on postmodernity), namely, an analysis of postmodern architecture. His sense of the Los Angeles Bonaventure hotel yields a now widely cited image of postmodernity: '[T]his latest mutation in space – postmodern hyperspace – has finally succeeded in transcending the capacities of the individual human body to locate itself, to organize its immediate surroundings perceptually, and cognitively to map its position in a mappable external world.'[37] But now this notion of 'hyperspace' becomes a metaphor of sorts for the experience of the individual who finds himself in 'the whole new decentered global network of the third stage of capital itself';[38] 'it is precisely this whole extraordinarily demoralizing and depressing original new global space [i.e., 'hyperspace'] which is "the moment of truth" of postmodernism'.[39] I am not inclined to dispute Jameson's analysis of an economic existence which leaves people in 'unmappable space' – as they worry about their job security, and as governments of every political stripe join with business concerns in the doubtful ideologies of rationalization, privatization, commodification.[40] Of course what I do wish to say (again) is that this is scarcely a new condition in itself: only in its proportions.[41] Charles Taylor urges that one of the chief marks of modernity was (or is!) its transubstantiation of qualitative values into quantitative ones.[42] That is why every value in the world – retribution for past wrongs, compensation for death or physical impairment, whatever – now has to be denominated in quantities of money.[43] But this is hardly new; as Taylor says, it was built into modernity from the outset.

The clearest indicator, however, which ties our age back into the modern paradigm seems to me to be its steadfast repudiation of religious conviction as a source of meaning. Whatever signs can be assembled to show a shift in popular sentiment in the latter part of the twentieth century, at

---

37. *Ibid.*, 44.   38. *Ibid.*, 38.   39. *Ibid.*, 49.

40. On this last term see particularly, Lyotard, *The Postmodern Condition*. On the universal adoption of 'market force' ideologies in the concluding decades of the century, see Jameson's eighth chapter in *Postmodernism*, 'Postmodernism and the Market'.

It is perhaps precisely the sign of the bewildering times in which we live that my sentences, written sometime in 2000, in 2003 have a 'dated' feel, in light of the corporate collapses witnessed through 2002.

41. Already in the period of high modernity, Weber had remarked on the depersonalizing forces of the market. See ch. 7 (pp. 635–640) of *Economy and Society*: 'The Market: its impersonality and ethic'.

42. Taylor, *Human Agency*, 17; see also 46–7.

43. Peter Skagestad, in an essay on the computer age ('The Mind's Machines: the Turing machine, the Memex and the personal computer', *Semiotica* 111 3/4 (1996), 217–43), puts the point of view that computers are not simply tools but have entered into the ways in which people think.

least *this* pattern – I mean the erosion of credibility of any religious 'grand narrative' – must be seen to have proceeded steadily, if not at first all that obviously, almost from the beginning of the modern period. The importance of this for the project of meaning in worship suggests that it needs greater detail than space has allowed in my overview of the postmodern condition generally. I will therefore devote my next section to it. To summarize this section (and still holding open the question whether any great thing is accomplished in being able to put a name on our time), in view (i) of the changes in available meanings we experienced in the latter part of the twentieth century and (ii) of the continuation and intensification of features already apparent in the earlier stages of modernity, it strikes me as better to describe our age as 'late modern' than in the near ubiquitous term, 'postmodern'.

Religion in late modernity

Jameson writes: '[I]n ... an uncontested postmodernism, more effortlessly secular than any modernism could have wished ... religious traditionalisms seem to have melted away without a trace ... while the wildest and most unexpected forms of what is now sometimes called "fundamentalism" flourish, virtually at random and seemingly obedient to other climacterics and ecological laws.'[44] Perhaps another, different, representation of the status of religious conviction in our age is to be seen in the replacement of the traditional honorific statue in the public space of the Stuttgart Gallery (built in 1977–84) by 'a functional, if also aesthetically designed, *drain*'.[45] The commentator makes the point that as part of modernity we no longer know, as other ages seemed to know, how to represent the sacred.

Of course, Jameson is scarcely an unbiased observer. There are other voices. For example, the entire point of this book is to attend the fact that there continue to be communities of people who assemble on Sundays with the expectation that religious meanings can help to shape the meanings of the week which lies before them. Yet only in less than sanguine moments can we avoid the truth of Jameson's generalizing comment. There can be few administrators of liberal or mainline churches who do not every month have to wrestle these dismal statistics: falling numbers, ageing

44. Jameson, *Postmodernism*, 387.
45. Rose, *Post-modern and Post-industrial*, 148 (my emphasis).

membership, receding budgets. The litany is as melancholy as Matthew Arnold's 'long withdrawing roar' of the sea of faith now more than one hundred years ago. There is doubtless a library of reasons which could be (and are!) given for the demise of institutional Christianity in our time. A thesis which runs through this book is that the meanings to which people are exposed daily, hourly, in the world all around them cannot possibly be insulated from those same people's religious readings of the world. That is, the corrosive effects of secularism are not left in the church foyer. They are insistently part of the available meanings with which people have to construct their world.[46] And, as I shall say in more detail in a moment, they are inimical to a religious reading of the world. Accordingly, the meanings which are proposed in the liturgy are bound to engage in one way or another with the meanings offered to people in their larger 'lifeworld'. The teasing question for designers and leaders of worship is: how shall this be effected? By shaping the meanings of worship more nearly to *accord* with the meanings to which people are daily exposed? Or by offering *alternatives* to these? Or by some *via media*?

Charles Taylor, in his comprehensive account of the forming of modern identity, *The Sources of the Self*, has traced the slow but apparently unstoppable progress of modern 'disenchantment', the transmogrification of what was belief in an enveloping cosmic order, able to 'define the good for us',[47] into a 'sense of the superiority of the good life ... [as coming] from the agent's sense of his [*sic*] own dignity as a rational being'.[48] So gradually incremental has been this process that it must startle the modern Christian to realize that it has *not* always been a matter of faint embarrassment to confess one's religious persuasion, that there was a time – not so long ago in the scale of these things – when 'the spiritual dimension in human life just seemed inexplicable to [people] in the absence of a God'.[49] Yet the consequences of this transformation of our cultural landscape are momentous. It is possible, probable in fact, that ours is the first major civilization to attempt to sever itself from all religious dependencies; that is, to locate all its personal, relational and ideational resources within itself. There can thus hardly be a more radical opposition than between a culture 'defined by the fact that man [*sic*] becomes the centre and measure of all beings',[50] and one which confesses that 'dependence is perhaps the only

---

46. I take this up in much greater detail in chs. 7 and 8, below.
47. Taylor, *Sources*, 149.   48. *Ibid.*, 152; see Taylor's chs. 8 and 9 particularly.
49. *Ibid.*, 309.   50. Habermas, *Philosophical Discourse*, 133 (citing Heidegger).

possible truth of religion'.[51] Yet – this is the condition which is so close it has become invisible – so deeply immersed in modernity are believers, not just as its inhabitants but precisely as its products, that the ideological dissonance in this, their doubled meaning-system, is doubtfully clear at the best. I want to say that the complications – should I rather say, hazards? – of the disenchanted world are for Christians in western societies twofold: one trap lies in the insinuating power of the modern paradigm; the other lies in the dangerous liaisons between Christianity and this which threatens to overwhelm it.

Periodically, the clash of values in which believers in a modern world are implicated does manifest itself. As a relatively benign example, individual Christians may still find themselves caught between Sunday loyalties and alternative claims (the question, that is, as to whether one is simply 'free' to 'please oneself'). More pointedly, church executives may feel obliged to withdraw their funds from an ethically doubtful investment scheme. Or, catching the dilemma accurately I think, congregations will pray for a terminally ill member while they anxiously await the doctors' verdict. But for most of the time I would say the conflict of cultures is not apparent. An Australian contextual circumstance (which I think will still be transparent to readers in other contexts) perhaps helps to sharpen the point. In this country, both those congregations of Christians deriving from European ancestry, and the indigenous people whose land they now share, profess their belief in God and in a system of values other than, or overriding, the consumerist values of the dominant society. Yet, even where there is sympathetic intention towards the values of the aborigines (which is by no means frequent) westernized Christians find themselves barely able to comprehend, let alone subscribe to, the semi-sacral reverence of the earth and the non-commercial values which generally guide these people. The two systems of value and meaning grind on each other like tectonic plates, so that precisely here is disclosed the depth to which the one group is embedded in western sources of significance. The cultural prerogatives of objectivization, of personal ownership, of reward for labour and of property values have been fused with, and profoundly inform, the European Christians' credal affirmation. Faith in God is undoubtedly one such source within their constellation of available

51. Ricoeur, *Ideology and Utopia*, 32; a full citation reads: 'When placed in contrast to the assertion of radical autonomy, dependence is perhaps the only possible truth of religion, an avowal of an element of passivity in my existence, an avowal that in some ways I receive existence.'

meanings, *perhaps* the definitively important one, but, given the power of our cultural conditionedness in shaping our view of God,[52] can we reasonably suppose that this remains immune from the scientific world view, the instrumentalist view of reason, and the immanentist ideologies with which we are on every side surrounded?[53] It seems to me inconceivable that a contemporary (i.e., western) Christian is not simultaneously and equally a modern person. But, I reiterate, this entanglement of values (meanings) is barely, if at all, apparent to the people who embody it.

I said that the state of disenchantment holds a twofold hazard for those who are its inhabitants but who also believe in a transcendent deity. I have spoken just now of the powers of insinuation on the part of the secular paradigm. The other side of Christian precariousness, however, is the historical and material affiliations between Christian belief and secular (un)belief. Taylor's analysis shows not just that there occurred the 180 degree shift in values we noticed earlier, but that the modern syndrome actually *derives from* Judaeo-Christian axioms. Further, at significant points in the process, it was Christian theologians who aided and abetted the transfiguration.

The marks of the new humanism, Taylor thinks, can be summarized under the following heads: a moral imperative to reduce suffering, a positive evaluation of ordinary life, the ideals of universal benevolence and access to justice, and the freedom of the individual.[54] These ideals, forged in the eighteenth century, struggled for in the nineteenth and established as at least necessary goals in the twentieth, are bound to be espoused by every political leader in modern democratic societies, irrespective of his or her faith in God. They are also the values (available meanings) which frame the working decisions of ordinary people in such societies. God

---

52. See, e.g., David Pailin, *The Anthropological Character of Theology: conditioning theological understanding* (Cambridge University Press, 1990).

53. Bridget Nichols has a striking example from Anglican liturgy. The baptismal service from the 1662 Book of Common Prayer leaves no doubt as to the radical and eschatological nature of baptism: 'Dearly beloved, forasmuch as all men are conceived and born in sin . . .'; the Alternative Service Book of 1980, on the other hand speaks of welcoming the child into 'the Lord's family . . . children of the same heavenly Father, inheritors together of the kingdom of God'; Nichols, *Liturgical Hermeneutics*, 155–86.

See also Marsha G. Witten, 'Accomodation to Secular Norms in Preaching: findings of a study of sermons from the Presbyterian Church (USA) and the Southern Baptist Convention', *Homiletic* 19 2 (1994), 1–3; and B. D. Spinks, 'Christian Worship or Cultural Incantations', *Studia Liturgica* 12 (1977), 1–19.

Finally, though her review of the interrelatedness of worship and technology is not restricted to the modern era, still a good many of the examples adduced by Susan J. White (*Christian Worship and Technological Change* (Nashville, TN: Abingdon Press, 1994)) are with respect to the impact of modern technologies on worship practices.

54. Taylor, *Sources*, 394–5.

as a meaningful option has evaporated – or is at best a personal (incidental) option; the humanizing values once inherent in that faith, now shorn of theistic reference, continue. At critical points it was theologians or philanthropic Christian leaders who facilitated the change,[55] but this means that both overtly Christian and non-believing-but-caring people in late modern societies have the greatest conceivable difficulty in saying wherein 'Christianity' properly, or basically, consists. All Christian denominations have powerful agencies for justice, peace and humanitarian care. Many of them receive substantial government subsidies; and precisely therein they are scarcely distinguishable from non-church benevolent instrumentalities. In Australia at any rate, governments are wont to refer to 'the churches and charitable organizations' in one collective reference. But now, when this inherited ambiguity between a humanitarian church and a just and caring, but disenchanted, populace is coupled with the insinuation into faith by the secularist spirit of the age to which I earlier made reference, the result is congregations of people still meeting ostensibly as 'Christians' but wholly unsure as to what that term means any more.

Liberal Protestant Christianity is especially exposed in all this. Taylor locates one of the most powerful impulses towards the immanentist values of modernity (what he calls 'the affirmation of ordinary life') in the flattening of distinctions between the sacred and the ordinary by the Protestant reformers: 'By denying any special form of life as a privileged locus of the sacred, they were denying the very distinction between sacred and profane and hence affirming their interpenetration . . . The entire modern development of the affirmation of ordinary life was, I believe, foreshadowed and initiated, in all its facets, in the spirituality of the Reformers.'[56] In this connection, one can then hardly fail to recall Max Weber's thesis, citing the Protestant ethic as the capitalist seedbed, an ethic in which the notion of 'vocation' shifts from a calling to the religious (monastic) life to the puritan's 'serious attention to this world, his [sic] acceptance of his life

---

55. *Ibid.*, e.g., 161, 191, 215, 230, 249, 272, 315, 405.
56. *Ibid.*, 217–18. Carlos M. N. Eire, in his treatment of Protestant iconoclasm (*War Against the Idols: the reformation of worship from Erasmus to Calvin* (Cambridge University Press, 1986)), insists that the Protestant objective was to achieve not the immanence of God but a form of Christianity 'surging with transcendence' (*ibid.*, 2, and frequently). It is perhaps a matter of judgement. But the movement he describes (on p. 63, for example: the singing of popular songs in church, the wearing of street clothes by ministers, the abolition of a confession, and the addressing of worshippers as fellow lay members) seems to bespeak more nearly the tendency described by Taylor than a movement towards transcendence in worship.

in the world as a task'.[57] One remembers, too, that it was liberal Protestant scholarship which from the eighteenth century embraced so whole-heartedly the new humanist methods for studying ancient texts, dismissing as 'intellectual timidity' questions concerning their appropriateness for sacred scriptures.[58] To be sure, significant voices of opposition have been raised against the secularist approach to Christian faith, most strikingly that of Karl Barth in the first part of the twentieth century, but at the end of the century it is mainstream or liberal Protestantism which appears barely distinguishable from the benevolent humanism by which it is surrounded. The chief 'meaning' of worship, for congregations in this tradition, often appears to consist more nearly in what is called 'fellowship', the encounter of people with people; and 'mission', as I noted, seems largely indistinguishable from the social justice programmes mounted by secular counterparts.[59]

Jameson, in the sentence I placed at the head of this section, notes the obvious exception to this general depiction: the conservative or evangelical styles of congregation. Again we appear to be engaging with questions of meaning or, more exactly, the viability of theistic meanings in a secular setting. If liberal Protestantism embraced the modern paradigm with the enthusiasm it did and now seems almost to have disappeared into that landscape, fundamentalist Christianity is able to sustain meaningful belief in God by encapsulating itself in a sort of pre-modern cocoon.[60] God is seen as intervening directly in human affairs; prayers are, or can be, answered miraculously; there is a strong sense of demarcation between the believing community and its unbelieving environment; the words of the Bible are regarded as qualitatively different from all other human utterances. It is just conceivable that, in an age of secularity, the *only* way of making sense of belief is to draw a kind of line around it, to mark it off, and to

---

57. Weber, *Protestant Ethic and Spirit of Capitalism*, 88. See also Deborah J. Haynes, *The Vocation of the Artist* (Cambridge University Press, 1997), esp. 33–44 on 'A History of Vocation'.

58. One recalls the sentence of Kornelius H. Miskotte (*When the Gods are Silent* (London: Collins, 1967)), 199: 'For later generations than ours it will be almost incomprehensible that academic scholarship was capable of reducing the sacral narrative . . . to little stories which . . . affect us less than the Greek or Teutonic myths and contain less wisdom than the Grimms' fairy tales.'

59. Flanagan, *Sociology and Liturgy*, 14–15, 28, is particularly critical of liberal theologians who, he thinks, 'in striving to make liturgy relevant to modern culture . . . have managed to make it peculiarly irrelevant'; see also his judgement (*ibid.*, 150) that 'since the Second Vatican Council, there has been a tendency amongst theologians and liturgists to give modern culture a benign, undifferentiated "reading"'. See also Saliers, *Worship as Theology*, 43.

60. See below, pages 233–44, for a more detailed analysis of the strategies for meaning in evangelical worship.

espouse some such pre-modern view of reality. At any rate, at the turn of the century it is a way of being Christian which seems to make better sense to more people than its liberal counterparts,[61] but it entails very considerable costs, too. A bifurcation, personal, conceptual and structural, is unavoidable. However greatly such believers may desire to construct around them a pre-modern world, they do, after all, live in the present. Thus, people who believe in inspired words also have to share with the rest of us the economic anxieties of Jameson's 'hyperspace'; those who suffer cancer must remain poised on a knife's edge between their confidence in miraculous cures and the statistical probabilities attending the disease; institutions which in their theology disregard modernity nevertheless put great trust in state-of-the-art communication systems. At the centre is this contradiction: it is a form of meaning which is at once most *opposed to modernity* and is simultaneously the most *advanced in the desacralizing tendencies* which Taylor or Weber have chronicled. Later in this chapter I shall want to speak of the meaning-making process as both 'making' and 'finding': meaning, I shall say, is neither the phenomenological 'constitution' of the world, nor is it a scientifically detached 'observation' of things, but both in synthetic fusion. In the case of conservative Christians one will say that often the *construction* of meaning triumphs over the *reality that is there*; when prayers seem not to be answered or, conversely when the most improbable circumstances coincide, we see (in conservative Christian circles) the victory of a human capacity for making meaning where frankly, to anyone else, none exists. But there is a limit to this capacity. Incredulity awaits. And, for the kind of Christianity we have been describing, the stakes are high. Some are left very disillusioned.

In concluding this survey of religious possibilities in the age of late modernity, and bringing it back to the question of meaning in worship, our overview raises – but in the meantime leaves unanswered – this tortuous question for the designers and leaders of liturgy: is the meaning of worship best shaped in terms of linking up with the desacralized meanings which are so immediately available to people in their everyday world? This is the (largely unconscious) strategy assumed by liberal or mainline Protestant leaders. It takes refuge within slogans such as 'relevance',

61. Langdon Gilkey, *Through the Tempest: theological voyages in a pluralistic culture* (Minneapolis: Fortress Press, 1991), 6–10, remarks on what, from a liberal point of view, must be regarded as an astonishing reversal of fortunes on the parts of liberal and conservative Christianity respectively through the twentieth century.

'meeting people where they are' and so on. It trades practically exclusively in immanent theology. It espouses 'issues' such as gender-free language and social justice causes. 'Mission' frankly means 'humanitarian help'. Clearly there is something important in such confluence of culture and belief: people have to be able to 'see the point', 'make the connection'. Yet we have seen that in shaping themselves in terms of 'more of the same', these are the churches which at the beginning of the twenty-first century are most vulnerable to the charge of having 'melted away without a trace'.

The conservative Protestant churches on the other hand, along with some styles of catholicism (who worry that the Catholic Church has become too much like the Protestants pictured above), propose not a continuity with, but a radical alternative to, the modernity by which they, we, are surrounded. This philosophy of worship is aligned more nearly with the convictions of Victor Turner, an anthropologist but also a conservatively inclined Catholic:

> If ritual is not to be merely a reflection of secular social life, if its
> function is partly to protect and partly to express truths which make
> men [sic] free from the exigencies of their status incumbencies, free to
> contemplate and pray as well as to speculate and invent, then its
> repertoire of liturgical actions should not be limited to a direct
> reflection of the contemporary scene ... The archaic is not the
> obsolete.[62]

It is not possible at this place to pursue in sufficient depth these questions concerning worship and late modern culture. I must postpone that to chapter 8, where I explore the conjunction (worship and modernity) in terms of 'identifiability' and 'difference'. Here I can only draw attention to the circumstance of Christians deeply ensconced within the paradigm, and the (often) hidden persuasiveness of the latter in decisions and actions which seem simply to be 'natural' or 'obvious'.

For the remainder of this chapter I wish to isolate some principles of meaning-making which flow from the above reflections on our social or cultural condition.

---

62. Victor Turner, 'Passages, Margins and Poverty: religious symbols of *communitas*', *Worship*, 46 (1972), 391. Kieran Flanagan, consequent upon the remarks I have cited in note 59 above, strongly urges a view of worship as *countering* the prevalent tendencies of late modern, secularist society; *Sociology and Liturgy*, *passim*.

Farewell to dualism

It is perhaps not too much to claim that modern thought generally was constructed on the basis of paired antitheses. I listed some of these earlier. In late modernity, by contrast, we have discovered that this approach leaves us anything but satisfied: 'dualism' and 'dichotomy' tend now to be terms of abuse. Our newer insight is that, upon examination, most of the realities we deal with contain within them *both* the abstractions we had supposed we could separate out: meaning, we now think, consists in both intellectual content and material signification; difference is built into identity; human beings are psychic/somatic wholes; and so on. It has also become clear that the 'objectivism' of the Cartesian paradigm is disastrously inimical to the planet. Accompanying this is a new-found popular demand for holism and multidimensional views of reality. Running through all these in one way or another was what I earlier called the 'chastening' of rationalism: a new awareness, first, that this is not a benign tool but marshals energies of its own to promote its preferred point of view[63] and, second, that such forces are inherently fissiparous rather than synthesizing.[64]

Thus is dualism now everywhere held in suspicion. In some of its expressions, however, the countermanding call for holism is not as judicious as it needs to be. In some cases, entities which properly must be distinguished ('self' and 'other', for example) are collapsed into an indistinguishable totality.[65] In others (the deconstructive strategy of which I

---

63. Toulmin, *Cosmopolis*, makes the point several times that rationalism was instrumental in promoting 'the received account' of itself as desirable; so, e.g., 81: 'Both the received view of Modernity, and the standard narrative of its origins, were thus rationalist constructions.' Similarly, pp. 16–17, 22, 41, 132, or 169.

64. Taylor, *Sources*, 500–1, lists approximately seven different sorts of tearing which the personal and social fabric suffers by the advent of what he describes as 'the instrumental mode of life'.

65. In their work with which I am broadly in sympathy and from which I have gained a good deal for my own reflections, Arbib and Hesse, *The Construction of Reality*, seem to me at this point to make a too sweeping claim. They say, 'the notion of [an] *essentially embodied subject* aspires to break the dualisms of mind/body, mind/brain, subject/object, materialism/idealism, self/other, and fact/value. It holds these dualisms to be untenable' (p. 38, their emphasis). For my part I would say it is injudicious to include the self/other relationship in this generalization. Certainly it is axiomatic in postmodernity that selves only know themselves *in relationship* to an other; but it is equally dangerous to *abolish* the distinction. Rowan Williams, for example, more carefully speaks of 'the overcoming of otherness not by reduction to identity but by the labour of discovering what understanding might be adequate to a conflictual and mobile reality without excising or devaluing its detail' ('Hegel and the Gods of Postmodernity' in (Philippa Berry and Andrew Wernick, eds.) *Shadow of Spirit: postmodernism and religion* (London: Routledge, 1992), 76). It is something of this 'mobile reality' within which I think we should comprehend 'self' and 'other'.

will speak in a moment), old (dualistic) purities are replaced by what is virtually a new totalization (purity). We do not want dichotomies. But if the stand-off between 'analytic' and 'Continental' styles of thinking which characterized the greater part of the twentieth century has anything to teach us, it is that the world may not be subsumed in 'consciousness' (as the Husserlian approach attempted to do), *nor* may it be reduced to sheer 'thingness' (as the positivists supposed). Both the constructive power of human 'constitution' *and* the objective reality of 'celestial bodies [which] will go on in their courses after mankind [*sic*] has vanished from the earth'[66] have to be taken in uttermost seriousness. That is, to totalize either subjectivism or objectivism at the other's expense is to perpetuate one or another version of the omnivorous ideologies we have known to our cost through the twentieth century. Of deconstruction, I shall accordingly want to say that, while it has shown us 'the dangerous supplement' always residing in whichever 'purity' it is we may have been interested in, it too demonstrates a seemingly irresistible tendency to valorize 'difference' over 'identity'.[67] Only very rarely, seemingly reluctantly, does Derrida allow that meaning or signification consists in the play of both identity *and* difference; but I will address this in greater detail in my next chapter.

In place of modern dualisms, then, we need not a monism of either or any kind, but a dialectical approach giving importance to both identity and alterity.

One such attempt has been what Hilary Putnam (following Kant, interestingly enough) calls 'dualities of experience': 'Note that Kant does not say there are two "substances" – mind and body (as Descartes did). Kant says, instead, that there are "dualities in our experience" (a striking phrase!) that refuse to go away. And I think Kant was, here as elsewhere, on to something of permanent significance.'[68] Putnam's editor expounds the notion of 'duality' 'not as a binary opposition, a dualism of two incommensurable kinds of entity, but rather as ... two complementary poles of a single field of activity – the field of human experience'.[69] A 'duality of experience', 'two complementary poles of a single field of activity', I shall

---

66. Schlick, 'Meaning and Verification', 168–9.
67. See my references, pp. 83–4 below, to authors who believe that Derrida's virtual totalization of difference over identity makes it (difference) in effect into a new transcendental principle.
68. The quotation comes from Putnam's *Exploring the Concept of Mind* (Iowa City: University of Iowa Press, 1986); it is cited by James Conant in his Introduction to Putnam's *Human Face*, p. *xxii*.
69. Conant, *ibid*.

say, is the field within which we now understand meaning-making to happen. Not an opposition of subject and world, of self and other, but each in complementary collaboration *with* the other is necessary where meaning will be found.

Another approach – one on which I will draw much more heavily – is the triadic view of signification formulated by C. S. Peirce, which, as I said above,[70] increasingly finds an acceptation as a, or the, alternative not just to the impasses of modernity but to the meaning-denying deconstructionist theses. One of Peirce's most widely cited, and characteristic, remarks is: 'It seems a strange thing, when one comes to ponder over it, that a sign should leave its interpreter to supply a part of its meaning' (CP 5.448, note 1). The sentence reflects Peirce's view that signification – meaning, we can as well say[71] – is not concluded within the relationship of signifier and signified but consists in a third element, which dimension of every sign Peirce called its (the sign's) *interpretant*. In forming a sign, its producer certainly has a meaning in mind; that is to say, anticipates the sign as containing a given interpretant. But, said Peirce, the sign-producer has only some degree of control over this; the sign *recipient* equally brings to the sign an interpretant which may or may not closely approximate to the interpretant foreseen by the sign's producer. Hence the sentence about the interpreter 'supplying a part of the sign's meaning'. This means, however, that the meaning of signs (Peirce thought there was no meaning *not* given in signs) is a collaborative undertaking *between* a sign's producer and its interpreter. But this, in turn, means that the 'otherness' of the interpreter's involvement in interpretation is irreducibly *part of* the construction of the sign's meaning. The recognition of 'thirdness' – the third element, the interpretant – in every act of signification thus moves Peircean semiotic theory beyond the dualistic frames of high modernity.[72] It also ensures that meaning is irrevocably dialogical in character.[73]

Meaning as consisting in both identity and difference will enter into a consideration of liturgical meanings in yet another sense (looking back

70. Above, pp. 29–30.
71. One of the most eminent present-day scholars of Peirce's work, T. L. Short, notes that Peirce 'seldom used the term "meaning" in his semeiotic writings, and when he did, it was usually defined as an interpretant'; T. L. Short, 'Interpreting Peirce's Interpretant: a response to Lalor, Liszka, and Meyers', *Transactions of the Charles S. Peirce Society* 32 (1996), 521–2.
72. 'Thirdness' thus becomes the hallmark of Peircean semiosis; see further, below, pp. 121 (esp. n. 11 on that page), 136–7.
73. Thus have Peircean scholars such as Augusto Ponzio and Susan Petrilli been able to draw detailed comparisons between Peirce's semiotic and the thought of Emmanuel Levinas in which the dialectic presence of 'the other' forms so central a part; see particularly, Susan Petrilli, 'About and Beyond Peirce', *Semiotica* 124 3/4 (1999), 351–60.

to my previous remarks on religion in late modernity and forward to my extended reflections in Part III): liturgical meanings need to be both *recognizable* (identifiable) from within the condition of modernity and yet be clearly *different* from the prevailing axioms of secularism. I hope to show that most of the standard ways of accounting for the theistic references of worship (the current liturgical theologies) still assume one or the other of the two 'purities', and thus seem not to see that each is implicated in the other.

Meaning is making and finding

This insistence on meaning's dialectical[74] nature is directly connected with a further specification in late modernity: meaning entails both 'making' and 'finding'.

In speaking of conservative Christians, I said that their religious system quite often demands a 'suspension of disbelief' in order to hold in one configuration their pre-modern religious views and some aspect of reality in this late modern world. But this capacity for seeing what one wants to see is scarcely confined to Christians of that persuasion; it is a human trait which they happen to exemplify rather clearly. The making of meaning, I said much earlier, *is* the construction of an habitable world. The world does not present itself passively for our exploration and measurement. Precisely in measuring it (to take an almost innocuous example) we are already making it mean something: as Merleau-Ponty says, quoting Malraux: 'There is signification when we submit the data of the world to a "coherent deformation".'[75] On the other hand, not infrequently the world confronts us in an implacable 'thereness'. In the case of the Christians I was discussing, I said that scepticism always threatens: people die, because in the world as it is presently constituted cancerous cells cannot be stopped; people lose their jobs because of international economic forces; prayers go unanswered – at least in the sense of something happening which could be read as divine intervention. At such points the human capacity (and near insatiable desire) to render such reality meaningful is met by stubborn reality: there must follow either disbelief (in the religious proposal of

---

74. I use the word with some qualification. It was customarily used in classical modernity in terms of the binary oppositions assumed at that time. Self-evidently, I hope, I wish it to signify the 'conversational' relationship of 'the two complementary poles of a single field of activity' as sketched above.

75. Maurice Merleau-Ponty, *Signs* (Evanston, IL: Northwestern University Press, 1964), 54.

meaning), or a rationalizing construction which still manages to encompass the recalcitrant fact within the favoured system of meanings. In any case, meaning lives between making and finding.

Our newer perception of the play of construction/reality (making and finding) in human meaning-making is a product of the cleavage between, and then reconciliation of, the dominant intellectual methods noticed earlier. For the positivists, meaning consisted univocally in 'discovery': in reading as accurately as possible the data 'which have no owner'. For phenomenologists, meaning was the individual's construction of a meaningful world. We have slowly learned we cannot have one of these without the other: meaning is both 'making' *and* 'finding'.

As it happens, the insight that meaning is both construction and discovery was there for theorists to have availed themselves of throughout the period I depicted.[76] Terence Hawkes, for example, draws attention to the principle of *verum factum* in the writings of Giambattista Vico (at just about the time Descartes was formulating his ideas) namely: 'that which man [*sic*] recognizes as true (*verum*) and that which he has himself made (*factum*) are one and the same. When man perceives the world, he perceives without knowing it the superimposed shape of his own mind, and entities can only be meaningful (or "true") in so far as they find a place within that shape.'[77] The point of view was reiterated in Kant's 'Copernican revolution'[78] in the latter part of the eighteenth century, according to which 'principles and facts mutually establish one another'.[79] And perhaps we can make mention of Karl Mannheim, writing in the early part of the twentieth century but scarcely noticed in the polarizing climate of the time, whose 'paradox' was the insight that 'ideology includes the one who asserts it.'[80] The age was ruled by the natural sciences, however,[81] which meant that this 'dialectical' way of construing reality found little degree of acceptance before Thomas Kuhn's groundbreaking work on 'scientific paradigms' in 1962,[82] including his famous near-concluding sentence: 'There is, I think,

---

76. This observation possibly lends weight to Toulmin's thesis that the cleavage into objectivist and subjectivist polarization was the effect of external forces (see above, p. 21, or n. 35 of this chapter).

77. Terence Hawkes, *Structuralism and Semiotics* (London: Routledge, 1977), 13. See similarly, Janet Martin Soskice, *Metaphor and Religious Language* (Oxford: Clarendon Press, 1985), 76.

78. Immanuel Kant, *Critique of Pure Reason*, Bxvi–xvii, B167 (the edition I am using is Norman Kemp Smith's translation (London: Macmillan, 1992)); the reference to Kant's 'Copernican revolution' is on p. 22 and the statement of it is on p. 174.

79. Norman Kemp Smith, *A Commentary to Kant's 'Critique of Pure Reason'* (New York: The Humanities Press, 1950; first edition 1918), 36.

80. Ricoeur, *Ideology and Utopia*, 158; see Ricoeur's ch. 10, *passim*.

81. Gadamer, *Truth and Method*, e.g., *xi, xvii*, 23, 58, 75, 214.

82. Thomas Kuhn, *The Structure of Scientific Revolutions* (University of Chicago Press, 1962; the second, definitive version was published in 1970).

no theory-independent way to reconstruct phrases like "really there"; the notion of a match between the ontology of a theory and its "real" counterpart in nature now seems to me illusive in principle.'[83]

Now there is a plenitude of such recognitions, ranging, shall I say, from the Sapir–Whorf hypothesis of language ('the language of an individual partially determines the world view and the conceptual system of an individual. Individuals who speak different languages, therefore, view the world differently with different conceptual systems')[84] to the recognition of the 'cut' between the system and the observer in quantum-mechanics theory – wherein, as Putnam observes: 'a great dream is given up – the dream of a description of physical reality as it is apart from observers'.[85]

Needless to say the dissipation of the 'great dream' has raised for many people the spectre of relativism. Is everything now simply 'in the eye of the beholder'?[86] The question pushes us back to an insistence on the indispensably *collaborative* nature of the undertaking: 'making' points to an acknowledgment of the human presence in every act of rendering such a world meaningful; but 'finding' means taking with utmost seriousness a world which *is* there, a world which *will be* there when its human observers have departed the scene. This is why science 'advances'. The expectations of researchers can be, and regularly are, overturned by what they discover; equally, new ways of seeing have at least as frequently enabled such discovery.[87] So, in the quaint formulation of Arbib and Hesse, what we require is 'a spiralling set of nested feedback systems';[88] or as Janet Martin

83. *Ibid.*, 206; see similarly, 52, '[The] distinction between discovery and invention or between fact and theory will . . . immediately prove to be exceedingly artificial', and p. 66, 'The impossible suggestion that Priestley first *discovered* oxygen and Lavoisier then *invented* it has its attractions' (my emphases).

84. MacCormac, *A Cognitive Theory of Metaphor*, 70. The same conviction lies near the heart of Gadamer's hermeneutics of mediation: 'Language is not just one of man's [*sic*] possessions in the world, but on it depends the fact that man has a world at all', *Truth and Method*, 401.

85. Putnam, *Human Face*, 11.

86. With respect to this question as relating to the Sapir–Whorf hypothesis, see Lyons, *Semantics*, vol. I, pp. 245–6.

87. Thus Putnam vigorously resists the notion that his 'internal realism' accommodates a relativistic view; see, e.g., his *Reason, Truth and History*, 54–5, or *Human Face*, e.g., 21–6. See also T. L. Short, 'David Savan's Defense of Semiotic Realism', *Semiotica* 98 3/4 (1994), 243–63, who defends the semiotics of C. S. Peirce against the notion that 'semiotic systems can be playfully altered *ad infinitum*, and worlds created and destroyed in the process' (p. 261). On Peircean semiotics as a form of 'making and finding' see especially Jørgen Dines Johansen, 'Let Sleeping Signs Lie: on signs, objects and communication', *Semiotica* 97 3/4 (1993), esp. p. 292: 'without semiotic processes no interpretation would take place, the world would become incognizable, and, as an ultimate consequence, life would cease . . . even robins would not mate. On the other hand, if nothing existed but the sign function . . . then many physical phenomena and processes . . . would be inexplicable.'

88. Arbib and Hesse, *The Construction of Reality*, 8. Putnam, *Human Face*, 25, similarly speaks about a 'feedback loop'. Thomas Sebeok, *The Sign and its Masters* (Lanham: University Press of America, 1989), 33–4, speaks of 'a need for the maintenance of homeostatic equilibrium.'

Soskice puts it more prosaically, '[The practitioners of science] must as-sume not only that the world, its structures, and relations exist indepen-dently of our theorizing but also that our theorizing provides us with ac-cess to these structures, limited and revisable as that access may be at any given time.'[89]

Meaning is something we do

Making and finding are actions. Their collocation thus leads me to stress the active (verbal) dimension of the word 'meaning' over its nominal qual-ities. In brief, people have to mean things before there can be meaning. In English, 'meaning' is a gerund, a verbal noun, but in both popular as-sumption and technical discussion the sense of meaning being *a thing*, a puzzling phenomenon for which an account is to be sought, carries a near-irresistible force. Perhaps one impulse in this apprehension of the word lies in the 'objectivism' at the heart of English language philosophy – the supposition that the world consists in a finite number of objects – so that meaning is assumed to sit somewhere in the relationship between lan-guage and world.[90] However that is, the tendency is unmistakable. One (trivial, perhaps) manifestation of it lies in the clever title devised by Ogden and Richards for their book *The Meaning of Meaning*, wherein precisely the success of the *mot* heightens the nominal sense of the word and renders its verbal sense virtually invisible.[91] More substantially, in his generalizing survey of the theories of meaning emanating from analytic philosophy, Jonathan Cohen claims – their internal complexity notwithstanding – that all such theories conform to one or the other of two types: either de facto theories (meanings come about as the result of certain causal circum-stances) or *de jure* theories (meaning is rule-governed). The point of interest for us is that *both* categories see meanings as entities – either the effects of causes or the products of rule-governed behaviour.[92]

It is scarcely insignificant for the point of view I am promoting that the problems encountered in each of the various kinds of analytic the-ory eventually pushed this way of theorizing meaning *towards* (one cannot

89. Soskice, *Metaphor and Religious Language*, 122.
90. Pickstock, *After Writing*, 89ff., esp. p. 92, is particularly critical of 'the prioritization of the noun in modernist poetics and contemporary discourse'.
91. Ogden and Richards, see ch. 1, n. 99 above. On the other hand one must acknowledge, too, Richards' revolutionary contribution to a *triadic* understanding of the sign and signification; see Ann E. Berthoff, 'I. A. Richards: critic, instructional engineer, semioticist', *Semiotica* 90 3/4 (1992), 357–69, esp. pp. 363–4.
92. Cohen, *The Diversity of Meaning*, 24 and 26.

say more than this) a phenomenological approach. It is reflected, for example, in P. F. Strawson's famous rejoinder to Russell: 'It is people who mean, not expressions.'[93] It may be seen in Paul Grice's interest in 'intention' in utterance.[94] And, most auspiciously, John Austin's 'speech act theory' pressed towards a notion of meaning as something undertaken rather than as an entity to be accounted for.[95]

In truth, it is not difficult to see how 'meaning' comes to stand as a reification, some sort of ideal entity, inhering in words, events and symbolic artifacts. One easily imagines a worshipper puzzling over some obscure part of the liturgy: 'I couldn't see its meaning', he will say. I made reference much earlier to Lawrence Hoffman's *range* of meanings: 'private', 'official' and so on. In all of this it seems to me of the greatest importance, however, to see that these are the *products* of people's meaning-making and meaning-grasping capabilities. People 'get the point', or they 'make sense' of something; or perhaps they experience the process more passively: 'the penny dropped' or 'it suddenly occurred to me'. But, patently, these are actions. In all the forms of its expression, I want to say, there is meaning when, or because, people mean things.[96]

Meaning is our biosphere

The entire period of classical modernity was characterized by its anxiety for certainty, its obsession with finding the one true basis on which we

93. P. F. Strawson, 'On Referring' in (G. H. R. Parkinson, ed.) *The Theory of Meaning* (London: Oxford University Press, 1968), 69.

94. H. P. Grice, 'Utterer's Meaning, Sentence Meaning, and Word Meaning', *Foundations of Language* 4 (1968), 225–42; also 'Utterer's Meaning and Intentions', *Philosophical Review* 78 (1969), 147–77.

95. Austin, *How to Do Things with Words*. These tendencies notwithstanding, the objectivist inertia in analytic theory ensured that, by the time it reached its point of exhaustion, a conception of meaning as the relationship between words and world was as firmly in place as ever. John Searle is generally regarded as Austin's successor in speech act theory. Yet Searle's book on the subject begins precisely with the question: 'How do words relate to the world?' (*Speech Acts*, 3). And at, or near, the heart of his answer is what he calls 'the speech act of referring' (*ibid.*, 28). In his *Expression and Meaning*, Searle undertakes a revision of Austin's taxonomy of illocutionary acts. This book, too, turns around the question of 'the fit between words and the world' (*ibid.*, 3ff.). But the entire point of Austin's work had been to break away from what he called the 'constative' notion of language (e.g., *How to Do Things with Words*, 1). For similar criticisms of Searle, see particularly James DuBois, 'The Empty Promises of Speech Act Theory', *Semiotica* 103 3/4 (1995), 369–84.

96. This is especially apt if we are to think of semiotic meanings. T. L. Short, 'Semeiosis and Intentionality', *Transactions of the Charles Peirce Society* 17 (1981), 202, writes: 'Nothing is a sign in itself . . . [S]omething's being so interpreted is the *process* which Peirce named "semeiosis" (e.g., at *CP* 5.473). Therefore Professor Max Fisch was surely right when he stated that "the fundamental conception of semeiotic is not that of the sign but that of *semeiosis*"' (my emphases).

can philosophize. For objectivists this was to be a 'God's Eye View' of the universe; for phenomenologists, it would be found in the unbreachable citadel of consciousness. Modernity did, in fact, believe we could discover the foundational principles according to which the universe functions. Perhaps, in its own way, it was the modern equivalent – though pursued with infinitely more frenzy – of the ancient question: where is the navel of the earth? From what does everything depend?[97]

At the end of the twentieth century we think that both these routes to the centre, or to the origin, have been blocked to us: the violent eruption of modernity left us bereft of the ancient paths to wisdom; but now these we have hewn of our own energies and by our best lights have petered out as well. There is no Archimedean point from which to gain a purchase on the whole. We confront the fact that we inhabit our own meanings.

At one point in their work Arbib and Hesse offer this phrase as an image of our condition: 'the platform of reality'.[98] I have gladly taken over their metaphor as one organizing picture of meaning in late modernity: meaning is a platform on which to live which we construct in space. Or perhaps another picture is the one offered as the heading of this section: our meanings are a filament or membrane, a great biosphere, which we have spun around us forming a perfectly (no, tolerably) good living condition, one which we must constantly keep in as good repair as we can, but from which there is no way of emerging to see what the whole looks like from the outside.[99] There are yet other ways of imaging the circumstance;[100] another, at least as evocative I would say, is attributed by W. V. O. Quine to Neurath: 'I see philosophy and science as in the same boat – a boat which...we can rebuild only at sea while staying afloat in it. There is

97. Mircea Eliade, *The Sacred and the Profane: the nature of religion* (New York: Harper Torchbooks, 1961), 42–7; or John F. Baldovin, *The Urban Character of Christian Worship: the origins, development and meaning of stational liturgy* (Rome: Pontificum Institutum Studiorum Orientalium, 1987), 48.

98. Arbib and Hesse, *The Construction of Reality*, 108.

99. Cf. Deely, *New Beginnings*, 218–19: 'Each individual as [German biologist, Jakob von Uexküll] explained, is surrounded by an invisible bubble within which alone the environment is rendered meaningful. Von Uexküll also compared the world of experience to a web . . . I think it is helpful to combine these two notions of bubble and web into a single model of a kind of geodesic sphere whose interior as well as its surface consists of a series of intersecting lines . . . At the centre of such a three-dimensional spider's web, by maintaining and elaborating it, we live our lives.'

100. Putnam places some considerable importance – as part of our new epistemological circumstances – on our ability to *picture* our reality; see *Human Face, lxii*: 'Such descriptions seek to help us to *see* the world differently, to render what is right before our eyes visible to us' (his emphasis), but: 'what is bad is to *forget* they are pictures and to treat them as "the world"' (p. 40, my emphasis; see similarly *ibid., liii*, 20, 32, 42).

no external vantage point, no first philosophy.'[101] The same idea inheres in Gadamer's conception of 'effective historical consciousness' or 'the fusion of horizons', in which understanding is achieved not in the mastery of fixed reference points but in the sense of the constantly moving relationship between that of which understanding is sought and the one who is seeking to understand.[102] However we picture it, the thing we have come to understand is that *there is no foundation*.[103] In the ensuing pages I make a number of expository points about this new state of affairs.

The first thing, I suppose, is to acknowledge the sense of terror, weightlessness or vertigo which this idea induces in us at first acquaintance. Whether we have been shaped in the essentialist myths of modernity, or whether we have sustained ourselves by one of the religious mythic systems, the sense that we have no ultimate point of reference is, for most of us, frankly unnerving. But, in attending to our discontent, we need to be aware that it is modernity itself which has bred in us this obsession with what is 'really there'[104] and is consequently responsible for our perturbation at the prospect of never knowing this. One insight into our modern anxiety with what is 'really there' comes from Hans Frei's erudite study of biblical interpretation during the 'critical historical' period of biblical scholarship. Frei shows that, assuming the critical method, interpreters consistently looked for the meaning of texts not in terms of the texts' own narrative representations – 'an interpretation . . . for which the narrative shape, theme and course are of the greatest interest because they constitute the story's meaning'[105] – but either in an 'idealistic reference' (reference to some universal, religious truth) or in an 'ostensive reference' (the

---

101. W. V. O. Quine, epigraph to *Word and Object* (Cambridge, MA: MIT Press, 1960); I am indebted to Professor J. C. O'Neill for pointing me to the source of the citation.

102. Gadamer, *Truth and Method*, 267ff.; see esp. 273: 'Understanding is always the fusion of [the] horizons.'

103. Another picture is given by Clifford Geertz in his famous essay on 'Thick Description': 'There is an Indian story – at least I heard it as an Indian story – about an Englishman who, having been told that the world rested on a platform which rested on the back of an elephant which rested in turn on the back of a turtle, asked . . . what did the turtle rest on? Another turtle. And that turtle? "Ah, Sahib, after that it is turtles all the way down"'; Clifford Geertz, *The Interpretation of Cultures*, 28–9. The image turns out to have a wide currency: Mark C. Taylor, 'Discrediting God', *Journal of the American Academy of Religion* 62 (1994), 616, says, 'In the absence of a foundational signified, it's signs all the way down.' And Charles Taylor, *Human Agency*, 191, cites Hubert Dreyfus' 'evocative term, they [human beings] are interpretation all the way down.'

104. Conant in his Introduction to Putnam's *Human Face*, xliv–xlv.

105. Hans Frei, *The Eclipse of Biblical Narrative: a study in eighteenth and nineteenth century hermeneutics* (New Haven, CT: Yale University Press, 1974), 134.

factuality of the events being narrated).[106] Contrariwise, Frei claims for the reformers, Luther and Calvin, what Stephen Toulmin does for the contemporary humanists, Erasmus and Montaigne, namely a freedom from the modern anxiety about reference and about certainty.[107] Indeed, both scholars go on to deplore the (fiercely ironic) *truncation* of meaning when attention is distracted by matters of certainty or of reference. I cannot think that we would wish to, even if we could, go back to pre-modern, pre-critical ways of reading scripture.[108] But it is also clear that in recent years many people have discovered it *is* enough, in reading Scripture for example, to listen to *the texts in themselves* and *for their own sake*, to find the stories' meanings not in truths external to them but rather within their own narrative configurations of reality. Our dizziness on learning that we inhabit our own meanings is understandable. But it is part and parcel of a general, cultural tendency inherited with our modernity. If we can maintain our poise for more than a moment, it is possible that we shall even come 'to celebrate the loss of essence'[109] in the same way in which we have learned to read ancient texts without the nagging question: what really happened?

A second point to make is that though we may not know what holds the whole thing up – to pursue my picture of the platform in space – we must fabricate the platform *as well and as carefully as we can*. This is our living place! We have to make the best sense we can of our history, the world as we encounter it, the human condition as it makes itself apparent to us. The imperative is not just an individual one; we owe it to each other to build with as much care – we might even say here, with as much 'objectivity' – as we are able. Wittgenstein's dictum about language, 'There is no private language,' applies no less to meanings: meanings are made in community.

This was the reason, though the reason was misunderstood, that rationality was afforded the importance it was in public discourse throughout the modern period. It was seen as being grounded in the 'timeless' – i.e., wholly impersonal – laws of logic and what were supposed to be 'data

---

106. See, *ibid.*, 119–20, for a survey of the positions reached by approximately the end of the eighteenth century. By exactly the same token, but, shall we say, from an opposite direction, this is also the period in which theories of verbal inspiration come into vogue.
107. Toulmin, *Cosmopolis*, 22–30; see p. 25, 'Human modesty alone [the humanists argued] should teach reflective Christians how limited is their ability to reach unquestioned Truth or unqualified Certainty over all matters of doctrine'; and see Frei, *Eclipse*, 23–4, 'The literal or grammatical reading . . . was for both [Luther and Calvin] usually identical with the text's subject matter, i.e., its historical reference, its doctrinal content, and its meaningfulness as life description and prescription.'
108. It must be said that Frei does not commit himself in this.
109. Conant, Introduction to Putnam's *Human Face*, xxi; cf. Putnam, *ibid.*, 88.

which have no owner'. Each new reading of reality imagined it was a
step closer to finished truth: eventually such reasoning would give us
the definitive picture. The dream has dispersed; but that should not obscure from us the abiding value which it enshrined, namely, that meaning is a *public discourse* and it depends upon the clearest reasoning and
the most fluent articulation of which each of us is capable. If I indulge
my metaphor a little, and say that if or when the fabrication of our living place is faulty – when part of it breaks off, or fissures open beneath
us – we are at risk of plunging to oblivion, then that is not *just* a figure of
speech. In perfect realism, entire generations of human beings have been
condemned to death or misery when human ideology has triumphed over
human reasonableness. The imperative to be as clear and as truthful in our
meaning-making as we can, both personally and communally, is always
upon us.

I advert then, by way of a third point of exposition, to Charles Taylor's
idea of our responsibility to give the 'Best Account' of reality we can:

> What better measure of reality do we have in human affairs than those
> terms which on critical reflection and after correction of the errors we
> can detect make the best sense of our lives? 'Making the best sense'
> here includes not only offering the best, most realistic orientation
> about the good but also allowing us best to understand and make sense
> of the actions and feelings of ourselves and others. For our language of
> deliberation is continuous with our language of assessment, and this
> with the language in which we explain what people do and feel.[110]

As its complement, I want to link with Taylor's insight one of Ricoeur's:
the idea of an account's 'followability'. I will introduce this notion in a moment; it will subsequently feature in my own account of the production of
liturgical meanings.[111]

Classical modernity, in its dedication to certainty, based itself on ide-
alizations: singular truth and mathematical-type rules of proof. It consequently induced an all-or-nothing approach in intellectual method,
what Putnam calls, 'a craving for absolutes'.[112] A point of view had to be

---

110. Taylor, *Sources*, 57; for additional references to Taylor's 'Best Account' idea see, above,
ch. 1, n. 89.
111. Ricoeur's definitive discussion of 'followability' comes at volume I, pp. 149–52, of *Time
and Narrative*, but, as my references will indicate, it is influential in numerous places in the
work. I take up the idea under the heading of 'The responsibilities of sign-producers', below,
p. 196.
112. Putnam, *Human Face*, 131.

adjudged wholly right or simply not countenanced. There could be no room for partialities or probabilities (even though, as Stephen Toulmin showed in an early work, this is how people ordinarily construct their 'most reasonable' account of things).[113] An adjacent aspect was modernity's determination to decontextualize both the process of such labour and its products: a methodical ignoring of the historical, personal and physical circumstances of the thinker, as if thought were some wholly disembodied energy.[114] Taylor's 'Best Account' thesis, contrarily, connects the *many* languages in which people organize the meanings they inhabit: the languages of deliberation, of assessment, of explication (see the citation above). In a word, it is the person 'making the best sense' he or she can of the world and of her or his place in it, in all the many dimensions in which the word 'sense' ('meaning'!) obtains: socially, personally, historically, emotionally, *as well as* thoughtfully or rationally.

Such embeddedness entails, of course, that the account will never, can never, be a finished version. Such beginnings and endings as we may draw will inevitably have about them a degree of arbitrariness. Our lives, corporately and individually, are in endless flux. The sins of forebears may well redound beyond a third and fourth generation, but so do their achievements of good, their visions of value and truth. In all this we are incontestably the inheritors of meaning as well as meaning-makers. In the middle, we do it as well as we can. I am thus not surprised to discover that John Austin – whose wonderful vision of the plasticity of language, I said above, was a harbinger of a new way of conceiving meaning – could say, 'Enough is enough, enough isn't everything.'[115] What we have at any given moment is not finality, it is enough; it is the 'Best Account' we can render.

Of course, the spectre of relativism enters here, as it did earlier in the point about 'making and finding'. 'Best Account'? By what standard, and on whose showing? This is the question to which 'followability' will undertake to offer an answer. Followability is an idea which Ricoeur gratefully appropriates[116] in his desire to bridge the divide – held in high modernity to be uncrossable[117] – between history and fiction.[118] Followability is a

113. Toulmin, *The Uses of Argument*.
114. This is a point stressed in Toulmin's much more recent work on modernity; see *Cosmopolis*, 21, 24, 30–5, 81, 104–5.
115. Putnam, *Human Face*, 121, 131.
116. Ricoeur has borrowed the term from W. B. Gallie, *Philosophy and the Historical Understanding* (New York: Schocken Books, 1968).
117. See my reference, n. 28 above, to John Searle's *Expression and Meaning*.
118. *Time and Narrative*, vol. II, 156: '[T]hese two analyses, dealing respectively with configuration in the historical narrative and with configuration in the fictional narrative,

rationality of a kind;[119] but it is *not* that kind of rationalism that depends on rules of deduction,[120] and which, I have now said several times, we have learned more recently to distrust. It is rather the *sense of assent* which a reader or listener either gives or withholds in the receiving of an account – irrespective of whether the account is history, fiction, or some kind of amalgam of the two. In a word, someone following the story will make up her or his mind about *which rules* for followability apply as *the story itself unfolds*. For storytelling which undertakes to offer history, for example, the story's followability depends upon the degree to which the storyteller (in this case, 'historian') 'renders an account' (or fails to render it) of the known 'traces': eyewitness accounts, surviving artifacts, and so on.[121] Stories which offer themselves as 'fiction', on the other hand, even though their *kind* of truth claim is different, must yet be 'credible', 'believable', 'followable', and this in the manner of fiction.[122] Ricoeur will even claim that fiction has its own kind of 'reference' – the so-called 'world before the text.'[123]

Followability, then, is the critical complement of 'Best Account'. It is the regulative principle which resists a relativizing 'any point of view is as good as another'. 'What is real is what you have to deal with, what won't go away just because it doesn't fit with your prejudices', says Taylor;[124] or, as Hilary Putnam says, in an age of constructed meanings there are still better and worse arguments;[125] even *within* the systems of meaning we

strictly parallel each other and constitute the two sides of one and the same investigation into the art of composition'; the ensuing pages of Ricoeur's text go on to show 'the several reasons why we should not be surprised by this congruence between historical and fictional narrative'.

119. It is intriguing to notice how frequently Ricoeur avails himself of the notion 'quasi-': 'quasi-event', 'quasi-character', etc. See the index to *Time and Narrative*, vol. I, also vol. II, p. 57; *The Symbolism of Evil* (Boston: The Beacon Press, 1967), 255–8; again in *Essays on Biblical Interpretation* (London: SPCK, 1981), 128, 130, 133; and, not least, *Oneself as Another* (University of Chicago Press, 1992), 110. The need to speak so frequently of the quasi-nature of reality links Ricoeur to Taylor's idea of a 'Best Account' and to Peircean 'abductive' reasoning.

120. See Ricoeur's discussion of the 'covering law' model of historiography made famous by Carl Hempel originally of the Vienna Circle; *Time and Narrative*, I, 112–20.

121. *Time and Narrative*, III, 152.

122. For fiction Ricoeur introduces the notions of fidelity and trust on the parts of the author and the reader respectively: 'The question of reliability is to the fictional narrative what documentary proof is to historiography', *ibid.*, 162.

123. E.g., *Hermeneutics and the Human Sciences*, 141: '[T]here is no discourse so fictional that it does not connect up with reality.' On Ricoeur's insistence on the referentiality of fiction see, notably, Kevin Hart, 'Ricoeur's Distinctions', *Scripsi* 5 (August 1989), 103–25, but particularly 112–18.

124. Taylor, *Sources*, 59. Taylor's hostility to relativism appears constantly in his work. See, e.g., the essay on Foucault in *Human Sciences* (ch. 6) or 'What's Wrong with Negative Liberty?' (ch. 8).

125. *Human Face*, 114.

inhabit, we still speak meaningfully of 'getting [something] right or getting it wrong'.[126]

A fourth expository note – staying for the time being with my 'platform' metaphor – is that one can actually approach the platform's edge. There is a vertigo which overtakes us when we apprehend that, at a certain point, meaning ceases and we are confronted by that which is not of our own making, not under our control. Perhaps it is a redundancy to say that the entire programme of classical modernity was dedicated to the concealment from ourselves of this human circumstance. Its means of doing so were several and they acted in collusion. We have touched on some of them. I mention here, by way of concluding example, the positivist stratagem of drawing a line (another binary opposition!) between 'facts' and 'feelings' and then dictating that everything which could not be a 'fact' was thus literally meaningless. Religious awareness – at any rate as signifying anything important – was thus eliminated at a stroke.[127] Relegated as wholly outdated, irrelevant, were the ancient mythic intimations of the uncanny, the limit, the otherness which confronts us when we turn from our (modern) obsession with ourselves.[128] The savage irony that attends our civilization is the now nearly universally acknowledged fact that in our modern 'emancipation from age-old dependencies'[129] meaning has become, if not quite lost, at least severely debilitated: 'In the absence of an overarching framework, questions of meaning and motivation become unanswerable and the problem of legitimation becomes irresolvable.'[130] This analysis suggests that meaning has become for us as problematic as it is *because* modernity worked as tirelessly as it did to conceal from itself its own, our, inherent boundedness.[131] Without a horizon from which to work there can be no orientation, no sense of one's place, no meaning.[132]

---

126. *Ibid.*, 122.
127. Ayer's *Language, Truth and Logic*, 104, puts the point as conveniently as any: 'We shall set ourselves to show that in so far as statements of value are significant, they are ordinary "scientific" statements; and that in so far as they are not scientific, they are not in the literal sense significant, but are simply expressions of emotion which can be neither true or false.'
128. Ricoeur, *Symbolism of Evil*, 306, 347–55, or *Conflict of Interpretations*, 269–86, 287–334. See, similarly, Polanyi and Prosch, *Meaning*, 146–7.
129. Habermas, *Philosophical Discourse*, 83.
130. Mark C. Taylor, 'Postmodern Times'; see above ch. 1, n. 9.
131. Gadamer, whose notion of 'effective historical consciousness' depends on a sense of one's own (historical) finitude says quite bluntly that the experience of human finitude is a religious experience and that it is learned through suffering; *Truth and Method*, 320.
132. Gadamer again: 'A person who has no horizon is a man [*sic*] who does not see far enough and hence overvalues what is nearest to him. Contrariwise, to have an horizon means not to

I have urged that meaning is made; but it is not made *ex nihilo*. It is also a taking of bearings and a finding of identity. Accordingly, in introducing his aptly named *The Limits of Disenchantment*, Peter Dews cites Theodor Adorno: '[M]eaning... implies *givenness* – it is something we encounter and experience, not something we can arbitrarily posit... And this very givenness seems often to be regarded as an affront to [modern] human powers of self-assertion.'[133]

Among such writers there appears a gathering consensus that an awareness of an 'edge' or 'limit' to what we can humanly fathom is properly to be described as a religious awareness.[134] It is presumably not coincidental, then, that this is how some liturgical theologians describe the task or vocation of a worshipping assembly: Aidan Kavanagh says that 'liturgy leads [its practitioners] regularly to the edge of chaos, and that from this regular flirt with doom comes a theology different from any other'.[135] In the same vein, Rainer Volp writes: 'When the language [of the liturgy]... wishes to be effective, that is, when it constructs symbols which will not, for God's sake, keep silent with respect to life's boundaries, then these become the inexhaustible *interpretant* of the boundary situation assigned to the world – at a border which is both insurmountable and surmountable.'[136]

These are the voices of some theorists of meaning and some theorists of worship. Over against such theoretical opinion, I expressed earlier in this chapter my misgivings about what I think is an infiltration by the secularizing spirit of the age of much ordinary Christian consciousness.

be limited to what is nearest, but to be able to see beyond it. A person who has an horizon knows the relative significance of everything within this horizon, as near or far, great or small'; *ibid.* 269.

133. Dews, *The Limits of Disenchantment*, 2 (his emphasis).

134. Dews, *ibid.*, 210, cites Habermas on 'contact with the extraordinary' [*das Außeralltägliche*]: 'Philosophy, even in its postmetaphysical form, will be able neither to replace nor suppress religion as long as religious language is the bearer of a semantic content which is inspiring, and... continues to resist translation into reasoning discourses.' Putnam, *Human Face*, 135, says of questions of ultimacy, 'of course, [such a question] was a religious remark.' And Charles Taylor, in concluding his study of our modern sources of self, writes: 'adopting a stripped-down secular outlook, without any religious dimension or radical hope in history, is not a way of *avoiding* the dilemma, although it may be a good way to live with it. It doesn't avoid it, because this too involves its "mutilation". It involves stifling the response in us to some of the deepest and most powerful spiritual aspirations that humans have conceived. This... is a heavy price to pay' (*Sources*, 520, his emphasis).

135. Aidan Kavanagh, *On Liturgical Theology* (New York: Pueblo Publishing Company, 1984), 73 (with an acknowledged dependency on Urban Holmes).

136. Rainer Volp, 'Grenzmarkierung und Grenzüberschreitung: der Gottesdienst als semiotische Aufgabe' in (Wilfried Engemann and Rainer Volp, eds.) *Gib mir ein Zeichen: zur Bedeutung der Semiotik für theologische Praxis-und Denkmodelle* (Berlin: Walter de Gruyter, 1992), 185 and, more extensively, 175–86.

If I am right about this, then it may be that it is in the gap between, on the one hand, what these recent theorists both of meaning and of liturgy are saying and, on the other, the actual weekly experiences of worshipping congregations and their leaders that a recovery of meaning in worship is to be located. To put it so must amount to yet another promissory note, hopefully to be redeemed in Part III on the theology of worship.

3

Comprehending meaning

Theories of most kinds, but particularly the kind which propose a definitive explanation of phenomena, are now in disrepute. We have settled, instead, for an ongoing *process* called 'theorizing', for series of *pictures* of reality, for an achievement of the *best account of things* we can manage. In the previous chapter I drew some possible pictures of meaning: the human biosphere, or a platform we construct beneath us. In this chapter I explore another picture: in this case a picture not so much of what it is we construct, but how it is that we construct it, whether by way of proposal ('this is what I mean...') or in its apprehension ('Oh, I see what you mean'). The act of meaning, I shall say, is one in which we 'grasp together' conceptual elements, bits of awareness, significations or factual data which we had hitherto not seen as linked, but which, in the generation of meaning, we do now so see. To give it its latinate name, it is the act of comprehension.

This way of characterizing our human capacities for meaning is to be credited, to the best of my knowledge, to the theorist Louis O. Mink.[1] Significantly enough, Mink belonged to a group of people, at about the third quarter of the twentieth century, interested in moving beyond the then still regnant positivist theories of history-writing gaining emblematic status in Carl Hempel's 'covering law' model of historiography.[2] Others who shared a similar interest at the time were W. B. Gallie, whose notion of the 'followability' of narratives we have already met,[3] Arthur Danto with his thesis that narrativity is already an explanatory mode of representing

---

1. See particularly, Louis O. Mink, 'History and Fiction as Modes of Comprehension', *New Literary History* 1 (1970), 541–58, see esp. pp. 548–9.
2. See notably Carl G. Hempel, 'Explanations and Laws' in (Patrick Gardiner, ed.) *Theories of History* (New York: The Free Press, 1959), 344–56. Hempel's essay was first published in 1942.
3. The reference to Gallie's work is given above at ch. 2, n. 116.

events,[4] and Hayden White.[5] All of these laid down lines of approach which would be drawn into Ricoeur's account of the contiguities between history and fiction.[6] Whether or not it was apparent at their time of writing, then, it is now clear that in their own way they were importantly involved in helping to effect the transition from mid-century positivism to that new kind of intellectual method for which I have borrowed the term 'late modernity'.

As a simple translation into English of the verb 'comprehend', the notion of 'grasping together' scarcely pretends to offer some kind of conclusive explanandum of this human faculty. However, what it does do – productively! – is alert us to the pictorial power latent but unrealized within the defunct metaphor (i.e., 'comprehend'). To be reminded – indeed, to be told anew, given the lexical opacity of the latinate form – that to comprehend something is to 'grasp together' its various signifying elements into a synthetic whole is to open our eyes to a process concealed within the now dead metaphor. Admittedly, to shift 'meaning' apparently sideways into the 'comprehending' semantic field may seem to amount to little more than the substitution of one elusive category for another synonymous with it. Such disappointment betrays the hold on us of the old classical modernity – with its supposition that our language can make percentage gains on how things really are. The late modernity which we inhabit, contrariwise, has taught us that all we have – but what we have – are our metaphors.[7] And to repristinate a metaphor which has become obtuse – in other words, to recover its genuinely pictorial power – may be no slight achievement.[8]

It is entirely likely, in fact, that we will never be able to give a good, much less final, account of how it is that human beings make this mental

4. Arthur C. Danto, *Analytical Philosophy of History* (Cambridge University Press, 1965). See particularly p. 217.

5. Hayden White, *Metahistory: the historical imagination in nineteenth-century Europe* (Baltimore: Johns Hopkins University Press, 1973).

6. All these writers are reviewed in detail in 'History and Narrative', Part II of Ricoeur's *Time and Narrative*, vol. I, pp. 111ff.

7. So, particularly forcefully, Derrida in *Margins*, 219ff., esp. perhaps p. 224, 'the "founding" concepts (*theoria, eidos, logos*, etc.) . . . already have their own metaphorical charge'; or *ibid.*, 262, where he speaks of 'the metaphoricity of the concept, the metaphor of the metaphor, the metaphor of metaphoric productivity itself.' While I concur with Derrida that all language is ineluctably metaphorical in its origins, I shall want sharply to distinguish myself from him in saying that we can, all the same, recognize when words are being *used* metaphorically and when they are functioning in a literal sense (see below, pp. 86–7).

8. On the rejuvenation of old (which is to say, lexicalized) metaphors by the expedient of breaking them into their constituent parts or, as here, the translation of them into equivalent terms, see Ricoeur, *The Rule of Metaphor*, 292.

leap which enables them to link or fuse two hitherto dissociated ideas so as to yield a third, until now unseen, idea. If intellectuality does indeed consist in this power of grasping together, then, I suppose, we would be watching the process trying to observe or explain itself. It is at any rate instructive that accounts which set out to show the cognitive processes involved in apprehending metaphor – which, I shall say, is a primary case of the art of grasping together – regularly lapse into elisions such as 'somehow', or the description 'mysterious', 'metaphors of metaphor'.[9]

The context of Louis Mink's discussion was, as I noticed, the new exploration of narrativity being undertaken in the 1960s–70s as an alternative to the 'covering law' model of historical explanation. 'Grasping together', he claimed, is what both storytellers and listeners to stories do, as they comprehend a story's numerous divergent threads within the synthetic whole which is a narrative.[10] But it was also clear to Mink that his 'grasping together' formulation far outruns just this form of human comprehending:

> It is operative, I believe, at every level of consciousness, reflection and inquiry. At the lowest level, it is the grasping together of data of sensation, memory and imagination, and issues in perception and recognition of objects. At an intermediate level, it is the grasping together of a set of objects, and issues in classification and generalization. At the highest level, it is the attempt to order together our knowledge into a single system – to comprehend the world as a totality.[11]

I would follow Mink less than confidently in his three-tiered taxonomy; and the notion of 'comprehending the world as a totality' now sounds more like a classically modern than a late modern idea. But that, when we strain for the meaning of something, we are attempting to find the ways in

---

9. See, for example, Earl R. MacCormac, *A Cognitive Theory of Metaphor*, e.g., 18, 136, 140 (for the adverb 'somehow'), or p. 148 (for the description of the metaphorical process as 'mystery'). The irony of the usage, rather obviously, is that MacCormac's intention in his book is to offer a 'cognitive theory' of metaphor. 'Somehow' crops up in Ricoeur, *Rule of Metaphor*, too, p. 80: 'The two thoughts in metaphor are somehow disrupted'; or see, similarly, *ibid.*, 193: 'What constitutes the metaphoricity of metaphor? Does the notion of resemblance have the power . . .? Or must one rather admit that it just hides the initial embarrassment of a definition and an explanation that can produce nothing but a metaphor of metaphor?'
10. Ricoeur treats this synthesizing quality of every narrative under the term 'emplotment': it is what 'brings together factors as heterogeneous as agents, goals, means, interactions, circumstances, unexpected results'; *Time and Narrative*, vol. I, p. 65. Umberto Eco also draws upon Aristotelian 'emplotment' in his analysis of a television director selecting and 'configuring' the broadcast image from the multiple images being fed from several different cameras; Umberto Eco, *The Open Work* (Cambridge, MA: Harvard University Press, 1989), 107–10.
11. Mink, 'History and Fiction', 548–9.

which its parts form some kind of significant whole and then the ways in which that whole hangs together with whatever else we know of the world, seems to me the most instructive picture of the process we are likely to get, given the ideas available to us in this cultural moment. And, on the other side of meaning's construction, as authors, as speaking subjects, as liturgical leaders intent on making ourselves as understandable as we can, that we, too, 'fasten together' language or pictures or actions such as will best 'make sense' or 'be comprehensible', seems also to be a picture of what we do. To own it again: clearly, the language circles endlessly – 'to make sense', 'to be comprehensible', 'to grasp the point', 'to see the issue' is (it could be said) simply to exchange metaphor for metaphor. But, if it is the case that we inhabit our own formulations, if there is no way of slitting the membrane of meaning or of looking under the platform, then, while *owning* our metaphors, to have them *illumine* our practice is what we must above all hope for. And that seems to me to be what happens when we envisage the meaning-making, meaning-grasping act as an action in which two or more elements of the known world are comprehended ('grasped together') so as to yield a way of seeing the world differently.

In following the lead given by the particular metaphor ('grasping together'), in the sections that follow I attend first to the *apprehension* of meaning by a recipient: a reader, one who listens to a story, or one who attends worship. This grasping of meaning, 'getting the point', cannot on any showing be supposed to be a passive role. We have learned from numerous directions in recent years of the active contribution which a reader, for example, brings to the appropriation of a text. It is this kind of 'grasping together' to which I will chiefly attend in the first section below. Of course, there can be no grasping of a point if none has been offered. So, in the second section, I turn to the *authoring* of meaning – a controversial point of view, given the consistent degrading of the author's role in structuralist and formalist theories and carried forward virtually unchanged in deconstructive styles of postmodernity. Admittedly, meaning production and meaning reception stand in symbiotic relationship, not easily separated as we shall notice (the construction of metaphors will be one such case; and the so-called 'narrative account of personal identity' is even more fluid). It still serves some purpose to approach the grasping of meaning from the two perspectives. In a third section I touch briefly on *jokes* as a particularly direct form of 'grasping together', one which certainly involves a cognitive dimension but which also shows how the entire human person is affected when a point has been grasped – I have in mind, of course, the 'series of convulsive movements of the diaphragm, causing spasmodic expulsions of breath, with jerky sounds, accompanied by movements of facial muscles'[12] which grips the entire body when we 'get' the point of a joke.

Grasping together identity and difference

In describing the experiences of a person attending worship in a place not familiar to her, I said that questions of meaning will arise as she sets in juxtaposition such features as she can identify – about the building, the people and their actions – with those aspects of the same things which strike her as strange, unrecognizable. It is important that we allow both the identifiable *and* the puzzling dimensions of her encounter each to have their part in the question of, and then the production of, meaning. It is true that it is the enigmatic side of the homology which seems to push forward more urgently our questions (with respect to the meaning of something). But we have learned that without some degree of recognition (precognition) not even the question would be possible. The circumstance has become known to us as the hermeneutic circle. To ask what is something's meaning requires that we have some conception of what that something is, what is the range of *possible* meanings among which to search for one – or *the* one – which seems most satisfyingly to meet the question. If, shall I say, my visitor were not at a Christian liturgy but at a Shinto shrine, it is likely that questions of meaning would be largely overwhelmed by her incomprehension. Thus some degree of familiarity is a precondition for questions of meaning. But it is equally possible to see that it is the *un*familiarity of proceedings which either sharpens meanings or provokes such new meaning as may emerge. That is, we can say, on the one hand, that she brings meaning across with her from her customary practices, and that to this degree meaning is not an issue, that the meaning of things is settled and clear. On the other hand, such meanings are threatened precisely by their familiarity; they may well be comfortable, consoling, consolidating, but they are also likely to have a low-level capacity to penetrate one's awareness, to be 'meaning*ful*' if we may so move from a qualitative to quantitative dimension of meaning. Meaning therefore appears to be constructed by the drawing together in one configuration of both the known and the unknown, or of similarities and differences.

---

12. Joyce O. Hertzer, *Laughter: a socio-scientific analysis* (New York: Exposition Press, 1970), 11.

To organize a discussion of meaning in terms of the play on each other (the grasping together) of sameness and difference is, I think, an approach shaped by the strictures of late modernity. For classical modernity, as I have now said often enough, meanings were assumed to be stable entities, recognizable and therefore trustworthy across any number of divergent contexts. Thus was meaning conceived wholly in terms of identity. The trait is disclosed, for example, in Frege's disconcertment that words can (but really ought not to) change their *Sinn*, their sense. It was presumed by the philological style of linguistics attacked by Saussure which took it for granted, first, that meanings remained stable across the centuries of a language's existence, second, that there was a 'natural' affinity between signs and their signification, and, third, that some meanings were therefore more 'proper' for a given word than others.

We have heard from the beginnings of structuralism – the note is sounded even more strenuously by its post-structuralist offspring[13] – that it is not identity which is the principle of signification but difference. That is, meanings do not inhere in words, meaning is not 'present' to its vehicle as classical thought supposed. Rather it is yielded in the play of differences *between* words or signs. Such difference thus evades conceptualization; it does not 'exist' anywhere but comes to our notice only by that which is not; that is to say, through our observation that this word, this sound, this sign is *other than*, *differs from*, other words, sounds or signs. It is for this reason – its non-locatableness, its non-identifiability – that Derrida forms his famous neologism, *différance*, the (non)sense of which he gives in this equally famous passage:

> 'Older' than Being itself, such a *différance* has no name in our language. But we 'already know' that if it is unnameable, it is not provisionally so, not because our language has not yet found or received this *name*, or because we would have to seek it in another language, outside the finite system of our own. It is rather because there is no *name* for it at all, not even the name of essence or of Being, not even that of '*différance*', which is not a name, which is not a pure nominal unity, and unceasingly dislocates itself in a chain of differing and deferring substitutions.[14]

---

13. G. B. Madison calls Derrida a 'hyperstructuralist', on the grounds that Saussure's thesis 'serves as the basis for [Derrida's] entire philosophical "system"'; G. B. Madison, 'Merleau-Ponty and Derrida: *la différEnce*' in (M. C. Dillon, ed.) *Écart & Différence: Merleau-Ponty and Derrida on seeing and writing* (New Jersey: Humanities Press, 1997), 98. See also the citation from John Sheriff, p. 84, below.
14. Derrida, *Margins*, 26 (his emphases).

In a constant effort to prevent difference – or, as he prefers to call it (in order to keep this non-identifiable energy from being identified with what we think of as simple difference), *différance* – becoming hypostasized, and hence identifiable and manageable, Derrida resorts to any number of forms of expression for it: grammatology, dissemination, fold, graft, iterability, spacing, supplement are some of these. In such variable forms, Derrida is constantly about his project of dismantling the classic assumptions pertaining to meaning: its identity, its stability, its propriety, its self-sufficiency and originality. On the one hand, it is not, as commentators remind us, that Derrida has no room for meaning.[15] On the other hand, he does insist that 'what is called "meaning" . . . is already, and thoroughly, constituted by a tissue of differences.'[16]

To recognize the differences she encounters as constituting at least one dimension of the meanings being proposed in the liturgy the person is visiting, is thus to move the discussion beyond the modern syndrome where meanings were held to be stable and identifiable wherever they should be met. But to speak of meaning as the grasping together of difference *and* similarity is also to distinguish the point of view from the now well-established moves of deconstruction, at least as these are regularly undertaken in Derrida's version of it. Kevin Hart makes the point several times that, in principle, deconstruction is not *a* position among others, but constantly equivocates, directing itself always 'to the deconstruction of dogmatic critique'.[17] But such is Derrida's animus with respect to the long-entrenched position of identity or presence, that in any comparison of difference and identity there will be no question as to the preferred option: '[T]he deconstruction of this hierarchy reveals that both identity and difference, as defined within metaphysics, are in fact conditioned by a form of pure negative difference – *différance* – so that both identity and difference can be said to be determined modifications of *différance*.'[18] Accordingly, there is hardly any passage in Derrida – known to me at any rate[19] – in

---

15. See, e.g., Dews, *The Limits of Disenchantment*, 3–4. Further references can be seen at n. 60 of ch. 1, above.

16. Derrida, *Positions* (The University of Chicago Press, 1981), 33; similarly, *ibid.*, 26: '[The] principle compels us . . . to consider every process of signification as a formal play of differences.'

17. See Hart, *Trespass of the Sign*, 107–8, or, similarly, *ibid.*, 67–8, 75, 127, 132, 157–8.

18. *Ibid.*, 133.

19. I know of two exceptions: in *Grammatology*, 244, Derrida allows that 'supplementarity . . . is neither a presence nor an absence, is neither a substance nor an essence of man [*sic*]. It is precisely the play of presence and absence'; and in *Writing and Difference*, 292, we read: 'Play is always play of absence and presence.' But that the positive term is here allowed concessively, and that Derrida's interest is wholly in the difference of signifiers, can scarcely be in doubt.

which signification or meaning is allowed to be the mutual and dialectical interplay of the known and unknown, i.e., a play between such aspects
of new circumstances which can be identified by their similarities with
other occasions, and such aspects which impact by way of their strangeness
or difference. In brief: we hear only ever about 'the play of differences'.[20]
Not a few commentators, however, have charged that this virtually absolute preference given by Derrida to difference over similarity transforms it,
wholly ironically, into a new principle of transcendence: 'What is at work
in the argument strategy relative to *différance* is something akin to a transcendental argument Kantian style, and Derrida, it would seem, is the current keeper of the transcendental question.'[21] But this virtual apotheosis
of difference – in place of the various 'purities' of high modernity – no
more yields an account of meaning than they did, or could. John Sheriff
writes accordingly:

> Derrida's deconstruction, as he himself claims, is already implied in
> the antitheses within which he works out his theory. The dyadic
> character of the sign that makes oppositions irreducible and makes
> everything in opposition mutually dependent on each other for
> meaning makes inevitable the conclusion that every sign is always
> already a sign of its relation to its other . . . That is why *Of Grammatology*
> is filled with statements such as the signifier is always already the
> signified, presence is always already absence, reality is always already a
> sign . . .
>
> Both structuralism and deconstruction are theories of the 'gap'
> inherent in the dyadic conception of the sign. The principle difference
> between the two is that the first tries to account for what fills the gap,
> what structures are in place, whereas the second maintains that no
> conceivable science or ontology can study the movement of the trace
> within the gap.[22]

In contrast, a Peircean style of postmodernity, we have seen, in theorizing the presence of 'thirdness' in signification – the presence in any given
sign of the constructive energies both of its producer and its interpreter –
builds into its account of meaning both identity and difference; on the one

---

20. Note 16 above; see also *Of Grammatology*, 7, 50, and frequently (other important passages
on 'play' are found in *Writing and Difference*, 260 and 292).
21. Patrick Burke, 'The Flesh as *Urpräsentierbarkeit* in the Interrogative: the absence of a
question in Derrida' in (M. C. Dillon, ed.) *Écart & Différence: Merleau-Ponty and Derrida on seeing
and writing* (New Jersey: Humanities Press, 1997), 61. In the same volume the charge that
difference has been elevated into a transcendental principle will be found on pp. 62, 69, 72,
82, 96, 99, 223 and 226–7.
22. Sheriff, *The Fate of Meaning*, 46–7.

hand, that is, the requirement that the sign be cognizable, able to be identified, and, on the other, the fact that its interpreter has some say in how the sign will be interpreted. Augusto Ponzio summarizes the case so: 'the sign is a dialectic unit of self-identity and otherness.'[23] More elaborately:

> One of the fundamental problems of the sign is that of establishing in what way we might reconcile similarity and difference, stability and transformation, uniqueness and polysemy, identity and alterity. The symbolic universe is not stable, uniform and monolithic. It is made of deviations, differences, deferments and *renvois*, displacements and transformations. In other words, we need to explain in what way alterity is able to infiltrate the very sphere of the symbolic. It is precisely the semiotics of Peirce that offers a possible solution to the problem, especially because in his theorizations the symbol, the sign *par excellence*, is such because alterity and identity co-exist in it. In the Peircean conception of the symbol, alterity is constitutive of the very identity of the sign.[24]

In the next several pages I exemplify this essentially late modern way of conceiving meaning – I mean, meaning as the act of grasping together identity and difference. Metaphors, I will say, are a primary case; but a similar play on each other of identity and difference can be seen in our late modern understanding of the self; our acts of perception are another primary site; and I shall return to the question of signification.

Metaphorical process

Our experience on encountering a new or striking metaphor serves me as a case study in meaning in a number of ways. Most directly, it is one of the clearest examples of the human capacity to grasp together an identifiable form of language with one hitherto not associated with it, so as to yield a new insight on the world,[25] what Owen Barfield wonderfully described as 'the pleasure of a felt change of consciousness'.[26] Second, a renewed interest in metaphors and metaphoricity is a mark of the shift in cultural and intellectual awareness during the seventh and eighth decades of the past century to which I have already drawn attention as forming some kind of watershed. Third, I will allow our experience of metaphors to stand as

---

23. Ponzio, *Man as a Sign*, 257.
24. *Ibid.*, 197; see also Petrilli, 'About and Beyond Peirce', 305: 'The sign's identity is grounded in the logic of alterity'; and, more extensively, *ibid.*, 351–60.
25. I find it entirely significant that the subtitle of Ricoeur's treatment of metaphor is 'multidisciplinary studies of *the creation of meaning in language*'.
26. Owen Barfield, *Poetic Diction* (London: Faber & Faber, 1952), 48.

a kind of paradigm case for our *apprehension* of someone else's meaning (what in Part II I shall call 'the act of sign-reception'). This is to stand in contrast or comparison with the *construction* of such meaning, to which I will turn later in this chapter under the heading 'Authoring meaning'.

It would not be untoward to see Ricoeur's entire study of metaphor built around a sentence taken from Aristotle's *Poetics*: '[A] good metaphor implies an intuitive perception of the similarity in dissimilars';[27] a modern version of the sentence would say 'to make a metaphor is to see two things in one'.[28] As with my reference back to the worshipper's experience in terms, simultaneously, of the continuities with her accustomed patterns and the discontinuities, so here both elements, the similarities and the dissimilarities conjoined in a metaphor, have to be given their equal weight. But then, of no less importance is their *fusion* in the new metaphorical configuration. Ricoeur's treatment, following Aristotle, is chiefly about the construction of metaphors; but, in keeping with my interest here (i.e., in the act of grasping together which is the *reception* of metaphorical meaning) he also says that it is 'the reader' – the recipient of a metaphor, we shall say – who must 'work out the connotations ... that are likely to be meaningful'.[29] The apprehension of a metaphor thus offers a vibrant case of 'grasping together' both known and unknown, like and unlike, as an act of meaning-making.

In attending, initially, to the 'similarities' which are brought across into the new synthesis of meaning, it is fundamental to Ricoeur's treatment of metaphor (and my theory of meaning!) that words be seen to be the repositories of stable meanings; that when we see or hear this or that particular signifier it carries for us a definite semantic content; that it is cognizable on the basis of its being recognizable. At the same time, this ability of words to be identified, to have semantic identity, is not at all to be confused with the old ideality of meanings, criticized no less by Ricoeur than by Derrida. If he draws on Aristotle for his central sentence, Ricoeur can equally say that Aristotle's views about the 'propriety' of words – i.e., that a metaphorical use of words is to use them improperly – would seal 'the destiny of metaphor ... for centuries to come'.[30] The centuries in question are all those up to the middle part of the twentieth century, in which metaphors were regarded as rhetorical devices, a decorative addition to language bringing to it ornamentation but not affecting

27. Ricoeur, *Rule of Metaphor*, 192, citing Aristotle, *Poetics* 1459 a 8; the same citation is made on pages 6 and 23 of *Rule of Metaphor*.
28. *Ibid.*, 24.   29. *Ibid.*, 95.   30. *Ibid.*, 14.

its 'proper' meanings. The stable meanings to which Ricoeur appeals are thus not 'proper', i.e., based in ideality or metaphysicality. They derive from the simple, pragmatic fact that, by reason of customary *use*, words come to *function* as stable units of meaning in a language: 'The word preserves the semantic capital . . . deposited in its semantic treasury. What it brings to the sentence is a potential for meaning. This potential is not formless: *the word does have an identity.*'[31] When language-forms – *forged* in metaphorical process unquestionably – have become sufficiently commonplace as to be arranged in dictionaries, they ought not any longer be considered metaphors ('the dictionary contains no metaphors');[32] they invite only confusion or worse when they are.[33] Lexicalization is thus the sign of a metaphor no longer new and accordingly no longer metaphorical: for a semantic unit (word or expression) to have become sufficiently identifiable as to be catalogued in lists of established meanings – which is to say, separately from any particular context – is the acknowledgment that such a word or expression has now achieved 'literal' meaning, a standardized meaning, a kind of common coin of the realm (it also means it is available to be drawn on for *new* metaphorical constructions).[34] Such a word or phrase is like the meanings that my worshipper carries with her from one place to another – recognizable wherever she meets them. All this has been with respect to the 'similarities' which the maker or recipient of

---

31. *Ibid.*, 130 (my emphases). See, further, *ibid.*, 66, 70, 112, 128.

32. *Ibid.*, 97, 162, or 170.

33. This accords with other theorists' opinions. MacCormac speaks of the critical importance of being able to draw a line between language being used literally and the same language used metaphorically. He also uses lexicalization as the criterion (*Cognitive Theory*, 14–15, and ch. 3, *passim*). Colin Turbayne, too, draws attention to our 'victimization' when we fail to see that our metaphors *are* metaphors; Colin Murray Turbayne, *The Myth of Metaphor* (Columbia, SC: University of South Carolina Press, 1970), e.g., 46, 51. The point is taken up again in particular circumstances by Ricoeur in *Ideology and Utopia*, 105, 153.

At the same time, it is not easy to withstand the point of view – offered, for example, by George Lakoff and Mark Johnson (*Metaphors We Live By* (University of Chicago Press, 1980)) – that even decayed metaphors can or do retain a cryptic but seminal power. This is precisely the point made, for example, by feminists with respect to masculine images of God – that such language *is* influential even when we take it as being dead; among many texts on the matter see Brian Wren, *What Language Shall I Borrow: God-talk in worship, a male response to feminist theology* (London: SCM Press, 1989).

34. On its lexicalization as the sign of decayed metaphor, see *Rule of Metaphor*, 99, 127ff., 130, 188, 237. I cite Ricoeur but the point of view is widely held. Barfield, for example, describes literal meaning as 'a . . . tissue of dead, or decayed, metaphors' (*Poetic Diction*, 63; see also *ibid.*, 131–2, and (citing Emerson) 179: 'Language is fossil poetry.'). Similarly, Philip Wheelwright (*The Burning Fountain: a study in the language of symbolism* (Bloomington: Indiana University Press, 1968), 120) speaks of 'the fate that eventually overtakes radical metaphors. They grow old and moribund, losing the vital tension of opposed meanings, dramatic antithesis, paradox, which was theirs at their inception. They become fossilized and enter into everyday speech as steno-symbols.'

metaphors brings to the metaphorical process. But what now of the 'dissimilarity' which he or she meets?

A metaphor is made – or, on its other side, is recognized – when words are assembled in a single configuration, whose established meanings entail only semantic dissonance. There is a clash of meanings which creates a crisis of a kind for the hearer or reader. Ricoeur (following Jean Cohen) calls this 'collision'[35] a 'semantic impertinence';[36] or, to catch the point more precisely, 'the metaphorical meaning as such is not the semantic clash but *the new pertinence* that answers its challenge'.[37] In an ordinary sentence (i.e., one offering non-metaphorical or literal sense) 'it is necessary...that all the [possible] acceptations...of the word under consideration be eliminated except one, that which is compatible with the meaning...of the other words of the sentence'.[38] Whereas, in the case of metaphors, 'the strategy of language at work...consists in obliterating the logical and established frontiers of language, in order to bring to light new resemblances the previous classification kept us from seeing. In other words, the power of metaphor [is] to break an old categorization, in order to establish new logical frontiers on the ruins of their forerunners.'[39] Ricoeur is in no doubt that a process of this kind – an energy of the mind in which it is always *looking for connections*[40] – is a genuine production of meaning, that is, of meaning which has not previously existed.[41] If we shall ask *how* the mind does this, we will find only more or other metaphors: 'Just as the plant reaches towards the light and into the earth and draws its growth from them...so too the poetic verb [metaphor] enjoins us to participate in the totality of things via an "open communion".'[42] Or, in only slightly more prosaic idiom, perhaps it is to Kant's 'productive imagination' that we might or should look: 'it constitutes the grasping of identity within differences and in spite of differences...[It] turns imagination into the place where the figurative meaning emerges in the interplay of identity and difference. And metaphor is that place in discourse where this schematism is visible, because the identity and difference do not melt together but confront each other.'[43]

35. *Rule of Metaphor*, 97.   36. See, *ibid*., e.g., 132, 134, 151–2, 154, 162, 194.
37. *Ibid*., 194 (my emphases).   38. *Ibid*., 131.   39. *Ibid*., 197.
40. *Ibid*., 82.   41. See, *ibid*., 65–6, 98.
42. *Ibid*., 249, citing I. A. Richards. One might compare Coleridge on the 'esemplastic power of the imagination'; see Basil Willey, *Nineteenth-Century Studies: Coleridge to Matthew Arnold* (Harmondsworth: Penguin Books, 1964), 19–35, but esp. 21.
43. Ricoeur, *Rule of Metaphor*, 199.

A recovery of metaphor was part of the transition from high modernity. 'These are good times for the friends of metaphor', enthused one conference participant in 1978.[44] I made earlier reference, however, to the totalizing rejection of all forms of identity undertaken within the deconstructionist approach, and – though it is admittedly difficult to weigh these things – it is probably correct to say that, by the end of the twentieth century, the deconstructionist approach had taken centre stage in western intellectual methods.[45] Such a judgement is reflected, for example, in Charles Winquist's sentence: 'Postmodernism . . . is . . . a way of thinking . . . governed more by metonymical constellations than by metaphorical constitution.'[46] And we have heard Jameson's (1991) pessimistic verdict:

> [R]eference and reality disappear altogether, and even meaning – the signified – is problematized. We are left with that pure and random play of signifiers that we call postmodernism, which no longer produces monumental works of the modernist type but ceaselessly reshuffles the fragments of preexistent texts, the building blocks of older cultural and social production, in some new and heightened bricolage: metabooks which cannibalize other books, metatexts which collate bits of other texts – such is the logic of postmodernism in general.[47]

The deconstructive critique was directed, as was Ricoeur's, against the 'propriety' of words and meanings.[48] But such was Derrida's disaffection for the notions of 'identity' and of 'presence' that, unlike Ricoeur, he would not allow the lexicalization of words to give them – so to speak – even a 'working identity' or 'temporary presence'. From his point of view, then, language never does escape its metaphoricity.[49] And, because there is

---

44. Ted Cohen, 'Metaphor and the Cultivation of Intimacy' in (Sheldon Sacks, ed.) *On Metaphor* (University of Chicago Press, 1978), 1.

45. Such judgements are inevitably impressionistic. Charles Reagan's sympathetic account of Ricoeur's work speaks much more positively about Ricoeur's influence, e.g. in terms of the rediscovery of his work among French philosophers in the latter decades of his life; Charles E. Reagan, *Paul Ricoeur: his life and his work* (University of Chicago Press, 1996), e.g., 48.

46. Charles E. Winquist, 'The Silence of the Real: theology at the end of the century' in (Robert P. Scharlemann, ed.) *Theology at the End of the Century: a dialogue on the postmodern with Thomas J. J. Altizer, Mark C. Taylor, Charles E. Winquist, Robert P. Scharlemann* (Charlottesville: University Press of Virginia, 1990), 15.

47. Fredric Jameson, *Postmodernism*, 96 (see ch. 2, n. 35, above).

48. On the affinities, but also the differences, between Derrida and Ricoeur, see Lawlor, *Imagination and Chance*, ch. 1 particularly, but *passim*.

49. See Gayatri Chakravorty Spivak's 'Translator's Preface' to *Of Grammatology*, p. *lxxiv*: '[D]econstructive criticism must take the "metaphoric" structure of a text very seriously.'

not even a temporary quality of identity attaching to the units of language we use, because there is *only* difference, meaning can only ever be at best elliptical, concealed, disseminated in 'differing and deferring substitutions' or a 'tissue of differences'. Certainly there can be no question of a 'production of meaning' as Ricoeur conceives it. For him, Ricoeur, it is a work, an active construction of the imagination; but, for Derrida, all we may speak about is the unpredictable play of signifiers – which accounts for Ricoeur's expostulation about the 'gigantic hole in [Derrida's] whole enterprise: because [he has] no theory of meaning'.[50]

Its fashionableness notwithstanding, we have seen that Derrida's is not the only formula for postmodernity, however. The citations I have adduced suggest it is not even the most fruitful way, that doubts can be raised as to whether in fact it escapes, as it seeks to do, an entrapment in the modern paradigm. My exposition here has aimed to show that it is not difference in itself that yields us meaning, but the grasping together of both difference and identity, and that our metaphors are primary examples.

The meaning of oneself

One of the casualties of the collapse of modernity was the Cartesian or idealist postulate of the self, an autonomous and apperceptive consciousness, able to make confident judgements about itself and thence with respect to the world about it. I traced some of the lines of attack made on such a presumption in my earlier account of the transition to our present state of awareness. The issue will arise again when I come to speak of the authorship of meaning. But it presents itself here, in the first place, as another primary case of 'grasping together' both like and unlike, yielding what we shall hear described as 'the narrative concept of selfhood'; second, this representation of 'self' stands, as a positive possibility, over against the deconstructionist judgement on 'the impropriety of the proper name'.[51]

The modern conception of a unitary self was an obvious target for deconstruction:

> I must first hear myself. In soliloquy as in dialogue, to speak is to hear oneself. As soon as I am heard, as soon as I hear myself, the I who hears *itself*, who hears *me*, becomes the I who speaks and takes speech from

Since metaphors are not reducible to truth, their own structures "as such" are part of the textuality (or message) of the text.' For Derrida on the metaphoricity of all our language, see the essay 'White Mythology: metaphor in the text of philosophy' in *Margins*, 207–71.
50. Lawlor, *Imagination and Chance*, 136.   **51.** Derrida, *Of Grammatology*, 111–13.

the I who thinks that he speaks and is heard in his own name; and becomes the I who takes speech *without ever cutting off* the I who thinks that he speaks. Insinuating itself into the name of the person who speaks, this difference is nothing, is furtiveness itself: it is the structure of instantaneous and original elusion without which no speech could ever catch its breath ... Henceforth, what is called the speaking subject is no longer the person himself, or the person alone, who speaks. The speaking subject discovers his irreducible secondarity, his origin that is always already eluded.[52]

But, as I noticed in my earlier discussion, the critique has come not just from deconstruction: it empowers itself from Freudian/Lacanian psychology, from Foucaldian genealogical and archaeological theories of knowledge, from Ricoeur's denunciations of both Cartesian and Husserlian presumptions. In one way or another we must now know that our conscious existence is heterogeneous and divided, socially constructed, mediated.

To accommodate ourselves to this (late modern!) view of ourselves, however, is not necessarily to capitulate to the deconstructive penchant for what John Caputo insists on calling 'cold hermeneutics': 'a shudder of recognition ... [which] resonates through our (non)selves, leaving us temporarily speechless, suffering from another bout with *Unheimlichkeit* and a Kierkegaardian trembling'.[53] Just as we saw with Ricoeur that it is possible to have a *working* theory of the meaning of words, so is it possible here to recuperate a theory of personhood, of personal identity, which – eschewing the old ideality and fully accepting our multiplicity and cultural embeddedness – yet recognizes that a human being is irreplaceably unique and has some sense of himself or herself *as such*. The notion of grasping together began with theories of narrativity. It is thus not surprising that this should be the leitmotif for a number of the accounts of personal identity in the late modern era. Alasdair MacIntyre is one such who asks: 'Am I the same man at fifty as I was at forty in respect of memory, intellectual

---

52. Derrida, *Writing and Difference*, 177–8 (his emphases). For summarizing statements of the postmodern deconstruction of the self, see Dews, *The Limits of Disenchantment*, 21–4; McGowan, *Postmodernism*, 20, 41–2; or Thomas McCarthy's Introduction to Habermas' *Philosophical Discourse of Modernity*, ix.

53. Caputo, *Radical Hermeneutics*, 200. It is, I think, instructive that the Heideggerian/ Derridean line which Caputo takes, professes to be a hermeneutics of play ('I ask to be pardoned if I temporarily adopt a serious and apocalyptic tone, it will soon pass', 225) and yet offers an almost wholly unrelievedly pessimistic view of human affairs. See, strikingly, the example of Caputo's meditation on the human face (*ibid.*, 272ff.) which he regards as consistently ambiguous and duplicitous.

powers, critical responses?' and answers, 'More or less.'[54] MacIntyre is clear that there is now 'no way of *founding* my identity – or lack of it – on the psychological continuity or discontinuity of the self'. He does not re-sile, however, from the possibility and importance of offering what he calls 'the narrative concept of selfhood':

> I am the *subject* of a history that is my own and no one else's, that has its own peculiar meaning . . . To be the subject of a narrative that runs from one's birth to one's death is . . . to be accountable for the actions and experiences which compose a narratable life. It is, that is, to be open to being asked to give a certain kind of account of what one did or what happened to one or what one witnessed at any earlier point in one's life.[55]

Daniel Dennett comes to the question of personal identity from a very dif-ferent angle, namely, that of neurophysiological research techniques. His picture of human consciousness is one of countless subordinate – largely self-sufficient – nervous systems creating for the overall organism what he calls 'multiple drafts', any number of partially complete nervous messages which usually do not need to get to the level of overt consciousness. Only in cases of urgency does the brain (the 'central meaner') coordinate such sys-tems as are necessary for the body's safety, survival or pleasure in what we are accustomed to call 'consciousness'.[56] But when he comes to the point of saying how this hugely complex and, for the most part, independent, system of nervous energies comes to regard itself as 'a self', he, too, resorts to narrativity:

> Our fundamental tactic of self-protection, self-control and self-definition is not spinning webs or building dams, but telling stories, and more particularly concocting and controlling the story we tell others – and ourselves – about who we are . . . These strings or streams of narrative issue forth *as if* from a single source – not just in the obvious physical sense of flowing from just one mouth, or one pencil or pen, but in a more subtle sense: their effect on any audience is to encourage them to . . . posit a unified agent . . . a *centre of narrative gravity*.[57]

54. Alasdair MacIntyre, 'The Virtues, the Unity of a Human Life, and the Concept of a Tradition' in (Stanley Hauerwas and L. Gregory Jones, eds.) *Why Narrative? readings in narrative theology* (Grand Rapids: Eerdmans, 1989), 102. The essay is a reprint of chapters from MacIntyre's book, *After Virtue* (University of Notre Dame Press, 1981).
55. *Ibid.*, 103 (his emphasis).
56. Dennett, *Consciousness Explained*; a 'thumbnail sketch' of his thesis is given on pp. 253–4.
57. *Ibid.*, 418 (his emphases).

A last witness to 'narrative identity' is Stephen Crites and his ground-breaking essay, 'The Narrative Quality of Experience':[58]

> Both mind and body are reifications of particular functions that have been wrenched from the concrete temporality of the conscious self. The self is not a composite of mind and body. The self in its concreteness is indivisible, temporal and whole, as it is revealed to be in the narrative quality of its experience. Neither disembodied minds nor mindless bodies can appear in stories. There the self is given whole, as an activity in time.[59]

Strictly, then, none of us is an undivided whole. But to live in community is to live 'as accountable' – which is to say, to be able and ready to 'render an account' of ourselves *in so far as* we know ourselves, and of our actions. This is already, in one sense, a deconstructed version of selfhood. It recognizes that our best account will only ever be that; that 'enough is enough, enough isn't everything'. This 'being accountable', the 'rendering an account of ourselves', I am saying with the help of my witnesses, is another way in which we grasp together the divergent strands of our lives into some sort of 'Best Account'.[60]

I noted earlier that a view of personal identity such as that offered here tends to blur the line I have been attempting to hold between meaning as construction and meaning's reception. 'Rendering an account' does, on the face of it, sound as if it belongs more appropriately to the construction side. But then I would say that the actual subject matter of such an account means that the process can hardly be categorically one or the other: in order to *tell* my story I have to *formulate* it. And an act – often perhaps subliminal but summoned to the surface of awareness under certain provocations – of grasping together the 'endlessly proximate situations of [a] life'[61] seems, rather self-evidently to me, an elementary part of offering one's best account of oneself.

---

58. In this case, too, I am working from a copy reprinted in Hauerwas' and Jones' anthology *Why Narrative?* (details above at n. 54). The essay was published originally in *Journal of the American Academy of Religion* 39 (1971), 291–311.

59. Stephen Crites, 'Narrative Quality' in Hauerwas and Jones, eds., 85.

60. See further, Bernard Harrison, 'Signs and the Self', *Semiotica* 104 3/4 (1995), 287–310, who thinks that the sort of narrativity we should be thinking of, with respect to the identity of the self, is not 'emplotment', which still carries too traditional ('premodernist') ideas of narrativity, but narrative as 'report': '[The self] is the point from which the reportable acts and utterances of a person continually emanate. It possesses integrity across time because the life of a person possesses intentional integrity across time' (p. 309).

61. See John Shea, 'Storytelling and Religious Identity', *Chicago Studies* 21 (1982), 23–43; the citation is from p. 24.

Perception

We are now in a position to approach the *analysis of the thing* as an *inter-sensory entity* ... [I]n so far as my hand knows hardness and softness, and my gaze knows the moon's light, it is *a certain way of linking up* with the phenomenon and *communicating with it.*

...

The passing of sensory givens before our eyes or under our hands is, as it were, a language which teaches itself, and in which meaning is secreted by the very structure of the signs, and this is why it can literally be said that *our senses question things* and that *things reply to them.*

...

The relations between things or aspects of things having always our body as their vehicle, the whole of nature is ... our interlocutor in a sort of dialogue ... To this extent, *every perception* is a *communication or communion.*[62]

In common with the theorists whose work we have been following, Maurice Merleau-Ponty brooks no patience with the supposition of a direct intuition or an immediate consciousness of the world. As with Ricoeur, Derrida, and the exponents of 'narrative identity' or of 'interpretation semiosis', our apprehension of reality is, according to Merleau-Ponty, always and necessarily mediate:

If we ... wish to characterize a subject capable of this perceptual experience, it obviously will not be a self-transparent thought, absolutely present to itself without the interference of its body and its history. The perceiving subject is not this absolute thinker; rather it functions according to a natal pact between our body and the world, between ourselves and our body.[63]

From this point of view, Merleau-Ponty's notion of the 'gap' or 'dehiscence' (*écart*) which always 'keeps [the perceiving subject and the perceived object] from collapsing into one another'[64] is regularly compared and contrasted with Derrida's *différance*.[65] There are similarities. But there are also critical differences. Analogously with Ricoeur's admission of lexical identity as an actual – though derived and temporary – property of words, and his consequent perception of meaning as consisting in the play of differences and identity, so, in the realm of perception, Merleau-Ponty

---

62. Merleau-Ponty, *Phenomenology of Perception*, 317, 319 and 320 (my emphases).
63. Merleau-Ponty, *Primacy of Perception*, 6.
64. Burke, 'The Flesh as *Urpräsentierbarkeit*', 66.
65. See, rather obviously, the volume edited by M. C. Dillon *Écart & Différence*. Nearly all the essays in the volume take up the comparison and contrast of the two themes ('gap' and 'difference') in Merleau-Ponty and Derrida respectively.

holds the physical ('fleshly') constitution of persons to be the 'reversible' site of identity-with-and-difference-from the world in which they find themselves:

> Visible and mobile, my body is a thing among things; it is caught in the fabric of the world, and its cohesion is that of a thing. But because it moves itself and sees, it holds things in a circle around itself...
>
> There is a human body when, between seeing and the seen, between touching and the touched, between one eye and the other, between hand and hand, a blending of some sort takes place – when the spark is lit between sensing and sensible, lighting the fire [of the body's animation] that will not stop burning until some accident of the body will undo what no accident would have sufficed to do...[66]

It is this curious 'reversibility' of the body ('seeing and being seen', 'touching and being touched') which, according to Merleau-Ponty, allows a presence to the world – 'the flesh as a fundamental presentability (*Urpräsentierbarkeit*)' – which, as at least one commentator has noted, is 'particularly repulsive to Derrida'.[67] The perceiving subject *is* present to the world; but in his or her paradoxically 'doubled' way: seeing and being seen, and so on.[68] This is the 'gap' which allows and at the same time limits perception: 'Thus there is a paradox of immanence and transcendence in perception. Immanence, because the perceived object cannot be foreign to him [*sic*] who perceives; transcendence, because it always contains something more than what is actually given... [These two elements of perception require] this presence and this absence.'[69]

It also effects the strikingly 'collaborative' act between percipient and the perceived which Merleau-Ponty has described in the paragraphs cited

---

66. Merleau-Ponty, *Primacy of Perception*, 163–4; the concluding ellipsis is Merleau-Ponty's.

67. Burke, 'The Flesh as *Urpräsentierbarkeit*', 69. Strictly, it is Merleau-Ponty's logocentrism which Burke says is so unacceptable to Derrida; but he has just identified this as 'the voice of primal presence'.

68. See, for example, this from *The Visible and the Invisible*: '[T]he flesh we are speaking of is not matter. It is the coiling over of the visible upon the seeing body, of the tangible upon the touching body, which is attested in particular when the body sees itself, touches itself seeing and touching the things, such that, simultaneously, *as* tangible it descends among them... This concentration of the visibles about one of them, or this bursting forth of the mass of the body towards the things... makes me *follow with my eyes* the movements and the contours of the things themselves, this magical relation, this pact between them and me according to which I lend them my body in order that they inscribe upon it and give me their resemblance, this fold, this central cavity of the visible which is my vision, these two mirror arrangements of the seeing and the visible, the touching and the touched, form a close-bound system that I count on, define a vision in general and a constant style of visibility from which I cannot detach myself... The flesh (of the world or my own) is not contingency, chaos, but a texture that returns to itself and conforms to itself'; Maurice Merleau-Ponty, *The Visible and the Invisible* (Evanston, IL: Northwestern University Press, 1969), 146 (his emphases).

69. Merleau-Ponty, *Primacy of Perception*, 16.

at the head of this section. In their own way, the paragraphs depict a 'grasping together' of external and internal reality; what I earlier described as 'making and finding'. So the percept is not passively objective as in the Cartesian schema; but then neither is the percipient masterfully active. Rather, there is a collaboration between what is given and how it is received; there is 'a communication and communion' in which 'our senses question things and things reply to them'. One may even say, we 'are brought to birth' in this collaborative act.[70]

Does this excursus into theory of perception seem tangential, at best, to a study of the meanings of the liturgy? If we shall allow ourselves to be led by Merleau-Ponty, we will see the particular form of comprehension which is perception – this human act of grasping together like and unlike[71] – as the form underlying all the others: 'By these words, the "primacy of perception", we mean that the experience of perception is our presence at the moment when things, truths, values are constituted for us; that perception is a nascent *logos*; that it teaches us ... the true conditions of objectivity itself; that it summons us to the tasks of knowledge and action.'[72] If this great student of human perception is to be trusted, then, somewhere near the heart of all meaningful engagement with the world is an action – intensely physical as well as intellectual – which looks something like the 'grasping together' we saw as characteristic of the play of similarity and difference in our apprehension of meaning in language, or which seemed to describe the responses of the visitor to an unfamiliar service of worship.

Grasping the meaning of signs

Charles Peirce's 'interpretation semiotics' also belongs within the post-1960s (late modern) paradigm; that is, within this new age in which we are not required to choose between 'the categories *ens reale* and *ens rationis*' (i.e., objectivity and subjectivity).[73] This is not yet the place to enter into a full-scale exposition of Peirce. My wish rather is to draw attention to the element of 'reaching for' or 'grasping of' meaning entailed in his semiotic theory closely resembling the metaphorical process I offered as a sort of paradigm of meaning construction and meaning apprehension.[74] One of

---

70. See *ibid.*, 181: 'The world no longer stands before [the painter] through representation; rather it is the painter to whom the things of the world give birth by a sort of concentration or coming-to-itself of the visible.'
71. One of Merleau-Ponty's favourite perceptual cases is the way we distinguish a subject from its ground; see, for example, *Phenomenology of Perception*, 3–4, 225–6, 304, 308, or 313.
72. *Primacy of Perception*, 25.   73. Deely, *New Beginnings*, 101.
74. On Peirce's view of metaphor as sign, see Jørgen Dines Johansen, 'Iconicity in Literature', *Semiotica* 110 1/2 (1996), 41.

the most succinct and widely cited of Peirce's numerous attempts at a definition of a sign runs: 'A sign, or *representamen*, is something which stands
to somebody for something in some respect or capacity. It addresses somebody, that is, creates in the mind of that person an equivalent sign, or perhaps a more developed sign. That sign which it creates I call the *interpretant* of the first sign' (CP 2.228). Thus it is stated that the Peircean sign is
not a single entity, but consists fundamentally in a relationship of three
things, *viz.*: (1) what Peirce at this stage was still calling the *representamen*
('that which stands for something'), (2) the sign's *object* ('that for which it
stands'), and (3) the interpretative element governing the relationship between them, the sign's *interpretant* ('in some respect or capacity'). It is this
last named element which elicits our attention here. By incorporating this
element into every sign constellation – and thus into every act of signification – Peirce means to say that there *can be no direct equivalence* between the
sign-vehicle (the *representamen*) and what it stands for (the sign's object).
The connection between them is always one of 'more or less' (recall the
question: 'Are you the same person ten years later?'). The specification 'in
some respect or capacity' means *there is work to be done* by the sign's interpreter or recipient; there is a *sifting* and a *grasping* to be undertaken if the
sign's meaning is to be apprehended, entirely analogous to the actions required of a person encountering a new metaphor. The Peircean exponent,
Susan Petrilli, articulates this explicitly:

> In Peircean semiotics the interpretant sign develops from the
> interpreted sign ... and may be considered as *grasping that sign to a
> certain degree*, with respect to which it is endowed with its own semiotic
> or signifying materiality.
>
> ...
>
> In the signifying universe thus conceived the imagination, both
> scientific and poetical, generates signs and *searches for an understanding* of
> the fact, for truth ... which is never ultimate nor determinate truth.[75]

A special note is perhaps called for on the disppointingly strained relationship between
hermeneutics, as it is represented by Ricoeur or Gadamer, and the proponents of a Peircean
style of semiotics (see, for example, Deely, *Basics*, 16, or his *The Human Use of Signs* (Totowa, NJ:
Rowman and Littlefield, 1993), 107–8; similarly, Wojciech H. Kalaga, 'Interpretation and
Sign: semiotics versus hermeneutics', *S: European Journal for Semiotic Studies* 7 (1995), 559–86).
The reason is that Ricoeur's engagement with semiotics was restricted to the Saussurean
type, of which he was consistently critical (see, e.g., the first three essays in *Conflict in
Interpretations*). This is then taken by semiotic theorists to represent an antipathy on Ricoeur's
part to semiotics per se (even though he offers the same kind of criticisms of Saussurean
semiotics as they do!) It is undoubtedly a matter for regret that Ricoeur has never directed a
serious attention to Peirce's writings (only the sketchiest references appear in his work). As I
go along, I shall try to give reasons for thinking that there is a much greater affinity between
semiotics, as it is now understood, and Ricoeur's style of hermeneutics.
75. Petrilli, 'About and Beyond Peirce', 301–2, 311 (my emphases).

'It seems a strange thing', we recall Peirce saying, 'that a sign should leave its interpreter to supply a part of its meaning' (CP 5.448, note 1). Significantly – in terms of our present inquiry into 'comprehension' – Augusto Ponzio would name this demand of the sign's recipient precisely 'an active form of answering comprehension'.[76]

Authoring meaning

I have attempted, though with only limited success, to hold separately from one another the production of meaning and its reception. There is a certain logic which suggests that the one precedes the other, according to which it might have made better sense to have treated production before reception. The difficulty I have had in holding the discussion within the prescribed demarcations already suggests that the logic is at best partial or apparent. The further consideration that a sign-*producer* has always to work towards the *reception* of his or her significations – attempting, that is, to speak as clearly, evocatively or persuasively as she or he can – means that there is no way of describing the one without having the other in view. I chose therefore to override the seeming logic of production/reception in order to attend first to our experience of 'grasping for' the novel meanings proposed, for example, in a new metaphor – a kind of paradigm, I have suggested, for so much of our meaning-making and meaning exchange. One who forges a new metaphor ('new' here is redundant since metaphoricity lies precisely in its novelty; but I let it stand to underline the point) and one who apprehends it engage in essentially the same work: namely, that of 'obliterating the logical and established frontiers of language . . . in order to establish new logical frontiers on the ruins of their forerunners'.[77] The grasping together of old and new, the identifiable and the puzzling, seems to me, however, probably more easily seen as we *encounter* new metaphors, new meanings. I thus let it have priority in a depiction of 'comprehension'.

On the other hand (obviously), there could be no apprehension if there were no proposal, and that is what I now turn to.

The heading 'Authoring meaning' is intentionally provocative. The 'death of the author' was vigorously prosecuted throughout the period of

---

76. Ponzio, *Man as a Sign*, 252. It is worth noting that Ponzio forms this expression directly in opposition to the structuralist (and, by extension, the post-structuralist) dyadic sign, in which a receiver's role is reduced 'simply [to] that of deciphering the message with reference to a previously established and unambiguous code' (*idem.*).

77. Ricoeur, *Rule of Metaphor*, 197.

formalism and is no less relentlessly pursued in post-structuralist, post-modern theses. The mid-twentieth century reaction to late nineteenth- and early twentieth-century notions of subjective expressiveness or authorial genius reached its sharpest articulation in judgements such as those of Wimsatt and Beardsley: 'The design or intention of the author is neither available nor desirable as a standard for judging the success of a work of literary art.'[78] Roland Barthes' brief essay under the title 'The Death of the Author' expresses the point of view as cogently as it may be (and also sounds prescient of much deconstructionist language): 'Who is speaking thus? Is it the hero of the story...? Is it Balzac the individual...? Is it Balzac the author...? Is it universal wisdom? Romantic psychology? We shall never know for the good reason that *writing is the destruction of every voice, of every point of origin.*'[79]

Derrida's campaign against 'presence', 'identity' and 'the proper' has continued this suspicion of authorial presence in, or in control of, texts:

> Henceforth, what is called the speaking subject is no longer the person himself [*sic*], or the person alone, who speaks. The speaking subject discovers his irreducible secondarity, his origin that is always already eluded; for the origin is always already eluded on the basis of an organized field of speech in which the speaking subject vainly seeks a place that is always missing.[80]

In the opposite direction to the way in which we are accustomed to think of authorship, then, we are invited in deconstruction to think of writing virtually writing itself through authors: 'the person writing *is inscribed* in a determined textual system';[81] 'it is ... a question ... of reading *what wrote itself* between the lines,'[82] all of which accords with the depopulated landscape drawn by Fredric Jameson: 'that objective mirage of signification generated and projected by *the relationship of signifiers among themselves*'.[83]

---

78. W. K. Wimsatt and M. Beardsley, 'The Intentional Fallacy' in (W. K. Wimsatt Jr., ed.) *The Verbal Icon: studies in the meaning of poetry* (Lexington: University of Kentucky Press, 1970), 3.
79. Roland Barthes, 'The Death of the Author' in *Image Music Text* (London: Fontana Paperbacks, 1984), 142 (my emphases).
80. Derrida, *Writing and Difference*, 178. See also *Of Grammatology*, 97–98, 111–13, for meditations on 'authorial presence under the sign of the proper name'; or, *ibid.*, 107ff., first, on the conventional connection between a proper name and proper meanings and then, 108–9, on the alleged 'obliteration' of this connection in the system of writing.
81. *Of Grammatology*, 160 (my emphasis).   82. *Ibid.*, 86 (my emphasis).
83. Jameson, *Postmodernity*, 26 (my emphasis). See Catherine Pickstock's trenchant critique of deconstruction (*After Writing*, 22): 'Derrida's written model suggests no people at all, only a word which comes from nowhere, an autonomous word which conceals or violently eradicates its origins and dictates to its "author" rendering him [*sic*] entirely passive before a disembodied ... power.'

Predictably this challenging representation of things finds rebuttal. Not that many theorists wish to gainsay the corrective point made by deconstructionists about the limits imposed on authors or speakers by cultural embeddedness, available language and personal complicity.[84] But, accepting these (in line with other acceptations of our late modern condition), people still wish steadily to insist: '[W]riting does not simply write itself; it takes a real human subject to write whatever it is that, as a matter of fact, gets written.'[85] Appropriating this to our purposes, we will, of course, say that neither does a liturgy come from nowhere. Taking into account the (hidden) labours of textual scholars and liturgical theologians, the patient work of drafting committees and so on ('and so on' means *almost* endlessly, except that it does momentarily reach an end of sorts: it actually yields an occasion of worship), a priest and people plan and effect the work which is a liturgy. Biblical words, traditional prayers, contemporary hortations are woven[86] into or with the occasion which is the day of the (liturgical) calendar and, not least, are shaped in accordance with the pastoral circumstances of the congregation: *someone does all this* in order to make meaning! When we come to it in greater detail, I will say it is not just in texts and music and so on that this meaning is fastened together; but that it is even or precisely in the 'facial expression, eye contact, gesture and body language, kinesics, tactile communication and proxemics' of the leader(s) or the presiding minister that people will receive the gift of meaning.[87] In large and in near-invisible detail, someone constructs the meaning of worship.

---

84. An exception might be George Steiner who wants to meet deconstructive fire with fire. He seems determined to reinstate the ideality of meanings: 'The break with the postulate of the sacred is the break with any stable, potentially ascertainable meaning of meaning'; George Steiner, *Real Presences* (University of Chicago Press, 1989), 132. On Steiner's equal extremism see, e.g., Giles Gunn, *The Culture of Criticism and the Criticism of Culture* (New York: Oxford University Press, 1987), p. *ix*; or Gillian Rose, 'Diremption of Spirit' in (Phillipa Berry and Andrew Wernick, eds.) *Shadow of Spirit: postmodernism and religion* (London: Routledge, 1992), 51–2.

85. Madison, 'Merleau-Ponty and Derrida: *la différEnce*', 100. Madison makes the wry comment that even deconstructive texts presuppose 'a subject who writes deconstructively'.

86. One of Merleau-Ponty's metaphors of the construction of meaning in language is that of weaving; Merleau-Ponty, *Signs*, 45.

87. See Ronald Sequeira, 'Liturgische Körper-und Gebärdensprache als Thema der Semiotik: Möglichkeiten und Grenzen' in (Wilfried Engemann and Rainer Volp, eds.) *Gib mir ein Zeichen: zur Bedeutung der Semiotik für theologische Praxis-und Denkmodelle* (Berlin: Walter de Gruyter, 1992). Strictly the citation (p. 207) is about the scope of a 'general semiotics'; but the burden of Sequeira's essay is to show how all of these semiotic dimensions of a presiding minister's 'presence' enter into the effectiveness (meaning) of a liturgical event. See also Sequeira's essay, 'Gottesdienst als menschliche Ausdruckshandlung' to which I have already drawn attention (above, ch. 1, n. 108).

Apart from these rather common-sense demurrals from the deconstructionist line, there are two aspects of the authorship of meaning which
demand more detailed attention. These are the questions of *agency* (to
whom does responsibility for the proffered signs revert?) and the actual
process of production (how is meaning generated?)

Agency

Charles Taylor and Paul Ricoeur have both made extensive studies of human agency.[88] Their interest has been drawn by what they take to be the
dangerous product of the trends just now surveyed, namely a view in
which actions are depersonalized and a consequent ambiguity is raised
about personal accountability. For both thinkers, the explicit target is not
so much literary deconstruction; it is more exactly English-language objectivism, or what Taylor calls naturalism (Taylor does have one essay on
Foucault).[89] But my recent references to the diminution of human initiative in the deconstructive 'play of signifiers' means that their disap-
probation could at least as well have been sent in this direction.[90] Taylor
particularly objects to the tendency of basing so-called 'human sciences'
on natural-science models, thus carrying across (into the former) quantitative judgements and the application of mechanistic styles of research.
In strong contradistinction he insists that 'the human animal is a self-
interpreting subject'[91] who must be regarded as a responsible agent acting out of 'certain strong evaluations which are inseparable from [him- or
her-]self.'[92] Ricoeur characteristically seeks 'a new alliance between the analytic tradition and the phenomenological and hermeneutic tradition'[93] –
in which, on the one hand, a person's *physical objectivity* allows us to single her out from all others ('a definite description . . . a class that has but

---

88. Charles Taylor, *Human Agency* and *Philosophy and the Human Sciences*. Though the essays of
the first volume are more specifically directed towards the question of agency, each volume
carries the same Introduction, in which Taylor outlines his thesis: 'A fully competent human
agent not only has some understanding . . . of himself [*sic*], but is partly constituted by this
understanding' (p. 3 of both volumes). For Ricoeur, the main text is his *Oneself as Another*.
89. 'Foucault on Freedom and Truth' in *Human Sciences*.
90. Taylor does have passing comment on Derrida's programme in his Introduction; he
regards it as 'close to an unmitigated disaster' (*Human Agency*, 10). The closest Ricoeur comes
(in *Oneself as Another*) to post-structuralism is a treatment of Nietzsche (*ibid.*, 12–16; see n. 20
on p. 13 for the identification of French writers with this tradition). But significant – in terms
of our interest in what I called 'the depopulated landscape' of deconstructionist
postmodernity – is Ricoeur's title for his third chapter, 'An Agentless Semantics of Action'
(directed towards Donald Davidson's views on intention and action).
91. *Human Agency*, 43 and frequently; see e.g., the chapter heading 'Self-interpreting animals',
pp. 45ff.
92. *Ibid.*, 34.   93. *Oneself as Another*, 114.

a single member'[94]), is joined, on the other hand, to the *uniqueness of vantage point* from which each person views the world.[95] These outward and inward dimensions of an individual Ricoeur calls respectively 'identity' (*idem*, 'the same' – 'is this the person who committed the alleged war atrocities forty years ago?')[96] and 'ipseity' (*ipse*, 'oneself' – 'am I the same man at fifty as I was at forty?'). Again, *identity*, in both dimensions, is directly linked with *agency*: '[It is not possible] to separate the "what?" of the thing to be done and the "why?" of the thing done from the "who?" of the action and of the reason for acting.'[97]

Self-evidently, the question of identity/agency has powerful ethical or moral ramifications; and conceivably these have a bearing on the actions and utterances made in the liturgy – that is, with respect to the moral responsibility carried by the priest or leader for her or his words and actions.[98]

Beyond ethics, there is, however, perhaps a more intractable problem with respect to the agency of liturgical meanings, namely an absence of mechanisms for monitoring or regulating the degree of congruence between an *intended* signification and its actual '*uptake*' (borrowing J. L. Austin's term). In my Introduction I said that this entire meditation on liturgical meanings in some degree sprang from such absence of purchase on our meanings as we pass beyond linguistic meanings.[99] Even in language, our most sophisticated signifying system, a complete coincidence between intention and interpretation is unlikely; indeed the possibility of rank – though honest – misunderstandings cannot be ruled out of account. This all becomes greatly more volatile, however, when we pass beyond language to our other signifying processes.[100] As a concrete example from personal experience, when I lifted the bread and the cup in the eucharistic prayer, I believed I was giving effect to the lines of the prayer which run: 'from the gifts you have given us, this bread and this cup, we

94. *Ibid.*, 28.

95. *Ibid.*, 54–5. Though he does not make the connection here (there is an allusive reference at p. 320) Ricoeur's thought is highly suggestive of Merleau-Ponty's 'fleshliness' of perception; cf., then, Merleau-Ponty, *Primacy of Perception*, 5: 'We grasp external space through our bodily situation ... Our body is not in space like things; it inhabits or haunts space ... We ... find that spatial forms or distances are not so much relations between different points in objective space as they are relations between these points and a central perspective – our body.'

96. *Oneself as Another*, 117.   97. *Ibid.*, 98.

98. See Flanagan, *Sociology and Liturgy*, ch. 5.   99. Page 1, above.

100. I am writing from a Protestant perspective where verbalization has always been awarded dominance. I presume, however, that even in those liturgical styles in which every last detail of the rite has been rubrically prescribed (see Flanagan again, *Sociology and Liturgy*, 179–80), the gap between intention and uptake is not eliminated.

praise and we bless you';[101] but my congregant supposed I was reverencing the eucharistic species. Or when the people stood as the Bible was carried in and the minister followed, some thought it was a mark of respect for the minister.

Usually, we shrug off – as a kind of inevitability – this cleft between proposal and reception: 'People always read things the way they will,' we say to each other. I will come back to this in greater detail later in my work under the headings 'Indexicality' and 'The responsibilities attending the production of meaning',[102] but to introduce the notion of agency here in a preliminary way is to claim that we are not as helpless before the inexactitude of non-linguistic signification as we had perhaps supposed. It is to bring to bear on the 'what?', as Ricoeur has it, the questions of the '"why?" and the "who?" of the action and of the reason for acting.' 'Intention' has had an admittedly chequered history in the theorization of meaning, but to link it here to the question of agency allows at least some level of access to the volitional dimension of the action; that is, it sets the action *not* in the field of a random play of signifiers but in that of *a human being wishing or intending to signify*. To ask about the intention of the sign-producer – accepting the still imprecise nature of 'intention' in these respects – is to open the way towards a critical assessment, first, of *the sign itself* (in terms of its suitability as the instrument or bearer of such an intention) and then, second, of the appropriateness or inappropriateness of the *recipient's construction of meaning* (in light of, or on the basis of, the sign). To say this slightly differently: as an action (i.e., as an agent's intentional act as opposed to something that simply happened), the publicly accessible sign can be held to exercise criterial jurisdiction *backwards towards the agent* (in terms of its adequacy as the sign of his or her intention) and *forwards towards the action's interpreter* (in terms of the adequacy of his or her apprehension of it as a sign).

Meaning production

The deconstruction of the author has led to a radical doubt about the *production* of meaning – that is, with respect to the achievement among us of new meaning. We are familiar with the standard motifs: 'the trace [which] is not a presence but the simulacrum of a presence that dislocates itself, displaces itself, refers itself ... properly has no site';[103] or the 'indefinite

101. See Max Thurian and Geoffrey Wainwright (eds.) *Baptism and Eucharist: ecumenical convergence in celebration* (Geneva and Grand Rapids: World Council of Churches and William B. Eerdmans, 1983), 122.

102. Below, pages 170–6, 192–5.   103. Derrida, *Margins*, 24.

referral of signifier to signifier.'[104] The principal reason for this condition we are told (often) is that the putative source for any such creativity is itself constituted, divided: 'There is no constituting subjectivity. The very concept of constitution itself must be deconstructed.'[105] An appeal to authorship, then, as the idea of someone generating some genuinely new vision of the world, is an appeal to 'the proper', 'the physics of presence . . . and of the subject'.[106]

One is again confronted with an all-or-nothing ultimatum. We saw, both in connection with 'narrative identity' and with the question of agency, that it is possible to hold a moderated view of personal identity; one can accept the individual and cultural limitations placed around our personhood, yet still be able (and actually required) to 'render an account'.

Another version of the objection, however (not, as we shall see in a moment, confined to deconstruction), is the old bogy[107] of prelinguistic thought. Deconstruction is certainly quick to take over the objection: since there can be no thought which is not already structured linguistically – hence is already constituted within 'the endless chain of signifiers' – it is 'irreducibly secondary.'[108] But the point of view has a wider provenance in late modern and postmodern thought. Terry Eagleton puts it as well as any:

> Perhaps the reader would care to experiment here by looking up from the book for a moment and 'meaning' something silently in his or her head. What did you 'mean'? And was it different from the words in which you have just formulated the response? To believe that meaning consists of words plus a wordless act of willing or intending is rather like believing that every time I open the door 'on purpose' I make a silent act of willing while opening it.[109]

One must say the experiment – to be more exact, the experiment's designer – entirely misses the point. Of course, expressible meaning will

---

104. Derrida, *Writing and Difference*, 25.
105. Derrida, *Speech and Phenomena*, 85 (n. 9 from p. 84).
106. Derrida, *Of Grammatology*, 246, and often.
107. See Dillon, 'Introduction: *écart & différence*', 8: 'The words "pre-linguistic meaning" seem to have magic powers to awaken ghouls in souls otherwise untroubled when they open their eyes and see the world. This phrase . . . causes specters to rise from the graves of philosophical history, to haunt the minds of the quick.'
108. *Writing and Difference*, 178. Or see *Margins*, 15: '[T]he subject . . . is inscribed in language, is a "function" of language, becomes a *speaking* subject only by making its speech conform – even in so-called "creation", or in so-called "transgression" – to the system of the rules of the language as a system of differences' (Derrida's emphasis).
109. Terry Eagleton, *Literary Theory: an introduction* (Oxford: Basil Blackwell, 1983), 67–8.

inevitably take the form of language – because it is expressible! To think of 'something', as we are invited to do, already takes for granted that that unit of language/meaning is in circulation, is available to be meant or thought. The point at issue is whether or not there is a human sense of the possible, an envisaging energy which is *not yet* expressible, and is thus not yet linguistically formed and, in a clear and true sense of the word, is not yet 'thought' (i.e., an articulable idea). Since it is not formulable it cannot be expressed and, strictly, cannot be thought (not yet!).[110] But I cannot imagine how any writer or speaker (writing is slower, has more time for deliberation, and thus allows the process to be seen more easily; but the principle applies to both) has not sat uncertainly, hands hovering over the keyboard or pencil poised, *waiting*: knowing there is something to be said but not yet knowing *how* it is to be said and thus not knowing either, with any clarity, *what* it is which wants to be said. One tries over various possibilities – either silently within, or in the external signs of writing or of speech – some of which seem suggestive but not yet 'right', and others of which are clearly inadequate in relation to that which awaits.[111] Eventually (most times, but not even this is assured) the form is found and the thought is identified. *Now* the assembling of signs which Derrida and others take so seriously can continue; but *that there was an energy* (Kant's 'productive imagination'?)[112] which was inexpressible, yet was *sufficiently definite as to exercise its power of veto or approval* over such language as was found for it, seems to me incontrovertible. Analogously with the 'rendering of an account of oneself' in terms of one's personal 'narrative identity', I call this the 'rendering' of meaning, the shaping of this inexpressible energy of insight into publicly accessible signs, linguistic or other.

Of the thinkers known to me, Julia Kristeva has theorized this best. At the stage of her work in which we are interested, Kristeva's desire was

110. Charles Peirce's thought is especially relevant here. On one side, Peirce was unambiguous in his conviction that 'all thought . . . must necessarily be in signs' (CP 5.251); see Petrilli, 'About and Beyond Peirce', 324, or Deely, 'Looking Back on *A Theory of Semiotics*', 84. On the other hand, Peirce's notion of 'Firstness' – the inarticulable possibility from which all signification derives, see below, pp. 135–6 – is entirely congruent with prelinguistic meaning; see, e.g., Sheriff, *The Fate of Meaning*, 81: 'It is impossible to talk about Firstness without losing it. When we try to bring the content of the present instant to consciousness, the sensation is past, has become the predicate of a subsequent sign, and "what remains is greatly metamorphosized" (CP 1.310).'
111. See Eco on Pareyson's theory of 'artistic trial', which process is 'guided by the work as it is to be'; Eco, *The Open Work*, 161.
112. Kant, *Critique of Pure Reason*, A 120, 123.

to pass beyond the then current preoccupation of structuralists and for-
malists with the interior organization of texts, and to offer an account
of the ways in which texts – poetic texts particularly – *in fact come into being*; in other words, to shift interest away from texts as 'products' and towards their 'production'[113] – or, as she described it in another place, to investigate 'the specific status ... of the speaking subject'.[114] In accord with
the transition from high modernity which we have identified with the
1960s, Kristeva was concerned to disrupt the solidity of selves as centres of
meaning:

> Our positing of the semiotic is obviously inseparable from the theory of
> the subject that takes into account the Freudian positing of the
> unconscious. We view the subject in language as decentering the
> transcendental ego, cutting through it and opening it up to a dialectic
> in which its syntactic and categorial understanding is merely the
> liminary moment of the process ... We will be attempting to formulate
> the distinction between *semiotic* and *symbolic* within this perspective.[115]

The last named distinction ('semiotic'/'symbolic'; the terms are used
idiosyncratically in Kristeva's work) refers to the disjunction (and then
conjunction) we experience in the gestation process, the 'rendering' of
prelinguistic intuition into publicly accessible signs which I tried to describe. The nebulous but unmistakable awareness of inexpressible meaning she calls (following Plato's *Timaeus*) 'the place', the *chora*.[116] It is in this
'place' that the 'rendering' happens: the formless energy (in her language,
'the semiotic') is fused with identifiable signifiers (what she calls 'the symbolic'). All signification, she says, will thereafter carry within it both these
dimensions – the chaotic, creative energy in which the sign was born,[117]

---

113. See, e.g., the account of Roland Barthes' comment to Kristeva: '[Y]ou have helped me to
change, particularly in shifting away from a semiology of products to a semiotics of
production', cited in Leon S. Roudiez' Introduction to Kristeva's *Revolution in Poetic Language*
(New York: Columbia University Press, 1984), 10.
114. Julia Kristeva, 'The System and the Speaking Subject' in (Toril Moi, ed.), *The Kristeva
Reader* (Oxford: Basil Blackwell, 1986), 32; or, from 'Semiotics: A Critical Science and/or a
Critique of Science', *ibid.*, 84: 'This seems to encapsulate the whole problem of contemporary
semiotics: either it continues to *formalize* the semiotic systems from the point of view of
communication ... or else it opens up to the internal problematics of communication ... the
"other scene" of the *production* of meaning *prior to meaning*' (my emphases).
115. Kristeva, *Revolution*, 30 (her emphases).   116. *Ibid.*, 24–5, and then frequently.
117. The *chora* can be described in womb-like terms: 'Plato himself ... calls this receptacle or
chora nourishing and maternal', *ibid.*, 26; see also Teresa de Lauretis in 'Gaudy Rose: Eco and
Narcissism' in (Rocco Capozzi, ed.) *Reading Eco: an anthology* (Bloomington: Indiana
University Press, 1997), 250. Kristeva's thought is comparable with Peircean thought at this
point, too; see esp. Petrilli, 'About and Beyond Peirce', 341–2, on Lady Welby's
correspondence with Peirce on 'mother-sense', particularly in terms of the generation of
meaning *ante litteram* (p. 342).

and the 'materiality'[118] of the signifying system which allows its utterance. Meaning, signification, consists in 'this *always split unification*'.[119]

I will want to say that our construction of meaning as liturgical leaders will similarly bear this double signification. Robert Hovda characteristically lays his finger on Kristeva's 'semiotic' dimension when he speaks of 'the presider's *spirit*' showing in and through the material signifiers;[120] but the materiality of eyes, face, tone of voice, demeanour and so on are the *public manifestations* (Kristeva's 'symbolic' dimension) of this person's act of meaning.[121]

I have been speaking of authoring meaning. How does someone mean something? 'Grasping together' has about it a vigour, violence even, that sits slightly oddly with the 'waiting', 'gestation', or 'rendering' I have been describing.[122] Still, it is not too difficult to imagine as a 'grasping' of sorts the semiotic energy which, in its wish to signify, reaches for its own most effective articulation. Our language has a few revealing descriptive terms in this respect: we speak of 'searching', of 'groping for words', or of 'struggling for the right expression'. I said that I thought the apprehension of someone else's meaning showed more readily the grasping together of familiar and unfamiliar. But in light of Kristeva's analyses, we can perhaps see that the actual construction of meaning follows a not dissimilar path.

The funny side of meaning

One of the most powerful expressions of the grasping together I am describing is what happens to us on hearing a joke. With truly extraordinary rapidity the brain ranges through the possible, the probable, and then the doubtfully probable implications of the conjunction of affairs proposed

---

118. *Revolution*, 28, 63 and frequently. We can usefully cite John Lechte (*Julia Kristeva* (London: Routledge, 1990), 101) in this respect: 'What Kristeva intends is that we should see a link between the *signifiance* [the double sided act of signification] and the materiality of language . . . in the sound and rhythm of words, and in the graphic disposition of the text on the page'; and (*ibid.*, 129): '*Signifiance*, Kristeva argues, is always present in the operations of the symbolic – such as in the everyday language of communication. For in all such speech-acts, timbre, rhythm, gesture, etc., are perceptible, but rarely noticed due to the dominance of the communicative function of language.'
119. *Revolution*, 49 (my emphases).   120. Hovda, *Strong, Loving and Wise*, 1ff.
121. I take all this up in greater detail under the notion of 'indexical' signs in chapter 5 (pp. 170–6).
122. Though one must say violence is not absent from Kristeva's view of the semiotic process. See, e.g., the references to the semiotic 'pulverizing' of symbolic structures cited at n. 11, ch. 6, below. The expression reminds one of Ricoeur's metaphorical 'obliteration' of previous senses in order 'to establish new frontiers on the ruins of their forerunners'.

in the joke and latches hold of the intended, but wholly improbable – ludicrous in fact – meaning of the joke-teller. An anatomical convulsion ensues: the diaphragm heaves, breath is expelled in sonic gusts, the trunk is very likely doubled or is at any rate shaken by the convulsion, and the facial muscles are contorted in the pattern familiar to us as laughter. The entire body enjoys a joke.

My purpose here is twofold: (i) to draw attention to this particularly striking example of our comprehensive powers and (ii) to allow laughter to direct us to the primitive nature, the deeply visceral nature, of the 'grasping' process. If, as I am mildly inclined to do, we were to see the joke as the clearest form of meaning transaction we have – showing the rapidity with which we 'hunt' for the connection between disparities – that should not be taken as implying the suggestion that humour in worship leads to more meaningful worship (that thesis is propounded in some quarters; there is good reason to see it as especially influenced by currently prevalent cultural dispositions).[123]

Human laughter is such an unpremeditated, reflexive action that it is difficult to suppose it is not a universal human trait. Most modern study of laughter seems so to assume and extrapolates from our own relatively recent (i.e., from the last three or four centuries) cultural mores in its theorizing of the phenomenon. This tends largely to be based on a connection between laughter and humour (though research does also attend to other stimuli such as tickling). Historical cultural studies such as the detailed work recently undertaken by Ingvild Gilhus show, however, just how dangerous such assumptions can be;[124] and, conversely, how culturally constructed is this which we imagine to be innate and utterly spontaneous. In ancient cultures, laughter is practically without exception – as shown in remnant texts at any rate; perhaps things were different for people at the time – depicted as sardonic, cynical, or mocking. Laughter is equally regularly the triumphant snarl of a superior deity over upstart mortals (among ancient texts the Hebrew scriptures turn out to be the most pronounced in this!).[125] In Christian mediaeval society laughter is regarded by teachers and those in authority as dangerously carnal and thus to be suppressed, whereas among lower orders of society it became an instrument

---

123. See Ingvild Sælid Gilhus, *Laughing Gods, Weeping Virgins: laughter in the history of religions* (London: Routledge, 1997), 114–16. On entertainment, as a seductive contemporary influence on worship, see, e.g., Lathrop, *Holy Things*, 114, 174, or the same author's *Holy People*, 3, 23, or 27.

124. Gilhus, *Laughing Gods, passim.*   125. *Ibid.*, 26.

of subversion.[126] But in either case it was associated with the body, with physicality; from the one point of view, negatively; from the other, positively.

All this warns us against too quick assumptions drawn from our own cultural evaluations. On the other hand, it is as modern people that we experience the phenomenon of laughter, and it is from this point of view that I will make my few remarks.

Modern laughter and humour theory (they are not the same thing) are generally said to fall into three camps. One of these, usually basing itself on remarks by Thomas Hobbes in the seventeenth century but possibly running as far back as the ancient sardonic laughter to which I referred just now, regards both humour and laughter to be the effect of a *sense of superiority* on the part of one person or group over another. Many jokes, on examination, turn out to depend on showing up the folly of weak or hapless people. They are wildly funny for those on the fortunate side of the joke, not nearly so funny for those on its other end. Racist or nationalist jokes are such.[127] A second cluster of theories is organized around our *sense of the incongruous* and our sense of resolution when we see the way in which the incongruity is resolved (i.e., in the punchline).[128] The third approach is based roughly on Freudian ideas of *relief from taboo subjects*; scatology offers itself here rather obviously.[129]

The different theoretical bases notwithstanding, it seems clear both from common experience and from clinical research that a joke depends on accumulating a psychic energy of some kind which is suddenly released in the climax of the joke, which is to say its point of resolution.[130] A fairly naive understanding (such as my own) suggests that the observed human response is a sharpened form of 'the pleasure of a felt change of

---

126. *Ibid.*, ch. 5.

127. This theory is expounded at length by Charles E. Gruner, *Understanding Laughter: the workings of wit and humor* (Chicago: Nelson-Hall, 1978).

128. See, e.g., Thomas R. Schultz, 'A Cognitive–Developmental Analysis of Humour' in (Antony J. Chapman and Hugh C. Foot, eds.) *Humour and Laughter: theory, research and applications* (London: John Wiley and Sons, 1976), 11–36; or, in the same volume, Mary K. Rothbarth, 'Incongruity, Problem-Solving and Laughter', 37–54, and Göran Nerhardt, 'Incongruity and Funniness: towards a new descriptive model', 55–62.

129. Herzer, *Laughter*, 66–7; the basic reference is Sigmund Freud, *Jokes and Their Relation to the Unconscious* (New York: Newton, 1960).

130. See Michael Godkewitsch, 'Physiological and Verbal Indices of Arousal in Related Humour' in (Antony J. Chapman and Hugh C. Foot, eds.) *Humour and Laughter: theory, research and applications* (London: John Wiley and Sons, 1976), 128, where various measurements of the physiological reactions of subjects (heart-rate, skin conductance), during the 'joke-body' and the 'joke punchline' respectively, are recorded.

consciousness' to which Barfield drew our attention much earlier in reference to poetic diction or the encountering of a striking metaphor.

Gilhus thinks that modern humour, in comparison with its mediaeval counterpart, is much more cerebral, depends much more on 'grasping a point' than the physical jests of 'the feast of fools' or of the morality plays. None the less, in comparison with the massively intellectual depiction of meaning which we have followed in the above three chapters, a form of meaning which elicits or induces the physical upheaval I described above must seem to involve a great deal more than just cognitive pleasure. On the one hand, the brain is not absent from this bodily mirth; it is what makes the connection, resolves the incongruity. On the other hand, the reaction is of the total human organism;[131] as I said above, the whole body enjoys a joke.

This leads me to ask whether *any* one part of the human person is to be more closely associated with the apprehension of meaning than another. We inherently think of it as an intellectual process, and much worship is predicated on this; notably, of course, Protestant worship with its celebration of verbal and doctrinal values. To address meaning through the joke and laughter, however, might be to bring major qualifications to such assumptions. The body's laughter might be held to be fairly proximate to other unpremeditated, physiological responses such as weeping, the keening of grief, shouts of rage or of pain, erotic climax and so on. When an entire sports stadium erupts as the home team scores the winning goal in the last minute of the match, people have not thought it through nor are bringing their considered response! As in laughter, here, too, the body convulses in pure spontaneity.

A consideration of meaning in terms of cry, shout, groan or laughter is thus leading me to ask whether the *music* of the liturgy – arguably much closer to these forms of human expressiveness than our shaping of meaning linguistically – might not be a more powerful medium of meaning than all, or many, of the verbal communications. Prudence (or are they simply western predilections?) suggests that it is the *words* of a hymn, song or chant that are crucial as the carriers of the song's meaning. Protestants have naturally insisted on this. But *why do we sing*? What does the actual musicality of the music do in terms of generating, or bearing, the meaning of the song? Why are sung responses almost always experienced as more meaningful than the same words spoken? Is music conceivably a deep and

131. I refer again to the essay by Michael Godkewitsch (n. 130 above).

ancient instinctive response to moments of high elation and terrifying solemnity?[132] Is this a form of 'grasping' lying deeper and more primitively than the kinds of meaning-making and meaning-appropriation we ordinarily identify, practically exclusively, with language?[133] Such are some of the possibilities for considering unreflective bodily responses such as laughter within the range of liturgical meaning-making and meaning-appropriation.

132. I refer to my discussion, below, p. 296, on music as a primary example of the 'intensification of ordinariness'.

133. Reference might be made here to Peirce's 'emotional' interpretant, which he identifies closely with the apprehension of meaning in music; see below, p. 145.

Part II

Signs of wonder
A worship service as a semiotic system

4

The liturgical sign (i)

Worship, signification and meaning

In my notebook for a certain Sunday I made the following observations:

> The minister leading worship today – an elderly man, retired I would
> say – sought to communicate a light-hearted, welcoming, personable
> style. But he managed it in such a way that it seemed (to this
> worshipper, at least) that this was an effect he desired rather than a fact
> he could assume. The actual communication seemed (to me),
> conversely, to be avuncular, saccharine, condescending; forms which
> attempted informality but which rather betrayed professional
> ineptitude, a style which attempted to make us present but which itself
> lacked 'presence'.

This [second] 'moment' happened in a Sunday-morning eucharistic service in King's College chapel, Cambridge, England:

> I had lined up with all the other visitors who had come to bathe
> themselves in the spectacularly fulsome aesthetic experience of vaulted
> stone and ethereal voices which is a chapel service at King's. That was
> my hope too, and I would have left, well-satisfied, had that been the
> sum of my experience. But there was more. One presumes, given the
> illustrious reputation of the place, that every aspect of the liturgy will
> have been meticulously rehearsed. I was therefore struck during the
> prayers of intercession, by the noticeably 'prayerful' quality of the
> prayers, and, on glancing up, realized that the chaplain, though he had
> manifestly prepared the *topics* of prayer, was in fact praying
> 'extempore'. The aesthetic experience moved through to a more
> exactly worshipful experience.

A third 'moment' occurred during a sermon in a Protestant church in Germany, which is a way of saying that, while I understood some of what the preacher was saying, I could by no means grasp it all:

> The building in which we were met was large, cavernous in fact; somewhat gloomy. It was approximately circular in shape, the cupola rising high over the modest congregation which occupied perhaps a third of its seats. Positioned as I was at one side of the pews, which ranged out from the pulpit in the circular configuration of the space, I was able to observe the texture, or the nature, or the quality, of the relation between preacher and people. The thought crossed my mind: 'They really want to hear what he has to say.'

Where does one turn in order to study the meaning(s) of worship? In choosing these autobiographical slivers of liturgical experience, I am rather sensitive to the fact – perhaps to the criticism – that in no way can they represent the deep or the high moments of the liturgy, those moments in which the drama achieves its climax or in which fundamental aspects of Christian doxology come to expression. In this sense, the levels of meaning involved were undoubtedly modest, trivial in fact; so personalistic and subjective as scarcely to be worth consideration as measures of meaning. On the other hand, these *almost* insignificant moments (from the point of view of liturgical theology) did prove highly influential in shaping at least this worshipper's experience of the events *as worshipful*. In choosing these over some of the textbook cases of liturgical significance (for example, the eucharistic prayer of thanks and praise, perhaps even assigning values within it),[1] I thus venture the possibility that such inconspicuous moments can prove to be quite critical in people's experience of the meaning and meaningfulness of worship. Of course, the major and minor significations need not be exclusive; one naturally hopes that worship's 'official' meanings will, in fact, be experienced *as* meaningful. But the simple possibility of distinguishing 'official' from 'public' meanings, or these from 'private' and 'normative' meanings, means that this cannot be presumed.[2] In any case, I do take such moments as I relate to have been transactions in meaning.

1. For example, the document *Baptism, Eucharist, Ministry* (Geneva: World Council of Churches, 1982), 12, can say, 'The *anamnesis* of Christ is the basis and source of all Christian prayer.' In his section on the theory of Protestant worship, Rainer Volp repeatedly calls on the anamnetic and epicletic dimensions of worship as its definitive marks (Volp, *Liturgik*, 909ff.; see, e.g., p. 915 and often). From a Catholic perspective see Kevin W. Irwin, *Context and Text: method in liturgical theology* (Collegeville: The Liturgical Press, 1994), 47–8.
2. The reference to the different kinds of, and levels in, the meanings of worship is to Hoffman, 'How Ritual Means', 79–84 (see p. 15 above).

Will it be any less controversial to claim that such meanings as were transmitted and then the degree of their meaningfulness – which I have said is a distinguishable item – were effected through various forms of signification? Some of the signs were linguistic ones; others were extra-linguistic. But, even with respect to the linguistic signs, the entire burden of Part I of my study was to show that by the end of the twentieth century we no longer felt we could subscribe to conceptions of meaning which attempt to split signification off from its material signifier. Liturgical significations are not exempt from this judgement.[3] My brief narratives thus show, I trust, that a good deal of the meaning and meaningfulness even of the linguistic signifiers happened through what in other places I have called their melismatic quality, that order of signification effected in 'the grain of the voice'. Other significations were more obviously related to the body or bodies of those from whom the significations emanated. Lacking the requisite professional competencies, I am unable to record here the kind of microanalyses as permit professional observers (of nonverbal signification) to say how these effects were produced. On the other hand, in common with most worshippers who form impressions of the meanings and degree of meaningfulness of worship, I can register such cumulative impressions as my stories indicate. I also register the conviction – in line with what I have just said on the materiality of all signification – that these impressions did not come from nowhere (none of them was anticipated or particularly looked for) but were effected through a multitude of tiny signals transmitted by their producers. It remains finally to note that some of these significations were consciously produced and transmitted; others were wholly involuntary. In at least one of the cases, had the sign-producer known about the signals he was sending and their effect on at least one of his congregation, he would have wished strongly to alter them.

While stressing that my impressions did not come from nowhere, neither – on the other hand so to speak – do I wish to underestimate my

---

3. So *The Documents of Vatican II* (Walter M. Abbott, ed.) (London and Dublin: Geoffrey Chapman, 1966), 'Constitution on the Sacred Liturgy', section 7 (p. 141): 'In the liturgy the sanctification of man [*sic*] is manifested by signs perceptible to the senses, and is effected in a way which is proper to each of these signs.' See also Sequeira, 'Gottesdienst als menschliche Ausdruckshandlung', 20: 'Human beings experience the world through their senses. With their senses they apprehend the world, the what and the how of others' self-expression; it is similarly through their senses that they bring to expression their own experiences and intentions. No less is the turning of God towards people, and people's believing, worshipping response, possible only through sensible media. Worship is therefore ordered in sensate forms of expression.'

own subjectivity in the signs' apprehension and in the construction of meanings formed on or around them. I have already cited Charles Peirce to the effect that a sign's recipient is deeply implicated in the sign's meaning, namely, 'It seems a strange thing, when one comes to ponder over it, that a sign should leave its interpreter to supply a part of its meaning' (CP 5.448, note 1). I urged above, in my more general considerations of meaning, that meaning is both found and made; that it is a question neither of phenomenological constitution nor of analytical objectivity, but each in a sort of collaboration. And now here, as we attend more directly to the role of the sign in the production, transmission and apprehension of liturgical meaning, we shall see that both the externality of the sign and the interior apprehension of it by its interpreter is each critically important in emergent semiotic theory.

Given the depth of antiquity during which biblical religion has treated the sign as a vehicle or medium of divine revelation – not to mention the importance of signs in liturgy[4] – it is perhaps surprising that recent liturgical study has not availed itself more than it has of the newly emergent discipline calling itself semiotics.[5] To some degree this may be explained by a lack of clarity within semiotics itself about its subject matter, its goals and its methods – which quandaries have begun largely to find resolution through the decade of the 1990s. It is not that there has been no interest in semiotics by liturgical scholars; but, given that the one regards itself as the subject area dedicated formally and consciously to the study of signs, and that the other depends so directly on signifying forms, one might have expected a greater degree of interchange than appears to have been the

4. In addition to the references of the previous note, see esp. Cyprian Vagaggini, *Theological Dimensions of the Liturgy: a general treatise on the theology of the liturgy* (Collegeville: The Liturgical Press, 1976), 22: 'all the elements which go to make up the liturgy, concretely . . . agree in one common essential concept, that of the *sensible sign*' (his emphasis); the entire second chapter of this work is an extended commentary on the sentence from the 'Constitution on the Liturgy' cited in the previous note. See also, e.g., A. G. Martimort, 'Structure and Laws of the Liturgical Celebration' in (A. G. Martimort, ed.) *The Church at Prayer: principles of the liturgy* (Collegeville: The Liturgical Press, 1987), ch. 4, 'Liturgical Signs', notably p. 174 'the entire liturgy is made up of signs'.

5. This should not be taken as overlooking the burgeoning interest taken in the phenomena of symbols and symbolism among liturgical scholars in the past two decades (I mention here just a few of the more widely cited works: Joseph Martos, *Doors to the Sacred: a historical introduction to the sacraments in the Christian church* (London: SCM Press, 1981); David N. Power, *Unsearchable Riches: the symbolic nature of liturgy* (New York: Pueblo Publishing Company, 1984); Bernard J. Cooke, *The Distancing of God: the ambiguity of symbol in history and theology* (Minneapolis: Fortress Press, 1990); or Louis-Marie Chauvet, *Symbol and Sacrament: a sacramental reinterpretation of Christian existence* (Collegeville: The Liturgical Press, 1995)). Theories of symbol, though adjacent to semiotic theory, are not identifiable with it, drawing as they do on much more general anthropological resources than does the newer, and more focussed, study of signs and signification. See, further, n. 83 below.

case.[6] Because my own study attempts a rapprochement (of liturgy and semiotics) I will attempt in the next few sections to situate each in relation to the other. Then, because it seems clear to me that the weight of opinion among semiotic specialists is moving towards consensus with respect to the superiority of one approach (that arising from the writings of C. S. Peirce) over competing approaches, I shall move to a more detailed exposition of this. In the subsequent chapter I shall attempt to see how the Peircean 'doctrine of signs' may help us understand the significations of worship.

Semiotics in the nineties

As mentioned, the decades in which semiotics has been a recognizable subject in the academic arena (the period coincides pretty well with what I am calling late modernity, i.e., since the 1960s) have been, for those within the discipline, a time largely of struggle over the nature of the subject, its scope and appropriate methods. Running across all of these, and often dominating the discussion, has been a contest between the advocates of two competing approaches: those coming to the subject from Saussure's theory of linguistic signifiers and those seeking to ground the discipline in the labyrinthine, often obscure, writings of C. S. Peirce. I shall sketch the differences between them as briefly as I can. Another aspect of semiotic studies, obviously important for liturgy, is that of nonverbal communication, i.e., signification that happens in or through gestures, proxemics, and so on. And yet a third issue of importance for the signs of the liturgy is that of the difference between intentional and inadvertent signs.

The two semiotic options
The most important circumstance in semiotics as an academic discipline has been the shift from a language-based theory of signs to a more general theory, of which language forms an important but clearly subordinate part. Through the 1970s and well into the 1980s the two approaches were pursued by their advocates and exponents largely independently of each other. One sometimes finds the analogy of the Cold War applied to the standoff between the Saussurean and Peircean adherents of that time. Because of its comparative simplicity, and because it was linked directly

---

6. I am aware of only a very few articles on liturgical semiotics in major journals on worship (such as *Worship* or *Studia Liturgica*). From the side of semiotics the silence seems even more deafening (see below, n. 40).

with structuralism – at that time enjoying considerable vogue as an intellectual method – it is probably fair to say that the European based, Saussurean style enjoyed an early pre-eminence. Even at the end of the century many people (outside the discipline) assume that this is what 'semiotics' means. For those working within, however, the centre of gravity has shifted, irrevocably they would say. Thomas Sebeok for example, perhaps the foremost commentator on the subject internationally, already in 1989 could write: 'American semioticians all but universally, and foreign semioticians increasingly, espouse Peirce . . . In short, the Peircean paradigm is now firmly regnant.'[7]

To say that the difference between the two approaches is between a dyadic view and a triadic view of the sign must seem to make the divergence insignificant if not trivial. In point of fact the consequences are major and the differences probably irreconcilable. We have already met some of them in preliminary sketches of both approaches. First, Saussurean semiotics ('semiology' is the name the exponents of this approach more frequently gave it) sees every sign as consisting in *two parts*: the signifier and that which it signifies – the familiar paradigm of materiality and intelligibility. But we have now seen repeatedly that accounts which assume a dualistic opposition between 'matter' and 'mind' cannot produce a theory of meaning; they will always expire in the unbridgeable gap they must postulate between the two. As we saw from the outset, the problem for these formulations will always be: *how* does language (or thought) 'hook on' to the world? The systematic dichotomization of reality at the heart of all Saussurean-type semiology ensures that it, too, in the end, will be bereft of an account of meaning. Second, the arbitrariness which Saussure was thus obliged to build into his theory of signs led him to see *codification* as the decisive semiotic mechanism: the sign-producer encodes meanings (i.e., within the established system conceptual significance is arbitrarily grafted on to a material signifier) which the sign-recipient (equally cognisant of the system) subsequently decodes. In this respect too, then, from a Peircean point of view, semiology is seen not as generating meaning but as acting simply as 'a tube for communication'[8] or as a system in which the encoded message is like 'a parcel dispatched by one post office

---

7. Thomas A. Sebeok, 'Semiotics in the United States', *The Semiotic Web, 1989* (Berlin and New York: Mouton de Gruyter, 1990), 329. See a similar judgement in Susan Petrilli, 'Dialogism and Interpretation in the Study of Signs', *Semiotica* 97 1/2 (1993), 103.
8. Thomas A. Sebeok, *The Sign and its Masters* (Lanham MD: University Press of America, second edition, 1989), *xvii*.

and received by another.'[9] Third, this semiotic exchange, based as it is on the arbitrariness of the sign, is bound to see the *linguistic sign* as the defining model for all signification. Semiology is thus an extension or extrapolation of linguistic signification to whichever other 'code' (gesture, proxemics, whichever) we wish to analyse; hence Roland Barthes' dictum: '[L]inguistics is not part of the general science of signs ... it is semiology which is a part of linguistics.'[10] Finally, again as the consequence of all that has gone before, semiosis on a Saussurean showing can only be conceived in terms of the *human* exchange of signs: only human beings are able, arbitrarily, to 'encode' the otherwise passive or mundane signifier with the intended signification. Thus is the entire world (of signification) viewed anthropocentrically – some would say imperialistically (the point will perhaps be clearer when I can range against it the Peircean alternative).

I am coming to a more extended exposition of the Peircean paradigm, but, with an eye on locating the recent relationships between liturgy and semiotics, I will here briefly match the points I have made about Saussurean semiology with their corresponding points in the Peircean 'doctrine of signs'. First, and most fundamentally, the Peircean sign consists in a relationship of three, not two, elements. It must seem astonishing that so simple a shift of perspective can effect such major changes in intellectual method. But such seems to be the case.[11] As noted earlier, Peirce's sign always consists in a dynamic relationship between the

9. Augusto Ponzio, *Man as a Sign*, 114, citing Ferruccio Rossi-Landi. See also, *ibid.*, 111: 'The semiology of Saussurean matrix conceives the sign in terms of equal exchange between the *signifiant* and the *signifié* and reduces the complexity of linguistic life to two poles between which all linguistic phenomena and, taking linguistics as their model, all semiotic phenomena are expected to be placed'; also pp. 117, 185f., 188, 251f.

10. Roland Barthes, *Elements of Semiology* (New York: Hill and Wang, 1967), 11.

11. The point is perhaps captured in a humorous narrative form. The following passage, then, is taken from an essay by Eugen Baer ('Tom Sebeok's Thomism', *Semiotica* 28 3/4 (1979), 352–3): 'What is the distinctive feature of the sign? The physicist George Gamow who liked to tell stories about Hungarian aristocrats begins his popular book, *One, Two Three ... Infinity* (New York: Mentor, 1959), with "a story about two Hungarian aristocrats who decided to play a game in which the one who calls the largest number wins. 'Well,' said one of them, 'you name your number first.' After a few minutes of hard mental work the second aristocrat finally named the largest number he could think of. 'Three,' he said. Now it was the turn of the first one to do the thinking, but after a quarter of an hour he finally gave up. 'You've won,' he agreed."' Baer goes on to comment: 'so, like Hegel, Peirce developed the category of thirdness as the distinctive semiotic category or, in a sense, as the largest semiotic number (*CP* 1.363). The third "bridges over the chasm" (*CP* 1.359) of sign-vehicle and denotatum, of signifier and signified, of yes and no, presence and absence, agent and patient, ego and non-ego, finite and infinite, life and death. It is the "process which leads from first to last" (*CP* 1.361), hence essentially mediation, interpretation, a kind of meso-scene. In its most elementary archetypal form, the mark of thirdness holds together a space which it severs and unites. By one and the same stroke, it cuts and glues, wounds and heals, separates and links.'

sign's *representamen* (that aspect of it which stands for something else), its *object* (that for which the sign stands), and its *interpretant* (that element which effects the meaningful relationship between the other two, to some extent supplied by the interpreter but also anticipated by the sign-producer). Peirce's notion of 'thirdness' is the element which breaks the dualistic impasse between subjectivity and objectivity (i.e., reality conceived as split between conceptual and material reality).[12] John Deely is one writer who sees this breathtakingly small-but-consequential step on Peirce's part to be one of the most important steps in western intellectual method.[13] Second, because the relationship between the material and the cognitive dimension of signs is bridged by the thirdness of the interpretant, the Peircean sign is freed from the arbitrariness with which significance must be grafted on to the signifier in the Saussurean model. Consequently the notion of 'codes' is radically downgraded in this semiotic style. It is not, doubtless cannot, be wholly absent. Thus, of Peirce's three basic sign-types – icons, indices, symbols – the third of these does explicitly depend upon 'convention' as that which supplies the interpretative dimension. The point, however, is that this is only *one* of the mechanisms wherewith semiosis is effected; iconic signs depend upon a perceived *resemblance* between the sign-vehicle and the sign's object, and indexical signs rely on a *factual* or mechanical relationship (clues at a crime scene, etc.). But, since even with symbolic-type signs the relationship between the sign-vehicle and the sign's object is not direct but indirect – i.e., mediated by the interpretant – the interpreter, or sign-recipient, is not exempted from participation in the meaning of the sign. Even here, then, it is not simply a matter (impersonally, as it were) of decoding the sign; here, no less, a sign-recipient actively 'grasps together' the sign's less than absolute signification[14] and, in this sense, joins the sign-giver in 'an active form of answering comprehension.'[15] Third, because the Peircean sign does not depend upon the arbitrariness of codes, language is not the only, indeed not even the primary, form of signification. Exponents of Peircean semiotics are keen to point out that meaningful semiosis was happening in the

---

12. See Deely, *Basics*, 17, 76; or the same author's *New Beginnings*, 101.

13. *New Beginnings*, 155: 'Earlier thinkers had . . . established firmly that the relationship in which a sign consists must be as such triaspectual. But no thinker before Peirce, as far as I know, had gone so far as to assign a name [i.e., "thirdness"] to this silent partner or third term essential to the sign–signified linkage.' See also, *ibid.*, 187, and *The Human Use of Signs*, 133.

14. On the inevitable unfinality of every sign, even of those that appear the least ambiguous, see W. C. Watt, 'Transient Ambiguity', *Semiotica* 101 1/2 (1994), 5–39.

15. Ponzio, *Man as a Sign*, 252.

world long before humans began to theorize it.[16] Which leads me to the fourth point of contestation between theories grounded in the arbitrary sign and those which see semiotic exchange happening at all levels of sentient life (i.e., certainly in all forms of animal life as far 'down' as monocellular organisms,[17] and *perhaps* also in plant life[18]); namely, the point of view (encapsulated in Peirce's famous, if enigmatic, remark that 'all this universe is perfused with signs', *CP* 5.448, note 1) that semiosis is an energy or process present in all life – of which communicating ability human beings are thus rather the inheritors than its inventors and masters. Thomas Sebeok is justly regarded as the semiotic theorist who has contended most indefatigably (and successfully) for the point of view that human beings are not to be seen as the *fons et origo* of signification but as its beneficiaries.[19]

The study of nonverbal behaviour and semiotic theory
It must be apparent that a great deal of the signification of worship happens in other than linguistic forms; that is, in what I earlier described as 'a multitude of tiny signals transmitted by their producers'. It is thus not surprising that some students of liturgical meaning have wished to direct attention to the 'performance' aspect of a liturgy as well as, or perhaps attributing to it a higher importance than, the text which underlies such performance.[20]

---

16. 'The ground tremor causing a hermit crab to draw back into its shell may or may not have been caused by a crab-predator, but such tremors are caused often enough by crab-predators to make it worthwhile for the crab, sensing the tremor, to forgo dinner a while longer, lest he become dinner'; T. L. Short, 'Peirce's Semiotic Theory of the Self', *Semiotica* 91 1/2 (1992), 116.

17. See, for example Sebeok, *The Sign and its Masters*, 42, 71. On what Sebeok has famously called 'zoosemiosis' (semiosis among animals) see more generally, *ibid.*, ch. 3.

18. A 1999 documentary produced by the BBC called 'The Supernatural' (screened by the Australian Broadcasting Corporation on 9 July 1999) showed acacias in Africa signalling by a change of odour the presence of grazing animals; whereupon all the trees in the vicinity inject a toxin into their leaves, fully effective within thirty minutes. As a consequence, grazing animals have learned that they have 15–20 minutes before needing to shift some distance to other herbage.

19. So on the opening page of Sebeok's *The Sign and its Masters* (p. 3): 'I shall . . . contend against the position of subjective idealism . . . embodied in that famous Sophist's [Protagoras of Abdera] arrogant adage that "Man is the measure of all things, of things that are how they are and of things that are not how they are not."'

John Deely has attempted to show that Peirce's 'Grand Vision' (as Deely calls it) extended even to inanimate matter (Deely, *New Beginnings*, ch. 7). T. L. Short, himself a consummate scholar of Peirce, adjudges Deely's thesis as 'not only false but useless' (Short, 'What's the Use?', 43).

20. Nichol's study, *Liturgical Hermeneutics*, is predicated on the 'general conviction that liturgy is text *and* performance, and that it is impossible to reflect on one without also taking account of the other' (*ibid.*, 9). Stringer, *On the Perception of Worship*, also gives considerable attention to 'performance' as a liturgical category; see e.g., pp. 35–6, 50–1. In his essay, 'Text, Context and Performance: hermeneutics and the study of worship', *Scottish Journal of Theology*

Needless to say, signifying forms other than linguistic ones have long been of interest equally to researchers coming to such signification from what we would now call a semiotic approach.[21] Since about the middle of the twentieth century,[22] this field of inquiry has developed an ever-increasing degree of sophistication and terminological exactness in such nonverbal forms of communication as one would deem crucial for the significations of worship: facial expression, kinesis, proxemics, gesture, and so on.[23] One thus naturally brings to this now vast literature high hopes for enlightenment on the meanings of worship.

Generally, however, this potential remains unrealized. From its beginnings practically until the present time, little attempt seems to have been made on the part of nonverbal behaviour researchers to find connections with, or an enveloping model within, a general theory of signs. Of course, in the earliest stages of the research this was fully understandable. In the 1950s semiotics had not yet been conceived as a field of study; then, in its 'cold war' period, semiotics perhaps scarcely suggested itself as a home for nonverbal behaviour theory. But in the more recent period, in which the Peircean model has gained widespread allegiance among semioticians as a viable working account of all semiosis, the continuing independence of nonverbal behaviour specialists comes as a surprise, not to say disappointment.

53 (2000), 365–79, Stringer criticizes Nichols' work on the basis that it appeals only to 'ideal' performances, not those which actually take place in churches; on the other hand, questions might be directed to Stringer about the selective use of Ricoeur on which he bases (some at least) of his criticisms. For issues of 'performance' see also Irwin, *Context and Text*, 53–5 (the 'context' of Irwin's title has largely to do with 'performance context', *ibid.*, 55).

21. In putting the matter this way I mean two things: one, that the study, so-called, of nonverbal behaviour begins in at least the middle of the twentieth century, thus anticipating the advent of the discipline calling itself semiotics; and, second, as I shall say in the body of my text, for reasons not apparent to me, most study of nonverbal behaviour, even by the end of the century, had not attempted to bring its material under a general semiotic theory – that is, within a theory of semiosis as meaning.

22. The notion of nonverbal behaviour is generally supposed to begin with the work of Jürgen Ruesch; see J. Ruesch, 'Synopsis of the Theory of Human Communication', *Psychiatry* 16 (1953), 215–43, and J. Ruesch and W. Kees, *Nonverbal Communication: notes on the visual perception of human relations* (Berkeley: University of California Press, 1956). Other definitive texts are Ray L. Birdwhistell, *Introduction to Kinesics: an annotation system for analysis of body motion and gesture* (Louisville KY: University of Louisville, 1952) and Edward T. Hall, *The Silent Language* (Garden City, New York: Doubleday & Company, Inc., 1959). For a comprehensive overview of the research up to 1981 see Adam Kendon's Introduction in (Adam Kendon, ed.) *Nonverbal Communication, Interaction and Gesture: selections from Semiotica* (The Hague: Mouton Publishers, 1981).

23. For an overview up till 1991, together with an analysis of how the research might apply to liturgical study, see Sequeira, 'Liturgische Körper- und Gebärdensprache als Thema der Semiotik'. In this essay, Sequeira still held hopes for a fruitful dialogue between the exponents of nonverbal behaviour and liturgy. In personal conversation he has subsequently acknowledged to me his disappointment that the discipline has not moved towards a general theory of semiotic meaning.

This non-convergence throws up three more-or-less distinguishable problems for someone looking for help with the meanings of worship. One of these is a terminological inconstancy. I have mentioned that one of Peirce's most elementary divisions is his threefold classification of sign-types – based on the kind of relationship between the sign's *representamen* and the sign's object – as iconic, indexical and symbolic signs. One can understand that the terms icon, index and symbol (together with many others) also offer themselves suggestively to analysts of nonverbal behaviour, but, because there has been, at best, very little attempt to align their work with Peircean method,[24] this terminology frequently sits askew of his or throws up ambiguities and inconsistencies.[25] For the same reasons, much of the descriptive language which has become standardized among nonverbal behaviour researchers – 'affective displays' (face), 'batons' and 'ideographs' (hands), 'regulators' (body movements to control or facilitate conversation), or 'adaptors' (adaptations of the body to its environment) for example[26] – though well-developed conceptual schemata, yet remain outside a general theory of semiotics.

A second difficulty in accounts of nonverbal behaviour is that much of the analysis assumes the anthropocentric view of signification which, I said, is antithetical to a Peircean approach. That is to say, similarly with but wholly independently of Saussurean semiology, *language* is assumed to be the definitive model – the term 'nonverbal' carries precisely this implication – for the study of signification.[27] It does seem to me conceivable

---

24. The almost singular exception to this, in the work known to me, is the essay by Barbara E. Hanna, 'Defining the Emblem', *Semiotica* 112 3/4 (1996), 289–358, in which she makes much the same kind of protest that I have, and then goes on to attempt an engagement between the notion of 'emblem' (a standard classification in nonverbal behaviour research) and Peircean categories.

25. For example, actions described in nonverbal studies as 'iconic' would often fit better into a Peircean taxonomy as 'symbolic' or 'indexical'. In their groundbreaking (and highly influential) study, 'The Repertoire of Nonverbal Behavior: categories, origins, usage and coding', *Semiotica* 1 (1969), 49–89, Paul Ekman and Wallace V. Friesen distinguish between 'extrinsic codes' ('one in which the act signifies or stands for something else') and 'intrinsic codes' ('in a sense no code in that the act does not stand for but is its significant'). The former may be 'arbitrarily coded' ('bear no visual resemblance to what they signify') or 'iconically coded' ('the nonverbal act . . . looks in some way like what it means') (*ibid.*, 60). On the basis of this taxonomy, Ekman and Friesen subsequently conclude that the act of pointing is 'intrinsic and iconic' (*ibid.*, 62). In Peircean terms, however, pointing is undoubtedly indexical and only secondarily iconic. In work much later than Ekman's and Friesen's, the notion of the 'iconic' continues to play a central role in nonverbal behaviour analyses, mostly with only a token acknowledgment if at all, to Peirce's understanding of semiosis (by way of near random example: Uri Hadar and Brian Butterworth, 'Iconic Gestures, Imagery, and Word Retrieval in Speech', *Semiotica* 115 1/2 (1997), 147–8).

26. Self-evidently, I presume, I table just a few of the simplest examples of nonverbal descriptions.

27. So Hanna, 'Defining the Emblem', 297–307.

that the human person, as an integrated organism, draws on both verbal and gestural capacities in the organization of her or his acts of self-expression,[28] but this is not at all the same thing as theorizing signification primarily in terms of linguistic signification, of which other forms are then somehow to be seen as derivative and degenerate. My brief excursus (in the previous chapter) into laughter yields at least the suggestion that underlying our linguistic competence one can trace a more primitive – and more corporeal! – form of human self-expression. This at any rate coheres with a perspective that sees much of our gestural signification as belonging with those aspects of semiosis which the human animal shares with the other animals on the planet.

In some ways encompassing both these difficulties is a third: one must conclude that the current versions of nonverbal behaviour study remain ensconced in a classical, modernist intellectual paradigm. Or perhaps another way of saying this is that the field continues to operate on the basis of a binary model of signifier/signified.[29] More and more sophisticated techniques in the observation, recording and analysis of a subject's self-expression or social interaction are devised. Detailed exploration of the precise musculature used in facial expression,[30] wide-ranging culturally specific surveys,[31] and split-second timing[32] are among the many devices invented or deployed in the research processes. All this is based, however, on an assumption that more and more accurate observation on the part of

28. There is an extensive and vigorously expanding literature on the relationships between linguistic utterance and gestural expression in human beings; see the numerous essays co-authored by Geoffrey Beattie published in *Semiotica* through the 1990s (references will be found in Geoffrey Beattie and Heather Shovelton, 'Do Iconic Hand Gestures Really Contribute Anything to the Semantic Information Conveyed by Speech? an experimental investigation', *Semiotica* 123 1/2 (1999), 1–30) or by Brian Butterworth (see Beattie and Shovelton's essay for these references also). For book-length studies see Pierre Feyereisen and Jacques-Dominique de Lannoy, *Gestures and Speech: psychological investigations* (Cambridge University Press, 1991); or David McNeill, *Hand and Mind: what gestures reveal about thought* (University of Chicago Press, 1992).

29. So Hanna, 'Defining the Emblem', 320: '[M]ajor problems remain: the influential definition [Johnson, Ekman and Friesen's definition of the "emblem"] is still firmly rooted in the tradition describing communication as the transmission of a message. That very powerful analogy . . . "the conduit metaphor" is at work here, and the danger of it is that the non-speaking, non-gesturing partner is figured as passive receiver, rather than active interpreter.'

30. E.g., Paul Ekman, 'Methods for Measuring Facial Action' in (Klaus R. Scherer and Paul Ekman, eds.), *Handbook of Methods in Nonverbal Behavior Research* (Cambridge University Press, 1982), 45–90.

31. Particularly: Desmond Morris, Peter Collett, Peter Marsh and Marie O'Shaughnessey, *Gestures, their Origins and Distribution* (New York: Stein and Day, 1979).

32. See, e.g., the linear graphs compiled by Adam Kendon to chart the facial actions of a couple kissing; or of people greeting one another; Adam Kendon, *Conducting Interaction: patterns of behavior in focused encounters* (Cambridge University Press, 1990), e.g., 134, 162.

a clinician will yield us objective insight. It may indeed be conceded that through this laudably meticulous research we now know better *what* such-and-such a gesture means in such-and-such cultural settings, but this is still a long way short of an account wherein we are helped to understand *how* we mean things gesturally, proxemically, or in any of the other forms of nonverbal behaviour which the field has so richly tabulated. The discipline (of nonverbal behaviour) still awaits, it seems, a theory of semiotic meaning.

Communication, information and semiotic theory

In at least one of my 'cases', I said, had the leader of the worship known the effect he was creating, he would have wished to have changed it – to have sent a different message or to have generated a different meaning. Though my other two sign-producers would presumably not have been displeased with the effects of their significations, in these cases, too, these were not something which they had foreseen or towards which they had particularly worked. All this catches the fact, apparent in all human interaction, that much of our communication is other than what we wish, intend or even cognize.

Intention and intentionality are/were standard problems for modern thought, given its in-principle distinction between ideality and materiality.[33] The question *always* was: how can purely mental states or events (someone's intentions) be reliably gauged on the basis of external (material) signifiers?[34] One response in the last stages of classical modernity, we have seen, was to abandon the question as meaningless ('the intentional fallacy') and to direct attention entirely to the structures of the work. A different approach, again in the last stages of modernity, was to attempt a distinction between 'information' and 'communication'. Drawing analogously on the principle of entropy (loss or wastage of energy) in the second law of thermodynamics, significations of intentional content were deemed to be 'communication' while those significations transmitted *over and above* the intended message were categorized as 'information'.[35] In terms of the three anecdotes given at the beginning of

---

33. See my references to Paul Grice at ch. 2, n. 94, above.
34. See Arbib and Hesse, *The Construction of Reality*, 175, for a representative statement of this.
35. For convenient summaries see Lyons, *Semantics*, ch. 2; or Umberto Eco, *The Open Work* (Cambridge MA: Harvard University Press, 1989), ch. 3. Eugen S. Baer, 'Some Elementary Topics of a General Semiotic Theory', *Semiotica* 29 1/2 (1980), esp. p. 348, gives valuable references for the development of this idea, as does Margaret Rucker, 'On the Principle of Disorder in Civilization: a socio-physical analysis of fashion change', *Semiotica* 91 1/2 (1992), 57.

this chapter, then, in one of the cases 'information' would have vastly dominated the whole transaction while in the others it would have been more evenly balanced with the intended 'communication'.

I shall want to argue (when I come to the matter of sign-production) that the intentions of the producers of liturgical signs are anything but unimportant – though I shall want to apply the notion 'intention' rather differently from the way it normally functioned within the modern paradigm. But here, where we are still considering semiosis generally, it must be clear that this (i.e., semiosis) includes *all* the signification which is produced (intentionally or inadvertently) and all the signification which is apprehended (justifiably or otherwise). Of course, this means that questions of semiotic mechanism ('*How* did she get that from what I said?') and of semiotic criteria ('Was I *justified* in taking that from what he said?') must be brought into play, but these are precisely the tasks (at any rate, they are included within the tasks) of a general theory of signs. I trust that we shall see well enough that a Peircean theory attends directly to them. The point must be: *semiosis includes all the signs sent and/or apprehended by sign-sensitive organisms*. As Eugen Baer says with customary clarity, the circumstance that smoke is not produced by a fire intentionally does not affect it as a sign of the fire; and that medical symptoms are not intentionally produced by a damaged organ does not diminish their importance to the physician in arriving at a diagnosis.[36]

These examples perhaps make clear that the attempt to draw in-principle distinctions between intentional and unintentional significations is yet another (one dares to say, almost classic) case of modern anthropocentrism (i.e., in its assumption that only human beings can 'intend' meanings to be invested in certain actions or things; or, in reverse, that only signs which were 'intended' can be significant). It also belongs to the Saussurean semiotic model of 'direct equivalence' in which ('intentional') messages are supposed to pass intact from sender to recipient independently of an active semiotic engagement on the part of the sign-receiver.[37] Such luxuries, however, are scarcely afforded the producer of liturgical signs (nor of signs generally). The meanings of signs will be constructed *between* the producer and the recipient – and on the basis of involuntary as well as intentional significations.

---

36. Baer, 'Some Elementary Topics', 349.
37. See Petrilli, 'Dialogism and Interpretation', 103, 106, on linkages between the 'communication-versus-information' model of communication and Saussurean semiology.

Liturgy and semiotics

In 1987 Gerard Lukken could say, 'Up to now semiotics has hardly made its way into liturgical science.'[38] In 1992 Ronald Sequeira would still lament the 'deficiency' in academic liturgical study of its acquaintance with the history and findings of nonverbal communication research.[39] Though some materials have been published in the intervening years, at the beginning of the new century the impression is still difficult to obtain that the study of liturgy has embraced the study of signs – at any rate as this is understood under the heading 'semiotics'. On the other hand, it is perhaps at least as curious, given the apparently omnivorous appetite of semiotic studies, that semioticians have avoided the liturgy even more comprehensively than liturgists have missed semiotics.[40]

In my introductory remarks to this chapter, I hazarded the guess that the lack of engagement between liturgy and semiotics might derive as much from the struggles for definition among semioticians as from an uncertainty or lack of conviction on the part of liturgists. Now that we come to a more detailed appraisal, one has the sense that the unsettledness within semiotics about a general theory of signs has had its effect on those expeditions into the subject undertaken from the side of liturgical studies. For whatever reasons, this has mainly been undertaken in languages other than English;[41] which is to say (in so far as the work is known

---

38. Gerard M. Lukken, 'Semiotics and the Study of Liturgy', *Studia Liturgica* 17 (1987), 112.
39. Sequeira, 'Liturgische Körper- und Gebärdensprache', 207.
40. In the voluminous journal *Semiotica* (since 1971 averaging four volumes per year, each volume of four parts and of more than a thousand pages) there has been, I think, no originative article on the semiotics of Christian worship, and only two reviews: Robert S. Corrington's 'Regnant Signs: the semiosis of liturgy' (*Semiotica* 117 1 (1997), 19–42, a review of Gerard Lukken's *Per Visibilia ad Invisibilia* (Kampen: Kok Pharos, 1994)), and M. Susan Ashbourne's 'Laetatus sum in his quae dicta sunt mihi: in domum Domini ibimus' (*Semiotica* 123 3/4 (1999), 299–325, reviewing Gerard Lukken and Mark Searle, *Semiotics and Church Architecture* (Kampen: Kok Pharos, 1993)).
41. The only published engagement with liturgical semiotics in English known to me is by Mark Searle. Searle's orientations appear to have been equally divided between the Dutch approach (see the previous note) and the code-based approach of the Germans (see, e.g., his essay 'Semper Reformanda: the opening and closing rites of the Mass' in (Peter C. Finn and James M. Schellman, eds.) *Shaping English Liturgy: studies in honor of Archbishop Denis Hurley* (Washington, DC: The Pastoral Press, 1990), 53–92). I do have in my possession copies of papers prepared for the 'Liturgy and Human Sciences Group' of the North American Academy of Liturgy in 1990 by K. M. Irwin ('Semiotics as a Methodology for the Evaluation of Liturgical Art'), Mark Searle ('Introduction to the Semiotics of Liturgy'), and by Joyce Ann Zimmerman ('Introduction to the Semiotics of Liturgy: clarification/response/reflection'). The papers, not subsequently published so far as I know, seem to me to reflect the then still unsettled position of semiotics as a discipline. Mention should also be made of Gerald V. Lardner, 'Communication Theory and Liturgical Research', *Worship* 51 (1977), 299–307, though the essay ranges between semiotics (of the Charles Morris style), through communication theory and non-verbal communication.

to me) in Holland and Germany. Given the transatlantic division between the Peircean and Saussurean approaches for so much of this time, it was perhaps only predictable that the European-based semiotic explorations of liturgy would follow the latter direction. But in light of a general acceptation only recently among semioticians that Peirce's model offers the more comprehensive account of semiosis, one might venture the opinion that for most of this time liturgy, too, was struggling (or perhaps inherited the struggle) to locate a general theory of signs within which to undertake its work.[42]

As mentioned, semiotic inquiry into liturgy has been chiefly undertaken in Holland and Germany. Since 1976 the Dutch studies have been centred on the 'Semanet' group (Semiotic Analysis by Dutch Theologians) at Tilburg Theological Faculty, of which Gerard M. Lukken has been the most prominent member.[43] The publications in German reflect a cluster of names rather than that of a particular leader (though Rainer Volp – prior to his premature death, Professor of Practical Theology in the Faculty of Evangelical Theology at Mainz – certainly appears to have been a catalyst and organizing force for the work). The names of Karl Heinrich Bieritz, Rudi Fleischer (= Rudolf Roosen), Herbert Muck, Günther Schiwy, Ronald Sequeira and Hans Erich Thomé appear variously frequently in this literature.

Each of the two groups shows a distinct tendency (the Dutch perhaps more cohesively than the Germans). The Semanet approach has been based, virtually exclusively one judges, on the semiotic theories of A. J. Greimas and his 'Parisian School'. Greimassian semiotics, in turn, represented a deliberate carrying forward of the Saussurean model. This predisposes it towards an unambiguously linguistic approach to semiotics; indeed, one dimension of the Greimassian approach has been to work towards a semiotic 'metalanguage' – a language in which to analyse linguistic, and then other, signification.[44] By all means this semiotic approach will extend its scope to 'architecture, painting, film, comics,

---

42. So, specifically, Rudi Fleischer, 'Einführung in die semiotische Gottesdienstanalyse' in (Peter Düsterfeld, ed.) *Neue Wege der Verkündigung* (Düsseldorf: Patmos Verlag, 1983), 101.

43. In addition to the essay mentioned in n. 38 and the two collections of essays referred to in n. 40, see Gerard Lukken, 'Die Bedeutung der Semiotik Greimas' und der Pariser Schule für die Liturgiewissenschaft' in (Wilfried Engemann and Rainer Volp, eds.) *Gib mir ein Zeichen: zur Bedeutung der Semiotik für theologische Praxis- und Denkmodelle* (Berlin: Walter de Gruyter, 1992), 187–206.

44. 'Natural language, the language we speak, is already freighted with secondary meanings, connotations and associations for it to function as the instrument of analysis'; Lukken, 'Die Bedeutung der Semiotik Greimas', 189.

theatre, music, rituals'; accordingly, 'as such, the metalanguage is applicable to liturgy as well'.[45] Lukken's application of Greimassian semiotics appears mostly to have been in terms of analysing the signifying relationships between liturgical *texts* and the spatial or *proxemic juxtapositions* within which the textual performance is set. This has yielded him, he feels, new dimensions of meaning with respect to the vertical (theological) and horizontal (the participants in the liturgy seen as actants) specifications of the liturgy. This briefest of accounts patently does less than justice to the complex procedure on which it reports. That acknowledged, it is nevertheless difficult to feel that such analyses as Lukken achieves go any great distance to answering such questions of meaning as posed by and for my subject in chapter 1, above, or in my brief vignettes at the head of this chapter.[46]

The German language writing suggests the influence of a different semiotic authority: that of Umberto Eco. Of course, Eco is a European and so could hardly not have inherited the structuralist influence of Saussure. But he also comes from Italy, which European country was singularly exposed to the writings of Charles Peirce and, in fact, those of Peirce's long-time correspondent, Victoria Lady Welby.[47] Eco's career as semiotician thus represents a steady passage from a Saussurean-type, structuralist preoccupation with language towards a Peircean view of the sign.[48] The publication of his extraordinarily influential *A Theory of Semiotics* during the 1970s[49] stands at something of a midpoint in this trajectory,

---

45. Lukken, 'Semiotics and the Study of Liturgy', 110.

46. In very general terms it must be said that the Greimassian style of semiotic analysis has not won for itself widespread acclaim. It scarcely escapes the problems inherent within the Saussurean model on which it is based, and indeed adds to these a formidable repertoire of idiosyncratic terms and concepts, much of which has been taken from the structural analyses of Vladimir Propp (see, e.g., Ronald Schleifer, *A. J. Greimas and the Nature of Meaning: linguistics, semiotics and discourse theory* (London: Croom Helm, 1987), notably ch. 3). Umberto Eco dismisses it briefly as 'an all-too-rigorous narratological grammar' or as 'an example of the Fundamentalist Fallacy' (Umberto Eco, 'Semiotics and the Philosophy of Language' in (Rocco Capozzi, ed.) *Reading Eco: an anthology* (Bloomington: Indiana University Press, 1997), 2, 7. More comprehensively, see Svend Erik Larsen, 'Greimas or Grimace?', *Semiotica* 75 1/2 (1989), 123–30, or William O. Hendricks, 'On Circling the Square: on Greimas' semiotics', *Semiotica* 75 1/2 (1989), 95–122.

47. See Teresa de Lauretis, 'Semiotics in Italy' in (R. W. Bailey, L. Matejka and P. Steiner, eds.) *The Sign: semiotics around the world* (Ann Arbor: Michigan Slavic Publications, 1978), 248–57; also, Ponzio, *Man as a Sign*, 94–148, and (as Appendix 1 to the same volume, 313–63), Susan Petrilli, 'The Problem of Signifying in Welby, Peirce, Vailati, Bakhtin.'

48. So Susan Petrilli, 'Toward Interpretation Semiotics' in (Rocco Capozzi, ed.) *Reading Eco: an anthology* (Bloomington: Indiana University Press, 1997), 121–7.

49. The book which I represent under its English title was published in several versions in different languages between 1967 and 1976: Umberto Eco, *A Theory of Semiotics* (Bloomington: Indiana University Press, 1976).

undertaking a mediating position between the two (then still deeply entrenched) semiotic traditions. On the one hand, *A Theory of Semiotics* extends the notion of semiosis well beyond language. On the other, it continues to draw the bulk of its explanatory power from linguistic models, most strikingly in the dominance it affords the code as *the* preeminent semiotic mechanism.[50] Closely related to this, but also betraying Eco's then interest in the information/communication disjunction,[51] Eco ties his semiotic 'systems' to questions of communication.[52]

Eco's presence, sometimes acknowledged but more often simply assumed, seems to pervade almost everything written on the semiotics of liturgy in Germany. Three elements, all just now mentioned, stand out. One of these is the stress placed by practically every writer (on the semiotics of worship) on the *communicative* nature of liturgy. The secular pressures faced by churches everywhere in the western world perhaps make an insistence on communication, as the – or one – ground structure of Christian worship, neither unexpected nor untoward. Yet the linkage of communication to semiotic theory seems too frequent for it to be the product simply of prevailing cultural circumstances.[53] Later on I shall suggest that – while understandable in present circumstances – the thoroughgoing adoption (or, at any rate, an uncritical adoption) of communication as a liturgical model is not without its perils.[54] A second theme present in this literature, practically without exception, is a *dependence on the code* as the channel within which semiotic exchange takes place. 'The code is the key concept of semiotics,' wrote Günther Schiwy in the Introduction to his influential *Zeichen im Gottesdienst*.[55] Rainer Volp would expand on this with

---

50. See, *ibid.*, ch. 2. Eco's attempt to draw a 'halfway' position (i.e., halfway towards a Peircean view) has drawn considerable criticism. See, e.g., Augusto Ponzio, 'Treating and Mistreating Semiotics: Eco's treatise on semiotics', *S: European Journal for Semiotic Studies* 9 (1997), 641–60, and Deely, 'Looking Back on *A Theory of Semiotics*', 82–110. Associated criticisms are made of Eco's treatment (in *A Theory of Semiotics*) of the pair 'connotation' and 'denotation' by Beatriz Garza-Cuarón, *Connotation and Meaning* (Berlin and New York: Mouton de Gruyter, 1991), 184–90.
51. See the reference above, n. 35, to his *The Open Work*.
52. *A Theory of Semiotics*, ch. 1.
53. See, e.g., Josef Schermann, *Die Sprache im Gottesdienst* (Innsbruck/Vienna: Tyrolia Verlag, 1987), ch. 2 (pp. 43–127, 'Liturgie-Kommunikation in Zeichen'); Karl-Heinrich Bieritz, 'Das Wort im Gottesdienst' in (H. B. Meyer, et al., eds.) *Gottesdienst der Kirche: Gestalt des Gottesdienst* (Regensburg: Verlag Friedrich Pustet, second edition 1990), vol. III (pp. 49ff., 'Gottesdienst als kommunikative Handlung', and pp. 53ff., 'Gottesdienst als Zeichenprozeß'); or R. Fleischer, 'Einführung in die semiotische Gottesdienstanalyse' (pp. 103ff., 'Das kommunikationstheoretisch begründete Zeichenmodell').
54. Below, pp. 162, 174–5.
55. Günther Schiwy, *Zeichen im Gottesdienst* (Munich: Chr. Kaiser Verlag and Kösel Verlag, 1976), 21.

his reference to the semiotics of worship: 'The notion of code has accomplished a universal character for liturgy.'[56] Again, dependence on Eco is either explicit or only just beneath the surface. In earlier sections I have assembled trenchant criticisms of a code-based semiotics on the part of those viewing it from a Peircean perspective. The claim is that this view eliminates the interpretative interaction of sign-producer and sign-recipient, reducing the transaction to an 'equal exchange' of coded signification. We shall have to see whether these criticisms are as damaging to a code-based theory of liturgical semiosis as such authors suggest.[57] At very least the criticisms warn of a precariousness or brittleness attending any representation (of semiosis) so heavily dependent on codes as these formulations have made themselves. A third note, related back directly to the preceding one, is the still unmistakable *linguistic orientation* of all the semiotic structures envisaged by this group of authors.[58] The 'codes' which are nominated (space, time, clothing, gesture, music, and verbal codes)[59] are in fact seen as either parallel to, or adaptations of, the principal human coding system, i.e., language. This comes out in numerous ways. Within one or other of the specified codes (gesture, music, whichever), for example, 'connotation' and 'denotation' are seen as the mechanisms accounting for differences of meaning between sign-producers and sign-recipients.[60] On a much larger scale, the meanings of worship are organized in terms of syntactical, semantic and pragmatic 'axes of meaning.'[61] Another indicator of the tendency is the use of the notions 'association fields' and 'semantic markers' by R. Fleischer in his important Mainz dissertation.[62]

It is impossible not to be indebted to this intellectual labour on behalf of the semiotics of worship. Though my remarks have carried a critical

---

56. Volp, *Liturgik*, 61.   57. See below, ch. 6, n. 88.

58. An exception is to be made of the writing of A. Ronald Sequeira who, over a long career and in numerous published works, has contended for the gestural or movement-oriented elements of worship. It is notable that in his work the idea of 'communication' is replaced by the notion of 'expression'; see particularly his 'Gottesdienst als menschliche Ausdruckshandlung', 13–18.

59. Volp, *Liturgik*, 121; Schiwy, *Zeichen im Gottesdienst*, 21, gives a slightly different list of codes: architecture, clothing, facial expression, gesture, rites, customs, pictures, decorations, sounds. See also the essay by Mark Searle, 'Semper Reformanda: opening and closing rites', e.g., pp. 57, 70–5.

60. Volp, *Liturgik*, 62, 96; see Eco, *A Theory of Semiotics*, 54–7.

61. Volp, *Liturgik*, 649, 913–61. Admittedly, the threefold schema, syntax, semantics and pragmatics, is taken not from Eco or Saussure but from Charles Morris; see Charles Morris, *Writings on the General Theory of Signs* (The Hague: Mouton, 1971), ch. 3–5.

62. Rudi Fleischer, 'Verständnisbedingungen religiöser Symbole am Beispiel von Taufritualen: ein semiotischer Versuch' (Mainz: Dr. Theol. Inaugural-Dissertation, Mainz University, 1984). For the use made of the ideas 'fields of association' and 'semantic markers' see particularly pp. 216–24.

tone, this is only possible in the light of recent shifts of opinion within semiotic studies generally. Still, from this vantage point, one will say of the work which I have so briefly summarized that the ghost of Saussure, wearing the habit of Eco, is much more evident than that of Peirce. Peirce is only seldom invoked, and when he is then only secondarily,[63] or in ways which conform him to the dominant linguistic paradigm.[64]

C. S. Peirce's 'doctrine of signs'

Against this background of the shared history of semiotics and liturgical study, I turn to a more sustained exposition of Peirce's semiotic theories in the expectation that these can provide some degree of help in resolving my leading questions: *when* may we say that a liturgical event has been 'meaningful'? *How* does such an event 'make sense' for its participants? And *whose* meanings are we talking about?[65]

Certainly there already exist both concise and more extensive introductions to Peirce's thought.[66] It seems redundant to repeat those here, and in a less expert way. But Peirce is not (or not yet) much known outside his circle of followers. In order, then, to make accessible my ensuing treatment of liturgical meanings, I feel obliged to give the next few pages to an introduction to his thought on signs and signification.

The categories
Peirce's earliest published work, 'On a New List of Categories' (published in 1867, now CP 1.545–67) shows that the theory of signs which puts us so deeply in his debt was in fact the product of a question with which in the preceding pages we have become more than familiar: how do we relate to the world? The term 'categories' deliberately echoes Immanuel Kant's 'Copernican revolution' according to which 'objects conform to concepts'

---

63. Volp, *Liturgik*, 97–8. But, as an exception, see Hermann Deuser, 'Christliche Religion: Zeichen unter Zeichen?' in (Wilfried Engemann and Rainer Volp, eds.) *Gib mir ein Zeichen: zur Bedeutung der Semiotik für theologische Praxis- und Denkmodelle* (Berlin: Walter de Gruyter, 1992), 31–43.

64. Fleischer, in his dissertation, appears to draw on Peirce but in fact conforms Peirce more nearly to Eco's schemata; see, characteristically, 227: 'In order to prevent misunderstanding, the Peircean concept "Symbol" will be replaced by the notion "arbitrary sign".' One must say that Fleischer's work nowhere attends to the Peircean 'categories' without which Peirce's semiotic theory cannot be properly represented.

65. See, above, pages 11, 30.

66. In addition to the work of John Deely, Susan Petrilli and T. L. Short which I have listed frequently in my notes, see the volume (Christopher Hookway, ed.) *The Cambridge Companion to Peirce* (Cambridge University Press, forthcoming).

rather than *vice versa*; otherwise said, the view that our 'concepts make experience possible'.[67] Following Aristotle, Kant had deduced a table of four 'Categories' within which our apprehension of the world takes place.[68] That Peirce calls his a 'new' list of categories indicates his dissatisfaction with the Kantian logic of reality.[69] Peirce's approach is to *think* about *attention*: in other words, to work out the logic of what happens when a human being attends to the world (*CP* 1.547).[70] The outcome of his reflection is the now famous series, Firstness, Secondness and Thirdness. One may say that these 'skeletons of thought' or 'moods or tones of thought' (*CP* 1.355) underlay and informed everything else Peirce ever considered. They are the soil in which the doctrine of signs grows.

Peirce attempted this 'logical analysis of thought' by a process of prescission: that is, attempting to say which dimensions of our encounter with the world we could 'suppose without the other' (*CP* 1.353) and, contrarily, which dimensions of our experience are *not* thus capable of prescission. For example: 'I can prescind . . . space from color (as is manifest from the fact that I actually believe there is an uncolored space between my face and the wall); but I cannot prescind color from space, nor red from color' (*CP* 1.549). In other words, since I can imagine uncoloured space, but cannot think of colour without thinking of a coloured space, space can be prescinded from colour but not colour from space.

Peirce considers that before I can encounter any *particular* thing, I have to allow the sheer *possibility* of its existence. This quality of possibility or potential, which preempts a thing's actual existence and thus can be prescinded from it, he names Firstness. Firstness 'is the mode of being which consists in its subject's being positively such as it is regardless of aught else. That can only be a possibility . . . The mode of being a *redness*, before anything in the universe was yet red, was nevertheless a positive qualitative possibility' (*CP* 1.25). Since Firstness only exists as potential, as 'freedom . . . as that which has not another behind it, determining its actions' (*CP* 1.302), we never do encounter it *as such*; we know it only as 'abstract

67. Kant, *Critique of Pure Reason*, B xvi, xvii; B166, 167.   68. *Ibid.*, B106.

69. See esp. Gayle L. Ormiston, 'Peirce's Categories: structure of semiotic', *Semiotica* 19 3/4 (1977), 211. Ormiston's essay in its entirety (pp. 109–231) should be consulted. A convenient summary of Peirce's treatment of the categories is given by Douglas Greenlee, *Peirce's Concept of Sign* (The Hague: Mouton, 1973), 33–42. Joseph Ransdell, 'On Peirce's Conception of the Iconic Sign' in (Paul Bouissac, Michael Herzfeld and Roland Posner, eds.) *Iconicity: essays on the nature of culture* (Festschrift, Thomas A. Sebeok) (Tübingen: Stauffenburg Verlag, 1986), 57–8, similarly has a brief but clear exposition of the Peircean categories.

70. Peirce's own description for this is: 'the logical analysis of thought . . . regarded as applicable to being' (*CP* 1.300).

potentiality' (*CP* 1.422); it is 'so tender that you cannot touch it without spoiling it' (*CP* 1.358). It is apprehended only in 'qualities...which, in themselves, are mere may-bes, not necessarily realized'. 'It is purely a question of what I can imagine and not of what psychological laws permit' (*CP* 1.304).[71]

Of course, something's 'may-be' quality of being is only realized when the thing assumes actuality. This mode of existence Peirce names as Secondness. Secondness is 'brute' existence. I encounter Secondness in putting my 'shoulder to a door and trying to force it open against an unseen, silent and unknown existence'. Secondness is experienced in the difference between an injunction for my arrest and 'the sheriff's hand on my shoulder'; it is just then that 'I shall begin to have a sense of actuality' (*CP* 1.24) It is thus Secondness which opens me to the irresolute *otherness* of the world I so encounter. Precisely in putting my shoulder to the door I meet the door's solid or actual resistance. But Secondness yields 'a double consciousness'. It is precisely in the resistance of the door to me that my own existence is disclosed:

> We become aware of ourself in becoming aware of the not-self. The waking state is a consciousness of reaction ... And this notion, of being such as other things make us, is such a prominent part of our life that we conceive other things also to exist by virtue of their reactions against each other. The idea of other, of *not*, becomes a very pivot of thought. To this element I give the name of Secondness.
>
> (*CP* 1.324)[72]

This last-named insight – awareness of self is given in the awareness of the other – is then the stepping-off point for Thirdness. There can be no encounter between self and other, between two or more things in their extant particularity, without relationship. And, just as potential may be prescinded from actuality but not *vice versa*, so potentiality and actuality can be prescinded from relationship but not *vice versa* (there can be no relationships without things actually to stand in relationship). Hence: Thirdness.

---

71. Joseph Ransdell, 'On Peirce's Conception of the Iconic Sign', 57, writes thus of Firstness: 'A monadic property is a wholly intrinsic property of a thing, which means that, in regarding a thing as having such a property, one is making no implicit reference to any second thing. In so far as we regard something in this way, we are regarding it neither as existent or as non-existent, as real or as unreal, since, to regard a thing only in respect of its monadic properties, is to regard it as if it had no relationship whatsoever to anything else (including oneself), whereas the ideas of existence and reality pertain to things in their relationships to one another. Firstness is [Peirce's] name for a property of this sort.'

72. On the importance of Secondness in Peirce's delineation of himself as against Kantian idealism, see Short, 'What's the Use?', 38–41.

The name should *not* however mislead us into seeing Thirdness simply in linear progression behind Firstness and Secondness. In terms of prescission, yes: it is Thirdness. But as relationship it essentially *mediates*, and thus stands *between* Firstness and Secondness: 'A Third is something which brings a First into relation to a Second' (CP 8.332).

> By the third, I mean the medium or connecting bond between the absolute first and last. The beginning is first, the end second, the middle third. The end is second, the means third ... Position is first, velocity or the relation between two successive positions second, acceleration or the relation of three successive positions third ... Sympathy, flesh and blood, that by which I feel my neighbor's feelings, is third.
>
> (CP 1.337)

Thirdness is thus essentially present in our apprehension of reality; yet it manifests itself only indirectly:

> the third category – the category of thought, representation, triadic relation, mediation, genuine thirdness, thirdness as such – is an essential ingredient of reality, yet does not by itself constitute reality, since this category ... can have no concrete being without action [Secondness], as a separate object on which to work its government, just as action cannot exist without the immediate being of feeling [Firstness] on which to act.
>
> (CP 5.436)

It is Thirdness which mediates the world to us and us to the world. That means that Thirdness encompasses the conceptual domain, the laws of nature which we formulate, indeed the entire world of thought, language, law and custom. Thirdness is inherently *interpretative*. And that is its irreducible function in semiosis.

A sign, we have earlier seen, is not a thing in itself, an entity. It is a relationship between three things, which three things we can now identify with the three modes of being: the sign-vehicle or *representamen* holds within itself the capacity for signification, it stands as Firstness to the other two elements of the whole sign-relationship. But this potential for signification will not be realized until it is brought into relationship with that to which it points, that of which it is a sign, the sign's object: 'A sign, or *representamen*, is something which stands ... for something', as Peirce's most famous definition has it (CP 2.228). This 'standing for something' is an actual relatedness, and the sign's *object* thus stands in a place of Secondness. But this 'standing for' is not simple, direct, or unambiguous.

All signification is polysemous as the definition goes on to acknowledge: 'in some respect or capacity'. It is thus the interpretant within the tri- adic relationship which will localize or specify in *which* signifying respect or capacity the sign-vehicle stands to the sign-object. It is the interpre- tant which mediates or relates the one to the other. Consequently is the interpretant Thirdness within the sign. We have seen previously that in some degree it is the sign-recipient who supplies the sign's interpretant, who 'understands' ('comprehends'!) that this sign-vehicle stands in this respect or capacity to that object as a sign: 'It seems a strange thing . . . that a sign should leave its interpreter to supply a part of its meaning' (*CP* 5.448, note 1). But, of course, the sign-producer was hardly absent from this ei- ther; in constructing and proposing the sign he or she must actively have *anticipated* which interpretant the sign-recipient would be likely to bring in completing the signification – anticipate, but not finally control. Thus is the sign a collaborative work between them. And thus, also, can we see how 'the doctrine of signs' could be the product of Peirce's reflection on the categories: Firstness, Secondness and Thirdness.

Peirce worked on his theory of signs for over forty years, and at the end still was not satisfied that he had thought it through to completion.[73] This warns the student of his writings against a monolithic reading, as if the ideas remained static across these forty years. It is nevertheless not much short of astonishing that the basic taxonomy of signs as iconic, indexical and symbolic already appears embryonically in the earliest published pa- per we have ('On a New List of Categories').[74] It is to this division of kinds of signs that we now turn.

Icons, indices and symbols

Firstness, Secondness and Thirdness are present in the sign not only in the nature of its three essential components. The three modes of being are also to be seen in the nature of the relationship *between* the elements. This applies in the first place to the relationship between the *representamen* (for which, in company of others, I shall henceforth mostly use Charles Morris'

73. See, e.g., Short, 'Interpreting Peirce's Interpretant', 530, n. 5: 'The very last entry in this Notebook, for 1 Nov. 1909, is particularly telling, even poignant. After trying several times to define "sign" (you would have thought that he would have had *that* down by this time!), Peirce wrote, "Well, on the whole . . . I think this won't do".'
74. At *CP* 1.558 (i.e., in 'On a New List of Categories') Peirce offers 'three kinds of representations': 'First. Those whose relation to their objects is a mere community in some quality, and these representations may be termed *likenesses*. Second. Those whose relation to their objects consists in a correspondence in fact, and these may be termed *indices* or *signs*. Third. Those the ground of whose relation to their objects is an imputed character, which are the same as *general signs*, and these may be termed *symbols*' (his emphases).

term, 'sign-vehicle')[75] and the sign's object. Then closely conjoined with this is the nature of the inferential relationship between the sign-vehicle and the interpretant.

Before I come to the details, it is of utmost importance to note that these relationships, and the sign-types they produce, are *never exclusive*. That is, there are no *purely* iconic, indexical or symbolic signs. Every iconic sign, for example, includes within itself some degree of indexicality and some symbolic signification; the same applies to each of the others. It is only ever a case, in any given triadic assemblage, of a *predominant* quality producing an *identifiable* distinction.[76]

Signs, then, according to Peirce, are more or less identifiable as icons, indices or symbols.

'An *Icon* is a sign which refers to the Object that it denotes merely by virtue of characters of its own, and which it possesses, just the same, whether any such Object actually exists or not' (CP 2.247). An iconic sign, in Peircean taxonomy, is one which signifies on the basis of a recognizable *commonality* or *similarity* or *likeness* between the sign-vehicle and the sign's object. The most familiar form of icon nowadays, I imagine, is the graphic representation on a computer screen of one or other of the functions which are accessible. Even as I write, on the screen before me there is a picture of something that *looks like* a half-open manila folder: I know it to be the icon for 'Open a Document'; beside it is the representation of a floppy disc which, I know, is the (iconic) sign for 'Save the Present Document'; and so on. Computer screen icons have become a sort of international language. In Peirce's day the closest he could get to this was the way in which a photograph or painting is an iconic sign of the person or thing of which it is the representation. Diagrams are also important examples for Peirce of iconicity: 'They exhibit the relations between parts of an object or between objects in sets';[77] as are algebraic formulae (CP 2.279). Maps are another fairly obvious example.

---

75. Peirce ceased from speaking of the *representamen* at a relatively early stage on the grounds that this dimension of the triadic sign is not always a representative one. Thereafter he spoke rather simply of the sign. This however seems to me to render less than clear that the sign, properly described, is a *relationship* between all three of its elements. I thus follow John Deely's recommendation: 'contemporary semioticians have learned to speak of "sign vehicles"' (*New Beginnings*, 156); the term 'sign-vehicle' comes from Charles Morris (see his *Writings on the General Theory of Signs*, e.g., 19).

76. See particularly Petrilli, 'Towards Interpretation Semiotics', 131. In what follows I am indebted to this essay by Petrilli, especially pp. 130–6. The point about the sign-types never being exclusive of each other is quite often made; see again, for example, Ransdell, 'On Peirce's Conception of the Iconic Sign', 70, 72, or Sebeok, *The Sign and its Masters*, 19.

77. Johansen, 'Iconicity in Literature', 40.

The iconic sign depends on similarity between the sign-vehicle and the object of which it is the sign. The iconic sign is thus characterized by First-ness. This can be shown in at least two ways. A computer icon or a photo-graph or a painting, for example, is 'identifiable' *as* the picture of that of which it is a picture. That is, the sign-vehicle (picture) and its object (that of which it is a picture) 'have a certain property in common'.[78] It is this 'property in common' (the likeness between them) which allows the one to be the sign of the other. But Peirce himself supplies the second reason in the sentence I cited above where he says a sign is an icon, 'whether any such object actually exists or not'. That is, a photograph is the photograph of my father (it has its own identity as a photograph of my father) irrespec-tive of the fact that my father died some years ago. The iconic sign (in ex-act contradistinction, we shall see, to the indexical sign) does not depend upon its object's actual existence. Patently, it could not be a photograph of my father had my father never existed; and herein is the point about none of the sign-types ever being wholly exclusive of the others.[79] In this case, the iconic sign (photograph) depends upon a *trace* of alterity and of actual existence (Secondness) which is in fact more exactly the mark of the indexical sign. Peirce also notes that iconic signs depend upon at least a modicum of convention (which is the characteristic of symbolic significa-tion) (CP 2.279). Most of us, that is, have had to become 'literate', as we say, with computer icons. Such 'traces' notwithstanding, iconic significations depend on a perceptible likeness between a vehicle and its object, even if the latter is purely imaginary.

Contrariwise, an *indexical sign* depends upon an actual contiguity be-tween the sign-vehicle and the sign's object: 'The sign and what it is a sign of are given together.'[80] Secondness, we saw, bespeaks concrete existence as a mode of being – for example, as contrasted with imagined existence or remembered existence. Accordingly, an indexical sign 'represents an ob-ject by virtue of its connection with it' (CP 8.368, note). In one of his de-scriptions Peirce says that indices may be distinguished from other signs in three ways: 'first, that they have no significant resemblance to their ob-jects; second, that they refer to individuals, single units, single collections

---

78. See Ransdell, 'On Peirce's Conception of the Iconic Sign', 63: '[I]n identifying something . . . as an icon . . . one is committed to the claim that sign and object really do have a certain property in common (since Peirce construes resemblance, likeness, or resemblance as identity in respect to some property).'
79. CP 2.247: 'It is true that unless there really is such an Object, the Icon does not act as a sign; but this has nothing to do with its character as a sign. Anything whatever . . . is an Icon of anything, in so far as it is like that thing and used as a sign of it.'
80. Petrilli, 'Towards Interpretation Semiotics', 131.

of units, or single continua; third, that they direct the attention to their objects by blind compulsion' (*CP* 2.306).[81] Peirce's well-loved example of an indexical sign is the weathercock, 'because in the first place it really takes the self-same direction as the wind, so that there is a real connection between them, and in the second place . . . when we see a weathercock pointing in a certain direction it draws our attention to that direction' (*CP* 2.286). Another example of the indexical sign is a knock at the door, telling us directly that there is someone outside who desires entrance (*CP* 2.285). This example also characterizes the index in that it forces our attention to itself, it 'directs attention to [its] object by blind compulsion'. All cause–effect relationships are indexical: smoke as a sign of fire, symptoms as the signs of disease, clues pointing to a criminal. Again, however, Peirce reminds us that 'it would be difficult, if not impossible, to instance an absolutely pure index, or [contrariwise] to find any sign absolutely devoid of the indexical quality' (*CP* 2.306). Signs which are *chiefly* characterized, then, as the effects of causes, or by a mechanical connection between the sign-vehicle and the sign's object, or which signify by directing our attention directly to their object,[82] may be regarded as indexical.

A sign which depends neither on a perceived similarity between the sign's vehicle and its object, nor on mechanical causation, but simply on the fact that it has become conventional to see one thing (a red traffic light) as a sign of something else (the requirement to stop) is called by Peirce a *symbol*:[83] 'The symbol is connected with its object by virtue of the idea of the symbol-using mind, without which no such connection would exist' (*CP* 2.229). Language is the most immediate and perhaps also the most

---

81. See Thomas A. Gouge, 'Peirce's Index', *Transactions of the Charles S. Peirce Society* 1 (1965), 53–4, for a list of six characteristic marks of the indexical sign. Short, 'Interpreting Peirce's Interpretant', 488–90, chronicles the development of the idea of the index in Peirce's thought and lists some of the implications thereof.

82. 'When a driver to attract the attention of a foot passenger and cause him to save himself, calls out "Hi!" . . . , so far as it is simply intended to act upon the hearer's nervous system and to rouse him to get out of the way, it is an index, because it is meant to put him in real connection with the object, which is his situation relative to the approaching horse' (*CP* 2.287).

83. It is just at this point that the discussion of Peircean semiotics is likely to become most confusing for those accustomed to the patterns of thought within which a discussion of the theory of symbols, as appertaining to the liturgy, was undertaken through the last quarter of the previous century. It was regularly assumed that 'signs' are sharply to be *distinguished* from 'symbols'; that 'signs' are univalent, pointing to some particular other object, whereas symbols are polyvalent, mediating some kind of 'presence' (so, e.g., James Empereur, *Worship: exploring the sacred* (Washington, DC: The Pastoral Press, 1987), 35). Occasionally attention was drawn to the fact that 'the two somehow coalesce . . . that the distinction is not as clear cut as it seems at first' (Power, *Unsearchable Riches*, 63). But such qualifications seem hardly to have been noticed in the enthusiasm for the antinomy. I am trusting that my exposition of Peirce makes it clear that, in his categorizations at least, 'symbol' is a subset of 'sign'.

copious source of examples of such signification (CP 2.292–6). But language is by no means the only kind of symbol. Further definitions make it clear that Peirce eschews the nature/law dualism which, for Saussure, promotes language as the primary semiotic form (and thus valorizes code over nature, or reads the world from an anthropocentric viewpoint):[84] '[A symbol] depends either upon a convention, a habit, or a natural disposition' (CP 8.335); 'A symbol is a *representamen* whose special significance or fitness to represent just what it does represent lies in nothing but the very fact of there being a habit, disposition, or other effective general rule that it will be so interpreted' (CP 4.447). As commentators point out, animals quite other than the human animal are capable of *learning* to associate one event with another and thus of forming semiotic *habits*.[85] That which allows us to see one thing *as* another, we saw in reviewing the categories, is Thirdness, that which mediates or interprets. All laws, customs, habits, codes, concepts, language itself – everything which functions as an interpretative screen between ourselves and external reality – thus partake of Thirdness; accordingly, so do symbolic signs.

Signs are iconic, indexical or symbolic according to the nature of the relationship between the sign-vehicle and the sign's object: in iconic signs this is a relationship of Firstness, in indices of Secondness, in symbols of Thirdness. But all such description is still at the expense of the third element of the semiotic relationship: the interpretant. Our discussion so far might almost have treated the sign as dyadic (signifier/signified) which, I have said repeatedly, can never yield an account of meaning. It is, in fact, the third element of the Peircean sign, the interpretant, which allows this account of semiosis to be an account of semiotic *meaning*: it is the interpretant which *mediates* between the sign's vehicle and object thus generating the signification found therein. The interpretant is accordingly not absent from the classification of the three sign-types. This is found in *the kind of inferential relationship* in which the interpretant mediates the sign-vehicle to the sign's object: in iconic signs the inferential process (that is, the basis on which I decided, or have figured out, that such and such is the sign's signification) is abductive; in indexical signs it is deductive; in symbolic signs it is inductive.[86]

84. See Joseph Ransdell, 'Some Leading Ideas of Peirce's Semiotic', *Semiotica* 19 3/4 (1977), 174; similarly, Ponzio, *Man as a Sign*, 265.
85. Short, 'Semeiosis and Intentionality', 208–9.
86. See particularly CP 2.96 for the association of the three kinds of argument with the three sign-types. See also the commentary by Petrilli, 'Toward Interpretation Semiotics', 134–5 (the same material is in Petrilli's 'Dialogism and Interpretation', 112–13).

In explication, I will take the three sign-types in order of their logical stringency. This will mean that indexical signs – characterized by Secondness, by factuality, by causal effect or mechanical contiguity – carry within them the highest degree of logical force. In this case the interpretant mediates the sign-vehicle to the sign's object *deductively*: 'The facts asserted in the premises oblige us to accept the interpretant-conclusion.'[87] Deduction – 'the application of general rules [the major premise: "all men must die"] to particular cases [the minor premise: "Enoch and Elijah were men"] in order to produce a conclusion ["Enoch and Elijah must have died"]' (CP 2.619f.) – is regarded by Peirce as the most secure but the least productive of the three forms of inference (CP 1.630; 8.383–8). Indexical signs, then, are least open to controversy or interpretative difference. Smoke pretty certainly is a sign of fire.

Induction is the inference of a major premise ('All the beans from this bag are white')[88] from a minor premise ('These beans are from this bag') and a conclusion ('These beans are white'). Here the inferential move has less stringency (CP 1.630) but yields more information (though of a probable, or statistical nature). It is 'where we generalize from a number of cases of which something is true, and infer that the same thing is true of a whole class' (CP 2.624). It is the kind of inferential move we make in the case of general laws, customs, projections. It is the inferential move within symbolic signs.

Abduction, however, 'depends upon altogether different principles from those of other kinds of inference'. It consists in 'the first starting of an hypothesis and the entertaining of it, whether as a simple interrogation or with any degree of confidence' (CP 6.525). It is akin to an informed guess[89] or to the Socratic dialogue.[90] It is thus a reasoning in possibilities, in imaginative speculation rather than in deductive certainty; yet Peirce will never concede that imaginative insight is other than reasonable![91] Iconic signification, depending on nothing other than likeness or similarity between its vehicle and object is abductive in its inferential processes. There is always a plenitude of ways in which likenesses may be interpreted;[92] the iconic sign is always open to conjecture and to disputation:

87. Petrilli, 'Towards Interpretation Semiotics', 134; similarly, Ponzio, *Man as a Sign*, 266.
88. See ch. 1, n. 91 above.   89. Fann, *Peirce's Theory of Abduction*, 35–8.
90. Jaako Hintikka, 'What is Abduction? The fundamental problem of contemporary epistemology', *Transactions of the Charles S. Peirce Society* 34 (1998), 519.
91. Fann, *Peirce's Theory of Abduction*, 36–7.
92. My friend's computer screen shows an icon which is not part of the display on mine: it depicts a pair of binoculars. But is this meant to represent (iconically) the command 'enlarge

> An originary Argument, or *Abduction*, is an argument which presents facts in its Premiss which present a similarity to the fact stated in the Conclusion, but which could perfectly well be true without the latter being so, much more without its being recognized; so that we are not led to assert the Conclusion positively but are only inclined toward admitting it as representing a fact of which the facts of the Premiss constitute an *Icon*.
>
> (CP 2.96)[93]

On the other hand, of course, the disputations will be themselves conjectural, lacking final determination. The iconic sign again thus manifests its Firstness.

The importance of the interpretant

In various places I have introduced Peirce's notion of Thirdness as the element which enables his to be a theory of semiotic meaning, whereas this eludes dyadic theories of the sign. Before leaving this exposition in order to attend more directly to an analysis of liturgical semiosis, it is perhaps desirable to say a little more about Peirce's interpretant.

It is the interpretant which stands in the place of Thirdness between the sign-vehicle and the sign's object. It is the interpretant which mediates the one to the other; otherwise said, it is the interpretant which effects the way in which the sign's object is apprehended, its meaning.[94] That much perhaps is clear, but, like every other aspect of Peirce's thought, his views on the nature and function of interpretants were subject to near endless expansion and intellectual experimentation (readers familiar with Peirce will know that at every turn I have given only the most elementary account of his ideas). His writings depict two different trichotomous divisions of interpretants, one of which seems to have been fairly stable for him, but the other of which shows much adaptation and experimentation.[95] The

the screen', or does it mean 'search' (or is it something else again)? It will be *something* like one of these. But without testing it, I can only guess.

93. See further, Petrilli, 'Toward Interpretation Semiotics', 135: 'In abduction the relationship between the premises and the conclusion is determined neither by the obligation of contiguity nor by the arbitrariness of conventionality. The premises *suggest* the conclusion, and simply through a relation of *relative similarity*: we start from a result which evokes a given law on the basis of which it is possible to explain the case in question. In this kind of inference the relationship between the premises and the conclusion is only probable: it is dominated by conjecture, by the inclination to guessing, and is variously risky . . . [G]iven the role played by similarity, abduction is predominantly associated with iconicity' (her emphases).

94. So Deely, *New Beginnings*, 222: '[the interpretant] is the fulcrum of semiosis in the writings of Peirce'.

95. In this account I am allowing myself to be guided by T. L. Short's exposition, 'Interpreting Peirce's Interpretant'; in his essay Short gives detailed accounts of other

more stable trichotomy sees interpretants as: *logical* interpretants (based in Thirdness, these effect their interpretation by way of thought or custom); *energetic* interpretants – an interpretant which is an action, or Secondness, such as the interpretant of a command: 'Ground arms!' (CP 5.473, 475); or as *emotional* interpretants, such as that which interprets to someone the 'meaning' of a musical experience, i.e., an interpretant grounded in Firstness (CP 5.475).

The other trichotomy – which, according to T. L. Short, it seems better not to try to assimilate to the first – is most usually called that of the immediate/dynamical/final interpretants (I said that Peirce played with many ways of naming this trichotomy). Here the *immediate* interpretant interprets the sign 'as it is meant to be understood' (the sign as its proposer understands it, we might say); the *dynamical* interpretant is the interpretant 'as it is produced' (the interpretant as seen by the sign's recipient); and the *final* interpretant is that which – after all the interpretational possibilities of the sign have been reviewed – yields the most finally acceptable or satisfactory interpretation of the sign.[96]

All of these, I think, are of potential interest for an account of the meanings of worship; for instance, the recognition of an 'emotional' interpretant immediately opens the way to 'meaning' which does not have to be reduced to linguistic categories (so that the possibility is raised of a hymn's *melody* contributing meaning, not just its words!).[97] For the moment, however, I want to pick up one of Peirce's attempts to render the second trichotomy, as offering an especially clear insight into the way in which the meanings of worship work:

> There is the *Intentional* Interpretant, which is a determination of the mind of the utterer; the *Effectual* Interpretant, which is a determination of the mind of the interpreter; and the *Communicational* Interpretant, or say the *Cominterpretant*, which is a determination of that mind into which the minds of utterer and interpreter have to be fused in order that any communication should take place. This mind may be called the commens. It consists of all that is, and must be, well understood

readings on the subject by way of arguing his own understanding which I have summarized in my text. He also modifies, in light of intervening criticisms, some of the views he had expressed in the 1981 essay, 'Semeiosis and Intentionality'.

96. See Short, 'Interpreting Peirce's Interpretant', 504–7.
97. Peircean semiotic theory has been frequently appropriated by musicians; see, among many possible references, William P. Dougherty, 'The Quest for Interpretants: toward a Peircean paradigm for musical semiotics', *Semiotica* 99 1/2 (1994), 163–84; or R. Keith Sawyer, 'The Semiotics of Improvisation: the pragmatics of musical and verbal performance', *Semiotica* 108 3/4 (1995), 269–306.

between utterer and interpreter at the outset, in order that the sign in
question should fulfill its function.[98]

Towards the end of the previous chapter I made reference to a couple of
liturgical incidents where intention and interpretation missed each other
by some distance (above, pages 102–3): people took my elevation of the eucharistic elements to be a reverencing of them; and people supposed that
the act of standing, as the Bible and the ministers entered the church, was
a sign of respect for the ministers. I said there that I thought the notion
of 'agency' offered some deliverance from a kind of helpless relativism
('people will see what they see in any case'). There are still things to say
about that in terms of the responsibilities of sign-production and sign-
reception; but, in the meantime, Peirce's analysis of interpretants gives us
a clearer idea of what is happening in such 'misses'. In so showing us how
it happens, he also opens the way towards at least a narrowing of the gap
between them, hopefully to the point where the interpretants proffered
by the sign-producer and brought by the sign-recipient, respectively, are
sufficiently close for there to be what, in the passage just cited, Peirce calls
the 'communicational' interpretant or 'cominterpretant'.

In the first case, the 'misses' occur because the interpretant of the sign-
producer (the 'intentional' interpretant) and of the sign-recipient (the
'effectual' interpretant) diverge:

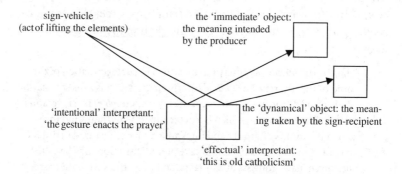

What is so greatly desirable, however, is the achievement of Peirce's 'communicational' interpretant in which there is sufficient coincidence of the

---

98. Johansen, 'Let Sleeping Signs Lie', 280, cites this passage from the Peirce/Welby
correspondence. See Short, 'Interpreting Peirce's Interpretant', 507, for a discussion of the
passage, and see his 'Semeiosis and Intentionality', 212–13, for a slightly different version.

interpretants to yield meaning satisfactory to both producer and recipients, and in which we can say 'understanding' or 'communication' has been achieved:

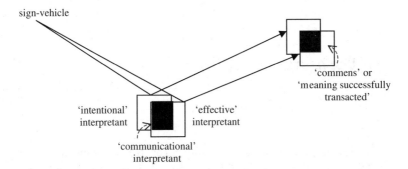

I will return to the interpretant in production and reception of signs in chapter 6. In the meantime we must see what iconicity, indexicality and symbolic signification can say about the meanings of worship.

5

The liturgical sign (ii)

How may the meanings of worship be constructed, transmitted and apprehended within the threefold ordering of signs as iconic, indexical and symbolic? This is the question to which I turn in this chapter. The *iconicity* of worship, I shall say, derives from its being seen as an event which takes place on some sort of boundary or frontier – at once imagined and yet altogether real – to what human beings can fathom as comprehensible; iconicity, that is, has to do with the degree that we can manage to generate a *likeness* or *similarity* between what we do on the known side of this frontier and how we imagine things might be on its far side. *Indexicality*, I shall suggest, has to do with 'truthfulness' or 'authenticity' in the words and actions of worship, an integrity between 'form' and 'performance', or what the Second Vatican Council's 'Constitution on the Sacred Liturgy' calls 'thoughts matching words' or 'participation which is knowing, devout, and active'.[1] The *symbolic* dimension of liturgical signification, I will say, comes from the fact that every liturgy draws on, presupposes, depends upon an incalculable depth of tradition in its construction of contemporary significations. All of these, need I say, are important strategies in, or for, the production of liturgical meaning.

Iconicity

Every act of worship, I postulate, assumes or represents some sort of 'virtual frontier' across which the divine–human transaction which is worship is undertaken. It is true that in all ordinary circumstances (apart from worship, that is) this boundary is not easily drawn. Daniel Hardy says

---

1. 'Constitution on the Liturgy', sections 11, 48.

quite simply: 'There is *no fixed boundary* either between God and creation, or within creation.'[2] Or Gordon Kaufman strenuously contests a 'dualistic way of thinking' which, traditionally, undergirded a separation of 'this' world from an 'other' world.[3] Again, one frequently encounters the puzzled question or objection (in speaking of a 'frontier', and of coming *to* such a frontier in worship) as to whether we can ever *not* be in God's presence. And finally – turning now explicitly to worship – one must admit that often enough worshippers come away with no particular sense of having approached a human–divine frontier. All this is duly acknowledged. But that human beings regularly run up against some kind of 'limit', that a sense of finitude is widely attested – not just in physical terms but in our abilities to manage our destiny–that eventually we reach a point at which we can speak only of 'mystery' or of 'the incomprehensible', seems not just to be inscribed indelibly in theistic accounts of our condition, but to be a nearly universal human trait:

> Now. When I have overcome my fears – of others, of myself, of the underlying darkness:
> at the frontier of the unheard-of.
> Here ends the known. But, from a source beyond it,
> something fills my being with its possibilities.[4]

It is then not surprising to discover that those many different representations of worship not drawing on a semiotic understanding,[5] nevertheless carry implicitly the idea of 'frontier' or 'boundary' or of 'boundary crossing'. Paul Hoon's 'Christological' representation, for example, in which the worship service is seen as 'God acting to give his life for man [*sic*] and to bring man to partake of that life' accords with the point of view insofar as it (a worship service) facilitates 'God's revelation of himself [*sic*] . . . and

---

2. Daniel Hardy, *God's Ways with the World*, 164 (my emphases).

3. Gordon Kaufman, *In Face of Mystery: a constructive theology* (Cambridge MA: Harvard University Press, 1993), e.g., 271, 301–2, 325–6.

4. Dag Hammarskjold, *Markings* (London: Faber & Faber, 1964), 77. Reference might be made to Langdon Gilkey's *Naming the Whirlwind*, where he traces intimations of alterity – 'this strange interloper into our secularity' – in ordinary life; see, e.g., *ibid.*, 253: 'This strange interloper into our secularity appears not so much as a new reality or being, as rather the ultimate presupposition for dealing with the ordinary relative realities we meet; not so much a presence . . . as a final limit and demand; not so much an answer as an ultimate question.'

5. James F. White, *Introduction to Christian Worship* (Nashville, TN: Abingdon Press, revised edition 1990), 25–30, and James Empereur, *Models of Liturgical Theology* (Bramcote: Grove Liturgical Publications, 1987), or (differently) in ch. 6 of the same author's *Worship: exploring the sacred*, compile comprehensive lists of ways in which the worship service has been understood.

man's response.'[6] Gordon Lathrop's 'juxtapositional' thesis[7] yields the idea of the worshipping assembly being or becoming 'a hole in the fabric of things, through which life-giving power flows into the world'.[8] Don Saliers' 'eschatological art' is in effect the frontier translated into a still outstanding future.[9] I. H. Dalmais, from a Roman Catholic perspective, speaks of 'the two movements recognizable in every cultic manifestation: the movement of human beings toward God in order to offer him [*sic*] their prayer of adoration and thanksgiving, and the movement of God to human beings, who look to him for the answer to their prayers.'[10] The 'Constitution on the Liturgy' speaks explicitly of the earthly liturgy sharing in the heavenly liturgy.[11] The number of liturgical texts which suggest either directly or implicitly that in worship we 'enter God's presence' must be practically innumerable.[12]

6. See White, *Introduction*, 25–6.

7. Gordon Lathrop's thesis is that the meanings, or significance, of worship are secured through the constant juxtapositioning of like with unlike – 'there is a design, an *ordo*, and it is one that is especially marked by juxtaposition as a tool of meaning' (*Holy Things*, 79; similarly, p. 170) – which juxtaposition ensures the 'breaking' of the univalency or reifying power of the symbols (e.g., *ibid.*, 80).

8. *Ibid.*, e.g., 212, 215, 222. It is important to say that Lathrop consistently sees the liturgy as grounded in, and pointing back into, this world: '[T]he stuff of Christian assembly is drawn from common experience and common life. That ordinariness is reflected in the ordinary words already chosen here as words for the beginning of interpretation: meeting, gathering, book, washing, meal, song, speech' (*ibid.*, 10; similarly, p. 87); or again, 'Go down your streets and into the meeting. You are not at a place especially sacred in itself; you are at a place in your town, a place used for the Christian meeting' (*ibid.*, 108). It nevertheless transpires that these 'ordinary' things and events admit to an 'edge' or 'limit' dimension of experience: 'The power of the loaf as symbol is [that] we eat to live . . . In eating we are at the edge, the limit of our possibilities' (*ibid.*, 91); 'the character of the speech we encounter in the liturgy will strike us as rare, even astonishing . . . it addresses God and other invisible realities directly' (*ibid.*, 98); 'For such meanings the appropriate figure needs to be direction away from here: all the members facing an open distance or the east or a wall standing for what is beyond here' (*ibid.*, 109).

9. Saliers, *Worship as Theology*, 9: 'This book proposes to rethink worship as an eschatological art', and cf. p. 102: 'Authentic prayer is born in extremity'; see particularly chapter 3 of the book for a more detailed exposition of Saliers' 'eschatological art' thesis.

10. I. H. Dalmais, 'Theology of the Liturgical Celebration' in (A. G. Martimort, ed.) *The Church at Prayer: principles of the liturgy* (Collegeville: The Liturgical Press, 1987), 230.

11. 'The Constitution on the Liturgy', section 8: 'In the earthly liturgy, by way of foretaste, we share in that heavenly liturgy which is celebrated in the holy city of Jerusalem towards which we journey as pilgrims.'

It is perhaps worth observing that the notion of boundary or limit is not by any means confined to liturgical theology. The systematic theologian David Tracy has explored the theme extensively as a theological motif (David Tracy, *Blessed Rage for Order: the new pluralism in theology* (Minneapolis: The Seabury Press, 1975), esp. chs. 5–7; and *The Analogical Imagination: Christian theology and the culture of pluralism* (London: SCM Press, 1981), pp. 160ff., and ch. 8. See also Pailin, *The Anthropological Character of Theology*, 69: 'the ultimacy of God not only provides the limits for understanding but is itself understood in terms of what we regard as those limits'.

12. *Uniting in Worship*, the book of services for my own church, The Uniting Church in Australia, includes in its list of suggested 'scripture sentences' thirty-six possibilities of

Peircean iconicity, we have seen, depends upon likeness or similitude between a sign-vehicle and that of which it is the sign. Bringing this form of semiosis into relationship with the notion of a 'virtual frontier' present in every act of worship gains the insight that signs fashioned in order, first, actually to generate some sentient awareness *of* such a frontier, and, second, to hypothesize how things might be on the farther side of such a frontier, is to put in place a far-reaching strategy for meaning in worship: *iconic signs invite us to imagine how things are in the presence of God!*[13] We observe this both negatively and positively. I noted a moment ago that it is possible – depressingly frequent, perhaps – for worshippers to come away with little sense of having encountered anything like a human/divine frontier: the 'edge of chaos', or 'a source [from which] something fills my being with its possibilities'. In this case we shall say that an iconic dimension in the liturgy's signification was either deficient or absent: the transaction (of worship) seemed mostly continuous with everyday events (the sermon was scarcely distinguishable from other exhortations to altruism; and the 'fellowship' could have been replicated in any social gathering). When, conversely, the iconicity of signs conveys the sense that the congregation is indeed summoned, invited, to join the song of the celestial company – as it is every time the *Sanctus* is sung[14] – the signs are undertaking to *show* the worshippers that of which the summons speaks!

Is this *genuine meaning*? Or is it no more, no less, than pious illusion? Three responses are perhaps in order. First, the *sense of boundary* which the iconic signs of worship bring into view – what I am calling worship's 'virtual frontier': the impression that every worship space is in some sense constructed at the edge of the known world – is *not imaginary* but witnesses to the universal sense of limit on which I touched and which I will develop at length in my concluding chapter. Second, we recall that iconicity partakes of Firstness, which means that these signifying forms have semiotic value whether or not any *actual* relationship obtains between the

---

which the greater proportion include the idea of 'coming into God's presence'. Among the first five of these, for example, are: Genesis 28:16f., 'Surely the Lord is in this place. This is none other than the house of God, and this is the gate of heaven'; Psalm 43:3, 'Send out your light and your truth that they may lead me, and bring me to your holy hill and to your dwelling'; and Psalm 122.1, 'I was glad when they said to me, Let us go to the house of the Lord.' See *Uniting in Worship: Leaders' Book* (Melbourne: The Joint Board of Christian Education, 1988), 558.

13. Perhaps there has never been a better exponent of this than John of Patmos; see, e.g., Richard Bauckham, *The Theology of the Book of Revelation* (Cambridge University Press, 1993), 31–5, 41, and ch. 3 *passim*.

14. See, e.g., Bryan Spinks, *The Sanctus in the Eucharistic Prayer* (Cambridge University Press, 1991), 194–5.

sign-vehicles and their objects.[15] It is true that we cannot really know what lies on the further side of the boundary to which the liturgy leads us; yet an iconic representation of that 'other' still offers meaning *as* an iconic representation of it: 'The value of an icon,' Peirce assures us, 'consists in its exhibiting the features of a state of things regarded as if it were purely imaginary' (*CP* 4.448).[16] In this connection we recall that the inferential process of iconicity is abduction. Abduction is the most open-ended, least assured of the three logical processes, not dissimilar to an educated guess or act of thoughtful imagination.[17] It is the riskiest of the inferential moves; but, because it depends least on information already within its premises, it also has the highest 'yield' in terms of the possible meanings it opens up before us.[18] Third, we may here recall that none of the sign-types is pure; that some indexicality and some symbolic signification inhabit iconic signs (and *mutatis mutandis*). This means that the iconicity of worship is never isolated from the vast complex of symbolic signs: those significations, that is, drawn into any particular worship service from the millennia-long stocks of memory shared by biblical communities. The iconic signs of worship *are* imaginary; but they are not the imaginings of an individual, or even of a group. They are the fruit of a long, dreaming – but active, too! – wisdom, carried in text, rite and symbols.

Where the iconicity of worship is brought off with any success, then, it is capable of great illumination: not just of that of which it is the sign (the 'other' at which we must guess) but of our lives on 'this side' of the frontier, too – that is, their reality before this great horizon against which they must be measured, their limitations but also their transcendental possibilities

15. Above, p. 140.
16. See Petrilli, 'About and Beyond Peirce', 316: 'An important consideration is that both [Peirce and Wittgenstein] believed that the sense of the world could be traced in the possibility of its iconic representation. And, given that what is manifested iconically is not necessarily utterable, both philosophers recognized in the world a margin of ineffability, traces of the unsaid, of the unutterable.'
17. Above, pp. 34–5, 143–4.
18. So Petrilli, 'About and Beyond Peirce', 335–6: 'On the level of inference, abduction is the name of a given type of argumentation, of development or transition from one interpretant to another foreseen by logic, but which – especially in its more risky expressions – supercedes the logic of identity in so far as it develops through argumentative procedures that may be described as eccentric, creative, and inventive. In abduction, by contrast with induction and deduction . . . the relationship between the interpreted sign and the interpretant sign is regulated by similarity, attraction and reciprocal autonomy . . . Abduction, therefore belongs to the side of otherness, of substantial dialogicality, creativity, it proceeds through a relationship of fortuitous attraction among signs and is dominated by iconicity. The abductive argumentative procedure is risky; in other words, it advances mainly through arguments that are tentative and hypothetical, leaving a minimal margin to convention and to mechanical necessity.'

which, all too often, our modern sophistication attempts to keep occluded.

The notion 'frontier' carries within it the connotations: space, time, embodiment, movement. Thus, one comes *to* a frontier; perhaps even passes *beyond* it, and *returns*. One comes to a frontier at specific *times*, and there is *duration* between coming to and moving back from such a dividing line. The spatial and temporal references then refer us to the condition of *embodiment*: it is the body's physicality which commits it to such localization. But the body does more: it is the *body's form* which *orients* it in space and time: being ourselves constituted, that is, in terms of 'frontness' and 'backness' is what gives us directionality, tells us which way is 'forward', what is 'behind', how to turn right or left. It is the form of the body, similarly, which permits and invites us to direct attention 'towards' someone or something, and, correlatively, to turn away from, turn our backs on, persons or circumstances. It is, then, an extrapolation of bodily form which lends 'frontness', 'backness' and 'sides' to built spaces, as to vehicles, and to locomotion generally (for that matter it is bodiliness which similarly gives us 'upward' and 'downward' – and then a whole constellation of religious sensibilities).[19]

Iconic liturgical significations of 'boundary' or 'frontier', and then of the Other which lies beyond the frontier (implicit, I am saying, in all language which speaks of 'God' and 'humanity') will thus necessarily be heavily impregnated not just with spatial, temporal and movement *imagery* (which it is), but with *actual, physical* movement and directionality. Of course, all such construction draws on both realism (finding) and imagination (making): space and time are already both real (i.e., dependent on cosmic factors wholly independently of human presence)[20] and dependent on powers of human artifice;[21] the frontier is both real and yet it cannot actually be located anywhere; as I say, it is a *virtual* frontier, posited as 'all the members [face] an open distance or the east or a wall standing for what is beyond here' (note 8, above). Iconic signs of worship thus mediate the real and the imaginary, but this, we recall, is precisely its (the iconic sign's)

19. See esp. Edwyn Bevan, *Symbolism and Belief* (London: Collins [The Fontana Library], 1962), esp. chs. 1 and 2; also Lakoff and Johnson, *Metaphors We Live By*, ch. 4.
20. See (above, p. 61) the reference of Moritz Schlick to 'celestial bodies [which] will go on in their courses after mankind [*sic*] has vanished from the earth'. On the dialectic of 'subjective' and 'objective' time see Ricoeur, *Time and Narrative*, vol. III, ch. 2.
21. Lathrop, *Holy People*, 218: '[N]ow it is with Japanese-made watches that we calculate our variations from Greenwich Time.' See also Regis A. Duffy, 'American Time and God's Time', *Worship* 62 (1988), 515–32, esp. pp. 526ff.

character: ['It exhibits] the features of a state of things . . . as if it were imaginary.' In brief: in worship it is *as if* we come into the presence of God!

How shall 'entrance to', 'being in' and 'departure from' God's presence come to expression? One element of this, I have said, is an (iconic) realization of the frontier which eventually distinguishes our mode of existence from God's. Another, deriving from my remarks just now on bodily constitution in movement and direction, will be an actual *locomotion* from space to space. Concordant with that will be what we may describe as *liturgical direction*: a sense of whence the action or utterance comes and where (to whom) it is directed; whether, that is, it is 'the movement of human beings toward God . . . [or] of God to human beings.'[22] Then, governed by the same bodily considerations, but now with respect to time, *temporal sequence* will be of importance: not just in terms of beginning (entrance), duration and conclusion (departure), but with respect to a *meaningful progression* of events within the time which is being configured as 'in the presence of God'.

The body exists simultaneously in both space and time, so it will be difficult to separate these out for semiotic analysis. In what follows I nevertheless attempt this finally impossible partition.

Iconic representation of worship's space

With respect to movement into, within and from the space designated for worship, the liturgy calls for many changes of place, or for actions at specific locations, all of which would be germane to the semiotics of worship.[23] I have here scope only to attend to the outermost brackets: movement *into* the worship space and exit *from* it. Then I will say something of what I have called 'liturgical direction'.

In the event which we call a worship service, 'entrance' will now usually involve two stages: initially people will enter the worship space and find themselves a place; subsequently there will be some sort of symbolic act which, as it were, officially gathers this group of assembled individuals

22. Dalmais, 'Theology of the Liturgical Celebration', 230. On 'liturgical direction' see particularly the articles 'Directions, Liturgical' and 'Orientation' in (J. G. Davies, ed.) *A New Dictionary of Liturgy and Worship* (London: SCM Press Ltd., 1986). And on the dialectic of *movement towards* the congregation (by God or Christ) and the congregation's *response*, see Daniel Hardy, *God's Ways with the World*, 11–13, and particularly p. 27: 'What occurs in Christian worship . . . is an ontological recognition of a God whose well-being occurs within relationality; and this recognition confers the same relationality on those who recognize it . . . [T]he relationality of God is not . . . inert . . . It is always a dynamic relationality'.
23. For comprehensive analyses of worship's space, see particularly White's *Introduction*, ch. 3; and his *Documents of Christian Worship: descriptive and interpretive sources* (Edinburgh: T. & T. Clark, 1992), in this case also ch. 3.

into *an* assembly, an action of some kind which indicates that *together* they now enter the space and time of the liturgy. To stay for the moment with the first stage, this is more or less informally done but, as I hope to show, is not the less semiotically important for that. 'Entrance' means to leave one space and pass into another. What iconic significance is thus generated for the worshipper as he or she passes from the space which is the church's vestibule to the space specifically designated for worship? If I may recall (from my opening scenes, chapter 1 above) the person whom I imagined as visiting a church not familiar to her, I said of her entrance to the worship space proper: 'Here, the *hushed tones of preparation* strike her almost physically in their contrast to *the buzz of conversation* with which she is familiar in her own place of worship.'[24] We are now perhaps in a position to 'read' these contrasting possibilities in terms of the iconicity of 'entrance'. The one which she encounters as striking seems to signify an understanding of the space – and thence of the worship which takes place within it – as *differentiating* itself from the ordinariness of familiar – I risk the description, 'secular' – space.[25] The set of significations with which she is more familiar, on the other hand, bespeaks a perception of *continuity* across the first and the second, the inner and the outer, spaces. The semiosis in both cases will be multiplex: the architecture and everything associated with built space (its height, its lighting, its so-called 'ambience', the arrangement and proportions of its interior spaces) will be of overriding importance,[26] but the texture, quality and disposition of the furnishings and appointments will come close behind in signifying power. And the manner or demeanour of the people already within the space or at its entrance,[27] will be similarly powerful signs of how worship is understood (what it means) in each place and among the people whose space it is. In the first case, the space and everything within it wants to signify 'difference': it will not be mistaken for living-room space.[28] It will manifest itself as a space intended neither for business transactions, nor for education, and not even

---

24. Above, p. 12.

25. Catherine Vincie, 'The Liturgical Assembly: review and assessment', *Worship* 67 (1993), 136, speaks of 'the violent rupture required for entrance into the assembly and for dismissal from it'.

26. See particularly Gerard Lukken's essay 'Die architektonischen Dimensionen des Rituals' in *Per Visibilia ad Invisibilia*, 359–74, together with his introductory chapter, 'Semiotics of Architecture' in Lukken and Searle, *Semiotics and Church Architecture*.

27. See Lathrop on 'door keepers'; *Holy Things*, 128.

28. Lathrop, *ibid.*, 125–6: '[T]he meeting must never feel like a living room'; see also, *ibid.*, 117–19, on the dialectic of 'warning' and 'invitation' as attending the awareness of entering liturgical space.

for socialization.[29] Its design will attempt to suppress tendencies to chatter, a sense of 'the everyday'. Conversely it will seek to induce feelings of the unusual, of reverence, of the uncanny (worship spaces are not unique in this: museums, art galleries and war memorials seek similar ends).[30] What, by way of contrast then, is signified by the visitor's more regular experience? Much earlier we heard Charles Taylor (and Max Weber) describe the concerted effort on the part of the sixteenth-century reformers to '[deny] any special form of life as a privileged locus of the sacred . . . [to deny] the very distinction between sacred and profane and hence [affirm] their interpenetration'.[31] Assuming the validity of this analysis, we may now say that for someone to pass from vestibule to worship space with the most minimal, if any, consciousness of a difference between them – so that conversations continue on the one side as on the other, so that an atmosphere of sociability dominates each of the spaces indistinguishably – is the long-term effect of a collapsing of the sacred into the ordinary such as Taylor describes. Here, too, many semiotic media will be in concert. For example, my own experience of Protestant worship spaces constructed in the last three or four decades (the experience is limited but I think not unrepresentative) is that they wish to minimize in so far as they can a sense of alterity and, conversely, strongly encourage a sense of sociability, of 'at-home-ness', of familiarity, of intimacy.[32]

Many such spaces are, in fact, intended to be 'multifunctional', with religious symbols and appointments at one end and a performance platform at the other. Thus the building itself is a manifestation of the immanentist convictions of those who constructed it. But now, in turn, it silently yet powerfully corroborates the notion that 'nothing special' is expected of the people who enter it, nor perhaps of what will happen within it. A question may be asked about what feats of imagination are called for by a space in which people have attended a play, or concert, or social gathering on Saturday night, then, with the seats turned around, are asked to

---

29. Lathrop, *Holy People*, 23: 'According to the classic description of this basic symbol [i.e., the assembly itself] this meeting is not – or ought not be – a crowd, a cheering section, a gathering to hear a lecture or a sales pitch, an audience. It is not a collection of consumers come to an expert, a gathering of the uninvolved come to be entertained.'

30. See particularly Rudolf Otto, *The Idea of the Holy: an inquiry into the non-rational factor in the idea of the divine and its relation to the rational* (Oxford: Geoffrey Cumberledge, 1923), 68–70, 132. See also K. S. Inglis, *Sacred Places: war memorials in the Australian landscape* (Melbourne: The Miegunyah Press, 1998); and John K. Simmons, 'Pilgrimage to the Wall', *Christian Century* 102 (1985), 998–1002.

31. Taylor, *Sources*, 217 (see above, p. 56).

32. See esp. M. Francis Mannion, 'Liturgy and the Present Crisis of Culture', *Worship* 62 (1988), 107ff., on what he calls 'the intimization of society'.

worship on Sunday morning; what claim upon the imagination, but then also, in classically Protestant style, what diminution of *actual* (i.e., physical, sentient) signification?

I said that liturgical 'entrance' will be in two stages: people have to enter the space individually; but then they have to '*be* gathered' into a corporate entity. The semiotics of this stage, too, are decisive (i.e., in terms of enabling a 'boundary' experience). To stay with the latter case, where the sense of 'threshold' has been reduced practically to imperceptibility, the second-stage entrance will often be equally curmudgeonly. Any actual or literal movement (I said that locomotion is an integral element of entrance; one cannot enter while remaining stationary) will be minimal, perhaps wholly absent. It may amount to no more than someone standing and turning to face the people. Or there may have been movement which was considered *not* to have been movement, such as the minister moving to the pulpit or table from the vestry door, and the choir moving to their places while the worshippers were still finding their seats, which movement however is deemed not to 'signify' as an act of entrance.[33] In these cases the second-stage 'entrance' will be effected perhaps by the announcement of scripture sentences or the singing of an introit. This *may* work effectively as an iconic signification of entrance. On the other hand, one can hardly fail to note, again, the extensive disembodiment that such practice signifies and a corresponding weight of dependence on verbal signs.[34] One risks the judgement that here 'entrance' has been wholly spiritualized, something done purely in imagination but not in any degree of physicality. From the point of view of semiotics, at any rate, something is seriously missing.[35]

In other traditions, of course, the formal entrance is effected by physical signs: in various degrees of ceremonial procession – ranging from a carrying of the Bible into the church and the placing of it on the lectern, perhaps followed by choir and other ministers, to an incensed procession of all the

33. James White and Susan White, *Church Architecture: building and renovating for Christian worship* (Nashville, TN: Abingdon Press, 1988), 27, affirm that 'movement [in the worship service] is not simply a matter of convenience [but is] an important ingredient of worship'. Their subsequent remark, (p. 28) that 'a choir procession has no real significance as an act of worship' then stands to the former at least curiously.

34. See Gregory Dix's bitter lament that the legacy of Puritan convictions is 'worship [as] a purely mental activity' in subsequent Protestantism; Gregory Dix, *The Shape of the Liturgy* (London: Adam and Charles Black, 1945), 312. More recently, see Xavier John Seubert, 'The Trivialization of Matter: development of ritual incapacity', *Worship* 67 (1993), 38–53.

35. See Volp, *Liturgik*, 79–80: 'This figure of thought [worship as 'gathering' and 'sending'] encompasses a fundamentally *spatial* dimension. A festival does not just reinforce memory and hope, but *distance* and *proximity*' (p. 79, his emphases).

lay and ordained ministers accompanied by organ and singing – the leaders of the worship will *enact* by means of walking, and the manner of their walking, an iconic representation of 'coming into the presence of God'.[36] That is not to say, however, that processionals are without problems for Christianity in late modernity. The semiosis requires that an actual *distance* be traversed. Modern democratic ideals, however, militate against the idea of people being widely separated from the sanctuary[37] and perhaps even more against the idea of priestly privilege which determines who may and may not enter such space.[38] In some styles of Christianity, there may be resistance against the affording to some (the leaders) a representative role on others' behalf. The desiderata of late modern Christian sensibilities are not distance but immediacy, proximity, access. Whether these preferences should be allowed to erase the iconicity of movement 'to the frontier' or 'into the presence of God' seems to me, on the other hand, dubious. So to do seems like a capitulation to the immanentist ideologies of the age which either complacently assume the holy is already among us or, alternatively, that we know how to find our way to it without impediment. Effective representation of 'entrance' will continue to need, I am suggesting, an *act* of movement from one place to another (the back of the church towards its front) and some significant degree of distance to cover. We need regularly to be reminded that the form of existence known to us is an existence which is bounded, which keeps bumping up against that which it is not, is constantly confronted by its 'other'. How might this be done in

36. I cite again the words of Cardinal Guardini: 'How can the act of walking become a religious act, a retinue for the Lord progressing through his land, so that an epiphany may take place?' (given by Mark Searle, 'Liturgy as Metaphor', 115). See similarly Sequeira, 'Gottesdienst als menschliche Ausdruckshandlung', 26: 'In liturgical celebration movement is not an end in itself but is a symbol for the experiencing of salvation or its prayerful response' and, *ibid.*, 31, 'In the form of the procession [walking] may become a symbol for the pilgrim people of God.' See, too, Lathrop, *Holy Things*, 129: '[The procession] moves through the people, as if visually to pull them along.'
    On the matter of effective procession, see Robert Hurd, 'A More Organic Opening: ritual music and the new gathering rite', *Worship* 72 (1998), 290–315, esp. 294–5; and, on procession *within* the worship service, see Irwin, *Context and Text*, 67.

37. So James White and Susan White, *Church Architecture*, 31: 'The least satisfactory [shape for a contemporary worship space] is the longitudinal, or basilican, plan with the congregation stretched out in a long tunnel-like nave'; similarly, *ibid.*, 32. The tendency is not just a 'Protestant' one: Mark Searle speaks of the reluctance in North American Roman Catholic congregations 'to ritualize the entry procession'; see his 'Semper Reformata: opening and closing rites', 84; also Irwin, *Context and Text*, 160. And see Lawrence Hoffman, *The Art of Public Prayer: not for clergy only* (Washington DC: Pastoral Press, 1988), 162, 172–3, on the contemporary cultural prerogative for 'intimacy, not distance' (p. 173).

38. See Janet Walton, *Art and Worship* (Wilmington: Michael Glazier, 1988), 31–45, on the political power symbolized by access to the sanctuary far removed from the place for the people in the nave of a mediaeval church.

churches without the traditionally extended nave? Perhaps a configuration in which the people gather in a separate space and enter *together* into
the space of worship becomes the most desirable form.[39] Or, since entrance
into holy space is not just to be seen as 'approaching the edge of chaos' but
is also seen massively in the tradition as a matter of ecstatic joy, congregational *dance* is another option.[40]

If, by way of declaring our militancy against the all-pervading immanentism of modernity, it is necessary clearly to mark the *entrance* to the
space and time of the liturgy, the exact counterpart of that must be the
preparation of people to *pass back* across the 'boundary' of such space and
time into the world and the week which awaits them. It can then only be a
matter of deepest regret that this 'boundary crossing', too, seems so badly
provided for iconically in many traditions. Otherwise expressed, it seems
a pity beyond the telling if all the presiding minister can manage to signify
is that 'it's all finished now'. In this respect, I have in mind an often-cited
passage from the pastoral psychologist, Paul Pruyser:

> Over the years, in attending worship services, I had gradually become
> accustomed to ministers terminating their services with a rushed and
> hardly audible benediction, uttered on the way out from the back of
> the sanctuary where nobody could see them. And if the benediction
> was pronounced from the pulpit, audibly and visibly, the spectacle for
> the beholders was often little more than a slovenly gesture, consisting
> of only one arm raised half-heartedly and only half-way up, against the
> force of gravity to which that poor limb would quickly succumb
> again.[41]

I have allowed the sense of the vertiginous edge (Kavanagh's 'edge of
chaos'; Otto's *mysterium tremendum*)[42] a dominance over the sensibilities of

---

39. See James White and Susan White, *Church Architecture*, 21–2; similarly Lathrop, *Holy Things*, 129.

40. See, e.g., A. Ronald Sequeira, *Klassische indische Tanzkunst und christliche Verkundigung: eine vergleichende religionsgeschichtlich-religionsphilosophische Studie* (Freiburg: Herder, 1978), esp. 225ff.; and his 'Liturgy and Dance: on the need for an adequate terminology', *Studia Liturgica* 17 (1987), 157–65, and 'The Rediscovery of the Role of Movement in the Liturgy' in (Luis Maldonado and David Power, eds.) 'Symbol and Art in Worship' (*Concilium*, February 1980) (New York and Edinburgh: Seabury Press and T. & T. Clark, 1980), 112–19. See also Doug Adams, *Congregational Dancing in Christian Worship* (Austin, TX: The Sharing Company, 1971), and J. G. Davies, *Liturgical Dance* (London: SCM Press, 1984).

41. Paul Pruyser, 'The Master Hand: psychological notes on pastoral blessing' in (William B. Oglesby Jr., ed.) *The New Shape of Pastoral Theology: essays in honour of Seward Hiltner* (Nashville, TN: Abingdon Press, 1969), 353.

42. Kavanagh, *On Liturgical Theology*, 73. Kavanagh has several ways of expressing the idea: 'The liturgical assembly's stance in faith is vertiginous, on the edge of chaos. Only grace and favor enable it to stand there; only grace and promise brought it there; only grace and a rigorous divine charity permit the assembly, like Moses, to come away from such an

elation, festivity and restoration (Otto's *fascinans*)[43] which are at least as importantly a part of 'coming into the presence of God'. Let me then correct that here with the recollection that pretty well the last responsibility of the presiding minister in any given worship service is to *bless* the people (invoke over them benediction!) as they prepare to leave the space and time of the liturgy. That is, the blessing requires to have about it an iconic quality such that it enables the people to *go back* from the encounter with the 'other' who is God, carrying within and about them the sense of promise, of absolution, of the empowerment and the blessing which belongs in and flows from this encounter.[44]

Of course, now the iconicity of 'entrance' is repeated here in reverse: so that the sense of 'holy presence, of blessing and reconciliation' can hardly easily be sustained when the same buzz of conversation which filled the room right up until the official 'call to worship' now breaks out with unabated intensity immediately upon the pronouncement of the benediction. Alternatively, for the entire company to recess with organ, choir and dancers carrying the benediction back 'out' into the space of the familiar world is powerfully to signify the depth, beauty and wonder of the event now concluding which purported to be at our human 'edge'.

The iconicity of 'spatial presence to God' is not only accomplished in movement, it also turns around what I have called 'liturgical direction': *whence arises* the action/utterance of the liturgy and *in which direction* is it sent? The possibility of signifying this dimension of the liturgy derives, too, from the fact that a human body is so formed that it has both forward and backward aspects: it faces and it faces away from.

It is a commonplace that the liturgy is dialectic in its structure: '[I]n its actual celebration the liturgy is truly a dialogue between God and his

encounter, and even then it is with wounds which are as deep as they are salutary' (*ibid.*, 75); 'That it never crosses our minds that a liturgy or an icon should cause us to shiver only shows how we have allowed ourselves to tame the Lion of Judah and put him into a suburban zoo to entertain the children' (*ibid.*, 94). For Otto, see his *The Idea of the Holy*, 12ff.

43. *Ibid.*, 31: 'The "mystery" is for [the creature] not merely something to be wondered at but something that entrances him; and besides that in it which bewilders and confounds, he feels a something that captivates and transports him with a strange ravishment, rising often enough to the pitch of dizzy intoxication; it is the Dionysiac-element in the numen'; see also pp. 120 and 145. The point is also beautifully caught in the subtitle of Rainer Volp's great work: 'Liturgy, the art of celebrating God' (*Liturgik, die Kunst, Gott zu feiern*); see, for example, 91–2: 'The securing of inner and outer, of self-presence (*Selbstdarstellung*) and self-emptying (*Katharsis*), a deepened recollection and a sensitivity for the new, the overcoming of estrangement and the discovery of the stranger – all these are the hallmarks of the religious, indeed of the biblical, festival, which we have nominated as the empirical basis of the worship service.'

44. See William Willimon, *Worship as Pastoral Care* (Nashville, TN: Abingdon Press, 1979), 210.

people'.[45] It is not difficult to see this as an extension of the 'border-crossing' imagery. The question raised to us by semiotics is: how *apparent* is this dialectical quality of the liturgy to those who are its participants? Otherwise expressed, does the iconicity of 'frontier', of 'dialogue across the boundary' come sufficiently to attention?

In the liturgy, 'Our dear Lord himself speaks with us through his holy Word and in response we speak with him through prayer and praise' (note 45 above). This is the dialogue which is envisaged. God speaks, and the assembled company makes reply. But because, as we heard much earlier, all the significations of worship require to be articulated in sensible signs (that is, in this case through human agents), some*one* has to speak on God's behalf; and someone has to speak the human response. In the latter case, *some* of these (human responses) are undertaken by the gathered congregation – Luther's 'Lobgesang' (hymns of praise) catches this well enough. But not *all* of the 'human response' side of the conversation is articulated by the people; some of it at least (the prayers, to stay with Luther) is usually voiced aloud by one person in everyone else's stead. All this still leaves God's side of the dialogue needing expression: *someone* has to speak *in God's place*, or *in persona Christi* as one formulation has it. The fact, then, that leaders – often but not exclusively the presiding minister – must sometimes speak for God and sometimes as the people's spokesperson means that their role oscillates. Sometimes, so to say, they speak *from* God's side *into* the assembly; and sometimes they are speaking *to* God from *within* the congregation. There will be times when this fluctuation of responsibilities must happen quite quickly. For example, in prayers of confession the leader has the responsibility of articulating the people's penitence. But in the very next action of the liturgy the same person (usually) will have the responsibility of speaking God's (or Christ's; see note 47 below) gracious words of forgiveness. Or again, the sermon is – presumably – the attempt to speak 'our dear Lord's holy Word' to the people; but if – as often, and most appropriately happens – the preacher concludes the sermon

45. A. G. Martimort, 'Structure and Laws of the Liturgical Celebration', 131 (and see ch. 3, 'The Dialogue Between God and His People', *passim*). Martimort's sentence is in fact a paraphrase of a widely cited sentence from the 'Constitution on the Liturgy', section 33: '[I]n the liturgy God speaks to His people . . . and the people reply to God both by song and by prayer.' Karl-Heinrich Bieritz, 'Das Wort im Gottesdienst', 61, under the heading 'Die dialogische Struktur der Liturgie' remarks on the close proximity of this sentence to one of Martin Luther's: 'Our dear Lord himself speaks with us through his holy Word and in response we speak with him through prayer and praise (*Lobgesang*).' See, further, Irwin, *Context and Text*, 86–90, and see finally, Empereur, *Worship*, 131: '[T]he principle that all liturgy is structured according to a proclamation/response pattern is valid for all services of worship.'

by leading the people in prayer, we must be clear (hopefully the person undertaking it will be) that in this moment the 'liturgical direction' changes.[46]

It is my impression that the iconicity of liturgical direction is often blurred, both in the minds of leaders and then, consequently, in the minds of the worshippers. This can happen on several different grounds. One such cause is an ambiguity inherent in a Christological interpretation of the worship service: is Christ supposed to speak from the people's side, as mediator? Or is Christ the second person of the Godhead who speaks God's grace and favour to the people?[47] Is Christ God's Word?[48] If a leader understands herself or himself as occupying a role *in persona Christi*, is that then an acting from God's side, the people's side, or somewhere between them?[49] Perhaps an even more fertile source of confusion is the seemingly unassailable idea: 'communication': '[Christian worship] reaches its highest degree of effectiveness *as a communicative event* in that, joined with the divine saving Word, it constantly newly makes present the fundamental act of salvation, so binding the assembled people in one structure of relatedness which can be described theologically as "the body of Christ" or "the people of God".'[50] The problem is that 'worship as communicative event' leaves seriously indeterminate who is communicating what with whom. Under the heading 'Worship is a Communications Event', for example, Rudi Fleischer goes on to speak of the importance of the people's active participation in worship (about which no one will argue) but this turns out to be a matter of communication between the *liturgist* and the

---

46. Empereur, *ibid.*, 132, produces a table charting the alternation through the liturgy between 'proclamation' and 'response'. I agree with the dialectical conception itself; but I find a good many of Empereur's judgements – as to which is which – difficult to understand.

47. In *Uniting in Worship*, the worship book of the Uniting Church in Australia, the form of the absolution is: 'Hear then *Christ's word of grace to us*: Your sins are forgiven' (my emphases); *Uniting in Worship: Leaders' Book*, 84.

48. The *Basis of Union* of the Uniting Church in Australia sees the sermon unambiguously Christologically or perhaps Christocentrically: 'Christ who is present when he is preached among people is the Word of God who acquits the guilty, who gives life to the dead and who brings into being what otherwise could not exist'; *The Basis of Union* (Melbourne: Uniting Church Press, 1992), 7.

49. A. G. Martimort, 'Structure and Laws of the Liturgical Celebration' in (A. G. Martimort, ed.) *The Church at Prayer: principles of the liturgy*, 158, writes: 'Whether as "Eucharist" or as "collect", the prayer of the priest is the high point of the celebration . . . It expresses the mediation that the priest . . . exercises *in persona Christi* between God and his people.' (see similarly I. H. Dalmais, 249–51, in the same volume). From a Protestant point of view (as reflected for example in the two previous notes) for the leader to assume a role *in persona Christi* is to assume unambiguously that he or she is speaking Christ's word *into* the assembly. This is rendered more ambiguous in Martimort's formulation.

50. Bieritz, 'Das Wort im Gottesdienst', 50 (my emphases).

congregation.[51] Or Bieritz (in the essay cited in note 50 above) goes on to say: 'The *Word of God* is enacted in, with and under *the answering response of the people*';[52] again it becomes practically impossible to know who is speaking what to whom. Finally, and in the same general direction, James Empereur writes: 'It is erroneous to say that liturgical prayer is addressed to God and so not to the people . . . [B]eing addressed to God, [prayer] is also addressed to people. Otherwise . . . there [would be] little concern for whether people hear and respond, whether they are touched or moved, whether they find that the prayers resonate with their problems and concerns.'[53] Speaking *for* people – making it thus entirely necessary for them 'to hear and respond' etc. – is an entirely different matter from speaking *to* them. Here, too, the question of liturgical direction is deeply compromised.

Is it all that important? Does it *matter* whether people think the actions/language are addressed to them or to God? Our subject generally is liturgical meaning and in this place particularly it is how that meaning is generated and communicated by way of liturgical signs. For both leaders and people to be unclear about the 'direction' in which the liturgy is oriented at any given moment is to allow the meanings of worship to be, or to become, indistinguishable from those of any other public event in which speeches are made, songs are sung and symbolic acts are undertaken. Ambiguity about 'direction', in fact, wholly vitiates the notion of the worship service as a 'dialogue'. It is to generate a semiosis in which all the action (communication) is effectively contained within the room itself: there is no semiosis of 'other', of 'beyond', of 'frontier', of 'engagement'.[54] On the other hand, an act of confession and absolution, for example, in which the prayer leader (in this case, I should say, the presiding minister) comes down *into* the congregation, turns *towards* the sanctuary area, and (assuming the acoustics allow it) offers the prayer of confession clearly as from *among* the people . . . and then at its conclusion steps up before them and, *now facing them*, declares God's tough patience and generous mercy, is to create – at least in part – by way of iconic signs of spatial reference the meaning of confession *before*, and then absolution *from*, Almighty God.[55]

---

51. Fleischer, 'Einführung in die semiotische Gottesdienstanalyse', 109–10. Later in his essay, the 'communicative programme' of the liturgy is construed as 'a symbolic dialogue between God and the congregation' (*ibid.*, 113); this still leaves a good deal of ambiguity about who communicates with whom and in which manner.

52. Bieritz, 'Das Wort im Gottesdienst', 62 (my emphases).   53. Empereur, *Worship*, 153.

54. See Lathrop's references, n. 29 above, to the marks distinguishing a liturgical assembly from 'a crowd, a gathering to hear a lecture, an audience' and so on.

55. See Nichols, *Liturgical Hermeneutics*, 71.

Not all the phases of the liturgy, admittedly, can be thus enacted in terms of their liturgical 'direction'; though the Prayer of Thanksgiving over the eucharistic gifts (God's gifts to us!)[56] is obviously addressed to God, none of us, I imagine, is going to relinquish the 'basilican' position in which the leader stands behind the table. Even so – recalling my judgement near the commencement of the previous chapter that 'the significations of worship are effected through a multitude of tiny signals transmitted by their producers' – for the 'leader [to know clearly that he or she] *speaks the prayer to God* even as the people reinforce it with their "Amen"'[57] is to generate this multitude of tiny iconic signs which leaves the people in no doubt about the source – and thence the 'direction' – of the utterance. They know that a prayer is not really for their 'consumption', but is spoken on their behalf by one who is, momentarily, their delegate. And, for leaders themselves, such consciousness must energize their utterance *as* prayer: it delivers them from temptations to 'theatricality' or 'performance', it confirms for them the delegated nature of this leadership, and it imbues their actual utterance (i.e., in the 'grain of the voice') with iconic indicators of 'utterance before the face of God'.[58]

The iconicity of temporal progression

Spatiality is not separable from temporality; we have already seen that the iconicity of *spatial* arrangements (the relationship of confession to absolution, for example) depends to some extent on the *sequencing* of the actions which happen within the spaces. Still, neither is the specific order of events through the time of the liturgy without its own meaning-giving importance. We approach and we *enter* the time which is the worship service, there is *duration* through which the sequence of events is not haphazard but is ordered or patterned according to a predetermined plan, and there is an *exit* from this time. The meanings which are foreseen and then realized in this ordering of events also derive, I shall say, from the iconic representation of 'boundary crossing'.

---

56. Empereur, *Worship*, 155. See also W. Jardine Grisbrooke, 'Oblation at the Eucharist' *Studia Liturgica* 3 (1964), 227–39, and 4 (1965), 37–55; or Colin O. Buchanan, *The End of the Offertory: an Anglican Study* (Bramcote: Grove Books Ltd., 1978).

57. Michael B. Merz 'Gebetsformen der Liturgie' in (H. B. Meyer, et al., eds.) *Gottesdienst der Kirche: Gestalt des Gottesdienst* (Regensburg: Verlag Friedrich Pustet, second edition, 1990), vol. III, p. 105 (my emphases); Merz seems to me to capture better than most the subtle dynamics of the relationship between prayer leader and congregation in terms of 'who is saying what to whom'.

58. Some of this signification, admittedly, consists in what I shall later describe as indexical; see both below, pp. 170–6, and above, ch. 1, n. 101, my references to Joyce Zimmerman.

If we had not previously known it, following Ricoeur's massive exposition thereof we can hardly now not understand that our apprehension of *the meaning of temporal passage* derives from *our capacity for 'emplotment'*. This is the particular form of human 'grasping together' which 'makes a story . . . out of action[s]', 'the operation that draws a configuration out of a simple succession'.[59] According to Ricoeur, time becomes a meaningful entity to the extent that we can 'render' it in – or into – narrative form.[60] The ordering of the actions of the liturgy is thus similarly an act of emplotment, a meaning-giving strategy; it is 'meaning [which] occurs through structure, by one thing set next to another'.[61] The question which yet remains is: *which* meaning(s) does this particular configuration of events set forth?[62] In Ricoeur's terms: what is the narrative configuration (story) which renders these events to be more than a random assemblage of actions? Or, in Peircean terms, what is the interpretant which gives the signs their meaning? I said earlier in this chapter that implicit in most of the several 'readings' of the meaning of worship is some general notion of 'frontier' between humanity and God which, in the liturgy, is represented in iconic signs, is approached by the worshipping people and, in imagination, is traversed. Within *this* 'narrative configuration' (of the actions in the liturgy) meaning is given in the fusion (grasping together!) of lived experience and transcendent vantage point, in the coupling of identity (a recognizable world) with otherness (our lives viewed from God's perspective), in an apprehension of our immediate moment from 'salvation history's' long perspective. Christianly, we call this time and space so configured 'the presence of God'.[63] The 'narrative configuration' ('emplotment'), then, which 'makes a story out of [the] actions [of the liturgy]' is the

---

59. Ricoeur, *Time and Narrative*, vol. I, pp. 44, 65.

60. So, *ibid.*, 53: 'Time becomes human to the extent that it is articulated through a narrative mode'; see similarly Ricoeur's essay 'Narrative Time', *Critical Inquiry* 7 (1980), 169–90, esp. p. 169. On the 'rendering' of an account, see *Time and Narrative*, vol. III, pp. 152, 177.

61. Lathrop, *Holy Things*, 33; see also *ibid.*, 82: ' "Meaning" is an abstract idea. In fact what the people grasp in the liturgy, what they become part of, is a palpable order and pattern, an order of service.'

62. It is not wholly clear to me that Lathrop pushes on to ask this question. His conception of 'juxtapositions', in which no single meaning or set of meanings ever achieves hegemony over others, yields a *sort* of deconstructionist view which leaves, as we have seen, 'a hole in the fabric of things, through which life-giving power flows into the world' (*ibid.*, 212). There is no doubt that, for Lathrop, the 'content' of this hole is God (*ibid.*, 135, 173, for example) or Jesus Christ (*ibid.*, 115). Perhaps this is as much as one can ever say. On the other hand, I have the feeling that at least the question, if not an answer, can be further sharpened.

63. Of course, there are numerous ways of naming it; see for example Bridget Nichols' frequent use of the idea that the liturgy 'proposes' or 'presents the possibility of the Kingdom'; *Liturgical Hermeneutics*, e.g., 53, 74, 83–4, 191, 255, 258.

sequence: 'entrance into, presence within, and return from' an encounter with the divine.

Across the remarkable proliferation of new orders of service in western Christianity through the concluding decades of the twentieth century – as a response to, and manifestation of, the so-called Liturgical Movement in the western churches – there is an equally remarkable uniformity, both in their basic, and in their more detailed, structures.[64] They are commonly arranged in four components: an opening or introductory rite, followed by what is called the Service of the Word, a rite for the celebration of the Eucharist, and a 'dismissal' or 'sending' rite.[65] The term *ordo* is sometimes invoked for this near universal 'shape of the liturgy' (as we have learned to call it following Gregory Dix's extraordinary influence in this respect). Dix was confident the pattern could be traced back to the early church; some share this general confidence,[66] others are more doubtful.[67] While no student of worship is *ever* free to disregard matters of historical provenance, in some respects my concerns need not await final settlement of those issues; my interest is in observing how Christians organize the time of the liturgy[68] in the dawning moments of the twenty-first century.

The 'Service for the Lord's Day' of the Presbyterian Church (USA) conforms closely to the pattern (*ordo*) I have described as now widely (ecumenically) accepted in the churches. It names its four definitive stages as 'Gathering', 'The Word', 'The Eucharist', and 'Sending'.[69] I shall accordingly allow it to be a representative example of this *ordo*. The *Book of Common Worship*, within which 'Service for the Lord's Day' is set, is further helpful

---

64. See, for example, John R. K. Fenwick and Bryan D. Spinks, *Worship in Transition: the twentieth century liturgical movement* (Edinburgh: T. & T. Clark, 1995), ch. 12.

65. The General Instruction on the Roman Missal (GIRM) specifies 'six structural units' for the revised Order of Mass (*Ordo Missae*), namely, introductory rites, the liturgy of the word, the preparation of the gifts and altar, the eucharistic prayer, the communion rite, the conclusion. Typefaces in 'The Order of Mass', *The Sunday Missal: texts approved for use in Australia and New Zealand* (Sydney: Wm Collins Pty Ltd, 1982), pp. 20–95, suggest five divisions: Introductory Rites, the Service of the Word, the Liturgy of the Eucharist, the Rite of Communion, and a Concluding Rite. Joyce Zimmerman's analysis of the Mass assumes four divisions comparable with the four found in the Presbyterian 'Service for the Lord's Day' which I shall follow here (Zimmerman, *Liturgy as Language of Faith*, 135, 139–65).

66. For example, Lathrop, *Holy Things*, ch. 2.

67. See Paul Bradshaw, *The Search for the Origins of Christian Worship* (London: SPCK, 1992), 139ff.

68. Not a few studies are devoted to what they describe in their titles as 'the time of the liturgy'. My impression is that these nearly all attend to *the time in which the liturgy is set* (day, week, year, cosmic cycles); I have not seen many attending to the way in which *time is organized within* the liturgy; the essays of James Empereur referred to above are valuable exceptions to this. See also, perhaps, Hoffman, *The Art of Public Prayer*, ch. 1.

69. 'Service for the Lord's Day' in *Book of Common Worship* (Louisville KY: Westminster/John Knox Press, 1993), 33.

in that its editors have supplied a succinct commentary, giving, as they perceive it, 'A Description of [the] Movement and Elements' of their order of service.[70] I will allow their insights to guide me.

Under 'Gathering', the *Book of Common Worship* is unambiguous about whence begins the dialectic of worship: 'Worship begins with God. God takes the initiative and calls us into being.'[71] Thus is the 'Call to Worship' – either constructed from or accompanied by scripture sentences – seen as God's initial summoning or invitatory word to the people.[72] On the other hand, it is at least interesting and perhaps significant that, with the boundary breached so to speak, quite the bulk of the action (utterance) of the 'Gathering' (in orders of service such as this) quickly passes to the people. There is an Opening Prayer ('Adoration is the keynote of all true worship, of the creature before the Creator, of the redeemed before the Redeemer'),[73] and/or a Hymn of Praise ('which tells of God's greatness, majesty, love and goodness').[74] This is followed by an act of Confession which now does elicit an answering response from God's side ('The assurance of God's forgiving grace is declared in the name of Jesus Christ').[75] Then follows the exchange of such reconciliation among the people themselves (more frequently the 'Kiss of Peace' is placed in the context of the Eucharist), which then gives way to a kind of shout of acclamation: 'With gladness, God is praised in song, for the gift of God's grace brings joy.'[76] It is on this note that the 'Gathering' concludes.

The second movement in 'Service for the Lord's Day', 'The Word', is more equally proportioned in terms of the divine and human interchange. It does begin with a prayer '[that we may be] receptive to the life-giving Word'. But almost the entire first half of the section is given over, uninterruptedly, to God's address both through canonical writings and the contemporary exposition thereof. Then at roughly midpoint the dynamic

---

70. *Ibid.*, 34–45; a note on p. 45 indicates that the materials are drawn from the Directories for Worship of the two contributing churches.

71. *Ibid.*, 34.

72. Is this perhaps a theological version of the point of view I described in earlier chapters as our now identifiable inability to cross the frontier, leave the platform, breach the membrane? The theology of the liturgy says that only as radical otherness *allows* itself to be approached, only as otherness makes itself cognizable – theologically, only by the grace of God, that is – can this dialogue across the boundary line begin. Thomas Krosnicki writing of the priest's greeting of the people in the Mass says: '[T]he specific function of the liturgical greeting is to mutually declare, affirm, and confess that the community has taken on a dimension bigger than itself. The eucharistic assembly is not simply a sociological grouping of individuals . . . it is the result of grace calling individuals to become the ecclesial Body' (Thomas A. Krosnicki, 'Grace and Peace: greeting the assembly' in (Peter C. Finn and James M. Schellman, eds.) *Shaping English Liturgy: studies in honor of Archbishop Denis Hurley* (Washington, DC: The Pastoral Press, 1990), 104.

73. *Book of Common Worship*, 35.   74. *Ibid.*   75. *Ibid.*   76. *Ibid.*, 36.

passes to the response of the people – 'in song, affirmation of faith, prayer and offering'.[77] The commentary never states it so, but the impression is available that the 'Word' section is somewhat more settled in the relationship (between people and God) than was the 'Gathering': there initiatives had to be taken on both sides, the relationship had to be established. The 'Word' section assumes that all that has now been resolved and, so to speak, a 'mature' conversation will ensue: God has something to say and the people are expected to make suitable response, to be 'responsible'.

The third section, regularly seen as paired with the second,[78] begins again with the divine initiative:[79] the gift of peace – as Dix memorably described it, 'the greeting of the Lord to his own'[80] – and the setting of the table (note 79 above). Thereafter, though, the action is mostly that of the people; Eucharist means 'thanksgiving'. This section of the liturgy therefore takes its character from the Great Thanksgiving prayer without which the meal would not be eucharistic. The people share the communion thus celebrated in the prayer, and then offer themselves for service in the post-communion prayer which, in Protestant euchology anyway, will almost always include an oblationary element.

The fourth part, 'Sending', is the counterpart of the first, 'Gathering'.[81] So then, as the dominant actions there were the people's acclamation, their act of contrition, and the reassurance of God's mercy – all this by way of taking their place in God's presence – so here the critical note is the divine blessing as people make ready to return to their familiar world. As the commentary has it: 'Assured of God's peace and blessing, we are confident that God goes with us to our tasks.'[82] By all means, 'mission' (i.e., people's glad acceptance of their responsibilities as disciples) is not out of sight in this section (the very name 'Sending', in its allusion to 'apostolicity', ensures this). But without the empowerment – and the grace of God – given in 'blessing', this can only be a variously resigned or strident

77. Ibid., 37.

78. Martimort, for example: '[T]he Lord passes by under the signs of the gospel and the Eucharist' ('The Dialogue Between God and His People', 151), or Lathrop, 'The ordo for the Sunday meeting is word service and meal' (Holy Things, 51).

79. 'Service for the Lord's Day' retains the point of view for so long popularized by Gregory Dix that the 'first action' of the Eucharist is an 'offertory'. That construal is now widely seen as mistaken (see n. 56 above) and has been replaced by a point of view which sees the 'Setting of the Table' as the reception into the community of God's eucharistic gift to the church.

80. Dix, Shape, 103.

81. So Nichols, Liturgical Hermeneutics, 113–15, 'Recrossing the Threshold: the Post-Communion' (Nichols, then, locates the 'return' slightly before the 'Sending' section; but her conception conforms exactly to the 'boundary crossing' notion I have employed).

82. Book of Common Worship, 45.

commitment to philanthropic humanism. Blessing is thus the *sine qua non* of mission.

Iconicity and liturgical meaning

Iconicity is semiosis effected on the basis of commonality or similarity between a sign's vehicle and its object. The iconicity of liturgical signs, I have suggested, depends upon their *offering a likeness* of how we imagine it might be to see the world from God's point of view. I have said that somewhere implicit in such signification is the notion of a human frontier; and I have said that this notion translates into actual iconic signs by drawing on spatial and temporal reference points. They effect the sense 'here' and 'there', of 'coming to' or 'coming away from' the particular otherness which we call 'the presence of God'. They give a 'narrative structure' to the time of the liturgy, such that one has the clear sense of 'entrance, duration, and exit'. Spatiality and temporality, in turn, depend upon or derive from human embodiment: we orient ourselves within space, and we differentiate one space from another, by way of turning the body or moving the body within and between spaces. Similarly the passage of time is experienced as the body anticipates the future and lives through presence into pastness. Though spatiality and temporality are decisive in the iconic representation of 'the presence of God' (as I hope I have shown), they are not, in fact, the only form or means of such iconic representation. Limitations of space prevented me from a further section on the relation of art and worship – art in terms both of visual spectacle and in musical audition. The deep and implicit kinship between the arts (visual and acoustic) and worship lies precisely in the 'boundary pressing' iconicity of the former.[83] These are media which directly effect a sense of 'limit' and of 'transcendence'; hence their long-established role in worship.[84] Of course, all these are accompanied by, and in large measure are interpreted within, the linguistic descriptions of God which are offered in worship; but this more properly belongs within the symbolic dimension of liturgical signification to which we have still to come.

A relation of similarity, however, is the least logically strenuous form of signification. A likeness cannot be 'proven' or 'established'; it must rest with the sign-recipient's ability to 'see' or 'comprehend' the suggested

---

83. From a vast literature on worship and the arts, I cite, purely representatively, the issue of *Reformed Liturgy & Music* 28 3 (summer 1994), 'Worship and the Arts'.
84. See below, perhaps, pp. 272–4, 278–9, where I adduce references to the proximities of art and religious sensibility.

similarity. The abductive inferential process, we recall, is logical – at any rate, not illogical – but with the logic more nearly of an 'informed guess' or 'imaginative presumption'. Iconic signs of worship can never 'demonstrate' that of which they are the signs. Thus does the iconicity of worship *suggest*, point to, that of which it is the sign – which is to say, this realm which is actually beyond us and which we can only apprehend in terms of our sense of boundary or frontier (again I mention that the way in which we 'clothe' this sense of radical alterity with our inherited images of God must await a treatment of the symbolic order of liturgical signification).

If abduction is the least logically stringent form of semiotic inference, it is also – in fact, correlatively – the most productive. In other words, here imaginative speculation (though disciplined under the sign) is allowed its greatest freedom; and this, in fact, is the source of the meaning effected in iconic liturgical signs. As the worshipper moves into space which is *perceptibly different* (visually, audibly) from the space from which he has just come, it becomes possible to suppose that *this might really be* how it is with 'God's space'; as the congregation is gathered in a great song of acclamation, it is not beyond imagination to suppose that it has indeed crossed the frontier and has joined some celestial choir; as the prayer-leader (presiding minister) actually moves from among the people, whence she has led the prayer of confession, to the raised sanctuary area, whence she now proclaims God's mercy and forgiveness, it is in some sense realistic to suppose that this is indeed 'Christ's word of grace to us'.[85] And so on, touching here only the initial movements. As Bridget Nichols has it: '[The liturgy intends] a gradually and carefully controlled metamorphosis of a congregation who have presented themselves in faith, in the presence of God . . . [before] . . . returning them finally to their secular lives charged with the weight of their liturgical experience.'[86] All this, I am suggesting, is the work of the iconic signs of worship.

Indexicality

From time to time I have drawn attention to the complicated relationship between 'meaning' and 'meaningfulness'. The former, I have suggested, tends to have a qualitative sense: one asks about *which* meanings and *whose* meanings; whereas meaningfulness has rather to do with quantitative

---

85. *Uniting in Worship: Leaders' Book*, 84.   86. Nichols, *Liturgical Hermeneutics*, 103.

dimensions: an action or utterance is rated as *more or less* meaningful.[87] The distinction thus allows us to speak of meanings as though the meaning-bearing signs themselves are relatively stable, and as if it is the articulation of them which is variously meaningful. From this point of view, a blessing would always be a blessing, but: 'the way he did it made it practically meaningless'. This is perhaps what we have in mind when we distinguish 'text' from 'performance'. But already we slip and slide. *Can* the action have been a blessing if no blessing has been received? Perhaps in the end *all we have* are signs, some of which are successful (a blessing in which people truly know they have been blessed) and other signs which do not achieve the semiosis which was hoped of them, or which was at least within their semiotic potential.

Complicated as it is, we do need somehow – if only for analysis, and then the correction of our habits – to distinguish between such sign as-semblages as I was describing in the previous section – the *formal structures* in which 'one thing is set next to another' – and the *performance or articulation* of those forms such that the semiosis inherent within them indeed comes to fruition. In at least two of the vignettes reported at the beginning of chapter 4, the *manner of their articulation* seemed to be determinative of the meaningfulness or otherwise of the liturgies under review. In one case, I thought, the leader supposed himself to be constructing significations of personal informality but instead communicated avuncular condescension; in the other, the manner in which the prayers were prayed signalled an unexpected authenticity – the prayers *were prayed* rather than read. In both cases, though with opposite estimations, I ventured the opinion that the manner of the articulation directly affected, first, the sense of meaningfulness which attended them and then, practically inseparably, the actual meanings which were conveyed. Yet, as I said just now, we somehow do feel the need to distinguish the meanings of the signs and the meaningfulness of their articulation. It is in this respect that I incline to think that Peirce's second sign-type, the indexical sign, can assist us.

The indexical sign is characterized by Secondness, by direct factuality. It 'represents an object by virtue of its connection with it' (CP 8.368, note). The index is 'like a pointing finger'; it 'directs [attention] to a particular object of sense'; it 'designates the subject of a discourse' (CP 8.41);

---

87. Roy A. Rappaport, *Ritual and Religion in the Making of Humanity* (Cambridge University Press, 1999), 52ff. (summary, e.g., p. 58) speaks of 'meaning' in terms of 'canonical rituals', and of 'meaningfulness' as 'self-referential ritual'; ch. 3 of his text is then given over to self-referentiality and ch. 4 to canonical rituals.

it 'assures us of a positive fact'(CP 4.448). Whereas an iconic sign can effect its signification quite independently of the object of which it is the sign, with an index this is wholly impossible: 'the index is physically connected with its object; they make an organic pair' (CP 2.299). For our purposes, perhaps, the most important aspect of indexical signification is that it is indices which ground signification in that dimension of reality we were inclined, in high modernity, to describe as 'objective' – a world other than oneself, not of our own making. It is the indexical dimension of signs, then, that secures the 'finding' side of the 'finding-making' dialectic which in earlier chapters I outlined as our present-day reckoning of the human apprehension of meaning (see pages 63–6, above). To encounter Secondness is to encounter that which is not myself; it is the experience of putting one's shoulder to a door which will not budge (CP 1.24), it is the 'hard fact' that 'we are continually bumping up against' (CP 1.324). T. L. Short, in an important discussion of Peirce's indexical sign, says it was his (Peirce's) discovery of Secondness that 'enabled him, finally, to escape Kant's idealism'.[88]

When a leader of worship undertakes some action which purports to be one of 'boundary crossing' (the most direct example is that of leading public prayer) yet in such a way that the worshippers have *no sense* of the iconicity inherent in the action, they will know that something is adrift; there will be at least some small crisis of meaning. The reason is that there is here a clash of semiosis: the iconic sign wanted to say 'crossing the frontier', but the indexical signs – the 'multitude of tiny signals' to which I made reference earlier – all signified 'language for this human audience'. It is not too much to say that this clash arises when the person himself or herself performed the action or announced the words while lacking any sense of their iconic (boundary crossing) meanings. *Indices*, we heard from Peirce, *tell us what is the case*, the index 'represents an object by virtue of its connection with it'. These, then, are the signs which tell us what is the case with respect to the mind, or spirit, or presumptions of the person so speaking or acting. It is the indexical signs which signal (usually pretty accurately, I would say) when 'the presider's spirit' has become detached from 'the presiding techniques';[89] or, conversely, they are the signs which surprise us into realizing that 'this prayer was actually prayed' when we supposed it would be read, or which tell us that 'we were truly blessed'.[90]

---

88. Short, 'What's the Use', 38; see esp. *ibid.*, 38–41.   89. Hovda, *Strong, Loving and Wise*, 1.
90. Willimon, *Worship as Pastoral Care*, 210.

It should not surprise us that many, or most, worshippers are unable to identify the seat of, or the reason for, their sense of not being blessed even as a blessing is being pronounced over them, or their feeling that the prayers were very beautiful but somehow 'formal' or 'unreal'. Peirce had already said that so close is the contiguity of sign-vehicle and the sign's object in indexical signs that 'the interpreting mind has nothing to do with this connection, except remarking it after it is established' (CP 2.299). Can we be mistaken? Can the person praying have become so professionally skilled that the language sounds exactly 'right'? Or, oppositely, can the person genuinely 'mean' what she or he is doing, yet give an impression otherwise? Of course. It is always the character of semiosis that it can deceive. We should not here allow ourselves, however, to be ensnared in the ancient enigma about intentionality: that is, how can one make decisions about the state of someone else's mind on the basis of signs external to that mind? *That is not the problem for us*. On the one side (that is, as worshipper) it does not really matter whether I correctly or falsely gauge the state of mind of the person leading the prayer or offering blessing: what counts for me as liturgical meaning is that the iconic signs and the indexical signs cohere – that the manner or bearing of the person signifies to me blessing or prayer (if I am deceived by professionalism, so be it; though I suspect this is a rarer event than may be supposed. Indexical signs are more reliable than we think). And, on the other side, what is critical for worship leaders is not whether or not we can 'bluff it', but that we should bend our energies *actually* to do what we are undertaking to do – that is: actually to offer prayer to God, actually to transmit God's absolution, or actually to bless people in God's name.

There are doubtless many factors which contribute to actions being formal signs, the 'meaning' of which has been betrayed or evacuated by the fact that such signs were not 'meant'. The most prevalent of these – the possibility or tendency must nearly be omnipresent – is what Max Weber described as 'routinization': this is when religious forms, forged in charisma, '[become] either traditionalized or rationalized or a combination of both'.[91] As Weber describes it, in religious devotion 'the rites [are] symbols of the divine'; but 'once it [devotion] is missing, only the bare and formal . . . ritualism remains'.[92] I should suppose that pretty well everyone

---

91. Weber, *Economy and Society*, 246.
92. *Ibid.*, 530. For Luther's protestations against a Protestant 'routinization', see Gordon W. Lathrop, 'New Pentecost or Joseph's Britches? Reflections on the history and meaning of the worship *ordo* in the megachurches', *Worship* 72 (1998), esp. 535–6.

who has ever had some experience of leading worship knows how difficult it is steadily to be 'conscious of and conscious to every person in the assembly'.[93] Perhaps the only thing more difficult is to be similarly conscious of and conscious to the *actions* and *words* one is undertaking on such an assembly's behalf. Without this consciousness, however, the signs will almost inevitably succumb to some degree of 'bare and formal ritualism'. The point I am making here is that this will certainly be signified;[94] and the signs will be indexical: indices of a presence or absence of the person's spirit *in* the liturgical actions he or she is undertaking.

Another contributing factor to an evacuation of 'presence' in, or to, the signs of worship one is undertaking is the juggernaut power of contemporary ideas concerning leadership roles in an assembly of people. If one is influenced (unwittingly, perhaps) by the idea that effective communication depends upon the entertainment of one's audience – this is more subtle than it sounds; how many worship leaders assess their work in terms of whether people 'liked it'? – one will scarcely be equipped to realize the meaning inherent in the iconic signs of 'boundary crossing' such as I described.[95]

A third influence for the evisceration of the liturgical signs' meaning is what Francis Mannion has called the 'politicization' of the liturgy. This is – again shaped by forces prevalent in contemporary society – the usurpation or exploitation of liturgical gatherings in order to 'redirect [the liturgy's] transforming operationality into political and legal channels'.[96] This happens whenever worship is used to 'make a point' extraneous to itself – even if the 'point' is entirely worthy (as, for example, in 'demonstration' liturgies).[97] We are reminded that worship can never be a means to some ulterior end; it exists as the Council of Bishops put it, 'for the sanctification of [people] and the glorification of God, to which all other activities of the Church are directed as towards their goal'.[98] A disparagement of 'politicization' in worship is *not* to say that worship will somehow be apolitical, having no critical 'edge' in terms of the culture in which it finds itself. We are reminded quite frequently that, to be true to itself, Christian

93. Hovda, *Strong, Loving and Wise*, 69.
94. Sequeira cites Erving Goffman to the effect: 'A person can stop speaking, but he [*sic*] cannot stop communicating with his body; in doing so he must say either what is right or what is wrong; but he cannot say nothing at all'; Sequeira, 'Liturgische Körper- und Gebärdensprache', 211.
95. See Lathrop, *Holy Things*, esp. 174–5; also *ibid.*, 144–6, and the same author's *Holy People*, 23 and 199.
96. Mannion, 'Liturgy and the Present Crisis of Culture', 118.
97. Lathrop, *Holy People*, 115.   98. The 'Constitution on the Liturgy', section 10.

worship will – inevitably – find itself in critical confrontation with prevalent norms.[99] Nor should we be under the illusion that liturgy is not itself a site of political contestation.[100] Recognition of the fact that it is so is not, however, warrant to *make* it so. I stand by my asseveration: when leaders or people are distracted from worship's fundamental intent – in my language, to bring us to the frontier – it, worship, is betrayed.

In summary, we need to be wholly vigilant to the traps contained in notions such as 'performance' and 'communication'; even 'education' and 'edification' are not beyond suspicion. These coalesce all too easily with the prevalent social tendencies I refer to, to gull worship leaders into a false sense that the action is contained entirely within the room; that is, that the language (prayers included) are for the people's consumption, that the actions are either those of entertainers making sure that their congregation should 'enjoy the show', or of agents of social change intent on making sure people 'get the point'. There is no iconicity here; and the indexicality will be disastrously revealing.

Given the difficulty which I suggested all liturgical leaders experience in holding steadily before them their need to be present to the people and no less present in their actions, is such presence just too much to ask, a counsel of perfection? I will return to this in greater detail in the next chapter where I come to matters of sign-production. For the moment, I shall admit that certainly it is difficult, it requires discipline, and is gained only with practice; but it is not impossible. In fact it is neither more nor other than the 'Constitution on the Liturgy' was looking for in its sentences about 'thoughts matching words', about 'full, conscious and active participation', and about pastors and other ministers being 'thoroughly penetrated with the spirit and power of the liturgy'.[101] Simply put, in order to lead worship, leaders *must themselves be worshippers*. And it is this, I have wanted to say, or its absence, which is signalled in the indexical dimension of their significations.

---

99. So, for example, Lathrop, *Holy People*, 165. Lathrop's 'juxtapositions' thesis leads him, throughout his books, to set the liturgy in critical interface with prevalent cultures (see particularly Part III of *Holy People*). On matters of worship and social justice generally, there is a vigorous literature. I cite, again representatively: Tissa Balasuriya, *The Eucharist and Human Liberation* (Maryknoll: Orbis Books, 1979); Mark Searle (ed.), *Liturgy and Social Justice* (Collegeville: The Liturgical Press, 1980); James L. Empereur and Christopher G. Kiesling, *The Liturgy that Does Justice* (Collegeville: The Liturgical Press, 1990); Kathleen Hughes and Mark R. Francis (eds.), *Living No Longer for Ourselves: liturgy and justice in the nineties* (Collegeville: The Liturgical Press, 1991).

100. Walter J. Hollenweger, 'Intercultural Theology', *Theological Renewal* 10 (1978), 2–14, see esp. p. 11; also, Michael Warren, 'The Worshiping Assembly: possible zone of cultural contestation', *Worship* 63 (1989), 2–16.

101. 'Constitution on the Liturgy', sections 11, 14, 29.

The indexicality of liturgical signs is not, however, the responsibility only of worship's leaders. Congregations also show in their significations the authenticity or otherwise of their words and actions. Gordon Lathrop thus writes: 'The exchange of peace, which links word and table, signs the community's desire to be mutually forgiving as an image of the forgiveness that they believe comes from God.'[102] And again, 'Concerning the Sunday meeting as sign: Is the Sunday meeting clearly people gathered graciously and peacefully around the two events of word and table?...Is the order [the] ancient one of scripture and meal? Is that what a visitor would say was going on?'[103] Lathrop's last question directs us, of course, to St Paul's interrogation of the Corinthian Christians, precisely we may now say, in terms of the indexicality of their liturgical significations: 'If...an unbeliever or outsider...enters...that person will bow down before God and worship him, declaring, "God is really among you".'[104] The semiosis in question *says what is the case*, it 'represents an object by virtue of its connection with it'.

Symbolic signs

The liturgy involves a 'border crossing', though reality dictates we never are able to leave the platform, penetrate the membrane of our own meanings. Whence then come the meanings of worship, the vast panoply of images, convictions, forms of belief which are the very weft and woof of the liturgy? Iconic signs, we heard from Peirce, 'consist in [their] exhibiting the features of a state of things regarded as if it were purely imaginary' (*CP* 4.448). We surpass the boundary, then, in imagination. But what makes these imaginings *Christian*, what makes them the *content* of a Christian act of worship? It is to this question that Peirce's third sign-type supplies an answer: the meanings of worship (at this level of the question) are both funded from the tradition and are accountable before the tradition. Iconic signs, we may say, allow or encourage an *experience* of the frontier; it is the symbolic dimension of the signs which *interprets* and *disciplines* this experience in the name of the tradition.[105]

102. Lathrop, *Holy Things*, 130.
103. *Ibid.*, 167; see 166–7 for several such sentences.   104. 1 Corinthians 14: 24f. (NRSV).
105. See, e.g., *Environment and Art in Catholic Worship* (The Bishops' Committee on the Liturgy, ed.) (Washington: The United States Catholic Conference, 1978), section 33: '[L]iturgy is more dependent on past traditions than many human activities are. Because it is the action of a contemporary assembly, it has to clothe its basically traditional structures with the living flesh and blood of our times and our arts.'

In the Peircean taxonomy the symbol is governed by Thirdness, that order of being which mediates the world to us and, *vice versa*, through which
we relate to the world. The symbol is thus that form of semiosis in which
the sign's vehicle relates to its object on the basis of convention, law, custom or thought:

> A Symbol is a sign which refers to the Object that it denotes by virtue of
> a law, usually an association of general ideas, which operates to cause
> the Symbol to be interpreted as referring to that Object.
>
> (CP 2.249)

> I define a Symbol as a sign which is determined by its dynamic object
> only in the sense that it will be so interpreted. It thus depends either
> upon a convention, a habit, or a natural disposition of its interpretant,
> or of the field of its interpretant.[106]

> The symbol is connected with its object by virtue of the idea of the
> symbol-using mind, without which no such connection would exist.
>
> (CP 2.299)

Symbolic signs, or the symbolic dimension of the signs of worship, then,
interpret to us the otherwise incomprehensible 'boundary' by which we
are met when we turn from ourselves and towards the otherness which
is 'God'; it is the tradition which in a sense 'clothes' for us this otherwise
blosses Daß, the 'mere that', of our boundedness. We 'know' and we 'name'
this limit in terms of our cultural stocks and resources. But it is then also
the tradition which calls for a degree of accountability in terms of the ways
in which we construct our understanding of our 'limit'. Iconicity helps us
imagine this; but the iconic is formed of Firstness, of that which is not otherwise grounded. The symbol – formed of Thirdness, of thought – brings
to these iconic imaginings a questioning critique. Again, such critical inspection derives from the tradition.

The conceptual content of the liturgy

The biblical scholar Christopher Evans once famously said, 'Christianity
[was] born with a Bible in its cradle.'[107] We could extend the metaphor
by saying, 'and it learned to pray at its mother's knee'. This nice idea is
absolutely *not* intended to obscure the uncertainties now attending the

---

106. Cited by Petrilli ('Towards Interpretation Semiotics', 131) from (Charles Hardwick, ed.)
Semiotic and Significs: the correspondence between Charles S. Peirce and Victoria Lady Welby
(Bloomington: Indiana University Press, 1977), 33.
107. C. F. Evans, 'The New Testament in the Making' in (P. R. Ackroyd and C. F. Evans, eds.)
The Cambridge History of the Bible (Cambridge University Press, 1970), vol. I, 232. I am indebted
to Professor Graham Stanton for directing me to the origin of this quotation.

historical question of formal dependence upon, or actual borrowings from, Jewish prayer by the earliest Christians.[108] It is, on the other hand, to register the fact that our perceptions of God do not come from nowhere. However much Christianity's belief in the resurrection of Jesus formed the lens through which the Bible was read, it was the 'book' which Christianity found in its cradle that provided the basic lineaments according to which it conceived and worshipped 'God'.

To put it like this is to avail ourselves of the 'cultural–linguistic' reading of religions generally – and Christianity particularly – formulated by George A. Lindbeck.[109] In contradistinction to two other conceptions of religion which he describes as 'propositionalist' (religion makes 'informative propositions or truth claims about objective realities')[110] and 'experiential–expressivist' ('doctrines [are] noninformative and nondiscursive symbols of inner feelings, attitudes, or existential orientations'),[111] Lindbeck proposes a reading in which 'religions resemble languages ... and are thus similar to culture (insofar as these are understood semiotically as reality and value systems, that is as idioms for the construction of reality and the living of life)'.[112] Though Peirce nowhere appears in Lindbeck's book and, as far as I can tell, has had no influence in Lindbeck's formulation, the sentence here cited shows not a little affinity with Peirce's Thirdness in so far as religion is seen as culturally formative and interpretative in the inculcation of people's values and world views. Grounded as it is in what seems still to be a structuralist–linguistic paradigm, Lindbeck's formulation seems to me to carry some serious deficits as an account of religion generally – notably with respect to its affective power, that is, what makes religion *more* than a set of rules for belief. Still, in terms of the question which engages us here – whence comes the conceptual content

---

108. See notably Bradshaw, *The Search for the Origins of Christian Worship*, ch. 1. Bradshaw is a self-confessed 'splitter' (*ibid.*, p. *ix*), on the whole highly cautious about finding primitive connections on the basis of later usage. Even so, while he may be right in the view that we are unable to identify specific euchological formulations prior to the Common Era (let alone point to Christian borrowings of them), Bradshaw does allow that 'general structure[s] and themes' (*ibid.*, 25; the particular reference is to the 'grace after meals', but for other prayer types see *ibid.*, 15ff.) are known to us from as far back as the second century BCE.

109. George A. Lindbeck, *The Nature of Doctrine: religion and theology in a postliberal age* (Philadelphia: The Westminster Press, 1984).

110. *Ibid.*, 16.   111. *Ibid.*

112. *Ibid.*, 18. The conception is described in slightly different form several times through the book; see, e.g., 32, 34, 40, or 80. This on p. 62 is perhaps as succinct and informative as any: '[The cultural–linguistic] picture of a religion ... is that of a system of discursive and nondiscursive symbols linking motivation and action and providing an ultimate legitimation for basic patterns of thought, feeling, and behaviour uniquely characteristic of a given community or society and its members.'

of the liturgy? – Lindbeck's 'cultural–linguistic' understanding of religion is instructive. Expanding on his 'coherence' notion of truth,[113] Lindbeck thinks that doctrinal discourse will seldom provide sufficient contextual referentiality for sentences such as 'Jesus is Lord' to be, or become, effective. Where this *will* happen, contradistinctively, is in worship: 'For Christian theological purposes, that sentence becomes a first-order proposition capable . . . of making ontological truth claims only as it is used in the activity of adoration, proclamation, obedience, promise-hearing, and promise-keeping which shape individuals and communities into conformity to the mind of Christ.'[114]

This philosophical-theological analysis of religion, in which 'system[s] . . . of . . . symbols . . . provid[e] . . . legitimation for basic patterns of thought, feeling, and behaviour . . . characteristic of a given community' (see note 112 above), thus accords with historical-biblical studies such as that of Gordon Lathrop in which the very notion of 'assembly' – 'the most basic symbol of Christian worship'[115] – is shown as being carried forward from one moment to another in the tradition, always gathering the past up into its new representation.[116] It also inhabits sentences such as: 'The business of this assembly will look more than a little silly . . . unless we know that the bread and wine, water and words are used here with historical intent';[117] and the idea that when Christians pray in public worship they are 'praying after' those who have already prayed the prayers before them.[118]

When the presiding minister stands before the people and summons them to worship, perhaps in words of scripture or with the ancient greeting, 'The Lord be with you', these words, these gestures *are already – instantaneously in fact – deeply imbued with meaning* for the people. The meaning comes from what Peirce describes as Thirdness: 'convention, habit', 'by virtue of . . . the symbol-using mind' (CP 8.335). These are the meanings which inhabit every move within the liturgy. They are still operative when

---

113. *Ibid.*, 64ff.
114. *Ibid.*, 68; so similarly, 69: '[According to the cultural–linguistic model] propositional truth and falsity characterize ordinary religious language when it is used to mold lives through prayer, praise, preaching, and exhortation.'
115. Lathrop, *Holy People*, 48, and frequently.
116. *Ibid.*, 31–43.   117. Lathrop, *Holy Things*, 100.
118. M. B. Merz, 'Gebetsformen der Liturgie', 113: 'To see the prayers of the liturgy as that which, generally speaking, has given form to the worshipping praxis of the church for centuries, yields for those who pray the role of those who "repeat in their turn" [*Nachsprechen*: 'to repeat after one']. Such a person prays . . . in forms and formulae that for long have been the words of prayer for Jewish and Christian people.'

the leader bids the people depart with God's blessing. It is the depth of the tradition which supplies this order of meanings.

Theological critique of the liturgy

Peirce's Thirdness includes 'thought'. The iconic representations of 'boundary crossing' are thus not exempt from reasoned or theological critique. This critique (the 'thought' which is brought to bear on the iconicity of worship) is also organized out of, and on the basis of, the tradition.

It transpires that Lindbeck's 'cultural–historical' construal of religion functions as actively in a critical capacity as it does in 'supplying idioms for the construal of reality'. 'The question', Lindbeck can say, 'is, "What is Christian?"'[119] It is this religion's cultural–linguistic dimension which supplies a 'frame' or 'screen' (Lindbeck prefers 'lens')[120] by which to assess the 'faithfulness' of any particular representation of it.[121]

In my development of the iconic semiosis of worship, I made a good deal of dependence on Aidan Kavanagh's sentence about liturgy leading its participants 'regularly to the edge of chaos'.[122] It is now necessary (correctively, I think) to observe that this sentence is offered by Kavanagh as part of his spirited *apologia* – following the great Orthodox theologian of worship, Alexander Schmemann;[123] Kavanagh's book is dedicated to Schmemann – of the view that the church's worship is its primary form of theology, the headwaters or the spring from which what we more ordinarily think of as theology (in these writers' terms, *theologia secunda*) should be seen to flow. To cite the sentence again, '[L]iturgy leads regularly to the edge of chaos, and from this regular flirt with doom comes a theology different from any other.' The present plight of the church, these writers maintain, derives from its elevation to a place of eminence that which *can* only ever be secondary: 'I maintain that our fall [from *theologia prima*] into *theologia secunda* has imperceptibly rendered us aphasic and inept in regard to it';[124] 'The served has become servant, mistress has become handmaid.'[125] From this perspective, Kavanagh is determined

---

119. Lindbeck, *The Nature of Doctrine*, 101.   120. *Ibid.*, 83.

121. See *ibid.*, 113–24 on 'faithfulness' as a critical test: 'The task of descriptive . . . theology is to give a normative explication of the meaning a religion has for its adherents'; see also 122. See similarly Irwin, *Context and Text*, 60–1, on 'the notion of the normativity of liturgical tradition'.

122. To give everyone their due, Kavanagh attributes the sentence to Urban Holmes; *On Liturgical Theology*, 73.

123. Alexander Schmemann, *Introduction to Liturgical Theology* (Leighton Buzzard: The Faith Press, 1966); see esp. ch. 1.

124. Kavanagh, *On Liturgical Theology*, 77.   125. *Ibid.*, 83.

to place the liturgical life of the church beyond the scrutiny of *theologia secunda*:

> Both liturgy and Word are called divine by Christians not because God is ultimate author of either, but because liturgy and Word, to a degree unique among all other human media of communication, have God's own presence at their core every time they are enacted. Neither liturgy nor Word can of themselves, therefore, lead the people who use them into those fatal pathologies which other human media lead people into. Liturgy and Word lead us inexorably home.[126]

Kavanagh's ebullient defence of his point of view is undoubtedly refreshing, and has won considerable sympathy among those writing recently on liturgical theology. It also attracts a clear note of caution, however, from those who think that any absolute position is precarious. From a Protestant point of view, where the very headwaters of theology arise *precisely* – albeit in part – from *perceived abuses in the Mass*, a confidence that our worship will 'lead us safely home' is to stretch credibility to breaking point! Geoffrey Wainwright thus writes:

> The Latin tag *lex orandi, lex credendi* may be construed in two ways. The more usual way makes the rule of prayer a norm for belief: what is prayed indicates what may and must be believed. But from the grammatical point of view it is equally possible to reverse subject and predicate and so take the tag as meaning that the rule of faith is the norm for prayer: what must be believed governs what may and should be prayed.[127]

One translates this into Peircean idiom by saying that – in worship at any rate – the imaginative, speculative, *iconic* quality of the 'border crossing' works in tandem with the critical, traditionalizing quality of Thirdness inherent in the *symbolic* ranges of semiotic meaning. Each is necessary to

---

126. *Ibid.*, 122. Cf. similarly, *ibid.*, 91, where, writing on the sentence attributed to Prosper of Aquitaine (*lex supplicandi legem credendi statuat*; 'the rule of supplication establishes the rule of belief'), Kavanagh says: 'the predicate *statuat* does not permit these two fundamental laws of belief and worship in Christian life to float apart or be opposed to each other . . . The verb *statuat* articulates the standard of believing and the standard of worshipping within the faithful assembly.' See also Kavanagh's essay, 'Primary Theology and Liturgical Act', *Worship* 57 (1983), 323–4; and Schmemann, *Introduction*, 15.

127. Geoffrey Wainwright, *Doxology: the praise of God in worship, doctrine and life* (London: Epworth Press, 1980), 218. See also Paul Bradshaw, 'Difficulties in Doing Liturgical Theology', *Pacifica* 11 (1998), 186–8, particularly p. 191: '*Lex orandi, lex credendi* is always a two-way street.' See, finally, Bryan D. Spinks, 'Two Seventeenth Century Examples of *Lex Credendi, Lex Orandi*: the baptismal and eucharistic theologies and liturgies of Jeremy Taylor and Richard Baxter', *Studia Liturgica* 21 (1991), 155–69. On the reciprocity of worship and doctrine, see further below, p. 227.

the other: without the one – iconicity – we have 'only bare and formal ritualism' (Weber); and apart from the other – the historical depth of symbolic meanings – we have no way of knowing whether our iconic signs are any longer 'Christian' (Lindbeck).[128]

Meaning in the liturgical signs

A worship service, and then each of its constituent parts, is a synthetic whole. It is not that iconic signs stand adjacent to indexical signs which then yield way to symbolic signs. *Each* of the actions, utterances, artifacts and spatial arrangements carries or combines within it *all* of these semiotic dimensions. But we have from the outset seen that there is another way in which the kinds of meaning sought in each of the moments, and in the event as a whole, are multiple: there are meanings resident within the *texts* being used; there is meaning, or its absence, in the *performance* of the leaders; there is meaning effected by the worship *space*, its textiles, furnishings and arrangements; there is meaning in the *music*, vocalized and instrumental; there is meaning in the *ordering of the events* one to another; there is meaning which consists in an *experience of the divine*, of God's otherness, of God's immediacy, of God's splendour and God's loving-kindness; there is meaning in the fact that those who undertake this action are an *assembly*, a gathered body of people. Not least there is meaning which enables participants to re-enter the familiar world better able to live in that world coherently and constructively. This near-infinite range in kinds of meaning are all desiderated of worship; the worship will be felt to be disappointing or less than adequate when any one of them is absent.

My analysis of the signs of worship has of necessity been brief and fragmentary. There may perhaps be aspects which have escaped my notice and which stand outside Peirce's threefold taxonomy of iconic, indexical and symbolic signification. Yet I think his schemata do take us a long way towards an understanding of the meanings of worship – perhaps better, of the way in which the meanings of worship are realized. The iconicity of the signs, we have seen, effects the sense of transcendence without which the

---

128. Further critical reflection is undoubtedly required on the *renewal* of the tradition; for example, precisely in terms of the replacement of uniformly male imagery and expressive forms with more evenly gender-balanced forms. My discussion of the tradition in terms of its 'calling to account' function leaves open, I hope, the possibility for its (the tradition's) renewal, more or less through the hermeneutical mechanisms I have invoked: i.e., a 'dependence upon' and an 'accountability before' which is not, however, simply a slavish 'appropriation of'.

event would perhaps be aesthetically pleasing, would entertain us for an hour, might give us precepts for life, but would not be a worship service. As I hope is now self-evident, the iconicity of 'boundary crossing' seems to me desirable in all the moments and actions of the liturgy (even though I was able to highlight only a few important cases in point). But, secondly, a clear sense on the part of worshippers that all these signs are 'meant' – that they are not simply formal undertakings or long-rehearsed routines on the part of those who lead them – seems also critically necessary. I have proposed that it is Peirce's indexical semiosis which effects this kind or quality of meaning for people. Finally, the signs have to bear meaning in terms of locating the language, the actions, and every other dimension of the worship in an identifiable context: the word 'God' has to be as cognizable as it can be; we need to know this is a 'Christian' liturgy to which we have come. This range of meanings, I have suggested, is that which derives from our conventional sets of religious references: the signs are both informed by, and scrutinized by, the meanings we have inherited by way of our membership in this particular 'cultural–linguistic' tradition. If – which is not to me a serious doubt – there remain dimensions of the worship service beyond the scope of this three-part analysis, that is unlikely to have been a question for Peirce. Whatever dissatisfaction he may have felt at the end about his mastery of the sign (see chapter 4, note 73), he at least was fully persuaded that all our meaning happens in signs, and that the ordering of these in Firstness, Secondness and Thirdness is as complete an account as we are likely to get.

6

Sign-production, sign-reception

An analysis of worship according to Peirce's three part taxonomy of sign-types perhaps gains for us some idea of the *kinds* of meaning generated in liturgical signs. It does not yet say *how* such meanings are generated, nor *whose* meanings they are. This is the task addressed in this concluding chapter on the semiosis of worship. Its thesis is that meaning is forged (fastened together) in signs, and that this is a collaborative task for which both the sign's producers and its recipients are equally responsible.

In addition to attempting thus to give some concluding account of the making of liturgical meaning, I hope to draw into relationship with Peirce's semiotic theories of meaning some of the strands of thought rehearsed in earlier chapters: meaning as both making and finding, meaning as 'Best Account', the reasonableness of the meanings of worship, and so on. In all this I am ruled by a degree of circumspection. It was something of a vogue in the 1980s to attempt to find the points of convergence between the Peircean and Saussurean approaches to semiotic theory. That undertaking now appears singularly unpropitious. On the other hand, as I have noted already in various places, many careful scholars of Peirce consider him to have been a forerunner of what we now call postmodernity or late modernity. Where I can, therefore, I shall attempt to draw connecting threads between his conceptions of meaning through semiosis and some of the writers on whose work I drew in the earlier, more general treatment of meaning-theory in our time.

As late as 1907, Peirce wrote: 'The action of a sign generally takes place between two parties, the *utterer* and the *interpreter*.'[1] The sentence pretty well exactly describes the case we need for the production of liturgical

---

1. MS 318. I take the citation from Short's essay, 'Interpreting Peirce's Interpretant', 489.

signs. It does require a certain scholarly gloss, however (Peircean scholars would put it more stringently). As it stands, the sentence seems to accommodate itself to the anthropocentric view (ensconced in Saussurean
semiotics, for instance) that it is humans who singularly produce signs for
other human beings. In the essay from which I have take the citation, T. L.
Short goes on to point out that this anthropocentric view was not Peirce's;
that one must insist that what is essential for his doctrine of signs is *not*
that every sign (necessarily, that is) is uttered, but rather that every sign *is*
interpreted.[2] Peirce in other places was quite clear about this: '[A]ll symptoms of disease, signs of weather, etc., have no utterer' (CP 8.185). It is
fundamental for a proper understanding of semiosis that we understand
that human beings are the *inheritors* and *refiners* of the capacity for meaning
in signs, not its inventors. Allowing all this then, still ours *is* a case of anthroposemiosis as it has been called;[3] the production of liturgical meaning
consists, I am arguing, in the production of signs by one or more persons
(the signs' utterers) for their reception by others (the signs' interpreters).

Every sign, we have learned, consists in a triadic assemblage of three
components: the sign-vehicle, the sign's object and its interpretant. It is
the last which mediates between the first two and it is this element of the
sign which allows the whole to be meaningful. But this, the sign's *meaning*,
is then necessarily a collaborative effect. For, on the one hand, the sign's
producer, in the utterance, has had a particular object, and therefore also
a particular interpretant, in view. But, on the other hand, in the act of
receiving the sign, the sign's interpreter brings *his* or *her* interpretant to
the triadic whole – which may or may not approximate to the interpretant foreseen by the sign's producer. Once again Peirce's seminal sentence
comes into play: 'It seems a strange thing... that a sign should leave its
interpreter to supply a part of its meaning' (CP 5.448, note 1). Successful
semiosis, a meaningful transaction of meaning, therefore depends upon
the ability of both producer and recipient to bring their respective interpretants sufficiently close for their mutual satisfaction.

It is the first side of the collaborative task which is liturgical semiosis to
which I turn in the ensuing section: how does the producer of such signs
undertake that responsibility?

2. Short, *ibid.*, 507; see also *ibid.*, 511–12, on the differences between Peircean semiotic and
Saussurean semiology.
3. For example, Deely's book *The Human Use of Signs* is subtitled: *elements of anthroposemiosis.*
T. L. Short, 'Semeiosis and Intentionality', 201, calls Peirce's anthroposemiosis his 'narrow'
conception of the sign; his 'broad' conception is that which ranges well beyond human
signification.

The responsibilities attending the production
of meaning in signs

Perhaps for the reasons just given, Peirce gave considerably less attention
to the production of signs than to their interpretation.[4] It is for this reason
that I here turn back to considerations already canvassed under the heading 'Authoring meaning' in chapter 3. There I drew upon considerations
of 'agency' offered by Charles Taylor and Paul Ricoeur; I also availed myself
of the semiotic theories of Julia Kristeva. All of these, we may recall, were
reactions against the then regnant positivist and structuralist ideologies
with their depopulated landscapes of 'worldless and authorless objects'.[5]
Taylor and Ricoeur argued forcefully that views such as these evacuated
from human meaning any order of accountability, of responsible agency.
Kristeva's interest was in restoring to poetics an account of the *process of production* in place of the dissection of literary *products*.[6]

Agency – that is, the *accountability* attaching to sign-producers in their
act of production – is by no means out of sight in the forming of liturgical meaning. But a treatment of this is presumably pre-empted by an account of productivity itself. I will attend first, then, to Kristeva's account
of semiotic production. Then I will say something of Peirce's notion of the
'determination' of interpretants, in order to secure the point that for him
the production of signification is not at all whimsical or arbitrary. Finally
I shall turn to the matter of agency as reflected in, first the identification of
person and role, second, the person of the sign-producer vis-à-vis the other
for whom the sign is produced, and third, the personal (that is, embodied)
competencies of sign-producers.

Julia Kristeva wrote out of, and into, the intellectual situation of Europe
in the 1960s and 1970s. Phenomenology and structuralism were the dominant methods. Peirce makes virtually no appearance in her work (or where
he does is lumped together with Saussurean semiology). Further, on the
one hand, her idiosyncratic use of terms is at odds with the Peircean
nomenclature. Hence the necessary circumspection mentioned in introducing this chapter. On the other hand, her impassioned opposition to
the hegemony accorded to consciousness and to rationality, to the perception of language as a static form, to the subsumption of speaking subjects
to signifying systems, and not least to the arbitrariness of the Saussurean

---

4. See Short, *ibid.*, 222, n. 15, on Peirce's subordination of production to interpretation.
5. Ricoeur, *Human Sciences*, 152.   6. See, above, ch. 3, n. 113.

sign tends towards an acceptation of the other – of alterity – in every sign, which characteristic is now also identified as a, or the, distinguishing mark of Peircean semiosis.[7]

Under the motif 'the speaking subject',[8] Kristeva takes up a campaign on a double front. On one side she attacks the universal assumption of high modernity that utterance is the undertaking of a fully autonomous, rationally governed being, that our language happens objectively 'out there in front of us' so to speak, that thought and language are synonymous. On the other hand, she opposes the formalist, structuralist (and post-structuralist) doctrines of authorless texts, of meaning as the product purely of systems. The *subject* of her programme thus counters the systematizing rigours of structuralism; the gerund *speaking*, conversely, directs attention to the always processual nature of this subjectivity, to the circumstance that a *speaking* subject is *not* complete, not assured in its utterance.

Kristeva is not in doubt that speaking subjects require systems. Only so can they converse; even more fundamentally, only so can they articulate to themselves their condition, their sense of themselves, their position in the world. But Kristeva insists that this latter, the subject's sense of himself, herself, is much deeper, undoubtedly prior to a systematizing of it in publicly accessible symbols. This place which – because it is anterior to language – is so hard to theorize, let alone describe, she calls (following Plato) simply the *chora*, 'the place', or perhaps better 'the space'. It is a space inhabited by instinctual drives and subliminal 'awareness':

> Discrete quantities of energy move through the body of the subject who is not yet constituted as such and, in the course of his [*sic*] development, they are arranged according to the various constraints imposed on this body – always already involved in a semiotic process – by family and social structures. In this way, the drives . . . articulate what we call a *chora*: a nonexpressive totality formed by the drives and their stases.

The *chora* is 'not a sign, nor is it a position'; it is rather 'an essentially mobile and extremely provisional articulation constituted by movements and their ephemeral stases.' It 'precedes evidence, verisimilitude, spatiality

---

7. See, e.g., Petrilli, 'About and Beyond Peirce', esp. 321, 351–60. Kristeva could perfectly well be included in the group described in the following sentence (*ibid.*, 322): 'In so far as it is unique, the self is ineffable (cf. CP 1.357); with Lévinas we could say that the self is saying beyond the said, a propensity for significance before and after words; with Oswald Ducrot, the self's specificity lies in the unsaid, the unutterable.' On alterity in Peirce see, further, Ponzio, *Man as a Sign*, e.g., 188ff., 197ff.

8. See above, ch. 3, n. 114.

and temporality'. 'Neither a model or a copy, the *chora* precedes and un-derlies figuration and thus specularization, and is analogous only to vocal or kinetic rhythm.'[9]

It is this inchoate, preconceptual, prelinguistic 'awareness' that is the seat of utterance, the seat of subjectivity. As I said in an earlier place, it is the energy known to every writer and every speaker which *presses* unmis-takably for articulation but which, equally undeniably, has not yet *found* the form it seeks. It is what Carl Raschke calls, '[T]he speaking of the un-spoken that writhes toward articulation.'[10]

Utterance from a Kristevan viewpoint thus depends upon, and consists in, two finally irreconcilable forces: the unsystematizable force which is subjectivity and the systematizing structures which alone give the subject access to utterance. Kristeva names the two forces inherent in utterance its 'semiotic' and its 'symbolic' dimensions. Each is inextricably entwined in the other; yet each is the other's opposite. The subliminal, creative force gathered in the *chora* restlessly pounds upon, 'pulverizes',[11] the very sys-tem on which it depends; conversely the system asserts its law-like force against that which is its only reason for existence.[12] Together they are 'this always split unification',[13] 'this differentiated unity'.[14] Thus, according to Kristeva, does utterance emerge into the world of public signification.

Kristeva's interest is poetics. Her project is thus to theorize the end-lessly surprising, unconventional, disruptive (un-ruly) energy of poetic discourse embedded precisely *within* the rule-governed, code-bound, con-ventionality of language: G. M. Hopkins' 'sprung rhythm' we might say,[15] but certainly, too, its endlessly unconventional (metaphorical) affiliations of words.[16] These 'semiotic' origins inscribed in the 'symbolic' structures

---

9. Citations from Kristeva, *Revolution*, 25–6.

10. Carl Raschke, 'Fire and Roses, or the Problem of Postmodern Religious Thinking' in (Phillipa Berry and Andrew Wernick, eds.) *Shadow of Spirit: postmodernism and religion* (London: Routledge, 1992), 100.

11. Kristeva's text is scattered with descriptions of the action of the 'semiotic' upon the 'symbolic' (page references are to *Revolution in Poetic Language*) such as 'tearing open' (62), 'pulverizes' (51, 63, 69), 'shatters' (60), 'disturbs, disrupts' (55), 'explosion' (69), 'assault' (69).

12. See particularly Juliet Flower MacCannell, 'Kristeva's Horror', *Semiotica* 62 3/4 (1986), 325–55, esp. 325–6: 'Listen to Julia Kristeva: no one else speaks so effectively and so passionately about and from the position of the subject, and no one else is as painfully attentive to the way it feels to be a *speaking being* . . . [T]he sense of the primordiality of language is total for Kristeva; an inescapable fact of being human, language deals the blow after it heals it, installing the human psyche as subject in a world it never made' (her emphasis).

13. *Revolution in Poetic Language*, 49.   **14.** *Ibid.*, 41.

15. See W. H. Gardner's Introduction to *Gerard Manley Hopkins: a selection of his poems and prose* (Harmondsworth: Penguin Books Limited, 1953), pp. *xxxi*ff.

16. James Joyce is an especially important source for Kristeva; see Lechte, *Julia Kristeva*, 54–5, 216ff.

of discourse Kristeva calls 'materiality' or 'musicality': these are the material forms of that turbulent energy which gathered in the *chora* and sought (demanded!) expression in the medium with which it lives so necessarily yet so restlessly:

> Mallarmé calls attention to the semiotic rhythm within language when he speaks of 'The Mystery in Literature'. Indifferent to language, enigmatic and feminine, this space underlying the written is rhythmic, unfettered, irreducible to its intelligible verbal translation; it is musical, anterior to judgement, but restrained by a single guarantee: syntax.[17]

> ... a resumption of the functioning characteristic of the semiotic *chora* within the signifying device of language. This is precisely what artistic practices, and notably poetic language, demonstrate.[18]

It is 'the semiotic' within the 'symbolic' structures of language which leap up to take us unawares every time we read a poem, irrespective of how often we have already read it and supposed we had 'understood' it. It is 'semiotic', Kristeva will say, which is responsible for Barfield's 'pleasure of a felt change of consciousness'. In different terminology, Kristeva calls it *la sig-nifiance* of language.[19]

Returning our attention to the production of liturgical meaning, what seems to me to be Kristeva's inestimable contribution in this is her insistence that the public sign (in her language, the 'symbolic' dimension of utterance) always bears indelible marks of the 'semiotic' energies out of which it was wrought. In her own way, Kristeva is naming what I have earlier called the iconic and the indexical aspects of liturgical signification. Kristeva set herself to theorize poetic diction. With reference to the liturgy we could without difficulty replace her 'musicality' with 'spirit'. When the publicly accessible signs of worship arise from within what we earlier heard described as 'the spirit of the presider' (except that the principle applies to every minister of worship) the one will carry the indelible signs of the other. For example, in the minister's awareness that she and the gathered congregation have come to the human frontier – or even, in some sense, that they have traversed it – the signs will be the icons thereof. Thus the 'gathering of the people' will carry the 'semiotic trace' (in Kristeva's sense of 'semiotic') or an iconic signification (in Peirce's) – not just of one person welcoming others to church but of a gathering of this assembly into

---

17. *Ibid.*, 29.   18. *Ibid.*, 50; on 'musicality' in language, see also *ibid.*, 63, 153.
19. See Lechte, *Julia Kristeva*, esp. 100–1, 129; the fifth chapter of Lechte's book gives a very accessible account of Kristeva's ideas on 'the semiotic' within language.

God's presence;[20] walking, as we heard from Guardini, has the chance of being an 'epiphany'; setting the holy table will signify that this is not a simple, pragmatic necessity but the reception into the assembly of God's eucharistic gifts; and blessings will actually bless people.[21] But, since these 'semiotic traces' are now *inscribed in* the public (i.e., in Kristeva's terms, 'symbolic') dimension of the signs, they are also *indices* of the leader's spirit or self-understanding in her or his act of production. As Kristeva says, all these significations are 'irreducible to [an] intelligible verbal translation'; they are what I described as 'a multitude of tiny signals' *almost* – but not! – imperceptible to ordinary awareness. They are the near invisible – but indispensable – residual marks of a *chora* (spirit, we may now more conventionally say) which 'spoke' – reached for utterance – *as* prayer, *as* blessing, or whatever.[22] Need I now say, then, that it was this 'dimension' or 'quality' or 'texture' of the chaplain's prayer which jerked my attention to the fact that we had met not just for a deeply aesthetic experience, but for worship? Even the seemingly more prosaic responsibility of reading scripture, I said much earlier, will bespeak either 'ministry' or 'pragmatic duty' (above, page 37, but also below, pages 193, 195). In these many different kinds of liturgical sign, we may hope, people will find actions which are 'meant'; which fuse inner and outer; which lead to the judgement that it was 'meaningful' worship.

If it can be supposed that the meaning of liturgical signs thus begins in the deep places of their producer's personhood, self-evidently it does not conclude there. Whatever else they are, the signs of worship are public artifacts. An inward disposition of liturgical intention, my discussion has suggested, is a *sine qua non*. It is at the level of *public* discourse, however, that the signs must effect their work of signification. In my initial attempt to list some of the necessary specifications of a theory of the meanings of worship, I said that the signs which comprise a worship service have to 'make sense' for the participants; so that one requirement of any putative theory is that it be able to say in which ways worship is 'reasonable' (above,

---

20. See my reference to Thomas Krosnicki, ch. 5, n. 72, above.
21. Ronald Sequeira's remarks on the 'human expressiveness' of liturgical signs are especially relevant here; see his 'Gottesdienst als menschliche Ausdruckshandlung', esp. pp. 13–23.
22. Should we be surprised that much of the meaning of worship remains at an intuitive or prelinguistic level? In his ethnographical study of perceptions of worship in four British parish churches, Martin Stringer (*On the Perception of Worship*) frequently found that there was 'something unsaid' (*ibid.*, e.g., 95) in people's accounts of their experiences of worship. Stringer thinks this inarticulate dimension is best not called 'meaning' but 'significance' or 'experience'. I return to his study later in this chapter.

pages 31–5). In another place I said that meaningful signification has to be 'followable' if it, signification, is not to sink into some relativistic swamp in which any meaning is as good as another (pages 72–3). The question now presents itself here in terms of the responsibilities which accrue to sign-producers.

Such responsibilities, from a Peircean perspective, are admittedly not absolute. Given that it is the signs' interpreters who carry their meanings to completion, only *some* control (hence, some responsibility) for this remains with the producer; the old presumption of an author's authority over the signification has been undercut. On the other hand, the producer does still have a collaborative role in this work; for the interpreter to bring *part* of a sign's meaning implies that *some* of its meaning has already been inscribed within the sign. Peircean theory will thus not countenance that abdication of responsibility which, with spread hands and shrugged shoulders, supposes 'people see what they want to see regardless'.[23]

It is of critical importance always to remember that Peirce considered his semiotic theory to be the extension of his study of logic (CP 2.227, for example). We need equally to recall that he found the prevalent notions of logic unduly restrictive, allowing essentially the formalization of that which is already known. Alternatively put, he held all meaning exchange to be fundamentally reasonable, though 'reasonableness' here had to stretch the canonical acceptations of 'reason' or 'logic'. One of the clearest indicators of Peirce's convictions about the 'goal-directed' nature of semiosis[24] is seen in his frequent use of the word 'determines' – or others like it such as 'produces' (CP 5.473), 'gives rise to' (CP 1.339) or 'creates' (CP 2.228)[25] – to characterize the relationship between a sign-vehicle and the sign's interpretant. For the interpretant to be *determined* within the triadic sign assemblage means that *that relationship cannot be random, fickle or arbitrary*. For semiosis to occur there is required (in the nature of the case, Peirce thought) an essential and perceptible reasonableness in the sign's inner relationships. The whole has to 'make sense'. For example: 'A Sign, or *Representamen*, is a First which stands in such a *genuine triadic relation* to

23. See Johansen, 'Let Sleeping Signs Lie', esp. pp. 278ff., where he gives 'three principle reasons why [according to Peirce] communication may succeed'.
24. Short, 'Interpreting Peirce's Interpretant', 524, insists that semeiosis (his spelling) is always and necessarily 'a goal-directed process'. Both in this essay (524–9) and in 'Semeiosis and Intentionality' Short deals extensively with the intentionality within Peircean semiosis.
25. I owe all these references, along with others using the word 'determines' to Greenlee, *Peirce's Concept of Sign*, 100. Greenlee counts ten occurrences of 'determines' or 'determination'.

a Second, called its Object, as to *be capable of determining a Third*, called its Interpretant, to assume the same triadic relation to its Object in which it stands itself to the same Object' (CP 2.274; Peirce's emphases deleted, my own added). It is thus precisely at this point that the sharpest conceivable differences are drawn between Peircean semiosis and Saussurean semiology, where everything is reduced to arbitrariness.[26] Peirce worked prodigiously for his entire career to articulate the immense variety of ways in which semiotic reasonableness or the logic of signification comes to expression. We have barely touched on this in the basic distinctions of sign-types (iconic, indexical, symbolic) and in the double trichotomy of types of interpretant (above, pages 144–7). The point here must be not the variety or complexity of possibilities, but that *all of them arise from his consideration of the 'categories' of existence and the logical derivations therefrom.*

Of course, as we have now heard often enough, the sign's interpreter will bring to the sign an interpretant of her or his own. We will thus, at the appropriate place, have to attend to the reciprocal responsibilities for semiotic meaning incurred by the sign-recipient. For the moment what is of definitive importance is that in *either* case – whether in terms of the sign-producer or of the sign-recipient – *the interpretant is 'determined'*. That is, it stands in an inferential (which is to say, logical, meaningful, not fickle or arbitrary) relationship within the whole. But this means (staying here with sign-production) that it is entirely within the capacity – and thus the agential responsibilities – of sign proposers to determine an interpretant within or for the sign, and hence also to be fully involved in the determination of its meaning – at least in so far as he or she is concerned.[27]

To eschew the idea that meanings fall where they will, I have said, is *ipso facto* to accept some significant degree of accountability for them. Peirce's preoccupation with the 'determinations' of interpretants thus carries across to more general questions of agency. Here a number of threads from earlier formulations are now tied together.

---

26. See my references to Short, n. 2 above.

27. One aspect of the responsibilities of liturgical sign-production thus becomes a responsibility for the maximization of 'communicational' interpretants and the narrowing of the gap between 'immediate' and 'dynamical' interpretants of the signs set forth (see my discussion above, pp. 146–7). This suggestion should not, on the other hand, be seen as diminishing that ambiguity necessarily inherent in liturgical signs – that is, in Peircean terms, their Firstness or iconicity; see Aidan Kavanagh, 'Thoughts on the New Eucharistic Prayers' now in (R. Kevin Seasoltz, ed.) *Living Bread, Saving Cup: readings on the Eucharist* (Collegeville, The Liturgical Press, 1982), 108, and Martin Stringer, 'Situating Meaning in the Liturgical Text', *Bulletin of the John Rylands University Library of Manchester* 73 (1991), 184–5.

First, agency and the question of personal identity: in our earlier re-view of Ricoeur's treatment of agency we heard him insist: '[T]he questions "Who? What? Why?"...form a network of interrelated meanings such that our ability to reply to any one of these questions implies our ability to reply to any other belonging to the same sphere of sense.'[28] In other words, 'what I do' is inextricably bound with 'who I am in the doing of it'. Charles Taylor puts the same point so: 'a basic, not further reducible distinction between *action* and what *just happens* is...ineradicable from our self-understanding *as agents*'.[29] According to this showing, then, when the lector moves to the lectern, it is impossible to separate *self-identity* from *appointed task*. Today this person is not simply 'Mary', or just 'Ken', someone who happens to be rostered on. He or she is the person to whom, today, this congregation entrusts the task of reading the church's scriptures meaningfully in their hearing. 'Who?' is implicated in the 'What?'[30] Similar considerations apply to every other role or ministry. *I am*: the door-keeper,[31] the people's minister of music, the one who today must articulate their prayers, the person who carries God's holy gifts of bread and wine to the table of communion. But now, since the dynamic is reversible ('Who? What? Why? form a network of interrelated meanings'), this self-knowledge inevitably flows back into the action. To know that today I am the lector (that I am entrusted with this role) must shape the execution of the task, and the signs will be formed accordingly. That is, *in* my reading there will now be embedded interpretants signifying that this is not just a task which I accepted good naturedly because someone had to do it; it will signify *as* the reading of holy scripture, and so on. I take it as now self-evident that all this semiosis is of the indexical type.

If identity is related to role, no less is it related to those on whose behalf the role is undertaken. This, too, is seen as a specification of agency: '[A]n agent must be able to designate himself or herself in such a way that there is a genuine *other* to whom the same attribution is made in a relevant manner.'[32] Here, in slightly different idiom, is everything Peirce had wanted to say about the alterity of semiosis. The work of sign construction is undertaken *with* and *towards* those whose work in some important sense

---

28. Ricoeur, *Oneself as Another*, 88; see a different version of this on p. 102 above.
29. Taylor, *Human Agency*, 79 (my emphases). On the connections between agency and responsibility see also Kaufman, *In Face of Mystery*, 143–7.
30. See Lonergan, *A Well Trained Tongue*, 3–6.   31. Above, p. 155.
32. Ricoeur, *Oneself as Another*, 98, some emphases removed. Of course, as the title makes clear, the entire burden of Ricoeur's book is to establish that *self*-identity is a meaningful notion only in the presence of *others* (see *ibid.*, 297, for an overview).

it also is – that is, those who must carry the significations to their completion. It is the collaborative, dialectical quality of semiosis which gives sign-production its directedness, the purposefulness, flagged in Peirce's 'determinations'. Christianly – in terms, that is, of the semiosis of worship – it is this awareness of the other, awareness of those on whose behalf the work is actually undertaken, which enables – demands in fact – a requisite *humilitas*, thus delivering the actor from illusions of grandeur and the action from 'performance' or 'entertainment'. Again: Who? What? and Why? are intertwined.

As a third dimension of agency, the assimilation into each other of person and role leads to the question of personal competencies. People are variously gifted: not everyone is suited to compose the prayers of the people, one does not call for volunteers to play the organ or form a children's choir. There is here a fundamental sense in which the question of agency is related to our embodiment. Ricoeur identifies the body as constituting our 'twofold identification' as agents: '[T]he body is at once *a fact belonging to the world* [people identify me as so-and-so] and the *organ of a subject* that does not belong to the objects of which it speaks [the sense of my own identity comes of not being just another object in the world].'[33] So, on the one hand, it is my sense of myself as minister (my body as the organ of an intentional subject) which fuses task and person as we saw a moment ago. On the other hand, it is my embodied being which – very considerably – determines positively and negatively my giftedness for some liturgical roles and not for others: if my *ear* is not attuned, I had better not lead the singing; if I have no *eye* for space, proportion, line and colour, it makes no sense to offer to design the Pentecost hangings. But, of course, there are few natural attributes that do not need enhancement through the acquisition of knowledge and the discipline of much practice (reading in public, for instance). And even here, natural giftedness and arduous discipline do not yet make me a *liturgical* musician; rhetorical flair is still only the *pre-requisite* for the ministry of lector. These disciplined gifts still require to be harnessed to both historical knowledge and practical understanding of the liturgy: its rhythms and its rationale, its heritage and its purpose. But to recover the point: all these skills, competencies and insights are accumulated in particular *bodies*. To link agency with embodiment like this, however, is to register again how far we have moved beyond questions of

33. Ricoeur, *Oneself as Another*, 54 (my emphases).

simple intention. The very best intentions, without the natural and accumulated competencies in whichever task or role it is I occupy as a minister of worship, will not suffice to generate the signs of worship.

There is an underside to agency, implicit in my treatment so far, but needing to be made explicit. Peircean semiotic theory includes *all* our significations whether we are conscious of them or not. To speak of interpretants being determined should not obscure from us, then, the fact that *not* all our significations will be intentional in the most usual sense of that word. For Short to say that semiosis is 'a goal-directed process' is by way of repudiating the arbitrariness (which is to say, capriciousness) assumed in the Saussurean model.[34] It is to say that when any sign is apprehended as meaning something, *causative origins* for that effect can be traced, not that all such causes were generated consciously (which is why Peircean theory is more interested in interpretation than in utterance). *Some* liturgical signification – and, in disappointing cases, perhaps *much* of it – will be signification other than that supposed, wished for or intended by its producer(s). I spoke, for example, of the lector's self-knowledge as he or she comes to the task of reading; but where such self-awareness is missing, where the person comes to the task unreflectively – 'well, someone has to do it and I'm happy to help out' – interpretants thereof will be in the signification. To suppose that I can undertake one or other of the liturgical ministries without diligence of preparation and a care-filled understanding of the liturgy will similarly manifest itself. *Agency means to accept responsibility for my actions.* My body – which is me in my public dimension; my interface with the world – sometimes says more than I know it is saying.

Positively, however, competence does not mean perfection. At this point, then, we remember Charles Taylor's late modern wisdom about a 'Best Account' theory of meanings. 'Best Account' is what we have learned to live with in the evaporation of modernity's 'great dream' that one day we shall find the finished answer, the last word. 'Best Account' is a reckoning with our human finitude, a repudiation of the 'craving for absolutes' which is how another late modernist characterizes the times in which he himself was formed.[35] Let me then recall Taylor's description of a 'Best Account', now in light of all we have subsequently learned about the collaborative nature of our signs:

34. See above, n. 24.   35. Putnam, *Human Face*, 131.

'Making the best sense' here includes not only offering the best, most realistic orientation about the good but also allowing us best to understand and make sense of the actions and feelings of ourselves and others. For our language of deliberation is continuous with our language of assessment, and this with the language in which we explain what people do and feel.[36]

Taylor, of course, is not speaking about worship. On the other hand, he sees a 'Best Account' as gathering into itself the many divergent kinds of assessment or valuation which people need to find in a religious reading of the world: 'actions' and 'feelings', 'ourselves' and 'others', 'language of deliberation' and 'language of assessment', 'explanations' (understanding, shall we say) of what people do and feel. Such is hardly a bad description of what the signs of worship have to do – have to propose – as the points on which people can hang their own cogitations, feelings and so on in terms of 'making the best sense' they can of God, themselves, their neighbour and the universe.

In my earlier treatment, I closely conjoined Taylor's 'Best Account' with Ricoeur's notion of 'followability', and this, too, now clothes itself in our more recently acquired language of signifying process. For worshippers to complete the meaning of the signs, for them to join their interpretants to our signs with some degree of mutual success, the sign proposals have to be 'followable'. I said in my earlier treatment: followability is the *sense of assent* which a reader or listener either gives or withholds in the receiving of an account.[37] I think it is now not out of the way to say: followability is the degree of ease with which worshippers are able to bring their meanings to the signs proposed, the degree to which they are able to join the proposer in a 'communicational' interpretant of the sign.

The last point I would make about the responsibilities of sign-production hopefully ties the discussion back to my treatment of iconicity and simultaneously anticipates themes still to come in Part III. In Ricoeur's idiom, the signs have to project a 'world before the liturgy'. In his introduction to Hilary Putnam's *Realism with a Human Face*, James Conant writes: 'Wittgenstein says that what we require in philosophy is not explanation but *description*', and links this to Putnam. '"The sorts of descriptions that

---

36. Taylor, *Sources*, 57; for additional references to Taylor's 'Best Account' idea see, above, ch. 1, n. 89.
37. Above, pp. 72–3.

we need..." Putnam writes, "are descriptions in the language of a sensitive novelist." Such descriptions seek to help us to *see* the world differently, to render what is right before our eyes visible to us.'[38] To philosophers and sensitive novelists we might add liturgists, leaders of worship: their task, too, is to 'help [the recipients of their signs] see the world differently, to render what is right before [their] eyes visible'. This exactly accords with Ricoeur's view: 'For what must be interpreted in a text is a *proposed world* which I could inhabit and wherein I could project one of my ownmost possibilities.'[39] And then Bridget Nichols, Kevin Irwin, Gordon Lathrop, Don Saliers and doubtless others see liturgy as doing exactly this. Nichols in her work makes extensive use of the notion 'threshold' with respect to the meanings proposed in worship: 'The working hypothesis [of her analysis of the eucharistic order of the Church of England's *Alternative Services Book*],' she writes, 'is that the performance of the rite is instrumental in placing the congregation in a threshold position with respect to the Kingdom.'[40] Lathrop sees liturgy's 'world proposal' this way: 'Christian ritual dialectic and its trinitarian faith propose a world larger than we had imagined',[41] and subsequently asks, 'What world does the liturgy... propose? How is it... a sanctuary of meaning?' and gives his next several pages to the 'world-making means' of the liturgy.[42] We are at the point of turning to the reciprocal task of sign-reception. Simply put, there can be no reception if there has been no proposal. The proposal, then, in its most fundamental and far-reaching proportions – as we have heard from these authors – is 'a world seen differently', a world in which 'we might project our ownmost possibilities', a 'sanctuary of meaning', perhaps indeed 'the Kingdom of God'.

38. Putnam, *Human Face,* p. *lxii;* Conant's emphases.

39. Ricoeur, *Human Sciences,* 142 (his emphases); see also his *Interpretation Theory: discourse and the surplus of meaning* (Fort Worth, TX: The Texas Christian University Press, 1976), 87–8: 'The sense of a text is not behind the text, but in front of it. It is not something hidden, but something disclosed. What has to be understood is not the initial situation of discourse, but what points to a possible world ... Understanding ... seeks to grasp the world-propositions opened up by the reference of the text. To understand a text is to follow its movement from sense to reference, from what it says, to what it talks about.'

40. Nichols, *Liturgical Hermeneutics,* 91 (emphases removed), and similarly frequently; see her glosses on 'appropriation' and 'threshold'/'threshold position', *ibid.,* 49–50.

41. Lathrop, *Holy Things,* 135.

42. *Ibid.,* 206–17. It is conceivable that Lathrop also has in mind Nelson Goodman's title: Nelson Goodman, *Ways of Worldmaking* (Indianapolis: Hackett Publishing Company, 1978). See also Irwin, *Context and Text,* 329ff., on what he calls liturgy's *lex vivendi*: 'the ethical demands inherent in liturgy as liturgy relates to life.' For Saliers, see his section 'Liturgy as Revelatory Art' in *Worship as Theology,* 197–202.

The completion of meaning in sign-reception

My desire is that this entire section might be seen as a kind of exposition of the scene drawn in the third of my 'moments' of liturgical signification at the beginning of chapter 4 (the faces turned attentively and expectantly towards the preacher, page 116 above). It is difficult for me to recall exactly what were those signifying marks – which we may now identify as indexical – which left the impression with me. But the impression itself is unforgettable: 'The people really wanted to hear what he had to say.' I suppose that perhaps here we see in its clearest form a manifestation of the 'grasping' which I proposed as sitting as near as we are likely to get to the centre of the phenomenon of meaning. The immobility of bodies, faces, eyes, as every attention seemed strained towards the person of the preacher, waiting for each sentence to reach its culmination, assessing how all this might be comprehended, how it should be woven back into the lives of each of them, is the demonstration, manifestation, of the energy we bring to the completion of meaning as it is proposed in signs.

It will perhaps be worth pausing briefly to consider whence comes this mighty energy – the power which drives the entire enterprise not just of meaningful worship but indeed the quest for meaning itself. I shall then want to ask where and how the meanings of worship are grounded, where we may say such meanings are completed. I will say a little on the relationships between proposals and responses; and I will say something more about the 'reasonableness' of the process, now in terms of the canons – such as they are – for a 'correct' completion of the meanings proposed in liturgical signification.

What is this energy which holds an unassuming congregation of ordinary people in its grip as in some sort of magnetic field? Whence comes the insatiable need for understanding? My interest here is not in attempting some sort of historical or evolutionary account of this which must be among the oldest, most intractable of questions. Even were I equipped for such an undertaking – which manifestly I am not – to attempt it here in half a dozen paragraphs would be more than faintly ludicrous. To raise the question is not to attempt an answer. It is to register the abiding importance to us of the question itself. Yet more critically, it is to see that it is this quest, or question, which holds proposers and recipients together in the mutual task of the construction of meaning. For, on the surface, it is not apparent just *why* they should join in the task. On one side, certainly, it is not difficult to account for the diligence of sign *proposers*: they have an agenda, a vested interest we might say, in securing the 'followability' of their meaning proposals. But sign *recipients* are not so clearly under constraint. On the face of things at least, there seems nothing that imposes on them the same disciplinary requirements; they seem free to bring any sandwiches they like to the picnic of meaning[43] (more prosaically: it might seem conceivable that they can join any interpretant to any sign proposal). Of course, they do have freedom; this is the risk to which every sign-producer exposes herself or himself.[44] The question is: how is it that this freedom is not ordinarily abused? How is that, on the whole, few sign-recipients willingly or knowingly distort the 'determinations' offered in the producer's proposal so as to find, willy-nilly, meanings they *wish* to find? (Of course I do not mean in this their frequent need to *disagree* with the proposal; that is quite different, that is to replace the initial proposal with a *counter* proposal. What I am speaking of here is a conscious and wilful *manipulation* of the same proposal.) This then is the question in its multiple forms: whence comes the intuitive self-restraint that actively seeks understanding? Why does the sign attract or elicit an 'answering comprehension'? What is the hidden guiding principle which joins producers and recipients in the absence of overt laws and sanctions? My answer to this question is anchored back to the question which appears to have no answer. It is the instinctive recognition that the human quest for meaning is too fundamental to our well-being, I will say, that (ordinarily) prevents us playing fast and loose with another's meaning and thus holds us to the collaborative task. It is our human need to *understand* (our condition in the world, each other, ourselves) which overrides an inclination to have meaning at any cost. To ask about those heads turned towards the preacher, to ask whence is this energy for the completion of meaning in signs, is to meet the other, more obdurate question about our need for meaning at all. And there is at least

---

43. The catchy idea that 'reading is a picnic where the author brings the words and the readers the meanings' apparently derives from, or about, Jakob Boehme. E. D. Hirsch, in his *Validity in Interpretation* (New Haven: Yale University Press, 1967), 1, cites Northrop Frye (without further attribution): 'It has been said of Boehme that his books are like a picnic to which the author brings the words and the reader the meaning. The remark may have been intended as a sneer at Boehme, but it is an exact description of all works of literary art without exception.' Ricoeur, *Time and Narrative*, vol. III, p. 169, uses the idea in a positive sense but without attribution. Umberto Eco in (Stefan Collini, ed.) *Interpretation and Overinterpretation* (Cambridge University Press, 1992), 23–4, cites Tzvetan Todorov – but 'quoting Lichtenberg à propos of Boehme'.

44. See Ricoeur on 'distanciation', particularly 'The Hermeneutical Function of Distanciation', ch. 4 of *Human Sciences* (also, above, p. 26); see also Merleau-Ponty on 'dehiscence', above, p. 94.

the suggestion that this question has at its heart a religious dimension. Let me then address this as briefly as I may.

At some primitive level our need to understand how it is with us in the world is presumably given with our animality. Daniel Dennett describes an essential requirement for the procreation of any given species – the need, that is, to be able to distinguish both potential mates and potential predators – as 'epistemic hunger'.[45] But now, for longer than anyone can remember, the 'hunger' of Dennett's vivid phrase seems far to have surpassed our elementary needs for survival. We need to know; but, more urgently, we need to *understand*. Putative answers to this quintessentially human question – wherein lies the difference between knowing and understanding? – will perhaps lie somewhere in our capacity for reflexivity, our identity in terms of what Ernst Cassirer called the *animal symbolicum*,[46] and Charles Taylor calls 'the self-interpreting animal'.[47]

We all know there is a sense in which the questions thus raised to us are inexhaustible: '[T]his question, once opened can never be closed', says Taylor of the self-interpretative human project.[48] 'It involves defining what it is we really are about, what is really important to us...[and]... a map of our motivations...we will never complete.'[49] That the 'assignment' (*Aufgabe*) of meaning-achievement is never completed[50] thus directs our attention to that sense of 'boundary' which, I was inclined to say, lies at the centre of all worship. Of course, any temptation to a religious imperialism, the conscription to itself of all who think about human finitude,

45. Dennett, *Consciousness Explained*, 180–1: 'Regular vigilance gradually turned into regular exploration, and a new behavioral strategy began to evolve: the strategy of acquiring information "for its own sake," just in case it might prove valuable someday . . . This marked a . . . fundamental shift in the economy of the organisms that made this leap: the birth of curiosity, or epistemic hunger.' A nice example of 'epistemic hunger' seems to be given in Peter Høeg's novel, *Miss Smilla's Feeling for Snow* (London: Flamingo/Harper Collins, 1993), 126: 'If you're hunting timid animals, like reindeer, you let them catch sight of you a few times on purpose. You stand up and wave the butt of your rifle. In all living creatures, fear and curiosity are neighbouring brain cells. The deer comes closer. It knows that it's dangerous. But it has to come and see what's moving like that.'
46. Ernst Cassirer, *An Essay on Man* (New Haven, CT: Yale University Press, 1944), 26; cf. p. 24: 'Man [*sic*] has, as it were, discovered a new method of adapting himself to his environment. Between the receptor system and the effector system, which are to be found in all animal species, we find in man a third link which we may describe as the *symbolic system*' (his emphases).
47. Taylor, *Human Agency*; see esp. ch. 2, 'Self-Interpreting Animals', but the idea occurs frequently through the book. Similar ideas are explored from a more explicitly religious point of view by Gilkey in his *Naming the Whirlwind*; see esp. pp. 335–6.
48. Taylor, *Human Agency*, 64.   49. *Ibid.*, 68.
50. Ricoeur, *Conflict of Interpretations*, 329: 'This is why reflection is a task – an *Aufgabe* – the task of equating my concrete experience with the affirmation: *I am* . . . [T]he positing of the self is not a given, it is a *task*; it is not *gegeben* but *aufgegeben*' (his emphases).

is to be resisted; many such will not be requisitioned. Yet the two – our quest for meaning and the question of God – may not be so far apart either, as some are willing to admit.[51] On the other hand, there is another sense in which meanings will *not* wait for ever: we have to 'make sense' of things here and now, I need to understand what it is you are saying to me, I have to comprehend the proposal of meaning in your sign. The infinite deferral of meaning, we shall hear from Peirce and others, is in the end the cancellation of meaning. The quest for meaning is conceivably at base a religious quest or question. Yet it needs practical, immediate (if temporary) applications.

In all this, as announced, I am less interested in trying to account for the phenomenon of meaning than in identifying it as the underlying power which holds proposers and recipients in their collaborative task. I return to my congregation with heads bowed towards a preacher and their clear signification: 'We really want to hear what he has to say.' The great human 'assignment' – that we may *understand* – is what turns us towards each other, prevents a wilful distortion of such signs as are offered us, and thus holds us in our joint project of the making of meaning.

Now, *how* is this meaning-completion effected, and in *which respects?* Postmodern deconstructionist theory, in its conviction that signification amounts to no more than 'this innumerable systems of marks',[52] rebuts the notion that meaning is ever completed. From within this conviction, deconstruction was keen to conscript to its purposes what it took to be Peirce's view of 'infinite semiosis'. In his earliest writings, Peirce did say something of the sort: he supposed that the interpretant of every sign constellation itself becomes the sign (sign-vehicle) of a further semiotic process, thus forming an infinite progression of semiosis. In 1902 he had accordingly defined a sign (CP 2.303) as: 'Anything which determines something else (its interpretant) to refer to an object to which itself refers

---

51. Gadamer, *Truth and Method*, 186, for example, thinks: 'This gives the word "understanding" its almost religious tone.' Perhaps the most articulate witness is Weber, *Economy and Society*, 451: 'The ultimate question of all metaphysics has always been something like this: if the world as a whole and life in particular were to have a meaning, what might it be, and how would the world have to look in order to correspond to it? The religious problem of prophets and priests is the womb from which non-sacerdotal philosophy emanated, where it developed at all.' See similarly his, 'The Social Psychology of the World Religions', 274 and 281. And see, finally, Kaufman, *In Face of Mystery*, 225: 'Today we can see that what was developing as "religion" was a sphere of culture within and through which humans would seek and find . . . a sense of the *meaning* of human existence' (his emphases).

52. Jameson, *Postmodernism*, 174, citing Achille Bonito-Oliva; see pp. 28–9, 89–90 above for more, and similar, deconstructionist estimations of signification.

(its object) in the same way, this interpretant becoming in turn a sign, and so on *ad infinitum*'. Derrida seized upon this early definition as supporting his own strategy: 'From the moment there is meaning there are nothing but signs.'[53]

The claim has earned the ire of Peircean scholars, however. Hanna Buczynska-Garewicz says that Derrida's invocation of Peirce 'can only be a misinterpretation' since deconstruction and Peircean semiotic theory 'are contradictory rather than complementary theories [of meaning].'[54] No less interesting, in light of the evolution of his own ideas, is Umberto Eco's judgement on what he calls deconstruction's 'hermetic drift'. Eco's trajectory began in an enthusiastic embrace, in the 1960s, of the then innovative idea of 'readers' response' ('the openness of a work of art is the very condition of aesthetic pleasure');[55] but by the 1990s he had come to the conclusion that 'in the course of the last decades, the rights of the interpreters have been overstressed'.[56] 'Hermetic drift', which he associates directly with deconstructionist theory, is 'the uncontrolled ability to shift from meaning to meaning, from similarity to similarity, from a connection to another'.[57] Students of his novels see there fictional accounts of the real and absolute dangers which befall people when the principle *tout se tient* ('everything is connected') is given unrestrained liberty.[58] Interestingly, given Derrida's original claim on Peirce, Eco now turns to Peirce by way of his *critique* of deconstructionist 'unlimited interpretation'.[59]

But it is the Peircean scholar, T. L. Short, who, in a series of essays from at least 1986, has attacked in sharpest detail the supposition that for

---

53. Derrida, *Of Grammatology*, 50.

54. Hanna Buczynska-Garewicz, 'Semiotics and Deconstruction' in (Rocco Capozzi, ed.) *Reading Eco: an anthology* (Bloomington: Indiana University Press, 1997), 163–72; citations from p. 163. See, similarly, Umberto Eco, *The Limits of Interpretation* (Bloomington: Indiana University Press, 1994), 34–7.

55. *The Open Work*, 39; *The Open Work* appeared in English translation in 1989, but the Italian version, *Opera aperta*, had been written in 1962.

56. Umberto Eco, 'An Author and his Interpreters', in (Rocco Capozzi, ed.) *Reading Eco: an anthology* (Bloomington: Indiana University Press, 1997), 59. Numerous essays in this volume (e.g., Anna Longoni, 'Esoteric Conspiracies and the Interpretative Strategy', 210–16, and Rocco Capozzi, '*Interpretation and Overinterpretation*: the rights of texts, readers and implied authors', 217–34) trace the evolution in Eco's thought from his acceptance of 'openness', through his misgivings with respect to the radical deconstructionists (Paul de Man, J. Hillis Miller, Stanley Fish for example), to his most recent position as delineated in the Tanner Lectures (Cambridge University) published in *Interpretation and Overinterpretation*.

57. Eco, *The Limits of Interpretation*, 26–7.

58. See particularly Peter Bondanella, 'Interpretation, Overinterpretation, Paranoid Interpretation and *Foucault's Pendulum*' in (Rocco Capozzi, ed.) *Reading Eco: an anthology* (Bloomington and Indianapolis: Indiana University Press, 1997), 285–99.

59. See esp. *The Limits of Interpretation*, 37–41.

Peirce 'every interpretant of a sign is another sign of the same object'.[60]
Short insists that it has long been apparent[61] that at about 1907 Peirce
radically revised his mind and thereafter 'deliberately excised that doctrine'. He did so, says Short, precisely because 'that which postmodernists
have found exciting and latched on to', Peirce himself now 'found ab-
surd and jettisoned.'[62] The reason for his 1907 revolution, Short says,
is that 'Peirce recognized that the *indefinite deferral* of meaning is the
negation of meaning';[63] 'the meaning of a word is not its translation into
other words but is the practical bearing of one's accepting its application to this or to that'.[64] We should not ever forget, Short thinks, that
Peirce's semiotic theory was grounded in his Pragmaticist philosophy,
the whole point of which 'is to break the circle of words by making
meaning to depend, ultimately, on possible practical bearings'.[65] Thus
it was:

> necessary to bring out, in one way or another, the fact that meaning
> does *not* consist simply in the translation of words into more words;
> that it is the practical rules of conduct, the actual habits of action, that
> certain words formulate, that are that without which there would be
> no meaning ... [T]he pragmatic maxim ... provides for a possible
> account of how beliefs connect to a nonverbal world and are tested
> against nonverbal experience of that world.[66]

This point – the point at which the sign translates into 'the *practical bearing*
of accepting its application to this or to that' – Peirce named as habit:

> In every case, after some preliminaries, the activity takes the form of
> experimentation in the inner world; and the conclusion (if it comes to a
> definite conclusion), is that under given conditions, the interpreter
> will have formed the habit of acting in a given way whenever he may
> desire a given kind of result. The real and living logical conclusion *is*
> that habit ... The habit alone, which though it may be a sign in some
> other way, is not a sign in that way in which that sign of which it is the

60. T. L. Short, 'What They Said in Amsterdam: Peirce's semiotic today', *Semiotica* 60 1/2
(1986), 114 (interestingly enough, this occurs by way of criticism of Hanna
Buczynska-Garewicz); on Peirce's alleged 'indefinite deferral of meaning' see also Short's
'What's the Use?', 8–16, and 'Interpreting Peirce's Interpretant', 516–24.
61. Short attributes the view to his teacher, George Gentry; 'Interpreting Peirce's
Interpretant', 516–17. Short says, '[T]he textual evidence is unambiguous ... The
fundamental change in Peirce's semeiotic that Gentry identified is explicable, traceable in
detail, and manifest in several ways' (*ibid.*, 517).
62. 'What's the Use?', 8.   63. *Ibid.*, 11 (my emphases).   64. *Ibid.*, 13.
65. 'Interpreting Peirce's Interpretant', 526.   66. *Ibid.*, 523 (his emphasis).

> logical interpretant, is the sign . . . The deliberately formed,
> self-analyzing habit – self-analyzing because formed by the aid of
> analysis of the exercises that nourished it – is the living definition, the
> veritable and final logical interpretant.
>
> (CP 5.491; his emphasis)

Peirce here names habit as 'the veritable and *final* logical interpretant'. Strictly, this does not accord with his wider usage. Short shows that a distinction can be drawn in Peirce's work between 'final' and 'ultimate' interpretants. 'Final' is more customarily used by Peirce to name 'the ideal interpretant that would be formed in the light of all possible information bearing on the interpreter's purpose'.[67] Final interpretants are thus thinkable, but probably unattainable in fact. An 'ultimate' interpretant (which is what Peirce *should* have said in the passage cited) is, by contrast, 'that logical interpretant which is not also a sign'; that is, it is 'the nonverbal logical interpretant',[68] the point at which the sign translates into 'the practical bearing of one's accepting its application to this or to that'. The translation of sign into life *is* an ultimate interpretant 'because it requires no further interpretation in order to confer meaning on the sign it interprets'.[69]

The terminological distinctions between 'final' and 'ultimate' doubtless appear abstruse. We have just seen that Peirce himself could confuse them, and most of his interpreters assume them to be synonymous, but the point of their distinction is of immense importance to us. I have urged that our postmodern, or late modern, condition does not permit us to see under 'the platform', to 'pierce the membrane'. I have shown, I hope, that deconstruction takes this to mean there is no meaning beyond signification, that what we have, and all we have, is 'innumerable systems of marks'.

The strange thing – strange on deconstructive presuppositions – is that *people do manage to mean things*. Every day, beneath the great canopy of meanings which permits among us commerce and community, people strain for the language or signs by which they may be understood and others strain to understand them. Stories are told, justice is transacted, information is shared. Occasionally people are caught in their exaggerations or downright lies and then sometimes they are not. But in this vast construction of meaning among us people are reaching for the 'Best Account', the

---

67. *Ibid.*, 521. See p. 145 above for a brief overview of Peirce's taxonomy of interpretants.
68. 'Interpreting Peirce's Interpretant', 520, 521.
69. Short, 'What's the Use?', 13; see also his 'Life Among the Legisigns', *Transactions of the Charles Peirce Society* 18 (1982), 288.

best sense of things they can manage. They undertake and they succeed – more or less – to mean things.

The meaning which we manage among us thus inhabits an intermediate place; it is *neither* the nihilistic world of 'innumerable systems of marks' *nor* a world of contextless ideality. Now, we shall say, it is to this world, the world I described as the place of more or less successful meanings, that Peirce's ultimate interpretant belongs. An ultimate interpretant is not a final interpretant. Final interpretants – 'the ideal interpretant formed in the light of all possible information' – do probably belong to a 'God's Eye View' of things. But ultimate interpretants are for the meantime. The ultimate interpretant of any given meaning exchange is 'that logical interpretant which is not also a sign' – in other words, where signification is translated into 'the practical bearing ... of accepting its application to this or to that'. Ultimate interpretants are the mechanism by which people translate signs into concrete decisions; they are the device by which – or the point at which – we 'comprehend' that small slice of the world for which we are responsible; they are the companion piece of a 'Best Account'.

As such, they are *the point at which the meanings proposed in the signs of the liturgy* are completed in the *concrete decisions*, in the *life habits* and the *value systems* which are formed, and are constantly being re-formed, in the lives of the sign-recipients. In some of my earliest remarks I said that the action in which my imaginary visitor to church had been participant finds its most far-reaching degree of meaningfulness in so far as it is able to interpret to her, or for her, some dimension of her lived experience.[70] This version of it coincides with Lathrop's 'world that is suggested [by the liturgy]': 'not the status quo, but an alternative vision that waits for God, hopes for a wider order than has yet been achieved'.[71] It is Nichols' 'reconfigured community that returns from worship to life in the secular world'.[72] It is Kavanagh's congregation coming back from its 'flirt with doom' bearing a theology 'different from any other'. Or, to recover our link with Peirce, it is 'the real and living logical conclusion [that] is the habit'. The meanings of liturgical signs are completed in the worshippers' lives in the days and weeks thereafter, and with reference to concrete decisions, in matters of perception or judgement, and in the formation of sets of values.

Is it possible to articulate in yet greater detail the nature of the collaborative work of sign-producers and sign-recipients? The dynamic quality

---

70. Above, p. 13.   71. Lathrop, *Holy Things*, 210.
72. Nichols, *Liturgical Hermeneutics*, 26.

of this relationship must reflect, at least as powerfully as any other feature of late modernity, the dramatic nature of the changes originating in the 1960s. A considerable variety of initiatives were put in place at just that time which have changed basic presuppositions about the nature of knowledge and insight, and the nature of its production and/or transference. The sites of this transition range from the most esoteric theories of language, literature and signification to fundamental classroom procedures. All of these in one form or another represented the dismantling or undercutting of an assumed monolithic source, from which information or insight was dispensed, and its replacement with a dialectical engagement to which teacher and pupil, author and reader, sign-producer and sign-recipient each brings a contribution. In pedagogy – as one manifestation of the syndrome – many of us teaching at the time had to be yanked (with various success) from the classical 'banking models' of knowledge in which we had been nurtured to the inductive models of Paulo Freire[73] and 'case study methods'.[74] Closely related, the same tendency was reflected in the collapsing of an assumed 'canon' of classical works in secondary and tertiary literary-studies curricula.[75] Similarly, but in a different direction, Hans-Georg Gadamer's 'fusion of horizons' view of meaning, according to which 'the discovery of the true meaning of a text or a work of art is never finished'[76] collided diametrically with E. D. Hirsch's conviction that valid understanding 'is a perception or construction of the author's verbal meaning, nothing more, nothing less'.[77] It is reflected in the critique we have already observed brought by Julia Kristeva to the high modern assumption that an author's authority lies in his or her fully conscious, fully controlled 'self' exercising mastery over her or his material.[78] 'Readers' response' has become something of an umbrella term, either within, or sometimes for, this comprehensive shift in understanding. It is perhaps worth noting that the impetus towards this view of textuality and reading was inspired directly – though perhaps not only – by Husserlian 'constitution', i.e., Husserl's view that 'I can enter no world other than the one which gets its sense and acceptance or status in and from me, myself.'[79]

---

73. Paulo Freire, *Pedagogy of the Oppressed* (Harmondsworth: Penguin Books, 1972).
74. For example, see Alice F. Evans and Robert A. Evans, *Introduction to Christianity: a case method approach* (Atlanta: John Knox Press, 1980).
75. Andrew Riemer, *Sandstone Gothic: confessions of an accidental academic* (Sydney: Allen & Unwin, 1998), 134ff., 170–1.
76. Gadamer, *Truth and Method*, 265.   77. Hirsch, *Validity in Interpretation*, 143.
78. Kristeva, *Revolution*, e.g., 7–8, 91.
79. Husserl, *Cartesian Meditations*, 60/21; see above, p. 23.

Both Roman Ingarden's idea of the 'gaps' or 'spots of indeterminacy' in literary texts,[80] which indeterminacies then require to be completed by the reader's 'meaning bestowing consciousness',[81] and Wolfgang Iser's 'wandering viewpoint', in which the reader 'travels' through a text (holding together the whole while constantly adding new viewpoints, exactly in the manner of Husserl's retentions and protentions),[82] are directly inspired by Husserl.[83] In the now three or four decades in which we have become accustomed to the notion that both writers and readers bring their contribution to the picnic of meaning,[84] there has had to be a good deal of fine-tuning of the precise nature of the relationships of author, text and reader,[85] and indeed there may yet be much to do in this. But the seminal influence of Husserl in the entire development means that what we have here is a very large-scale manifestation of the position I attempted to draw in earlier chapters, namely that meaning consists *both* in making and finding – in this case, the *discovery* of the meanings which have been written into the author's text, and the *construction* of the meanings effected by the reader in the act of reading.

What is surely interesting, is that all this which has exploded among us in the last several decades, shattering so many of our modernist assumptions, was clearly anticipated by Peirce. The definitive sentence we have now heard several times: 'It seems a strange thing...that a sign should leave its interpreter to supply a part of its meaning' (CP 5.448, note 1). The 'strangeness' is, of course, engendered by the modernist assumptions from which Peirce was labouring to extricate himself and in which we are still to some degree immured (notwithstanding the monumental shifts of the past forty years): namely, the ideality of meaning and the autonomy of the thinking subject. On the other hand, *much* of this has now been eroded,

80. Ingarden, *The Literary Work of Art*, 246–54 (it is worth noting that this book was published in German in 1931).
81. *Ibid.*, 101f.
82. Wolfgang Iser, *The Act of Reading: a theory of aesthetic response* (London: Routledge and Kegan Paul, 1978), e.g., 108–18.
83. It is wholly instructive that Iser places his discussion of the wandering viewpoint under the heading of 'the phenomenology of the act of reading' (*ibid.*, ch. 3). The term is appropriated by Ricoeur in his account of readers' response; *Time and Narrative*, vol. III, pp. 166–77.
84. Above, n. 43.
85. See Eco, *The Limits of Interpretation*, notably ch. 3, where he looks to distinguish between *intentio auctoris, intentio operis,* and *intentio lectoris*, the intentions of author, work and reader respectively. See also 'An Author and his Interpreters', e.g., p. 62. Finally, see Collini, ed., *Interpretation and Overinterpretation*, the first three chapters of which are dedicated respectively to: the intention of the work, the intention of the author and the intention of the reader (summary on p. 25).

of which Peirce's habilitation is precisely the sign. We are now able to see that of which he was so prescient: that meaning is a collaborative task.

Peirce has still one or two things to show us, however. My representation of the relationship (between producers and recipients) so far allows the possibility, I think, that there is some kind of meaning quotient resident within the sign jointly realized by its producer and recipient; that is, that the relationship between them is an incremental one in which the sensibilities of the recipient are *joined to* the insights and intentions of the producer. But this would greatly underestimate the productivity of the process. The process is not an additive one in which two things are laid side by side comparatively; rather it is their *fusion*, the product of which far outweighs their sum. Peirce himself saw this and formulated it so: 'It appears to me that the essential function of a sign is to render inefficient relations efficient – not to set them into action, but to establish a habit or general rule whereby they will act on occasion ... a sign is something by knowing which we *know something more*' (CP 8.332). John Deely catches the point I am reaching for when, on the basis of this passage, he writes: '[There is] a fundamental difference between a process in which, by the knowing of one thing, we merely know something *else*, and a process in which, by the knowing of one thing, we are led thereby to know something *more*.'[86] This is also what Augusto Ponzio is saying when, in comparing codification semiotics unfavourably with the Peircean model, he characterizes the recipient's response in the latter as 'an active form of *answering comprehension*'.[87] In code-based conceptions of the sign by contrast, he says, 'The [role of] the receiver ... is simply that of deciphering the message with reference to a previously established and unambiguous code.'[88] Of course the word 'comprehension' in Ponzio's formulation directs our attention

---

86. Deely, *New Beginnings*, 167–8 (his emphases).
87. Ponzio, *Man as a Sign*, 252 (my emphases).
88. In my brief overview of semiotic approaches to worship among German speaking theorists (above, p. 133), I noted that practically without exception these assign a central role to codification as a semiotic medium. In that discussion I also made reference to criticisms of code-based theories; and I said that we would have to ask how damaging, in fact, such criticisms are to the German-language analyses. We are perhaps now in a position to pursue that question. On the one hand, the criticism cannot be made as sweepingly as Ponzio's sentence suggests. Rainer Volp's analysis, code-based though it is, (*Liturgik*, 60–1, 120–1), nevertheless explicitly expects of sign-recipients an active interpretative process (*ibid.*, 90, and see *ibid.*, 96–7, on the 'selective and combinational' process required by connotative 'fields of association'). Volp's former student, Rudi Fleischer (subsequently writing as Rudolf Roosen) draws on the notion of 'association-fields' as calling for a process of sifting the significations and grasping for meaning ('Einführung in die semiotische Gottesdienstanalyse', 105; and see 'Verständnisbedingungen religiöser Symbole', 213–24).

 The point at which the critique has traction is, I think, precisely in terms of the point I am making about the *generation* of *new* meanings in the interchange of producers and

immediately to my earlier discussion of meaning as 'grasping together', where I drew heavily on Ricoeur's description of 'the new pertinence' of metaphorical meaning as our creative response to the collision (within the metaphor) of two established semantic conventions.[89] The new pertinence of metaphorical construction, we further recall, was what in other places Ricoeur calls a 'surplus of meaning'.[90] Now it is just this *surplus*, I am wanting to say, that is that which is generated in the fusion of meanings brought by the sign's interpreter with those proposed by its producer. 'Something more' comes into the world than had been known previously by each.

To conclude this reflection on the nature of the transaction between sign-producers and sign-recipients, I wish to illustrate the point about 'surplus of meaning' by drawing on the groundbreaking ethnographic studies of Martin Stringer. Stringer undertook this study of the meanings of worship as an anthropologist and sociologist. He began from the point of view that 'practically every writer on worship or ritual . . . has assumed that the real meaning of any rite exists primarily within the texts and/or the performance of the rite itself'. His questions, in contrast, were, 'How do ordinary members of Christian congregations in Manchester [England] understand their worship', and, 'does the "meaning" of that worship exist primarily within the performance of the rite, or should we aim to find it within the minds of those who attend the rite?'[91] Equipped with these questions and his grounding in ethnographic method, Stringer set himself to worship with four congregations of different denominational affiliation, widely divergent in ethos, for a period of six months in each. The book is the result of his findings.

It is true that Stringer inclines towards an affirmative answer to his question about whether the meanings of worship are to be found 'within the minds of those who attend the rite'.[92] To his annoyance, I imagine, my own sense of it is that his findings more nearly coincide with the point of view I have elaborated, namely that the meanings in question were the result of an interaction or fusion of those which had been *proposed* in the

recipients. The code-based semiotics of Volp, Fleischer/Roosen and others of this group, seem to me to envisage no genuine production of meaning; only of a process in which encoded denotations and connotations are sifted and selected. To this extent, the criticisms apply. But then the criticisms, too, needed to be drawn more accurately or comprehensively.

89. Ricoeur, *Rule of Metaphor*, 194; see above, p. 88.

90. Ricoeur, *Interpretation Theory*, 45–6.   91. Stringer, *Perception of Worship*, 3.

92. *Ibid.*, e.g., 3, 76, 199. See also his earlier essays, 'Situating Meaning in the Liturgical Text', 193–4, and 'Text, Context and Performance'.

liturgies and those *brought* to these by the worshippers. Admittedly, a conversation between Stringer and myself is made the more complicated by our divergent understandings of the word 'meaning'. He uses it 'almost entirely in its semantic sense'; that is, as implying 'a specific, definable something' which is 'what an action or statement "means"'.[93] 'Meanings' are thus articulable by definition. On Stringer's showing, to look for meanings seems to be much the same thing as looking for what people 'really think' about their own rituals;[94] it is to ask about their 'understanding' of such ritual actions in which they are participants.[95] But, since so much of what happens in worship is *in*articulable for people,[96] Stringer opts rather for 'significance'[97] and/or 'experience'[98] – which then always remain/s beyond an ethnographer's reach, he thinks[99] – over 'meaning'. Accordingly, 'the act of worship itself . . . is best understood as being *a space without meaning*'.[100] If one can speak about the meanings of worship at all – which has thus come to seem highly doubtful – 'then this meaning . . . is unique to the individual concerned';[101] worship is a 'space' (see the second previous reference) in which 'each individual creates their own very personal understanding of the rite which may be very different from that of others at the same event'.[102]

For my part, of course, I think the word 'meaning' works differently and much more comprehensively than Stringer allows,[103] and I think a different theorization is able to include this wider reference. Stringer's empirical cases thus seem to me not only to speak of 'meanings', but to depict this as the mutual construction of proposers and recipients. Such an operation is most clearly exemplified in Stringer's first 'case', that of a Baptist congregation for whom, he came to believe, the story or stories which had been recounted during worship (for the most part in the sermon) 'sat at the heart of every act of worship'.[104] Stringer then theorized that it was the fusion of the personal stories each worshipper brought with him or her *to* worship with the story or stories told *in* worship which 'creat[ed] a temporary bridge of significance between the two stories, inevitably

---

93. *Perception of Worship*, 211. I noted much earlier (above, ch. 1, n. 99) that Stringer's book would have been a good deal easier to read if this caveat had been made much earlier in it.
94. *Perception of Worship*, 87.   95. *Ibid.*, 85.   96. *Ibid.*, 95ff.
97. *Ibid.*, 212.   98. *Ibid.*, 205–6.   99. *Ibid.*, 199.
100. *Ibid.*, 218 (my emphases); Stringer's sentence adds 'in its linguistic sense' as epexegetic of 'meaning'.
101. *Ibid.*, 199.   102. *Ibid.*, 122.
103. Like the classical exponents of theory of meaning, Stringer knows that 'meaning' is *not* restricted to the meanings of words and sentences, and, like them, he chooses to overlook this; see *ibid.*, 211.
104. *Ibid.*, 97.

transforming both stories in the process'.[105] Stringer's predilections will, later in his book, lead him to speak of meaning (or 'significance') in the monist or solipsistic manner I have described, but here, in his first description, he reproduces almost exactly my own notion of 'grasping meaning together' in terms of likeness and difference, finding and making, and so on. He speaks quite explicitly of the two stories 'merging', 'creating a third and [thus] transforming the other two'.[106] Stringer would insist, I think, that whatever 'meaning' we can speak of here belongs wholly to the recipient, but I would say that the 'third' (the new meaning which 'speaks' to the person concerned) cannot, could not, have come into being without the fusion of *both* stories: the personal one brought by the worshipper *and* the public one recounted by the preacher. The case almost perfectly exemplifies Peirce's 'something more' and Ricoeur's 'surplus'.

Stringer's second, third and fourth examples are not so straightforward, but even in these I think one can find the 'grasping together' pattern of meaning construction and thus the production of 'something more'. In his second case, the worship of a Catholic congregation, Stringer observed what he believed were 'multiple levels of engagement' happening in the worship: some people were actively following the liturgy, others said they preferred to meditate on the readings, and yet others were content to pray the rosary. I am obliged to abbreviate his account, but Stringer finds a certain helpful analogy with a process described by the anthropologist Fredrick Barth with reference to New Guinea tribespeople: 'Certain key "symbols" are transformed by continual association and disassociation with others to generate a constantly shifting field of "meaning". One series of key elements are given significance at one point and others are illuminated at another, such that the cumulative effect is one of a gradual deepening and personalising of understandings over many years.'[107] Again, I would say, he is describing the interplay of what, in another place in his account he calls 'official' and 'individual' meanings.[108] In his third case-study, that of an Independent Christian Fellowship, Stringer finds that Christian significance was created for individual members in their personal interaction with what he describes as 'a "typical" story': a kind of basic outline of conversion experience, which turns out in every so-called 'testimony' to follow nearly identical lines. Here (as perhaps also with the Catholics) the meaning proposal being offered is not so much that of a particular person as that encapsulated in the archetypal story. Yet Stringer

---

105. *Ibid.*, 105.   106. *Ibid.*   107. *Ibid.*, 120.   108. *Ibid.*, 125.

himself recognizes similarities across his examples: in each case, 'it is the experience of response...that sits at the heart of worship'[109] – to which I want to say: there cannot *be* a response without something to respond to (in this case, the pattern of the 'typical' story) which thus makes it a collaborative arrangement. In the fourth case, that of an Anglican congregation, meaning or significance seems to have been generated in the play against each other of ordinary weeks and festival Sundays (or other festival days). Stringer thinks this reflects the play of 'official' (Christian) meanings against old, pre-Christian intuitions.[110] But again, I cannot help thinking, we see a play of the familiar with that which is different, of 'correct' meanings against 'illicit' ('impertinent'?) meanings. Reading each of these accounts from within my own frames of reference, I am bound to say they all sound like acts of 'comprehension' in which old and new forms of meaning are brought together, out of which encounter 'something new' is produced.

Martin Stringer is surely right in his judgement that virtually all writing on worship, and specifically on the meanings of worship, is undertaken not from the point of view of worshippers but from that of those (like myself) who approach from theoretical or doctrinal viewpoints.[111] All who do so write are thus challenged by, and are deeply indebted for, his patient research, careful observations and thoughtful reflection. I hope my extensive use of his material reflects my own sense of indebtedness. At just two points, but crucial ones, do I differ from him: meaning, I think, is not confined to linguistic meanings; nor do I think it belongs simply within personal experience. It is making *and* finding – which means that it is a collaborative arrangement in which something unforeseen either by proposer or recipient ('something new') comes into being.

Finally, however, by what principles is this collaborative project guided? Are there any controls or guarantees? Is the sign-producer wholly at risk that his or her proposal will or might be taken, not only to unforeseen places but actually to unwanted or objectionable places? Is there capacity in the process to say that a given interpretation of the sign is *wrong*, not just from the point of view of the sign proposer but, in some sense, objectively? The questions form an exact counterpart to the questions posed earlier about the 'reasonableness' of sign-production. To have spoken there (pages 191–2) about the 'determined' quality of Peirce's 'intentional

---

109. *Ibid.*, 167.   110. *Ibid.*, 176–7.   111. *Ibid.*, 7, 63–4.

interpretant' (the sign's interpretant as seen by its producer) is to see that exactly the same logical accountability is now asked of the 'effectual interpretant' (the interpretant brought to the sign by its recipient) (for the discussion of interpretants, see pages 144–7 above).

'A sign leaves its interpreter to supply a part of its meaning.' Thus is signalled the passing of classical assumptions about intact meanings and authors' authority. Thus are there no more cast-iron guarantees. Thus does the mark of alterity built into Peirce's semiotic theory distinguish him as a late modern or postmodern figure. To be delivered from one extremity, however, should not lead us to the embrace of another. Deconstruction is that other extremity. Deconstruction proposes, in essence, that there is *no* completion of meanings, that what we have and all we have is the endless play of signifiers. Peircean semiotic theory countenances neither extremity. The interpreter does supply part of the meaning. But Peirce's mature view, we have heard, was that an indefinite deferral of meaning is, in fact, the negation of meaning. The *freedom offered the sign recipient* in this new realization of things thus carries *its equal responsibilities*. It is the *sign's* meaning which is to be completed by its interpreter. That says: there is already within the sign a meaning proposal which its interpreter is now invited to bring to completion. There attaches to sign-reception something akin to the sign's exegesis; its meaning is to be 'led out', not changed, violated or distorted. Or (since neither have our notions of exegesis remained unscathed across the passage from modernity to late modernity or postmodernity) perhaps the better formulation is precisely that offered by Augusto Ponzio: they, the signs, call for 'an active form of answering comprehension'. If collaboration eliminates certainties, it equally means that an utterance and its interpretation do not simply drift, wholly unrelated. An 'answering comprehension' is therefore *attentive* to the sign or signs set before it; it is for *these* signs that it reaches, not wishing to supplant or eviscerate them. The dynamic is figured in the circle of heads bent towards the speaker which I posted as paradigmatic of reception's entire operation.

I said earlier that on the interpreter's side there are no external sanctions – unlike the constraints imposed on sign proposers. The motivating force holding the interpreter to the task of exegesis, I said, is simply the recognition among us – as 'self-interpreting animals' – of the inalienable values of 'meaning', of 'understanding', and perhaps of 'truth'. It is the recognition that a deliberate distortion or manipulation of each other's signs is counterproductive to the 'self-interpreting' project. It is to give preference to the desire for understanding over a competing wish or desire to score a point, or to further one's own interests. Needless to say, these latter possibilities are never behind us, but they will always come at the cost of meaning or understanding; and – sometimes anyway, maybe even mostly – meaning wins.

Semiosis, we heard, was for Peirce always and inherently grounded in reasonableness; it is guided by logical process towards the apprehension of meaning in signs. In supplementing the classical movements of deduction and induction with the move he called abduction, he was thus seeking at one and the same time to hold within the reasonableness of signification the kind of creative gestures we make in our 'reasoned guesses' *and* to expand the scope of rationality to accommodate this more comprehensive, probabilistic style of reasoning.[112] The process of sign apprehension mirrors both these dimensions of Peirce's work in logic. The relations within a sign assemblage are 'determined'; on the one hand, this catches directly at Peirce's commitment to the logicality of semiosis. On the other hand, the admission of alterity into signification means that the logic of semiosis cannot be of the same order as that logic which (simply) already contains its conclusions in its own premises. So, exactly as the sign-producer's interpretant was logically determined within the assemblage, no less do logical strictures apply to the interpretant supplied by the interpreter. There is thus likeness and difference in the sign as projected by its producer and apprehended by its recipient; we could say there is a 'restricted openness' (thinking of Eco's early enthusiasm for 'the open work'); we might say there is a grasping together of the sign as characterized by the determinations of its producer *and* as seen through the determinations of its recipient. An 'answering *comprehension*' can modify the interpretant to only some (logically acceptable) degree; but the fact that it is an *answering* comprehension (that it brings its own interpretant) means that its meaning will not be *exactly* that foreseen or intended by its producer. Semiosis, according to Peirce thus places constraints of intentional integrity on each partner in the collaborative construction of meaning.

It is therefore possible to determine – up to a point anyway – when a sign has been *wrongly* apprehended. T. L. Short writes:

> If the fanatic takes natural disasters to be signs of God's wrath, then we might say that they are signs *to him* of God's wrath; but it does not follow that we believe that they *are* signs of God's wrath. Hence, it is not

112. See above, pp. 34–5.

in virtue of any possible interpretant that a sign signifies what it does. Rather, there must already be some relation between the sign [vehicle] and its object which determines or justifies a specific type of interpretant.[113]

The same considerations apply to what Eco calls 'hermetic drift' and John Deely calls 'associationism':

[An] absence of external check is precisely why associationism or 'drift', in whatever form, cannot by itself constitute the process of semiosis. Proceeding toward the infinite is not the only characteristic of semiosis and not the defining one (. . . as Eco has well shown with his distinction of semiosis as such from the various forms of cancerous drift that have tried to claim the name for their own vagary).[114]

What both authors are saying is that Peirce's 'determinations' offer an external point of reference; they provide the degree of logical stringency which enables us to say when someone is just *wrong* in his or her appropriation of the sign. Meaning is not a free-for-all. To reiterate: it is a collaborative process in which the responsibilities (for meaning) are evenly shared between the producers and the recipients of signs.

Conclusion: signs of wonder

I return to my visitor (chapter 1, above). She enters this unfamiliar place. In a style we can now identify as 'reaching for' or 'grasping together', all her sensibilities strain to apprehend, make sense of, comprehend the sentient impressions which bear upon her. What shall be made of this space, its many different significations, the people within it, their demeanour, actions and utterances? She makes sense (the word 'makes' carries more than passing import here) of all this in so far as she can join with these unfamiliar impressions such references as she can identify; she makes sense of the new as she brings to bear upon it her familiar knowledge. It is certainly conceivable that the new may swamp the old; that the novelty of the new will be so overpowering, or so confusing, that the whole will for her be practically meaningless. It could also be, however, that the new will so radically transform her familiar experiences, that she will comprehend worship itself from a new vantage point. In any case, meaning will be generated in her act of 'grasping together' both old and new, the signs proffered

---

113. Short, 'Semeiosis and Intentionality', 199–200 (his emphases).
114. Deely, *New Beginnings*, 166; that part of the citation in brackets is given by Deely in a footnote.

and her completion of them, the 'world before the liturgy' and her own immediate circumstances.

These transactions will all happen, I have wanted to say, in the medium of signs. As the recipient of this panoply of unaccustomed significations, she brings to them her own interpretants. I admitted just now the possibility that she does not have sufficient or semiotically adequate interpretants at her disposal for the signs which are being proposed to her. If, on the other hand, what I have called the iconicity, the indexicality and the traditional (symbolic) dimensions of the significations have been successful, she will have seen her world, her self, her engagements and her possibilities opened to a new way of viewing all of these. She will have been brought to the edge of what we can think and must thereafter only imagine; she will have apprehended that such was the intentional ministry of those who devised and executed the words and actions; and she will have grasped that God, Christianly understood, was the innermost subject matter of all of these. Such, we may say, are the meanings of worship.

Part III

As in an alien land
Making sense of God in a disenchanted age

7

Liturgical theology

Introduction

Peirce believed, as has practically every semiotician since, that his 'doctrine of signs' encompasses every kind and level of sentient awareness: 'All thinking is performed in signs' (CP 6.481) and 'All the universe is perfused with signs, if it is not composed exclusively of signs' (CP 5.448, note 1). It might thus be argued that the meanings of worship are already accommodated within the semiotic web, so that – in principle, at least – there is no need for a supplementary account of the theological dimensions of liturgical semiosis.[1] I myself incline to this point of view. What necessitates a more intentional discussion of the theological competencies of liturgical signs – how may they signify transcendence? – is not so much the incapacity of semiotics (we recall that the mediaeval discussion of signs was grounded in sacramental theology)[2] as the difficulties incurred for inhabitants of modern (and postmodern) cultures in making sense of the notion 'God'.

Human beings construct their meanings (a meaningful world) from the meanings culturally available to them. That has been my guiding hypothesis. It is precisely this circumstance, I have urged, which generates

---

1. Daniel Patte, 'Religion and Semiotics' in (Walter A. Koch, ed.) *Semiotics in the Individual Sciences* (Bochum: Universitätsverlag Dr Norbert Brockmeyer, 1990), 1–24, explores the similar grounds covered by religious studies and semiotics. See also Deely, *New Beginnings*, 180, where he makes the case that the combination within signs of both intellectuality and materiality offers a new way of thinking that encompasses the entire range of human experience: 'The new era finds its limits only in semiosis itself which is coextensive both with thought and with the material universe not as two realms but as one reality of experience wherein the threads of what is mind-dependent and mind-independent are made to weave a common fabric of objectivity.'
2. Deely, *ibid.*, 58, 67; for the religious connotations of the notion *doctrine* of signs, see Deely, *Basics*, 72.

for the members of late modern societies a crisis in religious meanings; for the most basic axioms of such societies neither depend upon, nor have room for, theological readings of the world. That is not to deny that significant numbers of people in such societies do hold religious convictions of one kind or another. It is to argue that such people are thereby committed to finding for themselves some order of accommodation or reconciliation between the divergent sources of meaning to which they subscribe: their religious convictions, on the one hand, and, on the other, the sets of meanings in the larger society of which they are part and of which they are indubitably the products. In earlier chapters I tried, in so far as space allowed, to depict the great cultural shift which we can loosely call the advent of modernity: that is, the transition from a world view in which 'the cosmos [was] ... seen as the embodiment of meaningful order which [could] define the good for us' to one in which 'the good life ... must come from the agent's sense of his [*sic*] own dignity as a rational being'.[3] A religious believer continues to encompass these two world views. The means for effecting this reconciliation is the subject of these concluding chapters.

Another way of saying this – now from within Peirce's semiotic scheme – is that quite extraordinary tasks are thus assigned to the recipients of liturgical signs in being asked to bring the signs to their completion (finding, that is, from within their stocks of available meanings suitable interpretants for the signs which have been proposed). For, rather self-evidently, liturgical signs derive from a world view not now continuous with that from within which their recipients must find the signs' complementary or sufficient interpretants. The world assumed by liturgical signs continues to be one in which the notion 'God', as the maker and ruler of the universe, obtains. It is a world in which God actively intervenes, causing his Son to be born into human existence, to live among people revealingly, to die for them vicariously, and to be raised bodily from death into life. It is a world in which prayer to God, rather than technological self-sufficiency, still makes sense. It is a world in which God discloses God's self in human categories such as language, dreams, intuitions. None of these are meaning-making strategies available in the modern world *as such*. There, as I have earlier indicated, the strategies for meaning have become unambiguously humanly oriented: the sources of salvation are political, educational, economic, medical or otherwise technological. Another way, then, of framing the question for this final discussion of the meanings

---

3. Taylor, *Sources*, 149 and 152.

of worship is: how shall worshippers find within their world of available meanings the interpretants which might successfully bring to completion the signs proposed in the liturgy?

Or yet a third way of putting the question – reaching beyond the specifics of Peirce's semiotic but not in contradiction to it – is to ask: how shall modern worshippers *comprehend* ('grasp together' into a meaningful whole) the world of meanings irreducibly part of a worship service and the world in which these same worshippers must negotiate the joys and perils of being human, a world which we earlier heard Fredric Jameson chillingly describe as 'hyperspace'?

I have so far suggested that this is an assignment conferred on worshippers as recipients of liturgical signs. That perhaps suggests that the proposers of such signs (those who design orders of service in the first place, and then the priests, ministers, lay leaders and preachers who must bring these to expression) are spared from such world-spanning labours, that for them such signs are transparent and intact with respect to their meaning. Only in so far as such leaders will (usually) have had seminary training (tuition, that is, in the task of making sense of theistic faith in an age of uncertainty) does the assumption have some small degree of reasonableness. Much more fundamentally, of course, the leaders of worship are as deeply ensconced within the modern paradigm as are those for whom they are liturgical leaders (in fact, it is not inconceivable that seminary training has exposed them even more radically to the complexities of belief than those for whom they minister;[4] alternatively, perhaps, the professionalism of ecclesiastical office can equally conceivably cocoon leaders from the rigours imposed on belief). None of us who profess belief in God in our times, it seems to me, is relieved from the task of making *sense* of this belief, either as pastors or parishioners. Leaders incur some significant degree of responsibility in facilitating this on the part of their congregants, but, since they themselves are no less enveloped by, and exposed to, the suasions of modernity, the ways in which they will (instinctively) undertake these responsibilities will be those which seem best to have worked for them. Worship leaders and worshipping people are thus drawn with some kind of inevitability into effecting means of rapprochement between their theism and the secular values of their ordinary lives (though it will

---

4. As depicted in John Updike's character, the Reverend Thomas Marshfield: 'At all points, Ned, the world presses us towards despair and forgetfulness of God. At no point, perhaps, more than here, in this empty church' (John Updike, *A Month of Sundays* (London: Penguin Books, 1975), 63).

need to be said that some of the ways of doing this call for a greater or less bifurcation – for some degree of partition or confrontation – between faith and culture). In whichever ways it is undertaken, I take this to be the task of liturgical theology.

In what follows I shall suggest – in broadest generalization – that the task is presently undertaken in three different ways. The paradigms are not difficult to draw (though, predictably, their borders are fuzzy and there are points of commonality between them). What I have found more difficult is the naming of them. I should also say at this preliminary point that in constructing the three-part taxonomy I will want to say that limitations (as well as strengths) apply to all three approaches, and that a frame of reference more satisfactory than any of them thus needs to be found. This is what I shall attempt in the concluding chapter.

Of the three groups, the first is the only one which uses and discusses the term 'liturgical theology'. The approach of this group I describe as 'church theology'.[5] As far as I can see, the category includes most of those who write on the subject from within Roman Catholicism, but it also includes, notably and influentially, the Orthodox scholar and theologian, Alexander Schmemann, a number of Lutherans, and, again importantly, the Methodist Geoffrey Wainwright. Obviously the writers to whom I refer contend with each other over what 'liturgical theology' is, and how it goes about its task; but an assumption shared by all seems to be that the church's traditional liturgical formulations (thus inviting the description 'church theology'), when joined with an appropriate performance of them, may confidently be relied upon to effect their own meanings. Otherwise stated, no one of whom I am aware who writes explicitly on liturgical theology considers it necessary to attend equally seriously to the world in which late modern worshippers are set – the world, that is, from which such worshippers come *to* the meanings proposed in worship – as a constituent element in the achievement of liturgical meaning.

Though the writers I have named as 'church' liturgical theologians are those who ponder aloud the meaning of the term 'liturgical theology', it cannot be supposed that they are the only ones actually undertaking the task – at any rate as I have set it up. All who look for some way of comprehending the signs of worship in a setting now far removed culturally

---

5. Frank C. Senn, 'The Relation Between Theology and Liturgy', *Worship* 57 (1983), 329, says of Geoffrey Wainwright, a prominent member of this group: 'Wainwright's is a *churchly* theology' (his emphasis). But this, I hope to show, is perhaps the chief characteristic of the group as a whole.

from the original *locus* of those signs, I have claimed, are engaged in liturgical theology. If the first approach is roughly 'Catholic' (though including some Protestants), the second and third approaches are more identifiably 'Protestant'. The first of these I name – here, too, with some equivocation – as 'evangelical', meaning thereby the diverse conservative Protestant groups who regard the scriptures as an inerrant Word of God. By thus staking out an a-cultural, a-historical theological *datum* as their fixed point of reference, evangelicals in effect secure religious meanings by isolating them from the prevalent culture. They thus set up a basic cultural bipolarity in which religious meanings are held antipathetically in relation to the values of the surrounding culture. In Niebuhr's now classic analysis, this would be the clearest example of 'Christ against Culture'.[6] This always strikes outsiders as a perverse way to secure religious meaning. It does have a long pedigree, however; the powerful links between fundamentalist Christianity and apocalyptic thought are not coincidental. It does – inevitably perhaps – involve deep internal contradictions for those who espouse it. But – for its critics perplexingly and exasperatingly – at the opening of the twenty-first century it turns out to be one of the most successful ways of enabling people to make sense of faith (and thus of the signs of worship) amidst the culture of disenchantment.

My third designated approach to the meaningfulness of liturgical signs has, like the afore-mentioned approach, gone about this without general recourse to a 'theology of worship'. It has nevertheless been a major way of effecting religious meaning for the greater part of the twentieth century (and has roots stretching at least as far back as the Protestant reformers). Up to the middle of the past century or thereabouts, it would have been easy to identify this approach as 'liberal Protestantism'. At the opening of the present century, the notion of 'liberal' Christianity has become an outdated one, and in many respects it is this kind of Christianity which is most seriously vulnerable to the erosion of secularism. Nevertheless, this is the historical legatee of 'mainline Protestantism', and that is how I shall name it. Both mainline Protestantism and its evangelical offshoot are the

---

6. H. Richard Niebuhr, *Christ and Culture* (London: Faber & Faber Limited, 1952), 58–92. Geoffrey Wainwright, 'Christian Worship and Western Culture', *Studia Liturgica* 12 (1977), 20–36, in applying Niebuhr's analysis to some of the dominant forms of worship, thinks that 'a movement of "back to the Bible", even where successful, is not an unambiguous case of Christ against culture' (p. 22), on the grounds that the Bible is itself culturally embedded. This seems to me to miss the point, which is rather that fundamentalist Christianity *takes* the Bible to be an a-cultural, or supra-cultural, phenomenon. See, for example, William E. Hull, 'Response to Robert Preus' in *The Proceedings of the Conference on Biblical Inerrancy* (Nashville, TN: Broadman Press, 1987), 64.

descendants of the Protestant reformation. The point at which they divide (acrimoniously) is precisely the subject of our study: how to be Christian in relation to modernity. From its beginnings Protestantism has been implicated in the evolution of the modern spirit. In an earlier place we heard Charles Taylor name the reformers as chief agents in 'the affirmation of ordinary life' as the arena in which 'the fullness of Christian existence was to be found'.[7] Protestants eagerly espoused, for example, the new secular or humanist methods of investigating scripture. According to Karl Barth, Schleiermacher was someone who 'wonderfully ... [realized] the possibility of the theologian's being entirely a modern man, with a good, and not with a divided conscience'.[8] By the end of the nineteenth century, the strategy of identifying 'ordinariness' as the place and the mode of God's self-disclosure had gone so far, and was proceeding at such a pace, that the evangelicals sharply drew a line against it in terms, we have seen, of their doctrine of scriptural inerrancy. 'Liberal' or 'mainline' Protestantism, however, continued to pursue its basically immanentist approach through the remainder of the century (admittedly, allowing the irruption of 'neo-orthodoxy' and the 'biblical theology' movements) through various permutations: process theology, religionless Christianity and, more recently, the various styles of 'contextual' and 'liberation' theologies. Characteristically, this way of relating to modernity is to locate God ('God's Rule' or 'Values of the Kingdom') as present – albeit ambiguously – within such forces for tolerance, for human dignity and freedom, for justice and peace, and for care of the environment as seem to enshrine historic Christian values; this, irrespective of whether the agents thereof name themselves as Christian or even see themselves as religious. Almost diametrically oppositely, then, to the evangelicalism which divided from it, this strategy for religious meaning-making is to identify social benevolence wherever it is found in the enveloping culture as a sign of God's presence, and to see it as the point and object of the references of worship. Whereas evangelicalism is a way of securing religious identity *over against* the confusing claims of late modernity, mainline Protestantism has sought its identity *in and with* the humanizing tendencies of (some aspects of) modernity. At the end of the twentieth Christian century in the west, the former seems to have been much the more successful strategy. Institutionally, however, Protestant churches mostly remain under the influence of the mainline approach. This also continues to be the instinctive way in which many (now older) members of such churches bridge the gap

7. Taylor, *Sources*, 218.
8. Karl Barth, *From Rousseau to Ritschl* (London: SCM Press Ltd., 1959), 315.

between what they hear in church and the world in which they have to try to put it into practice.

In the remainder of the chapter I will examine in greater detail these three ways of comprehending the theistic references of worship, noting their strengths and also their shortcomings.

By way of drawing this introductory section to a close, however, it is perhaps important to remind ourselves that God always has been, and is by definition, a mystery to those who would name, and attempt to approach, him. In raising the question of how we shall do that from within our modernity, we need therefore to distinguish somehow that dimension of reality which Christianity (and indeed religion generally) has always acknowledged to be ultimately ineffable and the modern condition in which even the *idea* of God has been emptied of meaning. One way, perhaps, of construing it is to say that the modern (now postmodern) temper is either impatient before, or unable to contemplate, mystery as such; that even in our postmodernity the supposition perdures that, even if we cannot understand the universe, still, it is in principle explicable. Scientists and philosophers may or may no longer think like this, but as the discoveries of modern science keep rolling out before our bemused gaze (gene technology, medical advancement) the habit seems hard to break. There *are* points at which either mystery seems to crash in upon us or our confidence in human competencies is stretched so thin as to become transparent, thus disclosing the mysteriousness of our lives, of life, of the existence of anything at all. But, for the most part, inhabitants of late modernity are not well equipped to manage this when it happens; on the whole we prefer not to have to come too near the 'edge of the platform'; we prefer to be further back where we feel we have some control and where (mostly) we can 'make sense' of things. A theology of worship for postmodernity, I shall eventually try to say, explores precisely this sense of 'edge', of 'boundary' or of 'limit' where mystery is finally ineradicable.[9]

What is liturgical theology?

The 'church theology' approach

As noted above, it is this approach which alone poses the question: 'What is liturgical theology?'[10] Both elements of the term are important for the

9. See esp. Hardy, on 'The Bright Mystery of Faith', in *God's Ways with the World*, 17–19; or see Kaufman, *In Face of Mystery*, 359: 'a mystery within which we can feel "at home"'.
10. The question in just this form is the title of a book-length study by David H. Fagerberg, *What is Liturgical Theology: a study in methodology* (Collegeville: The Liturgical Press, 1992). Other

protagonists. The insistence on 'theology' is meant to ward off the suggestion that the study of liturgy is simply a rubrical, historical, or textual affair.[11] But the theology in question is not general, speculative, or systematic; it is the theology which comes to expression precisely, and concretely, in the church's worship: 'The concern of liturgical theology is liturgical rite as an instantiation of the Church's *lex orandi*.'[12]

Basically there are two stated agenda-items for those addressing the question of liturgical theology. On one they find general agreement; on the other they divide. The point of agreement is that the meanings of worship are not found in texts and rubrics alone, but in actual liturgical events. In a widely cited sentence, Robert Taft says, '[T]he only way to understand a top is to spin it':

> Liturgical history . . . does not deal with the past, but with tradition, which is a *genetic vision of the present*, a present conditioned by its understanding of its roots. And the purpose of this history is not to recover the past (which is impossible), much less to imitate it (which would be fatuous), but to *understand liturgy* which, because it has a history, can only be understood in motion, just as the only way to understand a top is to spin it.[13]

important monographs and articles are: Teresa Berger, 'Liturgy – a forgotten subject-matter of theology?' *Studia Liturgica* 17 (1987), 10–18; Mary Collins, 'Critical Questions for Liturgical Theology' now in *Renewal to Practice* (Washington: The Pastoral Press, 1987), 115–32; Kevin W. Irwin, *Context and Text: method in liturgical theology* (Collegeville: The Liturgical press, 1994); Aidan Kavanagh, *On Liturgical Theology* (New York: Pueblo Publishing Company, 1984) and, by the same author, 'Primary Theology and Liturgical Act', *Worship* 57 (1983), 321–4; Margaret Mary Kelleher, 'Liturgy: an ecclesiastical act of meaning', *Worship* 59 (1985), 482–97, and 'Liturgical Theology: a task and a method', *Worship* 62 (1988), 2–25; Catherine Mowry LaCugna, 'Can Liturgy Ever Again Become a Source for Theology?', *Studia Liturgica* 19 (1989), 1–13, and *God for Us: the Trinity and Christian life* (San Fransisco: HarperCollins, 1991), 335–50; Alexander Schmemann, *Introduction to Liturgical Theology* (Leighton Buzzard: The Faith Press, 1966) and 'Theology and Liturgical Tradition' in (Massey H. Shepherd, ed.) *Worship in Scripture and Tradition* (New York: Oxford University Press, 1963), 165–78; Robert Taft, 'The Structural Analysis of Liturgical Units: an essay in methodology', *Worship* 52 (1978), 314–29, 'Liturgy as Theology', *Worship* 56 (1982), 113–17, and 'The Response to the Berakah Award: anamnesis', *Worship* 59 (1985), 305–25; Geoffrey Wainwright, *Doxology: the praise of God in Worship, Doctrine and Life* (London: Epworth Press, 1980) and 'A Language in Which we Speak to God', *Worship* 57 (1983), 309–21.

11. So, for example, Taft, '[A]cademic liturgics does have a unity . . . [which] must come from a dialogue of methodologies all engaged in rendering intelligible the same glorious object, the worship of almighty God'; 'Liturgy, therefore, is theology' ('Liturgy as Theology', 117, 115).

12. Fagerberg, *What is Liturgical Theology?*, 67.

13. Taft, 'The Structural Analysis of Liturgical Units', 318 (his emphases). Similarly, Kelleher writes: 'The questions about assembly, symbols, and process which have guided my own studies emerge from a theory of liturgy as *ecclesial ritual action* in which the Church symbolically mediates its identity' ('Hermeneutics in the Study of Liturgical Performance', 299–300, my emphases). On questions of liturgical 'performance', see further, above, ch. 1, note 104, and ch. 4, n. 20.

Liturgy as rite (performance) leads, however, to the matter of contention, namely, the nature of the relationship between the theology effected in acts of worship and that in which theologians think more systematically about God, faith, the church and the world. Alexander Schmemann, Aidan Kavanagh and David Fagerberg (in approximately that order of influence) on the one side have energetically championed the point of view that liturgical theology (theology either discovered or effected in worship) is the church's *theologia prima*, from which is derived its capacity for speculative or doctrinal utterance, its *theologia secunda*. In Kavanagh's representation of the point of view: 'A liturgical act *is* a theological act of the most all-encompassing, integral and foundational kind';[14] and, in Schmemann's, 'The *leitourgia* – being the unique expression of the Church, of its faith and of its life – must become the basic source of theological thinking, a kind of *locus theologicus* par excellence.'[15] This means that critique may flow in one direction only: *theologia secunda* should be informed and controlled by *theologia prima* but not *vice versa*. On the other side of this debate, I noted earlier that the historical springs of Protestantism – i.e., where perceived abuses of the Mass were taken to be chief among the sources of the church's malaise – make this an unlikely thesis for Protestant writers.[16] Geoffrey Wainwright accordingly insists: 'worship influences doctrine, and doctrine worship'.[17] Resistance is not confined to Protestants, however. For example, Mary Collins writes: 'I suggest that the contemporary task of liturgical theology is preeminently critical: Is the faith vision being celebrated in the liturgy adequate? Is it congruent with human and ecclesial experience and expectations of the saving grace of Christ? The critical questions have gained in intensity in the past decade.'[18] And Catherine LaCugna says: 'the axiom [*lex orandi lex credendi*] means that prayer is a kind of norm for belief, and vice versa: what we believe about God, Christ, and the Spirit sets limits on how we can pray'.[19]

These aspects of liturgical theology have been well rehearsed over more than a decade, and there is no need for me further to pursue them here. Of much greater interest to me is the question flagged above, namely, that concerning the impact of the worshippers' modern condition upon their capacities or otherwise for liturgical meanings. Given that this question

14. Kavanagh, *On Liturgical Theology*, 89 (his emphasis).
15. Schmemann, 'Theology and Liturgical Tradition', 166 (emphasis removed).
16. Above, p. 181.   17. Wainwright, *Doxology*, 218.
18. Collins, 'Critical Questions for Liturgical Theology', 115.
19. LaCugna, 'Can Liturgy Ever Again Become a Source for Theology?', 2. See similarly Irwin, *Context and Text*, 16, 270. See also, above, ch. 5, n. 127.

seems almost never to be raised among those who discuss liturgical theology, it is likely to seem wrongheaded to its customary protagonists, if not plainly perverse. (But can I repeat my thesis: namely, that questions concerning the ways we attempt to make sense of God are as inherently theological as any in the curriculum, and that when these appertain to worship, they belong within a discussion of liturgical theology.) In this literature modernity is thus dealt with *in absentia*. This comes to expression in two different, though clearly related, ways. One takes the form of an apparently unquestioned optimism in the theological efficacy of the rites themselves (in performance, that is). So, according to David Fagerberg,

> the relationship [of a liturgical symbol to its meaning] is not logical (this stands for that), nor analogical (this illustrates that), nor causal (this generates that). The relationship is epiphanous: this communicates the other. Faith sees Christ on the table, at the altar, in the elements, with the Church, through the priest, within his Body the Church ... The Church's ritual liturgy is the epiphany of eighth-day existence which is eschatological life in the kingdom.[20]

Similarly Kevin Irwin believes: 'The Church at prayer is the Church in need of redemption; through the liturgy it experiences its hoped for redemption.'[21] Or again: 'Thus liturgy can be regarded as theologically appropriate in the way it gives voice to divine revelation and enables the Word of God to achieve its purpose as always inviting and involving God's people into an ever deepening relationship with him ... The liturgy constitutes the Church at prayer.'[22] Sentences such as these proliferate in the literature under scrutiny. This is not to overlook, I must immediately say, the care with which Irwin (and those like him) attends to the anamnetic, epicletic and ecclesiological dimensions of the liturgy in his/their account. When that is duly acknowledged, however, the liturgical signs are seen as effecting their own meaning; recipients are somehow written out of the account as contributors or agents. Perhaps, on reflection, one should not be surprised. Perhaps this representation of things is a continuation of classical doctrines with respect to the liturgy as *significando causant*.[23]

---

20. Fagerberg, *What is Liturgical Theology?*, 166; Fagerberg speaks similarly of the epiphanic quality of the liturgy on pp. 173, 195 and 223.
21. Irwin, *Context and Text*, 49.   22. *Ibid.*, 316; see, similarly, p. 320.
23. *Ibid.*, 297. See also the 'Constitution on the Liturgy' which says (section 7), 'To accomplish so great a work, Christ is always present in His Church, especially in her liturgical celebrations. He is present in the sacrifice of the Mass ... By His power He is present in the sacraments ... He is present in His word ... He is present ... when the church prays and sings.' Though participation on the people's part was, or is, one of the Constitution's intentional hallmarks (e.g., section 48), the notion that they might *bring* some part of the meaning to the rite still seems distant from these formulations. On the lack of precision in

The obverse or complementary side of this, then, is a seemingly complete unconsciousness of modernity as an issue. This achieves quite striking proportions in Irwin's text, given that its explicit theme is the bearing of contexts on the meaning of texts.[24] This long and detailed book not once, I believe, stops to consider what I take unquestionably to be the most preponderant circumstance of worshippers in western churches, namely the late modern society of which they are both inhabitants and products. Worship, we heard just now, is the *church* at prayer. So that the theology which provides the explanatory framework for the transactions therein is seen here exclusively from within the church's self-understanding as expressed through its liturgical and magisterial statements. In other words, any consideration of the church as consisting of actual congregations (perhaps better, congregations of actual worshippers) – people, that is, for whom the culture has rendered the notion of God at least elusive and possibly frankly meaningless – nowhere appears. This, dare I say again, in a book whose express topic is the context(s) of worship. The tendency is not confined to Roman Catholic writers (though it is found there consistently). The same is true of the much more self-consciously Protestant Geoffrey Wainwright, the description of whose theology we recall supplies the overarching designation of this style of theology (see note 5 above). Wainwright is not, in fact, entirely unconscious of the impact of culture on worship. He has published an essay precisely on this theme,[25] and a chapter of forty-one pages in his *Doxology* is dedicated to the subject.[26] Only the concluding eight of these pages, however – a compression of the earlier essay – deals with the *modern* cultural setting of western churches. Here Wainwright states his unambiguous preference for the fifth of H. Richard Niebuhr's five possible ways of Christians relating to culture, i.e., one which sees Christianity as exercising a transformative effect upon its enveloping culture. That is, Wainwright, too, instinctively assumes a position of belief, or thinks from within the church, and thus sees himself as speaking towards, or about, secular society.[27] Any suggestion that secular modernity might

---

the Constitution on wherein 'culture' consists, see Mark R. Francis, 'Liturgical Inculturation in the United States and the Call to Justice' in (Kathleen Hughes and Mark R. Francis, eds.) *Living No Longer for Ourselves: liturgy and justice in the nineties* (Collegeville: The Liturgical Press, 1991), 85–92, but esp. p. 92.

24. See Irwin, *Context and Text*, 291, for a clear summary statement.

25. Wainwright, 'Christian Worship and Western Culture' (see n. 6 above).

26. Wainwright, *Doxology*, 357–98.

27. On page 358 of *Doxology* Wainwright somewhat insouciantly reflects: '[I]t is not necessary to suppose that Christianity cannot benefit from a serious consideration of the questions addressed to it by cultural and epistemological relativists.' For criticisms not unlike those made here, see Hardy, *God's Ways with the World*, 6.

already have insinuated modern Christians' assumptions, and might on that account demand consideration as a factor in the meaningfulness or otherwise of their worship, seems innocently missing from Wainwright's perspectives on liturgical theology.[28]

In so saying, I do not overlook the ever-present danger of an enervating cultural assimilation, to which possibility I have already drawn attention,[29] and of which Wainwright importantly reminds us.[30] Nor, in bringing these critical questions to bear on the distinguished scholars and thinkers who have directed the discussion of liturgical theology, do I wish to overstate my case. Of course, the church's long quest for authentic forms of worship must be afforded massive weight in our own search. This was entirely, I think, my point about the traditionalizing dimension (Peirce's symbolic significations) when speaking of liturgical semiosis. Nevertheless, the question presses: can an account of liturgical theology, which somehow manages to ignore late modern religious disaffection, be sufficient for our times?[31] Can such be a sufficient account of liturgical theology – of the meanings of worship, that is – in the times in which we live? In distinction, then, to the writers I have mostly mentioned here, I press the point that our own cultural proclivities cannot be left out of the discussion.

Two different factors seem to me to substantiate the case, one empirical, the other expressly theological. First, as a matter of simple observation it seems to me as clear as it needs to be that the precepts of modernity have seriously undermined for vast numbers of people in the western world (and seemingly in the eastern world as well, if my next reference has validity)

28. A contrast perhaps can be made with Gordon Lathrop's treatment of worship and culture where, within Lathrop's 'juxtapositions' thesis, worship is seen as both borrowing from and criticizing prevenient cultures: 'The New Testament itself evidences an awareness that the cultural treasures of the nations are to be both welcomed and criticized in the life of the church'; Lathrop, *Holy People*, 183, and see generally ch. 7, 8 and 9 of this work. See also, pertinently, Daniel B. Stevick, 'Culture: the beloved antagonist', *Worship* 69 (1995), 290–305. A contrast is also to be made with Mary Collins' essay on 'Critical Questions for Liturgical Theology', where it is recognized that surrounding cultures *do* enter liturgical awareness, have done so from earliest times, and continue no less to influence worship practices and understanding today.

29. Above, ch. 2, n. 53.   30. Wainwright, 'Christian Worship and Western Culture', 24.

31. The question is posed in various degrees of stringency by the Roman Catholic writers, Mark Searle ('New Tasks, New Methods: the emergence of pastoral liturgical studies', *Worship* 57 (1983), e.g., p. 307), and Ralph Keifer and Mark Francis in the volume *Living No Longer for Ourselves* (details above, n. 23). The Protestant Langdon Gilkey is not in doubt: '[A]ny current theology . . . that does not recognize and seek reflectively to deal with this presence of secularity, of doubt, of skepticism, and so of a sense of the meaningless of religious language inside the Church as well as outside, and so inside the theologian and believer, is so far irrelevant to our present situation' (*Naming the Whirlwind*, 10; see similarly, *ibid.*, 240).

their confidence in a theistic reading of reality. Don Saliers' reference to an anecdote of Tolstoy's, brought to our attention in just this regard, thus seems pertinent:

> Leo Tolstoy, in his autobiographical essay 'A Confession,' relates how a friend once told him how he stopped believing the Christian faith: 'On a hunting expedition, when he was already twenty-six, he once, at the place where they put up for the night, knelt down in the evening to pray – a habit retained from childhood. His elder brother, who was at the hunt with him, was lying on some hay and watching him. When the younger man had finished and was settling down for the night, his brother said to him: "So you still do that?"
>
> 'They said nothing more to one another. But from that day he ceased to say his prayers or go to church. And now he has not prayed, received communion, or gone to church for thirty years. And this is not because he knows his brother's convictions and has joined him in them, nor because he has decided anything in his own soul, but simply because the word spoken by his brother was like the push of a finger on a wall that was ready to fall by its own weight.'[32]

As I suppose is apparent, this is a personalized account of the condition of which we are all cognizant, but which nevertheless seems difficult to quantify: our modern religious disenchantment. There is little doubt, I think, that our societies *function* without recourse to religion (though this varies, too; North American society gives signs of a much greater public religiosity than does Australian society and, I would say, that of western Europe). Yet one does not commonly meet people who have positively decided not to believe in God, and census results uniformly indicate more people believing than not. More pointedly, for large swathes of such people's existence the question of belief or disbelief is *simply not an issue*. David Pailin, a systematic theologian, says: 'The problem for theologians today . . . is that developments in scientific understanding seem to have so altered our view of the natural world that a theistic interpretation of it has become implausible . . . The current problem . . . concerns the fundamental possibility of an adequate and significant concept of God.'[33] The operative word here, perhaps, is 'implausible'. It may be a matter not so much of active disbelief, as of belief's general implausibility: either in terms – as Pailin says – of doubts about 'the fundamental possibility of an adequate and significant

---

32. Don E. Saliers, 'On the "Crisis" of Liturgical Language', *Worship* 44 (1970), 399, citing Leo Tolstoy, *A Confession, The Gospel in Brief, and What I Believe* (translated Aylmer Maude, London, 1940), 5.

33. Pailin, *The Anthropological Character of Theology*, 178.

concept of God' or in terms of the point, purpose and need of such belief.

It is admittedly hard to know how to measure such social facts in terms of those who attend worship. In Australia there has been a steady stream of statistical information from the National Church Life Survey, though up until 2001 this covered only Anglican and Protestant churches, where congregations conform more nearly to my second and third ways of making sense of God.[34] But the calm assumption on the part of liturgical theologians that all worshippers are as sanguine in their belief as is Aidan Kavanagh's 'Mrs Murphy', seems to me simply improbable.[35]

My second demurral (from the preferred stance of liturgical theologians), I said, is itself theological: there is no unmediated (uninterpreted) reality, not even, or perhaps particularly not, in the case of God. This, of course, is already a biblical conviction: 'No one shall see me and live' (Exodus 33:20), 'No one has seen the Father' (John 6:46). The point has become axiomatic through the twentieth century among thinkers of all kinds, not just theologians:[36] our thought consists in signs, said Peirce; there is no pure signified, said the deconstructionists; our meanings are both made and found, we heard attested by numerous thinkers in earlier chapters. The theological aspect of this is that some element of our own culturally shaped construction enters into any meaningful apprehension of God. I cite David Pailin again to this effect: 'Theistic understanding is inescapably conditioned by the structures of the understanding that produces it' and 'Theism will only be credible when it is conditioned by, and hence is relative to, our understanding of everything else.'[37] But perhaps

34. See, among others, Philip J. Hughes and 'Tricia Blombery, *Patterns of Faith in Australian Churches* (Hawthorn, Melbourne: The Christian Research Association, 1990); Peter Kaldor, *Winds of Change: the experience of church in a changing Australia* (Homebush West, Sydney: Anzea Publishers, 1994); Peter Kaldor *et al.*, *Views from the Pews: Australian church attenders speak out* (Adelaide: Openbook Publishers, 1995); Peter Kaldor *et al.*, *Shaping a Future: characteristics of vital congregations* (Adelaide: Openbook Publishers, 1997); Peter Kaldor *et al.*, *Taking Stock: a profile of Australian church attenders* (Adelaide: Openbook Publishers, 1999); Peter Kaldor *et al.*, *Build My Church: trends and possibilities for Australian churches* (Adelaide: Openbook Publishers, 1999).

35. Aidan Kavanagh, followed by David Fagerberg takes 'Mrs Murphy' to be a paradigmatic worshipper: '[A]s a consequence of her baptism, [she is] a primary theologian enjoying membership in that theological corporation . . . the church' (Kavanagh, 'Primary Theology and Liturgical Act', 322; Fagerberg, e.g., *What is Liturgical Theology?*, 211–12, 221–2). I have seen criticism of Kavanagh, to the effect that his projection condescendingly fails to suppose that Mrs Murphy lives with questions similar to, and of the same order, as he himself does. I fail to recall whose criticism this is.

    It is also into this context that Martin D. Stringer's important ethnographical observations of catholic worship need to be introduced; see ch. 5 of his *On the Perceptions of Worship*, notably pp. 115–16, on what he calls 'multiple levels of engagement'.

36. See esp. Taylor, *Sources*, 428, 469, or 471–2.

37. Pailin, *Anthropological Character*, 85 and 187. See similarly Kaufman, *In Face of Mystery*, e.g., 13–14, 243; also Hardy, *God's Ways with the World*, 119–20.

we needed only the percipience of John Calvin. So he begins his *Institutes of the Christian Religion*: 'Nearly all the wisdom we possess, that is to say, true and sound wisdom, consists of two parts: the knowledge of God and of ourselves. But, while joined by many bonds, which one precedes and brings forth the other is not easy to discern ... [T]he knowledge of ourselves ... as it were, leads us by the hand to find him.'[38] To know that something of ourselves is within any and all our apprehensions of God is not to capitulate to charges of 'projection' or 'invention'.[39] In the subsequent chapter I shall urge that there is an objective as well as subjective content in our encounters with ultimacy. For the moment, however, the other is the point at issue: that there is no 'finding' purified of our own constructive 'making'. The coils of modernity are thus not absent from our struggles to name God in the liturgy in our time. To the contrary, they are the condition within which this is undertaken.

Were I to suggest a naiveté about the theology which we seem mostly to meet in the writings of liturgical theologians, that would not be intended abusively. The suggestion is rather meant descriptively. It alludes to Paul Ricoeur's early work on symbolism, where he suggested that the advent of modernity undercut for ever the possibility of a naive (unreflective) assumption of a sacral world. He suggested that the recovery of such a world view could not be regained *simply by wishing it so*, but must pass through a chastened (eyes-wide-open) modernity to what he called 'a second naiveté'.[40] But what emanates from the liturgical theologians does seem more often than not to represent their wish for a world undamaged by modern doubt. Such must now seem a doubtful hope. What I shall eventually suggest is that liturgical theology must press on to a 'second naiveté', rather than assuming an old (first) naiveté as if untouched by the caustic effects of modernity. Before that, I must survey other ways Christians have found for effecting meaning in modern (late modern, postmodern) times.

Liturgical meaning from an 'evangelical' perspective

If 'church' theology (of worship) proceeds mostly unaware of modernity, the case could hardly be more different for the style of Christianity I am calling 'evangelical'. For these Christians, modernity is the foil against which to measure practically everything they stand for. Yet,

---

38. John Calvin, *Institutes of the Christian Religion* (Ford Lewis Battles, translator) (Philadelphia: The Westminster Press, 1960), I .1.1. (pp. 35, 37).
39. See Pailin, *Anthropological Character*, ch. 3.
40. Ricoeur, *The Symbolism of Evil*, e.g., pp. 351, 356. See further, below, pp. 287–8.

paradoxically, I shall say, evangelicals have managed to fuse their deliberate self-differentiation *from* modernity with elements *of* that world view,
the hybrid effect of which has yielded perhaps the most potent vehicle for
religious meaning in late modern times. Three notes are thus important in
the ensuing analysis: evangelicalism's explicit rejection of modernity as a
force fundamentally opposed to Christian values; the cultural contradictions in which evangelical Christians, as members of late modern societies,
can thus find themselves entrapped; and their paradoxical (but productive) utilization of modern styles in effecting meanings in worship.

One enters an unmapped (possibly hazardous) territory in attempting
to include evangelical Christianity in an account of liturgical theology.
That this style of worship is simply bypassed in discussions of liturgical
theology is only the beginning.[41] More pertinently, from their side, too,
evangelicals have steadfastly spurned the study of worship. An interest in
'liturgy', as a matter for historical inquiry, morphological analysis, or theological inspection, is seen precisely as characteristic of the kinds of Christianity from which they wish to distinguish themselves.[42] For evangelicals, worship is much more a matter of immediate, unstructured, informal
response to God. Accordingly it should *not* be analysed or theorized. A literature on evangelical understandings of worship is thus difficult to assemble. As a highly prominent way of making sense of 'God' in our times,
it nevertheless belongs in an account of liturgical meaning production.

Evangelicalism is for the most part an English-language phenomenon.
Given its chronically fissiparous tendencies, there is always the risk that
one or other of the versions envisaged here will take – or have taken –
exception to being included in a single generic grouping. There are sufficient 'family resemblances' across the diversity, however, to warrant
the identification. Its divergent tributaries doubtless beget its variety.
British sources included: the evangelical Anglicanism deriving from the
Puritan side of the English reformation together with Scottish equivalents, Wesleyan holiness tendencies, and the Darbyite millenarianism
represented by the Plymouth Brethren. The Inter-Varsity Fellowship
and the Keswick Convention, *inter alia*, gave institutional form to these

41. A nice exception is Lathrop's essay, 'New Pentecost or Joseph's Britches? reflections on the
history and meaning of the worship *ordo* in the megachurches'.
42. This could, in fact, change in the not too distant future. Robert Webber, Professor of
Theology at Wheaton College since 1988, has been responsible for a prodigious volume of
works introducing evangelicals to the benefits of liturgical worship, of which productions
the most spectacular perhaps is the multi-volume series (Robert Webber, ed.) *The Complete
Library of Christian Worship* (Nashville, TN: The Star Song Publishing Company, 1993–4).

various currents. North American derivations included the frontier or 'camp' meetings from the earlier nineteenth century,[43] and subsequently a millenarianism finding momentum through the latter decades of that century[44] and given doctrinal heft through the Princeton theologians, A. A. Hodge and Benjamin Breckinridge Warfield.[45] Another tributary was the pentecostalism stemming from the Azusa Street Mission of William Joseph Seymour and similar or derivative charismatic groups.[46] All these coalesce in some degree of uneasy alliance in the emergence of fundamentalism as a self-declared movement in the late second decade of the twentieth century and into the 1920s.[47]

In spite of their wide diversity (geographically and culturally) these evangelical origins brought a number of remarkably similar characteristics. Perhaps the first distinguishing sign is that, in their own ways, they were all movements opposed to the regnant *status quo*. They existed as statements of dissent either within or over against the denominational churches, for example, which seemed to them temporalizing and theologically moribund. Their millenarian tendencies led them to see the societies of their time – of which the churches appeared simply the religious extension – both as destructive and as set for destruction. Their literalist, commonsensical methods of biblical interpretation were diametrically opposed to the complex critical methods being developed in the denominational seminaries. In this respect, the 'Bible readings' being developed in the summer conferences – the Niagara Bible Conference in Ontario from 1883 was the first, and most influential, of these – were seen as the fruitful alternative to 'preaching'; that is, a method of actually engaging with biblical texts as opposed to a rhetorical device for the entertainment of effete congregations. The emergent estimation of 'teaching' as an expository method was then important in the establishment of the Bible Institutes which, by the turn of the twentieth century, had become the preferred alternatives to the highly distrusted seminaries. Though assuming

43. Lathrop, 'New Pentecost or Joseph's Britches?', 527–8.
44. Ernest R. Sandeen, *The Roots of Fundamentalism: British and American millenarianism 1800–1930* (University of Chicago Press, 1970), gives an especially detailed account of this movement.
45. *Ibid.*, ch. 5.
46. See Martin E. Marty, *Modern American Religion, volume 1: The Irony of it All, 1893–1919* (University of Chicago Press, 1986), 237–47.
47. For a convenient overview of North American fundamentalism, its origins, central tenets and political effects through the twentieth century, see Nancy T. Ammerman, 'North American Protestant Fundamentalism' in (Martin E. Marty and R. Scott Appleby, eds.) *Fundamentalisms Observed* (University of Chicago Press, 1991), 1–65. For the transmogrification of the various streams into a movement calling itself fundamentalism, see Sandeen, *Roots of Fundamentalism*, 233–50.

a different idiom, the same deep mistrust of rational methods was, of course, also the basis of the Pentecostalist desire for an immediate experience of the Spirit. In and through all this, modernist theology was the 'common enemy', a 'threat to the basic assumptions of their world view'.[48] The evangelical style of religion, then, carries within it a consistent strain of opposition: to what it sees as the moral, spiritual and doctrinal degradation of the churches; to the corruption of society; and to rationality as a mischievous source of untruth. In large measure it lives out of this self-perception as being rootedly opposed to the prevalent order; in brief: a not negligible source of its meanings comes from its sense of self-differentiation over against the norms of modernity.[49]

Second, and scarcely of less importance, is of course evangelicalism's biblicism. As Protestants, they had simply taken the Bible for granted as the basic point of departure in the pre-fundamentalist evangelicals' theology and self-understanding. To this they brought further assumptions about the literalness of the Bible's meanings.[50] Millenarianism inspired the search for connections of biblical references to datable, definable historical events.[51] The relative calm with which all this had been undertaken was shattered, however, by the new intellectual temper of the closing decades of the nineteenth century: the rise of science in the universities and the advent of so-called 'higher criticism' in the seminaries and faculties of divinity. The outcome on its evangelical side was the doctrinal conviction which has become the hallmark of fundamentalism: the inerrancy

48. Sandeen, *Roots of Fundamentalism*, p. *xvii*.

49. See Martin E. Marty and R. Scott Appleby, 'Conclusion: an interim report on a hypothetical family' in (Martin E. Marty and R. Scott Appleby, eds.) *Fundamentalisms Observed* (University of Chicago Press, 1991), 818: 'The reliance on religion as a source for identity explains a good deal about the *intentionally scandalous* aspects of fundamentalism. Lacking this redemptive identification with the transcendent Other, outsiders would not be expected to accept the trans-rational claims of the true believer; indeed they would find in them a trip wire, a stumbling block (Greek *scandalon*). Common to most of the movements portrayed in these pages are beliefs and behaviors that violate the canons of the post-Enlightenment secular rationality that has characterized Western thought over the course of the past three centuries. In securing an identity and a role in the cosmos immune to absorption, fundamentalists oppose "historical consciousness," especially as it is interpreted and translated by modernists into the foundational principles of relativism. Thus fundamentalists reject the notion that we know and believe and have our being within time and space as the sole arena of human agency; that belief and practice is therefore historically conditioned and contingent; and that, accordingly, as all belief systems are thus bound, no one of them holds an a priori advantage over any other in terms of cognitive truth claims' (their emphases). I will go on to say that many evangelicals repudiate the description 'fundamentalist'; notwithstanding, something of this characterization pertains to all the evangelical varieties.

50. See Mark A. Noll, *The Scandal of the Evangelical Mind* (Grand Rapids: Eerdmans, 1994), 83ff., 200–8, on the use of Enlightenment principles in evangelical biblical interpretation.

51. Sandeen, *Roots of Fundamentalism*, e.g., 4–8, 103–5.

of scripture. Evangelicals persist – strenuously – in the claim that their doctrine of scripture represents simply the continuation of classical beliefs of the church. More trenchant critics have shown, contrarily, that, in face of the inexorable pressures on tenets pivotal for their world views, the theologians of the time – most notably the Princeton Seminary professors, A. A. Hodge and B. B. Warfield – drew not so much on classical doctrines as on the rationalism of the late eighteenth century to forge a theory of scripture not previously held in the church.[52]

The intention, and effect, of the new doctrine of scripture was unambiguously to carve out from the doubtful flux of human affairs an irrefragable centre whence certain truth (truths) concerning the human condition might be drawn. But its presumed strength was, in fact, its liability. Even at the time, a Scottish evangelical theologian, James Orr, was pointing out its suicidal potentiality: 'It is urged, e.g., that unless we can demonstrate what is called the "inerrancy" of the Biblical record, down even to its minutest details, the whole edifice of belief in revealed religion falls to the ground. This, on the face of it, is a most suicidal position for any defender of revelation to take up.'[53] Evangelical writers in the latter part of the twentieth century have sought to limit the liability. Stanley J. Grenz, for example, in his treatment of the Bible seeks to make good on the evangelical claim to stand in the historic tradition of the church. He cites approvingly catholic or moderate Protestant authors such as David Tracy, Brevard Childs, David Kelsey and James Barr (a good deal of irony attaching to the last named, given his unrelenting criticism of evangelicalism).[54] Grenz elects for a more manageable language about the Spirit's co-equal inspiration (of texts) and illumination (of their readers), and of the 'trustworthiness' of the Bible in matters of Christian faith. He owns the culturally conditioned quality of the biblical writings and of

---

52. 'Since the modernists were relativists about authority, their critics had to be absolutists. Because the liberals favored dynamic and fluid views of history, the antiprogressives needed a stable and rigid superstructure. They found this in an assertion of the infallibility, or more scrupulously, the inerrancy of the canonical Bible' (Marty, *The Irony of it All,* 232). For a comprehensive account of the rationalistic origins, and the surreptitious methods, which Hodge and particularly Warfield used for the forging of their theory of inerrant scriptural autographs, see Sandeen, *Roots of Fundamentalism,* 114–31.

53. James Orr, *Revelation and Inspiration* (New York: Charles Scribner's Sons, 1910), 197, as cited by Alan Neely, 'James Orr and the Question of Inerrancy' in *The Proceedings of the Conference on Biblical Inerrancy, 1987* (Nashville, TN: Broadman Press, 1987), 268.

54. Stanley J. Grenz, *Theology for the Community of God* (Grand Rapids: William B. Eerdmans Publishing Company, 1994), 379–404. For Barr, see: James Barr, *Fundamentalism* (London: SCM Press Limited, 1977); Barr refuses to accept that 'evangelicals' are not more properly named 'fundamentalists', *ibid.,* 1–5.

their interpretation[55] and asserts 'we cannot follow the lead of those theologians who set forth the inspiration of the Bible as the first thesis of the
doctrine of Scripture.'[56] At the same time he by no means dismisses inerrancy; it is given an honourable place as having 'yielded several important conclusions'.[57]

In the end, the careful distinctions of the theologians may not be as important for evangelical believers as is the abiding sense that the Bible is to
be differentiated from all other writings, and holds an incontestable authority for Christians. These believers are likely to give simple assent to
the point of view that scripture,

> though written by inspired men and reflecting their style of writing,
> thought forms, and convictions, is not a human book or record like
> Caesar's *Gallic Wars*. The Spirit of God is the author of Scripture, and
> the Spirit does not have *tendenz* which may be corrected according to
> any theory concerning continuity and analogy within history.
> Furthermore, unlike Caesar's *Gallic Wars*, which deals with the
> activities of Caesar, a man, the Scriptures witness to the mighty acts of
> God, acts which transcend space, time, secondary causes, historical
> analogy, and everything else within our created order. The reader of
> scripture as he [*sic*] confronts the content of Scripture, God Himself and
> His mighty acts, can only accept the witness of the Spirit who testified
> through the writings of the prophets and apostles to these revelations
> of God's judgement and grace.[58]

We shall see, then, that evangelicalism is never really free of the contradictions which come of isolating their central *datum* – precisely as they have
isolated themselves – from the vagaries of cultural contingency.

Before coming to that however, I must make reference to a third characteristic which has allowed evangelicalism to be the force for religious
meaning which, I have said, it has shown itself to be. This feature derives directly, in fact, from those already mentioned, *viz.*, evangelicals'

---

55. *Theology for the Community of God*, 386 and 391.

56. *Ibid.*, 388. It is important that Grenz's treatment of scripture comes, in his systematic
theology, in the context of pneumatology, and not, as with earlier, fundamentalist, writers as
theology's first *datum*.

57. *Ibid.*, 401ff. Grenz and those like him represent one voice within late twentieth-century
evangelicalism. Beside them, however, must be placed the unbowed fundamentalists,
represented for example by a number of the protagonists in the 1987 'Conference on Biblical
Inerrancy' in the Southern Baptist Convention (see n. 53 above for reference to the *Proceedings*
of this conference), e.g., the powerfully placed Paige Patterson (on whom see Ammerman,
'North American Protestant Fundamentalism', 49), *Proceedings*, 86–94, or Kenneth Kanzer,
ibid., 111–25 and 153–63.

58. Robert Preus, 'The Inerrancy of Scripture' in *Proceedings*, 57–8.

separation of themselves, and their central source of religious authority, from circumjacent modernity. This, in a word, is the clarity of conviction, of self-awareness, the sense of spiritual completeness and deliverance from uncertainty, which these strategies yield. Modernity's threat to religion is, of course, its omnivorous relativism. The real, and realistic, fear of the conservatives was that the Christian God, the Bible, and Christian moral values would be entirely swallowed by the modernist monster. Meaning, I have said often enough, consists in facts and interpretation, it is finding and making. Religion generally, I suppose, but evangelical religion particularly, brings to its meanings a comparatively high degree of construction or interpretation. In the fraught situation of the late nineteenth and early twentieth centuries, and in the nearly constant social and political flux which has marked the twentieth century, there was, and is, a strong predilection for stability in convictions, values and behavioural norms. Evangelical Christianity, in its in-principle withdrawal from such flux, has provided at any rate the sense of such clarity and stability:

> For those who remained true believers, fundamentalism offered a comprehensive and satisfying explanation for the complexities of life. If the condition of society seemed to be deteriorating, then the Rapture must be near. If there were choices to be made, then the Bible surely had the answers. Where others might be preoccupied with change and adaptation, believers could rest assured in unchanging truth. While no one could know with certainty what the future might hold, believers were proud to sing that they 'know Who holds the future'. Individual lives in disarray were put right by the clear rules and discipline of a fundamentalist lifestyle. While a changing, ambiguous world tossed lives and expectations about like flotsam, fundamentalists claimed an anchor in the storm.[59]

Thus evangelical Christianity, throughout the expansion of twentieth-century theological pluralism, was able to offer security about God's certain providence, in spite, almost, of people's actual condition. In its demand for conversion from an increasingly post-Christian society, it gave clarity in terms of Christian identity.[60] And in its suggestion of direct access to divine guidance in the inspired writings – as distinct, of course,

---

59. Ammerman, 'North American Protestant Fundamentalism', 28.
60. See, e.g., H. Edwin Young, 'Response to J. I. Packer' in *Proceedings*, 147: 'Do you think it accidental that the churches who lead us in per capita baptisms and other churches who lead us in total baptisms are pastored by men who proclaim a Bible free from error? Is it coincidental that the churches which are dynamic, alive, exciting and involved in effective social ministries are pastored by men who hold a high view of Scripture?'

from the dubiety inspired by the arcane divulgations of the seminary professors – it offered refreshment of heart as well as mind.[61] But, by exactly
the degree to which evangelical meanings are constructed (of which an inerrant scripture is precisely a case in point), they are also brittle. There was
thus always a hidden cost attached to this certainty.

The clamp in which evangelical Christianity perpetually finds itself
is that it simultaneously wants to define itself over against modern culture and yet be convincing or persuasive with respect to that culture. This
is not *just* a matter of evangelism, of a converting persuasiveness. Evangelicalism's radical commitment to truth, while yet being exposed to an
enveloping cultural relativism, meant and means that it must find – or
construct – the grounds by which it may *itself* be persuaded: 'Habitually
reverencing the Bible as the Word of God, I yet often detected with pain a
latent scepticism in my mind, regarding its plenary inspiration…What
the mind craves…is *proof*, and nothing less than proof.'[62] It was this
craving for proof that Hodge and Warfield set about meeting in their attempted demonstration of an irrefragable source. Two circumstances have
been unfortunate for subsequent evangelicalism. One was the casuistic
style of rationality on which the Princeton theorists drew in the formulation of their theory of inerrant autographs. As Sandeen and others have
shown, Warfield constructed a case now recognized as unfalsifiable and
thus inoperable:

> Warfield…phrased his defense of the inerrancy of the original
> autographs in such a way that no further discussion was possible. In
> retreating to the original autographs, Warfield, whether intentionally
> or not, brought the Princeton apologetic to a triumphant
> conclusion…Since in order to prove the Bible in error it now became
> necessary to find the original manuscripts, Warfield might have
> concluded…by announcing that inerrancy could never be denied.[63]

The brittle casuistry inherent in the doctrine of inerrancy could be re-
produced even at the latter end of the twentieth century.[64] A prominent

61. Cf. the contemporary testimony of a conferee at the 1898 Niagara Bible Conference given
by Sandeen, *Roots of Fundamentalism*, 144–5: 'The Rev. Mr. Ayers, from Illinois, mentioned
how he had wandered through the mazes of the higher criticism until he came to disbelieve
in what he had held dear, and finally began to consider the question of leaving the ministry.
But God was very gracious to him and sent the showers of his Holy Spirit upon his dry heart.
He told of the refreshment of his spirit, his acceptance of premillennial truth, the full
inspiration of the Bible, the coming back of his love for the Word, and his faith in all he had
previously held dear, and now he was continually preaching the doctrine of the premillennial
coming of the Lord.'
62. Sandeen, *ibid.*, 112, citing a correspondent to a millenarian periodical in 1831.
63. *Ibid.*, 129–30.
64. See, e.g., the criticisms brought by John Lewis to the 1987 Inerrancy Conference;
Proceedings, 107–8, 129–34.

example is the unremitting pressure evangelical scholars seem to feel upon themselves to harmonize variant versions of biblical narratives and/or explain away discrepancies.[65]

The second unfortunate circumstance for evangelicals is that their high esteem for truth was being formed at just the time that 'truth' meant *correspondence* between verbal utterance and facts in the world. This has meant that – dedicated as they are to the truth of things, pre-eminently of the biblical accounts – evangelicals have invested prodigious energies in 'proving' such facts in the world as would substantiate the veracity of the biblical accounts, and thus of the Christian view of the universe generally. The most extraordinary statement of this is perhaps the late twentieth-century evangelical commitment to creationism;[66] but this simply exemplifies the deep structures, and the inherent fragility, of the position overall.

Yet, as noted several times in passing, evangelicalism has frequently surprised its critics. Thus has it emerged as a vehicle of meaning for a large, and now powerful, minority in pretty well all Protestant churches, not to mention western democracies generally. There are doubtless socio/political reasons for this;[67] I confine myself to reflections on the meaningfulness of worship for evangelical believers. Some of the reasons can be extrapolated from my account so far: evangelicalism offers its converts a clarity, a simplicity, an accessibility not obviously afforded in pluralistic societies, case-by-case decisions, and before the erosion of personal and public morality. The proffered clarity extends from evangelicalism's representation of God, through its call for a 'personal decision for Christ' and its preoccupation with 'righteous living'. Another aspect lies precisely in the bifurcation between faith and culture I have attempted to draw: James Barr says, '[T]he fundamentalist is often very much a secular [person], very much *at home* in a secularized world.'[68] That is, the partition of lived experience into religious and secular dimensions permits, on the one hand, a clarity of belief not so easily gained by someone attempting to locate God *in* the swirling indeterminacies of human existence, and, on the other hand, an uncomplicated involvement in secular matters. This is not (necessarily) to allege a hypocritical faith; on the contrary, evangelicals are notable for their 'seriousness' (with respect to standards), and in the

---

65. See particularly Barr, *Fundamentalism*, 55–72, esp. pp. 61–2.
66. Noll, *Scandal of the Evangelical Mind*, 188–200. David Pailin describes creationism as the attempt 'to preserve . . . a stage in a living tradition which has long left it behind'; *Anthropological Character*, 197.
67. Noll, *Scandal of the Evangelical Mind*, 164–73; Ammerman, 'North American Protestant Fundamentalism', 38–47.
68. Barr, *Fundamentalism*, 99 (my emphasis).

latter parts of the twentieth century have demonstrated an emergent social conscience. It is rather that the 'separation of powers' within which
evangelicals function more easily enables religious clarity.

The most potent factor (in so far as evangelical worship is concerned)
seems to me, however, to be the extraordinary combination which evangelicals have managed to fashion between their inherited or underlying
Protestant commitment *to* ordinariness and their religious differentiation
from ordinariness as the sphere of God's self-manifestation. I have earlier
said that Protestantism is inherently *part of* modernity. It represents the
breaking open of sacrality into ordinariness, the naming of every believer
as priest, the use of vernacular idioms as vehicles of worship, the rendering
of God accessible. The secular versions of these things are represented in
a dismantling of social hierarchies, in democratic political process, in the
collapse of protocols and in a seemingly unstoppable pursuit of egalitar-
ianism. It holds the dignity of the individual as of first importance; it believes in the triumph of informality over convention, and in the elevation
of popular entertainment over high culture.[69] All these are the meat and
drink, the weft and woof, the natural habitat of evangelicalism. Strict demarcations between ordained and lay leaders are imperceptible; the dominant idiom is informality – of dress, of personal manner, of forms of communication. Worship spaces are deliberately chosen or constructed to be
as 'irreligious' – i.e., as unlike traditional 'church' buildings – as they can
be; and musical idioms are directly continuous with their secular counterparts. In their introductory essay to the volume on global fundamentalism, Martin Marty and R. Scott Appleby observe: '[F]undamentalists
do not reject all features of the ways called modern. Rather, they exist
in a type of symbiotic relationship with the modern, finding, for example, technology, mass means of communications, and other instruments
of modernity congenial to their purposes.'[70] The assessment exactly fits
evangelical forms of worship. It is the paradoxical – hybrid – fusion of
separation from and *identification with* modernity which has given evangelical worship its power as a medium of meaning. My constant theme has
been that people construct their meanings from the meanings available
to them. Evangelicals seem to confirm the hypothesis: the media, styles,
forms of engagement are all directly continuous with prevalent cultural

---

69. See particularly Hoffman, *The Art of Public Prayer*, 173.
70. Martin E. Marty and R. Scott Appleby, 'The Fundamentalist Project: a user's guide' in
(Martin E. Marty and R. Scott Appleby, eds.) *Fundamentalisms Obsrved* (University of Chicago
Press, 1991), p. *vii*.

patterns. Theologically, the semiosis uniformly attests a God who is immediately accessible, who does not need priestly or ministerial intermediaries, and who does not stand behind or upon dignity. The 'separatist' dimension of evangelicalism, on the other hand, requires an actual, or distinguishable, conversion *from* ordinariness *to* discipleship. The ideology of a 'gathered' community imparts a sense of Christian identity not ordinarily experienced by members of 'mainline' congregations. For someone to be named publicly as 'a Christian' now almost certainly indicates membership of an evangelical church.

Evangelicalism has surprised people through the twentieth century; it may do so again. That said, there must be a question whether the current success of evangelicalism betokens a long term viability. Several dimensions of evangelicalism as it presently is give rise to doubts. One of these is certainly what I earlier called its conceptual brittleness; otherwise described, the disproportionately high level of 'construction' which is brought to external reality in the effecting of evangelical meanings (the need to harmonize scriptures, to make special pleading for theological incongruities, and so on). There come points in human life where 'we know Who holds the future' is barely distinguishable from a religious 'whistling in the dark'. Sophistries such as 'God surely means good to come of it' expose believers to terrible all-or-nothing systems of belief. Second, and closer to worship, there must be a question about how and where evangelicalism draws its elusive line between 'belonging' (to the prevalent culture) and 'separation'. In introducing the notion of 'human frontier' (above, page 148), I agreed that the 'boundary' between ourselves and God is not fixed or absolute. I also said, however, that, whatever else we must say of God, God is to us *as Other*. That means that signs of God's unequivocal 'difference', an actual semiosis of alterity, are foundational for all acts of Christian worship. This is the reason, of course, for worship's ritual elaboration, for definable spaces and for authorized leaders. Worshippers should not, may not, be left in doubt about 'who is saying what to whom' – about 'liturgical direction' – if we are to avoid the risk essentially of speaking to ourselves, of 'confessing our sins to ourselves and also granting ourselves absolution,' as Dietrich Bonhoeffer memorably put it.[71] In drawing cultural norms such as informality and immediacy as deeply into worship

---

71. Dietrich Bonhoeffer, *Life Together* (London: SCM Press, 1954), 90. See, similarly, the New Testament scholar Eduard Schweizer, 'Scripture–Tradition–Modern Interpretation' in his *Neotestamentica* (Zurich: Zwingli Verlag, 1963), 234–5: '[W]hoever believes in nothing but his [*sic*] own spirituality has . . . got salvation in his own possession. No longer is he forced to listen except to himself. No longer does he know a God outside his own soul, an incarnate

practices as they have, evangelicals risk a great deal at just this point. What seems at the moment to be its greatest strength could eventually prove to be this worship style's most critical weakness. Third, this leads to evangelicals' nearly singular dependence on language as their medium. When every other signifying medium is directly continuous with the secular environment – otherwise said, when ritual process, spatial semiosis and designated leadership have been written out of the equation – the one channel left in which to communicate 'God' or 'transcendence' or 'otherness' is the linguistic one. Music is a case in point. *Musically*, the music used in evangelical worship is practically indistinguishable from its contemporary, secular counterparts; its singular aspect defining it as 'gospel' is its *linguistic* component. An unqualified dependence on language is, of course, characteristically Protestant. It is a precarious dependence. A fourth dimension then has to do with evangelicalism's rejection of liturgical tradition (almost exactly the opposite point to my question about the 'church' theologians). This is another of evangelicalism's contradictions, or its questionable drawing of the line between cultural separation and cultural identification. That is, evangelicals are insistent that they are the carriers of orthodoxy, of the church's 'right belief'. In their ritual life, contradictorily, they categorically reject the church's worshipping history in the name of cultural immediacy and personal familiarity with God.[72] The long-term question, then, is: how long does a form of worship remain 'Christian' which untethers itself from Christian tradition[73] so forthrightly as evangelicalism has.[74]

'God' for 'mainline Protestants'

In the degree of generalization with which I am working, one may say that mainline Protestantism endeavours to make sense of God by reflecting *from within* its condition in modernity in order to say how and where

Word of God, and a word given to a Church which is greater than he. No longer is he a poor beggar expecting everything from his Lord.'

72. See, pertinently, Irwin, *Context and Text*, 269: '[I]t is worship . . . that is the most native and true generative source for Christian theology which, as derived from the liturgy, is both essentially orthodox and doxological.'

73. The reference is to Schweizer, 'Scripture–Tradition–Modern Interpretation', 204: 'There is no doubt, that all New Testament authors emphasize that any one who loses the connection with the original tradition will get lost like a child's balloon which is no longer held on its string.'

74. All this is predicated on the recent history of evangelical styles of worship. Things could change, as the references in my note 42, above, indicate.

God may be understood as fitting into this. Said again, Protestant theology assumes the modern condition as given and is then faced with the task – self elucidatory and apologetic – of explaining God's place and function in this.

Given that contemporary evangelicalism represents the disavowal of the tendencies already well under way in mainline Protestantism at the beginning of the twentieth century, there is a definite sense in which each stands to the other as its mirror-image. This account does need some qualification: on the one hand, evangelicals, I noted, are ambivalent about modernity; on the other hand, ageing congregations and diminishing resources have increasingly pressed mainline congregations towards the informality in worship styles seemingly so effective in the evangelical and charismatic churches. That said, the deeper, more substantial, differences remain: the one effects its meanings generally by *withdrawal* from modern culture, the other by an *espousal* of it.

William R. Hutchison names three defining characteristics in beginning his detailed survey of Protestant modernism in America: 'first and most visibly . . . the conscious, intended adaptation of religious ideas to modern culture'; second, 'the idea that God is immanent in human cultural development and [is] revealed through it'; and, third, the 'belief that human society [was] moving toward realization . . . of the Kingdom of God'.[75] Hutchison believes that by 1920 these ideas – assimilation to modernity, divine immanence and progressivism – were 'accepted and respectable' in more than a third of American Protestant pulpits and in at least half of those churches' theological and educational institutions. By this stage, however, one global war had already damaged confidence in a divine indwelling of western civilization and its accompanying cultural progressivism.[76] It was not accidental, then, that at just that time in Europe Karl Barth should drop his 'bombshell in the playground of the theologians'[77] and that – through the middle part of the century – the liberal ideas would be displaced by his theology of a self-attesting Word of God and its accompanying (though largely coincidental) 'biblical theology' movement. These were already carrying 'use-by' dates, however.

75. William R. Hutchison, *The Modernist Impulse in American Protestantism* (Oxford University Press, second edition, 1982; first edition, Harvard University Press, 1976), 2.
76. *Ibid.*, 3.
77. Karl Barth, *How I Changed My Mind* (John D. Godsey, ed.) (Richmond: John Knox Press, 1966), 25.

As early as the 1930s Bonhoeffer had queried Barth's *tour de force* as a 'positivism of revelation';[78] and by the 1960s James Barr and others were busy laying charges beneath 'biblical theology' and its vast monument, Gerhard Kittel's *Theological Dictionary of the New Testament*.[79] In their monolithic style and proportions both Barth's dogmatic theology and the *Theological Dictionary* – along with dozens of lesser, but still influential, productions such as the *Interpreter's Bible* commentaries[80] – now appear characteristically modernist; i.e., as measured against the postmodernist, diversified approaches to theology and biblical interpretation which were to follow.

The chastening of liberal optimism by the cataclysmic events of the century meant the stripping from it of its cultural progressivism. That still left it with its predisposition towards the shaping of religious understanding in terms of modernist presumptions, and its conviction that the ordinary life is the place in which God is to be sought and found.[81] The 1960s then – the decade of social revolution in so many respects – witnessed not just the expiry of confidence in the 'big' mid-century theological projects (of which Barth's *Church Dogmatics* must have been about the biggest). Suddenly, like a dammed river breaking through, there came a flood of theological texts, both technical and popular, proclaiming the meaninglessness of conventional religious practice, the 'death' of God as conventionally understood from within these practices, and the need to define faith and theology in terms of ordinary human intercourse. At the time, these seemed to everyone, their authors included, to be disturbingly radical utterances. In longer perspective, one may now say they represented the continuation and radicalization of the Protestant predilection for ordinariness as God's field of action. Books characteristically addressed

---

78. Dietrich Bonhoeffer, *Letters and Papers from Prison* (London: Collins Fontana, 1959), 91–2: 'Barth, who is the only one to have started on this line of thought, has still not proceeded to its logical conclusion, but has arrived at a positivism of revelation which has nevertheless remained essentially a restoration'; similarly, pp. 95, 109.

79. Gerhard Kittel and Gerhard Friedrich (eds.), *Theological Dictionary of the New Testament* (Grand Rapids: William B. Eerdmans Publishing Company, 1964–76) (ten volumes). See James Barr, *The Semantics of Biblical Language* (London: Oxford University Press, 1961), esp. 206–62.

80. *The Interpreter's Bible* (Nashville, TN: Abingdon Press, 1952–1957) (twelve volumes).

81. See Hutchison's concluding sentences (*The Modernist Impulse*, 311): 'For the time being . . . the acceptance of Christianity's cultural involvement persists without the comforts of the progressivist elation that first nurtured it – largely without the nineteenth-century liberal's "generous hopes of the world's destiny" . . . The other two modernist ideas – adaptationism and the sense of divine immanence that supported it – remain with us not as historical curiosities but as the main elements of a controversial, still-vital heritage from the decades of modernist enthusiasm.'

themselves to 'the secular meaning of the gospel'[82] 'the secular city',[83] the 'everyday God'.[84] Of course, the most widely known was John A. T. Robinson's *Honest to God*.[85]

I draw a line of continuity between recognizable Protestant tendencies and this new insistence on the secular as the arena of religion. Yet neither can the shocking – and, I will suggest, damaging – dimension of the new asseverations be overstated. They sounded in many ears as if the entire re-ligious enterprise had given way to some order of 'depth' humanism:[86]

> since the holy is encountered in and through the secular world, we now have to seek a worldly holiness, i.e., sanctity is to be so understood that it is seen to involve acceptance of and involvement in the world . . . Secular existence is the locus of the encounter – the holy gives it meaning and rescues it from sheer absurdity. Indeed one cannot have a 'spiritual' life apart from one's life as a human being in the world, because 'God is at the heart of every human situation, summoning man [*sic*] to the Kingdom through the mediation of human objectives.'[87]

> Intercession is to *be with* another at that depth, whether in silence or compassion or action . . . And this means seeing the diary *in depth*, preparing in the telephone to meet our *God*.[88]

> Standing in a picket line is a way of speaking. By doing it a Christian speaks of God. He [*sic*] helps alter the word 'God' by changing the society in which it has been trivialized, by moving away from the context where 'God-talk' usually occurs, and by shedding the stereotyped roles in which God's name is usually intoned.[89]

'Religionless Christianity', or the 'death of God' movement,[90] was a vogue that passed, to some degree, from the glare of public awareness. Its

---

82. Paul M. van Buren, *The Secular Meaning of the Gospel Based on an Analysis of its Languages* (London: SCM Press Limited, 1963).

83. Harvey Cox, *The Secular City: secularization and urbanization in theological perspective* (London: SCM Press Limited, 1965).

84. J. G. Davies, *Every Day God: encountering the holy in the world and worship* (London: SCM Press Limited, 1973).

85. John A. T. Robinson, *Honest to God* (London: SCM Press Limited, 1963).

86. See Alasdair MacIntyre, 'God and the Theologians' in (John A. T. Robinson and David L. Edwards, eds.) *The Honest to God Debate* (London: SCM Press Limited, 1963), 215: 'What is striking about Dr Robinson's book is first and foremost that he is an atheist.'

87. Davies, *Every Day God*, 216, citing R. Roqueplo.

88. Robinson, *Honest to God*, 99, 101, his emphases.   88. Cox, *The Secular City*, 256–7.

90. One strand of secularizing theology proceeded to the yet more radical 'a-theology' of Thomas Altizer and his successors, a kind of deconstructive move which holds that God can only ever be named by God's absence; see, as typical, the essays collected in (Robert P. Scharlemann, ed.) *Theology at the End of the Century: a dialogue on the postmodern with Thomas J. J. Altizer, Mark C. Taylor, Charles E. Winquist, Robert P. Scharlemann* (Charlottesville: University Press of Virginia, 1990).

place has been assumed by the various 'contextual' theologies: liberation, feminist, post-colonial and, most recently, so-called ecological theology. Rather obviously these developments exactly reflect the great sea-change in intellectual methods and cultural perspectives which swept the western world in the concluding decades of the twentieth century. It is neverthe-less difficult to suppose that the traditional Protestant predilection for the everyday world has been changed. I take as a case in point the most recent writings of one prominent Protestant theologian, Sallie McFague. This author's two newest books continue earlier lines of approach (notably, the metaphoricity of all language pertaining to God) but now apply this to the ecological crisis which has engulfed our planet.[91] The earlier of these pro-poses – an idea scarcely less startling than those of the older 'secular' the-ologians – that the universe is God's body. McFague's intention in this is to reverse the dreadful exploitation of the planet, not a little of which de-rives from Christian sources, and alternatively to inspire a reverence for and sense of connectedness with it. There is undeniably much that is ap-posite, moving and illuminating in her treatment. The point to make here, however, is that this author's identification of the universe as God's bod-ily form of existence attains some kind of extreme limit, one supposes, in the Protestant assimilation of God and the ordinary. Both *The Body of God* and *Super, Natural Christians* (but especially the second, as the title sug-gests) attempt to rehabilitate the notion of the supernatural by remarking on the truly wonderful dimensions of the so-called natural world when it is attended to closely and carefully. But, with respect, it must be doubt-ful whether much more than a linguistic trick has been invoked here: the natural world now appears as *super*natural. That can only mean either an apotheosis of the ordinary or the making of God continuous with the or-dinary. McFague wishes to avoid this impression. As a Christian theolo-gian she is at pains to distinguish her point of view from pantheism.[92] She names it, rather, panentheism, and proposes a doubtful conceit accord-ing to which God's *face* is to be distinguished from God's *body*: 'We would, then, have an entire planet that reflects the glory, the very being – though not the face – of God.'[93] But: learning to revere the creation *as* God's cre-ation is one thing – urgently and practically necessary. Identifying it *with*

---

91. Sallie McFague, *The Body of God: an ecological theology* (London: SCM Press Limited, 1993) and *Super, Natural Christians: how we should love nature* (Minneapolis: Fortress Press, 1997).
92. *The Body of God*, 149.
93. *Ibid.*, 132. See Bauckham, *The Theology of Revelation*, 50–1, for a critical response to what he calls 'a distaste for . . . the absolute dependence of the creation on the . . . Creator.'

its Creator, or, at the very least, rendering the relationship ambiguous, is another. Any notion of worship is then rendered void: that is, in terms of *whom* we should praise for creation's grandeur, or *to whom* we might pray, or *from whom* we were bound to seek absolution for the planet's rapine.[94]

With only the rarest of exceptions Protestant worshippers remain unaware of the learned articles and books produced by their confessional theologians. The exposure even of preachers to the literature is probably disappointingly low. Notwithstanding, the basic and pervasive instinct on the part of these worshippers and worship leaders follows faithfully the pattern inscribed in their now long tradition. Again, I am dealing in immense generalization; but my consistent experience is that when sermons of this tradition reach the point of asking: 'What does this mean for us?' or 'How then does God come to us?' an answer will be found in one form or another of God's immanence: 'God is encountered in unexpectedly beautiful moments of our ordinary lives', or 'God takes the form among us of human care and compassion', and again, 'We see the face of Jesus Christ in the face of the other, the stranger, the outsider', or 'In our darkest moments, we may be assured that God is already in the darkness with us.' So deeply instinctive are these responses, that I perfectly imagine the majority of Protestant preachers would wonder what other direction the sermon could take. To the extent that this is so, is the measure by which God as categorically other, God as the creator to whom we are in some way accountable for our actions, God as the 'bright mystery' by which our existence is overshadowed (note 9 above) has slipped out of the theological lexicon of Protestant preaching.

---

94. At various places in the two books mentioned, McFague invokes liturgical turns of phrase to express her felt response to nature. For example, in *The Body of God*, 112, she writes: 'To feel that we belong to the earth and to accept our proper place within it is . . . finally . . . an aesthetic and religious sense, a response of wonder at and apprehension for the unbelievably vast, old, rich, diverse, and surprising cosmos, of which one's self is an infinitesimal but conscious part, the part *able to sing its praises*' (her emphasis removed, mine added). On p. 187 of the same work she says that 'our oppressive misuse of the major part of God's creation in regard to our planet' involves 'a *confession of sin*.' And then in *Super, Natural Christians*, 29, she cites Simone Weil to the effect that 'absolute attention is *prayer*' (emphases added in both cases). One can hardly overlook the circumstance in this last example, that that to which McFague is exhorting an 'absolute attention' *is* the natural world; one is thus left in doubt as *to whom* the prayer is thus supposed to be addressed. But in the earlier cases, too, given the nearly indistinguishable line McFague draws between God and creation (the universe is God's *body*) the question remains more than ambiguous as to whom praise shall be offered or from whom absolution must be sought. On Simone Weil's expression, see Daniel W. Hardy's critical response in his 'Worship as the Orientation of Life to God', *Ex Auditu* 8 (1992), 64–5.

It is true, of course, that an 'incarnational' faith, from its beginnings, will have made the kind of connections as do the sermons to which I refer. It is also the case that a truly evangelical quality attends a proclamation of God's immanence (taking 'evangelical' now in a non-sectarian sense). William Hutchison cites Eugene Lyman of Union Theological Seminary, at the height of post-World War I scepticism, as affirming the point: 'Men [*sic*] at this tragic moment of history need a God who is accessible, who can enter into the most intimate relations with them.'[95] Nor can there be any question but that the 'secular theologians' of the 1960s were compelled by the desire to help people make sense of statements about God when traditional formulations no longer did so. And in the case of the newest stage of the trajectory, the 'contextual' theologies, the desire here, too, is that people will be enabled to construct their theologies in 'the language of the heart'.[96]

Over against these important positive considerations must be weighed the danger that people will in fact *mistake* ordinariness for God (or *vice versa*) resulting in the kind of 'apotheosis of our ordinary condition' as I thought to be the case with Sallie McFague. The danger (of mistaking God for the ordinary) seems to be realized in late modern Protestantism in two main forms. One of these is that God's presence will be identified (without remainder) with acts of human benevolence, especially for disenfranchised members of society. Charles Taylor – cited earlier in this respect – in his account of the emergence of modern ideals such as universal suffrage, human rights and basic social welfare, traces these to a complicated amalgam of nineteenth-century Christian reforming zeal and the ongoing legacy of Enlightenment humanism.[97] In a context of ceaselessly advancing religious disenchantment, on the one hand, and, on the other, a steady insistence on ordinariness as the theatre of religious life, it is scarcely surprising that both members of churches and those outside them should presume that to be 'Christian' *means* to be generously disposed to others, especially the dispossessed.[98]

The other form which a late modern Protestant commitment to God-in-ordinariness finds is in a prerogative importance on 'knowing one another'. In this country at least – I imagine it to be characteristic of churches

95. Hutchison, *The Modernist Impulse*, 245.
96. See, e.g., Clive Pearson, 'Christ and Context Down Under: mapping transTasman Christologies' in (Susan Emilsen and William W. Emilsen, eds.) *Mapping the Landscape: essays in Australian and New Zealand Christianity* (New York: Peter Lang, 2000), 317, n. 34.
97. Taylor, *Sources*; see esp. pp. 399–400.   98. Gilkey, *Naming the Whirlwind*, 24.

in western societies generally – one finds congregations advertising themselves as 'caring communities'. One may be pardoned for wondering
whether their motivation has as much to do with the need or desire to bol-
ster their membership as with genuine concern for those they are seeking to attract. In any case, the appeal is directed to a populace massively
destabilized by mobility of employment, the fragility of relationships and
personal isolation. Intimacy, or even community, however, is *not* the point
and purpose of an assembly ostensibly gathered for the worship of God.
By all means it may be a hoped-for byproduct of corporate worship, but,
when the priorities are reversed, the one becomes the other's sublimate.[99]
Gordon Lathrop, in an overview of misleading concepts of 'assembly', accordingly writes:

> we may [in trying to define 'assembly'] make use of a cultural idea that
> is practically universal at the present time. We may hope that this
> gathering will be that sacred thing so many of us, throughout the
> world, desperately long for: *genuine community*. Lacking any experience
> of public assemblies as reliable communities, we will imagine that
> 'genuine' community must mean intimate community, a collection of
> friends and lovers. Such an understanding of assembly can also be
> found to be shaping much current liturgical practice...
>   The question remains, what does this assembly or any of our
> assemblies have to do with God?[100]

Writing a decade earlier, and from within a Catholic rather than Protestant
perspective – thus demonstrating the susceptibility to the tendency across
all forms of western Christian worship – Francis Mannion similarly de-
cried the debilitating effects when intimacy becomes a primary liturgical
value: 'personality rather than rite tends to become the medium of liturgical communication and performance'; and worship itself tends towards
'an amplification of the "little pieties" and "brief rituals" focussed on moments of interpersonal sharing'.[101]

By way of concluding this section, the relative positioning of mainline Protestantism in Christian demographics over the latter years of the

---

99. The judgement of Martin Buber is pertinent: 'The true community does not arise
through peoples having feelings for one another (though indeed not without it), but
through, first, their taking a stand in living mutual relation with a living Centre, and,
second, their being in living mutual relation with one another. The second has its source in
the first, but it is not given when the first alone is given ... The community is built up out of
living mutual relation, but the builder is the living effective Centre'; Martin Buber, *I and Thou*
(Edinburgh: T. & T. Clark, 1937), 45.
100. Lathrop, *Holy People*, 28–9 (his emphases).
101. Mannion, 'Liturgy and the Present Crisis of Culture', 112, citing Erving Goffman.

twentieth century must leave a question as to whether these emphases have, in fact, helped its adherents weather the storms of secularization. I return to my leitmotif: people construct their meanings from the resources of meaning available to them. The problem or dilemma for theologians of this tradition is that the world to which they have earnestly directed people's attention does *not* offer religious meanings. It is a self-consciously *autonomous* world; it is a culture which has *deliberately renounced* religious dependency. Admittedly, the consistent approach of the theologians whose work we have so sketchily reviewed is that when it is attended to *in depth* ordinary existence discloses 'intimations of transcendence', 'rumours of angels' as one famous expression had it.[102] This approximates in some measure to what I have already suggested, and have yet to develop in detail, about 'approaching the edge' of our familiar existence. But there are significant differences: to conceptualize God as at the 'edge' of our known world is to posit that God remains to us essentially, or largely, *un*familiar, that God is fundamentally *other* to us, is *not* coextensive with known reality. That is not, I think, a point often allowed by the theologians in question. For them God is to be apprehended *in* ordinariness – albeit in its depth – not at the edge of ordinariness. The fact that at least those who undertook to propose a 'secular theology' in the 1960s and 1970s were constrained to show why and how theirs was indeed *Christian theology* and not simply a benevolent humanism, is suggestive.[103] Their intentions were unquestionably worthy, but, as noted, the material circumstances of most mainline Protestant churches at the turn of the new century suggest that the condition of disenchantment was not the direction in which to turn people as a source of religious life. Rather than deprecating the conventional forms, the ritual practices and the designated places through which, or in which, people have traditionally encountered God, instead of demolishing churches and replacing them with multi-purpose 'service centres', instead of transforming priestly ministry into vaguely religious forms of therapy or management styles of leadership, Protestant leaders might have done better in looking for the ways of *creating sanctuary* for people overwhelmed by ordinariness, in trying to *generate sacral spaces* as genuine alternatives to mundanity.[104] The point, however, lies not so much in criticizing mistakes of the past as in learning from them.

102. Peter L. Berger, *A Rumour of Angels: modern society and the rediscovery of the supernatural* (Harmondsworth: Penguin Books, 1970).
103. E.g., Cox, *The Secular City*, 257ff., but esp. p. 259; Robinson, *Honest to God*, e.g., 50–1.
104. See the citation from Victor Turner on p. 59 above.

Conclusion

My overview of the ways in which people have typically attempted to make sense of liturgical significations in a culture of religious disenchantment, to the extent that it is accurate, depicts a range or spectrum about as wide as it could be. One approach, the style I called 'church' theology, appears to hope that it can simply avoid the question of cultural disaffection. The 'evangelical' approach has responded to modernity basically by setting itself deliberately over against it, yet at the same time borrowing extensively from it. 'Mainline Protestantism' has consistently assumed the modern condition as a given and has then attempted to analyse our condition so as to locate within it signs of divine presence.

In criticizing all of these, I have been conscious of appearing to prepare the way for *the* wondrous disclosure, the solution which all of them, in their inadequacy, seemed to suggest. If that did seem to be the direction in which the discussion was heading, then at precisely this point my own working principle rises up like some familiar spirit: we can only construct our meanings from those available to us. For at least two hundred years, maybe longer, the greatest minds among Christian thinkers have bent before the task of saying how we may name God in our age. Only a condition of the most profound illusion could fail to see that.

In other words, it seems to me likely that no one really knows how we shall think out of our condition of modernity in order to offer an account of God.

In what follows, therefore, I set out the tentative or exploratory markers which have presented themselves to me by way of response to, or reflection on, these well tried paths people have taken through the twentieth century in attempting to make sense of liturgical signs. My discussion of the 'church' liturgical theologians should make it clear that it seems to me there is no future in an 'old' or 'first' naiveté that simply *wishes* modernity were not a factor. This seems to me to eviscerate everything we know, and which I tried to depict, about the work of meaning-completion which readers of texts, recipients of signs and interpreters of reality undertake in the construction of meanings. In our time, the recipients of liturgical signs *are* inhabitants of this modern culture and complete their meanings from within it. By the same token, the evangelical strategy of attempting to mark out an area or arena in the midst of an enveloping modernity, to which the canons of sense as we know them are refused admittance, is equally untenable. This is a different, now much more wilful or self-conscious, version of the naiveté which seemed to me to characterize the 'church' theology, the effect of which however is not especially different. Mainline Protestantism seems to me, contrarily, to fail by its quite opposite approach: if liturgical meaning cannot be effected by ignoring or repudiating the cultural resources out of which we construct our meanings, neither is it to be found by submersing oneself in the modern paradigm.

What the case requires, therefore, is a theorization which is recognizable from within present-day presuppositions while not remaining ensconced therein; which is clear-eyed about our dependence on late modern cultural forms and *at the same time* works towards the relativization of these in the name of a theistic reading of reality.

The only thing on which I would wish to insist in all this is that the entire project of making sense of the signs of worship is to be called liturgical theology.

8

At the edge of the known

'God' in two stages

The largest, and unquestionably most challenging, dimension of any putative theory of liturgical meaning in our time is to say how *God* can make
sense for people formed within late modern religious disenchantment. It
is to this that I turn in my concluding chapter. The analysis is best undertaken, I shall say, in two stages. I call these: 'the phenomenon of limit experience' and 'religious conviction as an assumed naiveté'. Two prefatory
notes will be helpful.

The play of identity and difference
In concluding my survey of the ways in which the theistic references of
worship are ordinarily undertaken, I said (page 254) that such references
require to be recognizable from *within* the prevailing cultural matrix, and
equally to show the *relativity* of those cultural assumptions. Another way
of saying this is that at the heart of a theorization of theistic references for
our time there will need to be a dialectic of identity (recognizability) and
difference (alterity). In earlier chapters we had seen that just this dialectic
is now admitted as at least one of the constitutive elements of meaning-
theory in late modernity. By contrast, classical modernity had committed
itself singularly to meaning's *identity* (in one or another of its various 'purities'). Thus was meaning presumed to be an intellectual or ideal commodity not contaminated by its material signifiers; it could be identified in
widely divergent empirical circumstances; its inherent rationality (better,
rational*ism*) obliterated or severely marginalized alternative viewpoints;
and so on. Conversely, the deconstructionist challenge – frequently but in-
accurately named as the (singular) postmodernist gesture – was dedicated

precisely to exposing the fissures covered over by modernity's totaliza-
tions. Its obsession was accordingly with *difference*. In contradistinction to
both of these we encountered not a few theorists, equally deserving the
soubriquet 'postmodernist', holding that for its part – wholly ironically –
deconstruction's virtual totalization of difference (as constituting whatever meaning there is) represented simply the exchange of one purity for
another.[1] More comprehensively (as just now hinted), according to its own
self-descriptions deconstruction was ready to resile from the project of
meaning per se. It professed itself reconciled to (it would say, it embraces
the reality of) 'innumerable systems of marks' or 'a tissue of differences' as
the closest we can get to an account of meaning.[2] In contrast, then, both
to modernity and to its deconstructionist antagonist, the schemata, variously associated with Ricoeur's 'long way around', with Merleau-Ponty's
modified phenomenology, or with Peirce's 'interpretational semiotics',
have theorized meaning in terms of the play *on each other* of identity and
difference. To recall one of my chief examples, it is the clash of identifiable lexical items in 'semantic impertinence' which yields the 'surplus'
of metaphorical meaning.[3] Or it is the fusion of personal accountability
('I am that person') with acknowledged change ('but I am very different
now') which allows the 'narrative concept of selfhood', to invoke another
such instance.[4] Or again, it is the presence of Thirdness, of the interpretant, which enables every successful semiotic exchange.

The problems encountered in each of the ways of undertaking liturgical theology depicted in my previous chapter ('church' theology, 'evangelical' theology and 'mainline Protestantism') have to do with the fact that
each in its own way assumes *either* its differentiation from *or* its identification with the modernity in which it is ensconced. Otherwise expressed,
in spite of their considerable variety, none of them attempts the dialectic which I am here claiming as a *sine qua non* for liturgical meaning in
late modern western societies (recognizability from within the cultural
paradigm together with a clear differentiation from it). Evangelicals, in
their hybrid aggregation of difference-from-and-similarity-to modernity,
could, I suppose, make some claim to such a dialectic, but, because the
conjunctions are not properly theorized, the relationship is perhaps better described as cognitive dissonance. More fundamentally, both 'church'
theology and the evangelicals either find or assume their meanings in

---

1. Above, p. 84.   2. See above, pp. 82–4, 201.   3. Above, pp. 88, 209.
4. See particularly pp. 90–3, above; and, more generally, pp. 81–98.

terms of their *differentiation from* modern culture, while mainline Protestantism pretty well takes for granted an *assimilation with* this culture. In each case we saw (though differently) that an absence of genuine engagement with its other – modern culture for the first two; God's alterity for the last – renders doubtful for the recipients of liturgical significations their capacity to complete the semiosis.

Liturgical meaning is effected at the extremity of what we can manage or comprehend as human beings. Worship is a journey 'to the edge of chaos'. It is something liminal, standing on the borderline of finitude and the infinite. It is both the terror and the ecstasy of coming to the edge of ourselves. It is thus that I shall argue that liturgical theology is equally *cognizable* from within universal human experience and, simultaneously, attends to the *inalienable alterity* by which we are confronted when we dare or are driven to approach this place of radical marginality.

Approaching God in two stages

One of the assumptions distinguishing our times from pre-modern cultures is that a dimension of reality transcendent of human limitations was then both unquestionable and unmistakable. The task of theology in that setting was thus to debate not so much *whether*, but *in what kind*, God should be discussed. Another way of saying this is that the conjunction of strangeness and similarity inherent in all human-limit situations was then more easily accessible than it has become for us. This means that, for us (now) to speak of God in terms both of recognizability and of strangeness or incomprehensibility, one must first trace the basic circumstances of the human condition which give rise to religious sensibilities; only then, in a second move, can one attend the great mythic and ritual particulars in which the major religions of the world have sought to 'clothe', to bring to symbolic expression, this basic religious susceptibility. It is this double movement which is represented in the two sections which follow and which, in their combination, form the central argument of this chapter. The experience or condition of 'limit', I shall say, is sufficiently common for us to assume it as virtually universal. It is this which locates the 'identifiable' dimension of theology generally and thus also of liturgical theology. This I call 'the phenomenon of limit experience'. The particularly theistic descriptions on which Christians depend by way of bringing this basic (perhaps quasi-) religious awareness to expression are, I shall say secondly, the exclusive stock of this confessional body. This dimension of theology I call 'religious conviction as an assumed naiveté'. It is in the joining of *religious experience* to *doctrinal conviction* that liturgical meaning is effected. That will be my thesis.

I take it as apparent that the organization of a discussion of worship in two stages like this has not the least bearing upon the event (of worship) as experienced; as I said just now, in any successful liturgical event the two dimensions are seamlessly fused. This notwithstanding, not a few of our confusions derive from the failure, conceptually, to distinguish the (near universal) *religious vehicle* from the particular *confessional speculation* to which it, the experience, gives rise and which it carries. The failure can entice the illusion that any performance of Christian rites yields a religious experience (this tends to be the more 'Catholic' danger); alternatively, and perhaps more frequently, it encourages the (imperialistic) supposition that any religious or quasi-religious experience must, at bottom, be somehow 'Christian' (which is, of course, the quicksand more characteristically awaiting liberal Protestantism).

Neither the idea of 'limit experience' as the opportunity for theology, nor the suggestion that theology must now be undertaken in two stages,[5] is unfamiliar to theologians of the late modern period – though my own way of combining these might be, I think. With regard to our periodic experience of the 'limit' or 'boundary' to human competencies, and the sense of 'the uncanny' or 'mysterious' which such experiences inspire, it is perhaps David Tracy who has explored these themes in greatest detail.[6] But Langdon Gilkey is another writer who has sought to trace what he calls 'the dimension of ultimacy' always deeply embedded in human experience but brought to the surface of consciousness in moments of extremity:

> In such moments of awareness, our fundamental human contingency, and the contingency of all that we men [*sic*] may make or create to protect us, become clear to us. An infinite or ultimate dimension has opened before us and we realize that there is simply no human guard against the infinite power of Fate . . . Put in the religious language of our tradition, we realize then that we are not and cannot be our own gods, the ground of our own being, or the source of ultimate security and value.[7]

---

5. In addition to the writers cited in the following notes, see also David Pailin, *God and the Processes of Reality: foundations of a credible theism* (London: Routledge, 1989), ch. 4, 'The Dipolar Structure of the Concept of God'.
6. Tracy, *Blessed Rage for Order*, ch. 5 (and particularly pp. 108–9); and *The Analogical Imagination*, 358–64, but especially p. 363.
7. Gilkey, *Naming the Whirlwind*, 326–7.

Or again, Gordon Kaufman, for whom the double reference point of the 'profound mystery' of human existence and our finitude before that impenetrable mystery is the starting point for theology,[8] also avails himself of the motif.[9]

While all of these writers are thus clear that theology can now only be written 'from below' – that is, out of a 'recognizable' world – it is Langdon Gilkey who best exemplifies the 'two-stages' approach I am advocating.[10] Though Gilkey undertook his work *Naming the Whirlwind* in response to the challenge posed by the radical (Death of God) theologies of the time,[11] and though this large book is dedicated almost wholly to tracing the 'dimensions of ultimacy' in ordinary experience, Gilkey explicitly does *not* see this task *as theology*. Such articulation, he says, can only be described as theology's *prolegomenon*.[12] In the ordinary experience of secularized people, the various intimations of ultimacy – 'this strange interloper into our secularity'[13] – remain as yet 'unthematized'; that is, in the absence from our cultural repertoire of any explicitly religious mythic and cultic structures, they present themselves to us simply as anxiety before an implacable Fate, as the need to amass power over others, as the choice between better and worse values and so on.[14] Indeed, the interior logic of secularism works actively to *suppress* the thematizing of these cultural phenomena as religious or theological issues.[15] This which is yet theology's prolegomenon

---

8. See for example Kaufman, *In Face of Mystery*, 6–7.   9. *Ibid.*, 213, 227–8.

10. For his part, Kaufman thinks we must approach what he calls 'the Christian categorial scheme' (theism) through six small, incremental 'steps of faith', beginning in the fundamentally historicist dimensions of human existence (our capacity to shape the future in terms of a remembered past) and leading finally to an acceptance of Jesus Christ as a key or clue to the human situation in God's presence (e.g., Kaufman, *In Face of Mystery*, 240, 244, 262, 294; see *ibid.*, 287, for a diagrammatic representation of the 'six steps').

David Tracy comes somewhat closer to my own scheme in naming 'Christian texts' and 'common human experience' as the 'two sources' of theology (see e.g., *Blessed Rage for Order*, esp. pp. 43ff.). On the other hand, he does not see these as standing in any sort of sequential relationship. On the contrary, each is implicated in the other: 'the model holds that contemporary fundamental theology is best understood as philosophical reflection upon both the meanings disclosed in our common human experience and the meanings disclosed in the primary texts of the Christian tradition' (*ibid.*, 237).

11. Gilkey, *Naming the Whirlwind*, 21–5.

12. *Ibid.*, e.g., 182–3, 232, 332.   13. *Ibid.*, 253.   14. See *ibid.*, Part II, chs. 3 and 4.

15. See *ibid.*, 40–61, on the commitment generally of 'the secular spirit' to contingency, relativity, historicity and to autonomy; and see *ibid.*, 293, on the suppression of religious awareness by the modern spirit: 'That region of experience with which religious language deals is constituted by a level of ultimacy or of unconditionedness; it is concerned with that which transcends and so undergirds the ordinary sequences and relations of life, with, therefore, the holy and the sacred. [But] this is . . . *precisely that system of language which has been effectively excluded from the realm of intelligible speech by the development of the secular spirit*' (my emphases).

becomes theology proper only when it is introduced to 'a second level, namely one of symbolic thematization'.[16] That is, the intimations of ultimacy become recognizable for what they are only when they are brought within symbolic and mythic frames of reference which allow them to be interpreted (or 'thematized'; Gilkey's term) *as* religious; i.e., as one primary element of theological reflection.[17]

My own representation of the theological task in two stages, then – first, as interrogation of our common encounters with a 'limit' or 'boundary' (as giving rise to general, or quasi-, religious experience), and then in terms of an acceptance of one religion's confessional repertoire (Christianity) by way of 'thematizing' or giving meaning to such experiences – thus coheres quite closely with Gilkey's model. It is also my way of securing what I hope is a dialectic between recognizability (more-or-less universal human experience) and difference (the naming of this experience from within Christian faith) as the constituent elements of theology – and thus of liturgical meaning – for our time.

The phenomenon of limit experience

Modernity is a cultural paradigm dedicated to the achievement of human autonomy. The dependencies from which release is sought are numerous and various, as are the strategies for their removal. As a first example, the term itself ('modern') bespeaks a rejection of ancient authorities in favour of one's own immediate judgements: 'tis better to own a Judgement, tho' but with a *curta supellex* [scant equipment] of coherent notions; then a memory, like a Sepulchre, furnished with a load of broken and discarnate bones.'[18] Thus is the stupendous edifice of modern scholarship built on the overthrow of yesterday's opinion; 'modernity' and 'novelty'

16. *Ibid.*, 419.
17. One might compare with this Rudolf Otto's remarks on Genesis 28:17 ('How awesome is this place! This is none other than the house of God'): 'This verse is very instructive for the psychology of religion . . . The first sentence . . . connotes solely the *primal numinous awe*, which has been undoubtedly sufficient in itself in many cases to mark out "holy" or "sacred" places . . . Worship is possible without this farther explicative process [in which his mere impression of the eerie and aweful becomes a "numen", and then "nomen", a divine power, a named power]. But Jacob's second statement gives this process of explication and interpretation; it is no longer simply an expression of the actual experience' (*The Idea of the Holy*, 130–1; Otto's emphases).
18. Joseph Glanvill, *The Vanity of Dogmatizing*, as cited by Basil Willey, *The Seventeenth Century Background* (Harmondsworth: Penguin Books, 1962), 166.

are virtually synonymous ideas.[19] Then, in a different direction, the flight
to modern self-determination is seen in its constant desire to overcome
the body's limitations: escape from its (the body's) confinement in space
and time, from its meagre physical strength and from its vulnerability
to disease and death. It will doubtless be said that such was the intention of even primitive technologies, whether we think of the invention
of writing (of language itself?), the harnessing of draught animals, or the
discovery of elementary machines such as levers and wheels.[20] But neither can it be denied that this basic human proclivity was given exponen-
tial acceleration in what Weber called 'occidental purposive rationalism'
(*Zweckrationalität*): an approach to the world where 'there are no mysterious incalculable forces that come into play, but rather [where] one can,
in principle, master all things by calculation.'[21] Then, related to our endeavours to overcome bodily constraints through technology, must be our
still wishful optimism that mass education (the wonder of the internet
in every classroom) will somehow push back prejudice and intolerance.[22]
Of course, neither will we omit political processes from the catalogue of
modern emancipations; in the modern and now postmodern world the
only forms of governance not dependent on popular mandate are military dictatorships. And then, still in this connection, the importance of
'the freedom of the press' demands attention: our insistence on the non-
interference of governments in the media, on the right of people to know
what in fact is the case, on freedoms of expression and so on. This, in turn,
draws attention to the relatively late development of 'civil rights': of access to justice for every individual, freedom from discrimination on bases
of gender, creed, or race, the rights of privacy. Finally, weaving its way

19. See, e.g., Dews, *The Limits of Disenchantment*, 59–60; Habermas, *Philosophical Discourse*, 34,
46, 71–2; or Polanyi, *Meaning*, 108, 115.

20. See for example, Marshall McLuhan, *Understanding Media: the extensions of man* (New York:
McGraw-Hill Book Company, 1964), notably pp. 3–6.

21. Weber, 'Science as Vocation' in (Gerth and Milly, eds.) *From Max Weber*, 139; see particularly
the comprehensive discussion of Weber on 'purposive rationality' in Habermas' *Theory of
Communicative Action*, vol. I, ch 2. Habermas says (*ibid.*, 157) that the question on which Weber
'endeavored throughout his life to shed light' was why, outside of Europe, '"Neither
scientific, nor artistic, nor political, nor economic development entered upon the path of
rationalization peculiar to the Occident?"' He goes on, 'In this connection [Weber]
enumerates a wealth of phenomena that indicate "the specific and peculiar rationalism of
Western culture."'

22. See Habermas, *ibid.*, 148, on the eighteenth-century optimism of the Marquis de
Condorcet: 'Among other things, he expects . . . the elimination of criminality and
degeneration, the conquest of misery and sickness through hygiene and medicine; he
believes "that the day will come when death will be due only to extraordinary accidents." In
other words, Condorcet believes in eternal life before death.'

through all of these in one way or another is the rejection by the modern spirit of religious dependencies: the repudiation, that is, of 'an avowal of an element of passivity in [our] existence, an avowal that in some ways [we] receive existence'.[23]

Thus is independence – freedom from external constraint whether of political, physical, intellectual, or of ideological/theological kinds – the hallmark of the modern paradigm. The great cultural sea change which overtook western societies in the latter decades of the twentieth century, on the one hand, did undoubtedly dent the unbridled optimism in which earlier generations of the modern period had dreamed of emancipation from disease, poverty, inequality and ignorance. On the other hand, many of the values and assumptions of modernity did survive across the paradigm shift: students (theological students no less!) are expected to be abreast of the latest opinions; we take for granted the right to elect our leaders; it is seen as perverse not to avail oneself of the newest technologies (in medicine, for instance). Late modern societies of the west, even in war-weary disillusion and gathering distrust of global economies, yet continue to trust the mechanisms of human devising (i.e., we reckon ourselves as *autonomous*, a law to ourselves)[24] as the sources of whatever salvation there is likely to be.[25]

We heard earlier that one change which has found acceptance among us as a result of the newer perspectives is that, in place of comprehensive *theories* of our condition, we have learned to live with series of negotiable *pictures*.[26] One way, then, of picturing the modern condition, a picture I introduced in my earlier treatments of meaning more generally[27] and which now forms the central motif of this concluding chapter, is that it is as if the meanings we manage to construct form a vast platform on which we find ourselves able – more or less successfully – to live and to communicate with each other. The modernity of which I speak, then, in its endless promotion among us of our own self-sustainability, encourages at every opportunity a

---

23. Ricoeur, *Ideology and Utopia*, 32; see the larger discussion, *ibid.*, 31–2, of the modern repudiation of 'heteronomy' in favour of autonomy. Perhaps the ultimate dimension of modern autonomy is its claim (or acceptance) of responsibility for putting God 'to death'; see Hardy, *God's Ways with the World*, 85.

24. See the reference in the previous note to Ricoeur's discussion of 'heteronomy' and 'autonomy'.

25. All this was written before the events of 11 September 2001. That we view the world differently since that fateful day is beyond question. Still, it is hard to say how I would now recast this paragraph.

26. Above, p. 68; see particularly n. 100 on that page.   27. Again, see pp. 67–76 above.

'forgetfulness'[28] of the platform's dangerous 'edge' – the fact that there are limits to our human forms of existence – and a consequent preoccupation with our own 'centre', the place in which the various technologies lend an illusion of safety and permanence. For, of course, it is the 'edges' which terrify, which induce in us a sense of powerlessness, of dread, of alienation (where we are confronted with what is alien, not of our own contriving and mastery). (The 'edge' or 'boundary' or 'frontier' is *also*, paradoxically perhaps, the place of exhilaration, of ecstasy; we will come to this too; I incline to think that westerners tend towards safety rather than to excitement – or better, to an excitement from which there is a good chance of a safe return.) As mentioned, it is the 'centre' that our technologies serve to secure and where they make predictable the desired outcomes. It is here that our steno-language functions:[29] trains are expected to run as the timetable says they will; the price advertised is what we expect to pay; this is the world of contractual obligation, of diary appointments, of systems of justice, of learned journal articles and of stable government. The need for a safe 'centre' such as this is not *unique* to modern society; at the same time, Weber's *Zweckrationalität* has made protection against the unknown one of our highest priorities and expectations.

In spite of our overwhelming desire for a mastery of our circumstances – for *freedom*, that is, from knowledge of life's contingency – from time to time an awareness of the limits of human competencies is driven in upon us. At some point, the best precautions notwithstanding, every person will find himself, herself, brought to the brink of what she or he can manage: emotionally, intellectually, in life skills, in contesting drugs, sickness or death. Since these experiences of limit were neither wished nor foreseen, I call them *inadvertent* boundary experiences. Alternatively, people do also turn deliberately to the frontier of the known: risking life and limb, entering emotional commitments, wagering the future on the roll of dice. These I call *advertent* experiences of the edge, a deliberate testing of limits.

---

28. In accordance with his remarks on 'heteronomy', just now noted, Paul Ricoeur speaks of modernity's 'forgetfulness' with respect to matters of human boundary or limitation: '[I]f we raise the problem of symbol . . . at this period of history, we do so in connection with certain traits of our "modernity" and as a rejoinder to this modernity. The historical moment . . . is . . . the moment of forgetting . . . forgetting hierophanies, forgetting the signs of the Sacred, losing hold of man himself [*sic*] as belonging to the Sacred'; or again, 'Hermeneutics, child of "modernity", is one of the ways in which this "modernity" overcomes its own forgetfulness of the Sacred' (*Conflict in Interpretations*, 288, 298); see similarly his *Symbolism of Evil*, 394. Hardy, *God's Ways with the World*, 43, also speaks of modern 'forgetfulness'.
29. See the reference to Philip Wheelwright, ch. 3, n. 34 above.

A number of points are important (for my account of liturgical meaning) about both these forms of boundary or limit experiences. First, both
involve a powerful intensification of otherwise familiar matters. That is:
emotions such as anxiety, doubt, joy or elation are highly quantifiable,
ranging from wondering whether I shall miss my usual train to work to
the prospect of becoming redundant in my workplace altogether, from the
mild intoxication of a spring morning to the wonder of learning that I am
loved utterly by the person in the world whom I most love. 'Edge' experiences *are* different from everyday experiences. But this is not – in the first
instance, anyway – a qualitative difference (such as, for example, 'sacred'
and 'secular' are supposed to be). Rather they represent the powerful –
sometimes nearly unbearable – intensification of otherwise thoroughly
recognizable phenomena. Second, such experiences regularly yield what
are perceptibly religious – at the very least quasi-religious – effects: awe,
horror, wonder or ecstasy.[30] Third, though I am insisting on the recognizability of such experiences from within ordinariness, when they are
brought to the degree of intensification I am describing, they serve to reveal a quality of vulnerability, an exposure to depths and possibilities,
which is or are occluded in that ordinariness. We may properly speak of
them as 'disclosure situations'.[31]

In what follows I shall attempt to analyse these three dimensions of
both inadvertent and advertent experiences of 'the edge' of human competencies.

Inadvertent experiences of 'limit'
I offer two imaginary but imaginable scenarios:

> The telephone on my office desk rings. I take the call expecting a
> student seeking an appointment or a colleague wanting to check class
> timetables. It is not. It is the Accident and Emergency unit of the city
> hospital to say that my wife has been seriously hurt in a traffic accident,
> and that they need my permission to rush her into surgery. At this
> point my world, quite literally, stops. My body takes some minutes to
> adjust itself to its new circumstances. The essay in which I had been

30. In this I am recognizably dependent on Rudolf Otto's analysis of 'the numinous' as both
mysterium tremendum, 'the daunting and repelling moment of the numinous', and as
mysterium fascinans, 'the attracting and alluring moment of the numinous'; see his *The Idea of
the Holy*, 144–5, where he draws connections between these and theological motifs such as, on
the one hand, God's wrath, and, on the other, 'all that we mean by Grace'.
31. See e.g., Ian T. Ramsey, 'The Logical Structure of Religious Language: models and
disclosures' in (Ian T. Ramsey, ed.) *Words About God* (London: SCM Press, Ltd., 1971), 202–23.
See also Tracy, *Blessed Rage for Order*, 106.

engrossed until that moment now lies open at the place, utterly forgotten. Eventually I make my way to the departmental secretary's office to have her cancel all my appointments for this day at least, and to announce the cancellation of my classes. She wants to drive me to the hospital, and is anxious that I think I can manage this myself.

Or again:

My second child, nineteen years of age, together with three companions, has now been overdue five days in their bushwalking expedition in the hazardous terrain of western Tasmania. Rescue services have been engaged in search operations for now three days but with no suggested sightings. At 7.00 a.m., the telephone rings; I leap to it; it is my child to say that they have all got out safely and are being cared for by the rescue service people. I am overcome with the relief of it; gradually the nightmares of the past days and nights dissipate. I go to the bedroom to tell my husband. He, too, is very relieved. And then asks me if the clothes I had taken earlier in the week for dry-cleaning will be ready today. I stare at him in incomprehension.

Both scenes depict people at, or near, the limits of what is humanly thinkable, manageable, or utterable. Both, I shall say, represent an involuntary intensification or particularization of ordinary human emotions, both are incipiently religious occasions, and both are disclosive of the unknown (the unknowable?) by which all human life is inhabited or surrounded. Their difference lies in the fact that the one is an intensification yielding terror, the other ecstasy.

First, then, both are cases of emotional intensity far in excess of levels normally experienced. And the intensification is inadvert; it is not planned or foreseen but is given to or imposed upon the patients. The nature of the intensification is as follows. We know it as a commonplace that when life is more manageable (further 'in' on the platform, less 'close to the edge') our minds range across many things at once, attending only casually or not at all to what is at hand, performing tasks pretty well 'by rote' or 'on autopilot': as is frequently noticed, I can drive perfectly competently through city traffic, all the while in earnest conversation with my passenger; or I can reasonably successfully go through the motions of attending to a conversation before realizing I know nothing of what I have been told; and so on.[32] In the occasions depicted, conversely, the entire human organism is suddenly, but totally, consumed into the moment: cataclysmic

32. See notably Dennett, *Consciousness Explained*, 180: 'Most animals, like us, have activities that they control in a routine fashion, "on autopilot", using less than their full capacities, and in fact under the control of specialized subsystems of their brains. When a specialized

in one case, ecstatic in the other. One subject instantly abandons the engagements in which, until that point, his day had consisted: everything is swept before the preemptory force of the new circumstance, such is his singular obsession with the one thing. For her part, the woman cannot credit that the mundanity of a dry-cleaning list can find entrance to this all-surpassing moment. So are energies intensified when we are involuntarily brought to 'edge' experiences.

Second, these are also inherently – perhaps better, potentially – religious experiences. Admittedly, so to describe them is quickly to encounter questions of definition: what *is* 'religion' and wherein does 'religious experience' consist? Most of the working definitions of religion assume a starting point from within what I am saying is a second level of analysis, i.e., what I called 'the mythic and ritual particulars with which each of the great religions has "clothed" a basic religious susceptibility' (page 257, above).[33] But the questions are further sharpened for us by two factors: one is the continuity I have insisted upon between 'ordinary' and 'edge' experiences, thus provoking the question as to where one ends and the other begins; the other arises from an element to which we have still to come, namely, the fact that modernity's repudiation of external dependence has spawned a host of what may conceivably be described as 'religious sublimates' (so-called 'civil religion' is one such; the religiously vicarious role of the arts is another).[34] On the one hand, it must be apparent that the involuntary experiences of my subjects are not yet overtly religious. On the other hand, the circumstances in which they find themselves, and the effects thereof, certainly do form *at least the substratum of religious occasions*

alarm is triggered . . . the animal's nervous system is mobilized to deal with the possibility of an emergency. The animal stops what it is doing . . . a temporary centralized arena of control is established through heightened neural activity – all the lines are open, for a brief period . . . These brief episodes . . . are probably the necessary precursors, in evolution, of our conscious states.'

33. Theorists regularly invoke Clifford Geertz' five-part definition of religion, namely: (1) a system of symbols which acts to (2) establish powerful, pervasive, and long-lasting moods and motivations in men [*sic*] by (3) formulating conceptions of a general order of existence, and (4) clothing these conceptions with such an aura of factuality that (5) the moods and motivations seem uniquely realistic (see, e.g., Tracy, *Blessed Rage for Order*, 92).

Another theorist, Ninian Smart, approaches the question through a list of seven 'dimensions' which most or all religions will display, *viz.*, (1) the ritual or practical dimension, (2) the doctrinal or philosophical dimension, (3) the mythic or narrative dimension, (4) the experiential or emotional dimension, (5) the ethical or legal dimensions, (6) the organizational or social component, and (7) the material or artistic dimension (Ninian Smart, *Dimensions of the Sacred: an anatomy of the world's beliefs* (London: HarperCollins, 1996), 10–11). As noted in my main text, these definitions belong more appropriately to what I am calling a second-level analysis.

34. See below, pp. 276–80, my discussion of 'degrees of alterity'.

(something like Gilkey's 'prolegomenon'). The man's experience is in every way akin to the 'awe-ful-ness', the 'shudder' of the uncanny, the dread recognition of one's powerlessness which are the hallmarks of Otto's *mysterium tremendum*.[35] And, equally, the *mysterium fascinans* – the 'beatitude beyond compare', the real nature of which a person 'can neither proclaim in speech nor conceive in thought, but may know only by a direct and living experience'[36] – clearly approximates to the wordless joy which overwhelms the mother on receiving news that her child is unharmed. By all means, the experiences have still to be 'thematized', brought, that is, within a specifically religious frame of reference (for example, wherein the man might address *God* in his fear and sense of helplessness; and the woman is able to render her relief into *thanks and praise*). Yet neither may such experiences be discounted from a religious or theological point of view. On the one hand, they are not so far away from *becoming* explicitly religious;[37] and, on the other hand – as I shall argue – worship, if it is anything at all, partakes of an 'awesome wonder' and an 'overwhelming joy'.

A third mark of the situations I am describing is that, although the progression from ordinariness to the extraordinariness of 'limit' or 'edge' experiences is continuous, and though the things which we learn in the latter are no less true of the former, yet the latter serve to expose or disclose that which is less than apparent in ordinary existence. In other words, our dangerous contingency and our capacities for elation are never actually absent, but our technological self-sufficiency (on the one hand) and our ability to fill our days with '*divertissement*, distraction, *Gerede* [chatter]'[38] (on the other) make it possible to dampen, if not quite conceal, both these dimensions of our human condition. It is the encounter with the boundary that exposes us to, and exposes to us, a dimension of existence which is other, alien, not at our disposal. It is thus at these points of fierce intensification that the dialectic of likeness and difference, present but suppressed in ordinariness, is finally shown in its fullest dimensions. Langdon Gilkey

35. See Otto, *The Idea of the Holy*, 13–28.   36. Ibid., 33–4.

37. In the past several years the Australian public has been exposed to a number of major catastrophes: a shooting massacre in Hoddle Street, Melbourne in 1987 resulted in six deaths; in 1996 a gunman ran amok at Port Arthur in Tasmania killing thirty-five people; a landslide at the alpine resort of Thredbo killed nineteen people in 1997; a train smash at Glenbrook near Sydney killed seven people in December, 1999; then in June, 2000, fifteen young people died in a fire in a backpackers' hostel in Childers, Queensland. In every case, services of religious worship were called for as a necessary and appropriate response.

38. Tracy, *Blessed Rage for Order*, 107. See also Hardy, *God's Ways with the World*, 18, n. 28: 'Triviality has replaced blasphemy as the main hazard of religious life.'

accordingly characterizes the intertwining of recognizability and enigma when human beings reach this point:

> The questions raised at this level – questions of an ultimate security, order, meaning, value, sovereignty, acceptance, and eternity – are raised precisely by the contingency and the helplessness of the finite itself. Since, moreover, these questions are raised by the essential character of finitude *as finite*, finitude can by itself at this level only generate questions; it cannot provide answers, and this is precisely what the experience itself communicates to us. It asks about an ultimate, about that which it itself is not.[39]

The knowledge of limit, suppressed by its sheer familiarity in ordinariness but exposed (alarmingly or wonderfully) in extremity, finds perhaps its most immediate form in the fact of our embodiment. So habitually do I associate my existence with this corporeal entity which is myself – 'a definite description . . . a class that has but a single member'[40] – that my boundedness in space and time is practically invisible. But this which is so apparent that I fail to notice it in everyday life becomes an issue of utmost urgency when I (my body) happen(s) to be in Europe and my father is dying in Australia. Now the circumstance of my bodiliness – dictating that I shall be in one place at one time – becomes a crucial barrier requiring to be overcome if I am to be with my parent in his extremity. Which leads directly, of course, to the other fundamental limit of the body: its fleshliness, which is to say its limited duration in time. The urgency of my situation (its 'boundary' quality) is that no technology yet devised can – ultimately – overcome the limit which is death. Precisely in our bodies do we thus learn about the givenness of limit; but usually only in their moments of extremity.[41]

There are other, more metaphysical, kinds of 'limit' experience. Every pastoral minister knows the boundary which those who meet with her or him in the church office are likely to run into in their abilities (actually, their inability) to comprehend each other's point of view; this, together

---

39. Gilkey, *Naming the Whirlwind*, 447 (his emphases). See also Kaufman, *In Face of Mystery*, 56: 'On the one hand, the traditional image/concept "God" was intended to symbolize that . . . which brings true human fulfillment . . . But, on the other hand . . . God was taken to be beyond human knowledge and understanding. There is a profound tension here which has not often been clearly recognized.'

40. Ricoeur, *Oneself as Another*, 28.

41. It is also through bodiliness that we encounter 'thresholds' of pain and of endurance generally; thus is the body the site of torture, extortion and manipulation. See, e.g., Michel Foucault, *Power/Knowledge: selected interviews and other writings 1972–1977* (New York: Pantheon Books, 1980), 55–62, and *The History of Sexuality* (London: Penguin Books, 1990), vol. I, pp. 59, 140–1.

with the minister's own powerlessness to help them overcome the aporia. Projected on to a larger (global) screen, this same refusal or inability to transcend personal and particular perspectives gives us the gap between rich and poor, the rape of the earth's resources, ethnocentrism, nationalism and, finally, the arms industry.[42] Akin to this, there are barriers or limits – even with roughly half a million English-language words at our disposal! – in knowing *how to say* what it is I most deeply feel; sometimes a gesture might do it, or a flower left on the kitchen table; but there are times when human beings are locked inescapably within their dumb grief. Finally, there is also a boundary to what we can think: when our most powerful intellects have thought as long, as deep, and as hard as they can, they eventually encounter the point at which 'the spade is turned'.[43] It is from this perspective that Hilary Putnam speaks of philosophy's 'regaining [a] sense of mystery',[44] or that Peter Dews should cite Habermas to the effect that 'only contact with the extraordinary [*das Außeralltägliche*] can renew the sources of meaning';[45] but, for one last time, our knowledge of such limits is usually given in moments of crisis or need.

Advertent encounters with 'the edge'

The experiences I have reviewed are passive, unintended. Even of the 'wonderful' (Otto's *fascinans*), we speak of 'falling' in love or 'striking' it lucky.[46]

---

42. So Tracy, *Blessed Rage for Order*, 214, 'A first step in that direction [towards belief in a suffering and loving God] can be taken when, singly and as a society, we admit to the reality of that central fact of our own experience which we name as evil or, in explicitly religious limit language, sin.' See also Hardy, *God's Ways with the World*, 84–6, on the human 'failure to orientate [our] interweaving with others to the active presence of God and the energetic order which that provides' (*ibid.*, 84).

43. See James Conant on Wittgenstein's aphorism: 'In declaring that his spade is turned . . . Wittgenstein is not announcing the absence of justifications so much as a perplexity concerning what could count as a further justification here . . . He has reached a point at which it is no longer obviously possible to continue to dig any deeper' (in Putnam, *Human Face*, p. lxx). On limits in thinking, see also Kaufman (in *In Face of Mystery*, 222–3) on 'unthinkable' questions such as the modification of human genetic structures to eliminate disease, abnormality, stress or anxiety. Nor, of course, should Tracy's analyses of 'limit-questions' be overlooked: *Blessed Rage for Order*, 97–104.

44. Putnam, *Human Face*, 118.

45. Dews, *The Limits of Disenchantment*, 210: 'Aware that only "contact with the extraordinary [*das Außeralltägliche*]" can ultimately renew the sources of meaning, Habermas describes a division of labour in which philosophy cannot entirely supplant religion: "Philosophy, even in its postmetaphysical form, will be able neither to replace nor to suppress religion as long as religious language is the bearer of a semantic content which is inspiring, and even indispensable . . . and continues to resist translation into reasoning discourses"'; the citation is from Habermas, *Postmetaphysical Thinking: philosophical essays* (Cambridge: Polity Press, 1992), 51; Dews, *The Limits of Disenchantment*, 10, cites the same essay at greater length.

46. So Tracy, *Blessed Rage for Order*, 106: 'In all such authentic moments of ecstasy, we experience a reality simply given, gifted, happened.'

There is also, however, a whole range of cases in which people turn wilfully towards the dubiously manageable. Sports endangering life and limb are among the most obvious of these, but, in fact, all sporting engagement wherein one 'pushes to the limit' in order to triumph over another is characterized by this determination to transcend a boundary (eventually, to 'break' the record). All such undertakings involve risk: the risk, that is, that one might be shown up as less than the best. One thus dares to expose oneself – often in public gaze – to some measure of excellence. But this consideration leads us to see that *all* public presentation, whether it be a concert performance, publishing an article, or applying for a new position, involves the risk of shortcoming and a concomitant anxiety about venturing oneself. Commitments to personal relationship, whether of such modest kind as engaging a newcomer in conversation or at the limit of pledging oneself in lifelong fidelity, are another form of deliberate risk-taking. Not absent from such a survey will be gambling.

I will say that the same features of intensification of ordinariness, of religious potential and of the disclosure of alterity apply equally to these encounters with 'limit', though their now intentional quality means that the three characteristics assume somewhat different forms.

First, as with our inadvertent 'limit' encounters, so also do our deliberate acts of turning towards the boundary of the manageable involve an intensification of ordinariness. But, whereas in the former case intensification is the *effect* of the circumstances in which we find ourselves, in the second case it is more exactly a *means* or a strategy we adopt in order to achieve the 'boundary' experience. That is, by deliberately intensifying aspects of our familiar world, we turn away from its safe and predictable 'centre' and towards its variously formidable (and/or exhilarating, breathtaking) margins. All the occasions I mentioned a moment ago exemplify this deliberate intensification of ordinariness by way of choosing the risky over the mundane: concert performers, however experienced, accept the sensation of 'nerves' before a performance as intrinsic to the artistic venture; every athlete elects the stress of competition over the ignominy of retirement; it is exactly the risk of the unknown which lures the gambler. The fascination which is *risk*, delivering its agent as it does from a familiar but uneventful world, mostly takes the form of an intensification of elements found precisely within that world.

I suppose that any or each of the advertent 'edge' experiences to which I refer would offer itself for analysis, but, given the long association between worship and the arts, it is the artist's modus operandi to which I shall look by way of exposition. Advertent adventures of the limit require an intensification of ordinariness, I have said, and deliberate risk-taking. The arts in whichever form – plastic, poetic, dance, music, whatever – demonstrate both characteristics.

It is thus something of a commonplace among aesthetic theorists that art finds its affectivity in its compression of, or focus upon, aspects of ordinary life which otherwise elude us precisely in their banality. G. H. Lewes, for instance, writes to the youthful George Eliot on the power of the novel: 'The true business of art is intensification, not distortion or falsification of the real.'[47] It is from this point of view that Philip Wheelwright gives several pages of his text on symbolic and literary language to 'particularity of reference' as the distinguishing mark of poetic or 'tensive' diction.[48] The idea similarly occurs not infrequently in Suzanne Langer's aesthetic philosophy.[49] Paul Ricoeur calls it 'iconic augmentation': '[L]iterary works depict reality by *augmenting* it with meanings that themselves depend upon the virtues of abbreviation, saturation, and culmination, so strikingly illustrated by emplotment.'[50] But it is perhaps David Tracy who has achieved the most exact statement of the principle:

> The difference between the artist and the rest of us is one of intense degree, not one of kind. The difference is one where the journey of intensification – a journey which most of us fear yet desire, shun yet demand – is really undertaken. The journey into particularity in all its finitude and all its striving for the infinite in this particular history in all its effects, personal and cultural, will with the artist be radically embraced . . .
>
> The sign of the artist may well be a willingness to undergo the journey of intensification into particularity to the point where an originating sense for the fundamental questions and feelings that impel us all . . . is experienced.[51]

47. G. H. Lewes, cited by Basil Willey, *Nineteenth-Century Studies: Coleridge to Matthew Arnold* (Harmondsworth: Penguin Books, 1964), 256.

48. Wheelwright, *The Burning Fountain*, 35: '[T]he first and most indispensable attribute of poetic language is its radical particularity of reference, its presentative immediacy'; see *ibid.*, 34–40, on 'confrontative imagining', esp. p. 37 on Coleridge's 'intensifying function of [secondary] imagination'.

49. For example, Suzanne K. Langer, *Feeling and Form: a theory of art* (New York: Charles Scribner's Sons, 1953), 243–4: '[T]he principle of condensation . . . is essentially a fusion of forms themselves by intersection, contraction, elision, suppression, and many other devices. The effect is usually to intensify the created image, heighten the "emotional quality"; often to make one aware of complexities of feeling.' See further, *ibid.*, 91, 212, 291–2.

50. Ricoeur, *Time and Narrative*, vol. I, p. 80 (his emphasis) and see *ibid.*, 82–83; see also his *Interpretation Theory*, 40–3. Similarly, Stephen Crites, 'The Narrative Quality of Experience', 85, describes narrative as a 'strategy of contraction'.

51. Tracy, *The Analogical Imagination*, 125.

If literature – the same applies to every artistic form – gains its effect *as* literature through strategies of intensification, then neither can there be a question of the inherent risks. It is scarcely a secret, that is, that in comparison with prosaic and discursive forms of utterance, art, music and poetry remain elusive in terms of both their meaning(s) and their value. The risk is in the first place for the artist: 'A courage to allow oneself to be played and thereby to play this game of the truth of existence must replace the fears and opinions of the everyday. The artist does not know where the journey will lead; one must wager and risk.'[52] But the risk is then inherited by the critic or interpreter: '[T]he cognitive role of the poeto-statement... is bound to be somewhat blurred...ironic...manic...paradoxical and inconclusive. Let us not deny or ignore these traits; they are part of the ambiguous delight of poetic statement. And they are useful in restraining a critic...from the *hybris* of excessive confidence in his [*sic*] own method.'[53] The venture of artistic expression is thus variously but inevitably precarious; with art, we *expect* to find ourselves in unknown territory: '[W]hen I recite a line of poetry or an entire poem, the words I utter cannot be immediately translated into a fixed *denotatum* that exhausts their meaning, for they imply a series of meanings that expand at every new look, to the point that they seem to offer me a concentrated image of the entire universe.'[54]

These references to the linking of intensification and risk in all artistic endeavour (as an example of advertent turning towards the boundary of the possible) lead me, second, to a consideration of the religious potential in this form of 'edge' experience. By all means, as in my account of unintentional encounters with ultimacy, we shall need here carefully to guard against overstatement: I speak deliberately of art's 'religious potential' or its 'religious affinity'. In this part of my discussion I am looking for such points of kinship or recognizability as offer themselves between modernity and an overt profession of faith. Subsequently (under the heading 'degrees of alterity') I shall want to advance much more stringent criticisms of what I dare to call modernity's 'religious sublimates'. Given the proximities of art and religion (on the one hand) and the modern repudiation of explicit religious dependency (on the other), it is scarcely surprising that from the earliest days of Enlightenment art was asked to assume this alternative role.[55] It is therefore common to meet accounts

---

52. *Ibid.*, 126.   53. Wheelwright, *The Burning Fountain*, 203.
54. Eco, *The Open Work*, 25.
55. See my discussion of art as 'religious sublimate', below, pp. 278–9.

which uncritically subsume religion into art;[56] indeed the examples I adduce themselves probably transgress in this respect, but, as noted, my purpose here is not so much to criticize as to find linkages between religion and modern sensibilities.

Thus it is not the least bit difficult to assemble a series of texts speculating the proximities of – or an identification between – art and religion. Rudolf Otto serves us as well as any: 'In great art the point is reached at which we may no longer speak of the "magical", but rather are confronted with the numinous itself, with all its impelling motive power, transcending reason, expressed in sweeping lines and rhythm.'[57] But perhaps the point should rather be made in the form of imaginative construction itself. I have in mind, then, the novel by the Australian Patrick White, *The Vivisector*.[58] Ben Nicholson's epigraph sets the direction: 'As I see it, painting and religious experience are the same thing, and what we are all searching for is the understanding and realization of infinity.' Thus is the book's main character an internationally renowned artist called Hurtle Duffield, now living in obscurity in a Melbourne suburb with his half-batty sister. Duffield is hardly a believer in any conventional sense. Yet for his entire life he has been driven by an unattainable goal: a vision of the colour blue, indigo in fact. Towards the end he suffers a stroke and can barely manage his brush. In one last terrible spasm of energy, he locks himself in his attic studio for upward of a week, scarcely stopping to sleep and only infrequently coming down to eat. These are the book's nearly concluding paragraphs:

> There was this day he sensed his psychopomp standing beside him. At once he began scrabbling according to direction on his rickety palette-table. He was mixing the never-yet-attainable blue.
>
> He pursed his lips to repeat the syllables which were being dictated: N-D-G-O. A thrumming of this stiff tongue. The gaps – nobody recognize. She insisted they would, apparently unaware of the precarious state of his faith.
>
> Whether it was she or he who knew better he took his broadest, though frankly feeble brush, and patted the blue on: brush was leaving its hairs behind, he noticed. All his life he had been reaching toward this vertiginous blue without truly visualizing, till lying on the pavement he was dazzled not so much by a colour as a longstanding secret relationship.

56. See, e.g., Hardy, *God's Ways with the World*, 69, n. 4, on George Steiner.

57. Otto, *The Idea of the Sacred*, 69; see *ibid*., 68–73, for Otto's treatment of 'means by which the numinous is expressed in art.'

58. Patrick White, *The Vivisector* (Harmondsworth: Penguin Books, 1973).

Now he was again acknowledging with all the strength of his live hand the otherwise unnameable I - N - D - I - G - O.

Only reach higher. Could. And will.

Then lifting by the hairs of his scalp to brush the brushhairs bludge on the blessed blue.

Before the tobbling scrawl deadwood splitting splintering the prickled stars plunge a presumptuous body crashing. Dumped.

Light follows dark not usually bound by the iron feather which stroked . . .

. . . Too tired too end-less obvi indi-ggoddd.[59]

White thus depicts – presumably is defending – a modern assimilation of art and religion: 'As I see it, painting and religious experience are the same thing.'[60] They are *not* the same thing, I shall insist. For the moment, though, it is enough to mark their affinity: both reach for the frontier of the imaginable; both entail an intensification of familiar things; both are risk-filled undertakings. In these respects religion and art (and other advertent ventures to human boundaries) share similar territory.

A third mark of boundary experience, I have said, is that it sharpens an awareness of the dialectic of identity and difference which, while never absent from human existence, is often or largely obscured precisely by the ordinariness of the familiar. It is not difficult to see that this sharpening is exactly the point of actions in which we wilfully embrace our limits. I have spoken of modernity's obsession with its autonomy. A deliberate encounter with danger thus involves something of an antinomy (itself a heightening of tensive forces): that is, the *dangers* to which we expose ourselves must be *controlled* (the roller-coaster operator must be licensed and the plant subject to daily inspection!).[61] Another way of saying this, I suppose, is that no one wants the *mysterium* which is truly *tremendum*: 'a terror fraught with an inward shuddering'.[62] In some cases, then, it is

59. *Ibid.*, 616–17.

60. For a period in his life Patrick White worshipped as an Anglican. I think this was not sustained, though his biographer speaks of a 'lifelong search for that fleeting presence [God]'; David Marr, *Patrick White: a life* (Sydney: Random House Australia, 1991), 282. White is regularly seen by Australian critics as an author exploring religious questions at their deepest levels; see for example Veronica Brady, *A Crucible of Prophets: Australians and the question of God* (Sydney: Theological Explorations, 1981) ch. 4, or ch. 3 of the same author's *Caught in the Draught* (Sydney: Angus and Robertson, 1994); also Michael Giffen, *Arthur's Dream: the religious imagination in the fiction of Patrick White* (Paddington NSW: Spaniel Books, 1996).

61. A most recent manifestation of our modern desire to *control* advertent *risk* is the practice of pre-nuptial contracts, already determining who shall get which assets in the event of the marriage's failure. Once, of course, we simply but soberly swore: 'With all my worldly goods I thee endow.' And we assumed that that meant, 'Till death do us part.'

62. Otto, *The Idea of the Holy*, 14.

more nearly the *illusion* of the terrifying (the roller-coaster ride, a horror movie) or in others it is the measured *possibility* of catastrophe (the lone ocean-going sailor) which gives to advertent 'edge' adventures their thrill, rush of adrenaline, escape from mundanity. Normally, we will say, it is the *mysterium fascinans* which entices people to abandon the certainties of the 'centre' and to venture the thrill of the 'edge', but this is precisely to sharpen the chances of either glory or disaster which, if not eliminated, are certainly inoculated in ordinariness. In risking death (at least its simulacrum), we know we are alive; in speaking out, we will be proved either right or wrong. The dangerous edge has a way of sharpening differences: 'Without alterity, experience becomes vacuous, our landscape a desert.'[63]

Experience of 'limit' as a component of worship

My analysis of the conditions within which liturgical meaning may be realized by late modern worshipping people is barely half accomplished. To the attempt thus far to trace points of identifiability between the modern condition and liturgical acts, I have yet to bring a dialectical rejoinder: namely, a *critique* of modern proclivities in the name of theism. Still, at this median point it will not be untoward, perhaps, to table some of the gains we have made.

'[L]iturgy leads regularly to the edge of chaos, and from this regular flirt with doom comes a theology different from any other.'[64] Thus does Aidan Kavanagh's bold sentence[65] anchor worship within the lived human circumstance I have called 'the phenomenon of edge experience'. Our survey of such experiences (of both involuntary and intentional kinds) has enabled us, I trust, to see that even in our radically secularized age there remains a residual awareness of the wonder and the dread of exposure to forces not of our own contriving. Every one of us, wholly irrespective of credal stance, knows – at least in part – how it must be, to be hurled into an abyss in the moment it needs to lift a telephone receiver. Everyone can imagine what it must be like, the specialist's eye averted, to hear that the tumour is active. In just the same way, we all know the rapture of a home team's winning goal in extra-time, the wonder of a newborn baby's fingernails and the beauty of a landscape freshly mantled in snow. Kavanagh's line sets worship squarely within this anthropological commonality.

63. Mark C. Taylor, 'Reframing Postmodernisms' in (Philippa Berry and Andrew Wernick, eds.) *Shadow of Spirit: postmodernism and religion* (London: Routledge, 1992), 21.
64. Kavanagh, *On Liturgical Theology*, 73; see my references to this sentence, above, p. 75 and ch. 5 n. 42.
65. More strictly Urban Holmes' sentence, according to Kavanagh's acknowledgment.

It does more than this, however: the identification of worship with such moments of intensification is (as Kavanagh certainly intended it to be) at once a judgement and a challenge to so much that goes in the name of worship. To include worship and the sorts of human encounter we have reviewed within a single frame of reference is to lay bare the conventionality, the domesticity and mildness into which worship so easily and routinely seems to descend. So distant from the sorts of terror and elation I have reviewed is the worshipping life of many (most?) Christians, that even Kavanagh's *description* is enough to elicit in many a thrill of fear and longing! Liturgical life does unquestionably contain this potential: its musical legacy even now supplies much of the repertoire for secularized concert-goers;[66] and its visual art stocks our galleries and continues to inspire.[67] But these are now mostly far removed from the regular experiences of late modern worshippers. The phenomenon of edge experience certainly links worship to universal human apprehension. It does more: it directs worship itself back to an original evocative power, a force which seems mostly to have been overtaken by the mundanity it was supposed to overcome.

Religious conviction as an assumed naiveté

A liturgical theology for late modern times must show how worship can 'make sense' for people shaped within the modern paradigm. My thesis thus far, then, is that worship's recognizability lies in its coherence with other human 'boundary' experiences. I have also urged, however, that worship cannot be *simply* coextensive with generalized human experience; that liturgical theology is bound to bring to human experience generally, and to a late modern infatuation with human autonomy particularly, a theistic alternative. Meaning, hence liturgical meaning, lies in the play on one another of similarity and difference. It is to the second part of the assignment that I now turn.

Degrees of alterity

One characteristic of 'edge' experiences, I said, is that these heighten or intensify – and in this way disclose – what has always been the case. The line

---

66. I recall my pain and confusion a year or so ago at the rapturous applause accorded a (religiously) spellbinding performance of Allegri's 'Miserere' in the Sydney Opera House (Concert Hall) by the Tallis Scholars.

67. I think of the celebrated passage in Chaim Potok's story of a Jewish artist who can find no other sufficient symbol of his mother's suffering than a crucifixion; Chaim Potok, *My Name is Asher Lev* (Harmondsworth: Penguin Books, 1972), 258.

of continuity which runs from everyday comfort to the terror of the un-
manageable (or to a dizzying elation) thus permits an infinite gradation: as
I noted earlier, perturbation can range in intensity from the annoyance of
missing my train to a disbelieving discovery that my job no longer exists,
and elation can be either the joy of a spring morning or being 'head over
heels' in love. But now this sliding scale between 'normalcy' and 'the extraordinary' also means that there are infinite degrees according to which I
will allow the *alterity* of 'the edge' to assert itself. In such circumstances as I
pictured as being at or near the 'centre' of our living-space platform, for example, it is clear that modern autonomy affords me much self-sufficiency:
I am free to order my life from its tiniest details (where I shall meet my
friend for lunch) to its largest (whom I shall marry, my career, who will
form the government).[68] Here no alien law or compulsion threatens. Yet,
we have seen, the sensed security can be illusory: it is possible to be hurled
from assured self-determination to an uttermost dread in seconds. Even
should I be so fortunate in life as never to have been plunged in crisis (an
unlikely idea), my equanimity conceals the fact of my 'thrownness': that
I had no say in whether and in which circumstances I would be born, nor
about my eventual departure. At the borders, exposed or concealed, I am
anything but in control; and at these (boundary places) whether of disaster
or fortune, it will be not uncommon to use language such as 'utterly un-
done', 'coming to pieces', 'at my wits' ends'. In a word, the alterity which
had been kept at bay in ordinariness is now terrifyingly (or wonderfully)
real. These are the recognizable end-points. What is perhaps not so apparent is that *the line which connects them is continuous*. This is more obviously
so in our deliberate ventures to the 'edge'. Mostly we have some power of
choice in electing for risk over retreat. Yet, of people overtaken in unexpected crisis, we will still speak admiringly of 'a wonderful composure',
of 'holding it all together', or of an 'impressive self-control'. We also recognize a point beyond this in which the person 'loses it' or 'comes unstuck'.
In advertent, but to some degree also in inadvertent, experiences of our
limits we recognize a graduated scale from well-secured autonomy to the
ravages of a fierce heteronomy.

Emmanuel Levinas is acknowledged as the thinker of our time who has
most persistently probed the nature of alterity, of the Other's 'otherness'.

68. So Taylor, *Sources*, 214–15: '[N]o one can be blind to the tremendous role [the new
"bourgeois" ethic] has played in constituting modern liberal society . . . with [its] ideals of
equality, [its] sense of universal right, [its] work ethic, and [its] exaltation of sexual love and
the family.'

In a moment I shall invoke his appeal to the human face as hypostasizing alterity. Here, however, it is his more fundamental preoccupation with what he calls western philosophy's 'endless return to the self' which engages our attention. In Levinas' view, philosophies of consciousness, which is to say, philosophy which assumes its starting point in the autonomy of the thinking person – the entire western tradition, in fact – cannot help themselves from usurping and suppressing the otherness of that on which the thinker thinks. To think something, to know something, is to encompass it within the field of the knowable and thus to reduce it to terms which are thinkable for the thinker: 'Western philosophy coincides with the disclosure of the other where the other, in manifesting itself as a being, loses its alterity. From its infancy philosophy has been struck with a horror of the other that remains other – with an insurmountable allergy.'[69] From this point of view, all knowing remains within itself. Plato's intuition about *anamnesis*, recollection, is well placed. Western thought rightly links itself with the myth of the eternal return; its leitmotif is Ulysses returning, after all his adventures, to his native land.[70] From this vantage point it becomes clear that the graduated range by which subjects are removed, either willingly or involuntarily, from a well-regulated 'centre' to a dangerous 'limit', is the measure either of their exposure to alterity or, oppositely, their 'return to the self'.

I have from time to time made passing reference to modernity's 'religious sublimates'; it is now time to inspect these in sharper detail. If Levinas supposes that the entire course of western thought evinces 'the return to the self', then modernity can only be regarded as its epitome: 'An unprecedented modernity, open to the future, anxious for novelty, can *only fashion its criteria out of itself*. The only source of normativity that presents itself is the principle of subjectivity.'[71] It was quickly clear – for reasons we have already traversed – that in the new era of Enlightenment art would assume much of the role previously ascribed to religion.[72] The tendency has remained entirely recognizable:

69. Emmanuel Levinas, 'The Trace of the Other' in (Mark C. Taylor, ed.) *Deconstruction in Context: literature and philosophy* (University of Chicago Press, 1969), 346.
70. *Ibid.* A useful *entrée* to Levinas' thought is given in Colin Davis, *Levinas: an introduction* (Cambridge: Polity Press, 1996); on 'the self and the other' see particularly pp. 38–47.
71. Habermas, *The Philosophical Discourse*, 41 (my emphases).
72. See e.g., *ibid.*, 45–6: '[In Schiller] art is supposed to become effective in place of religion as the unifying power . . . Hence [he] stresses the communicative, community-building and solidarity-giving force of art' (emphases removed); and see *ibid.*, 31–2, 139 for similar ideas in Hegel and Heidegger.

[T]he temptation to ascribe a quasi-sacred or religious office to certain kinds of literary expression is not restricted to a small and eccentric group of critics in the modern period. In a time when all forms of traditionalism are on the wane, a great many critics . . . like writers themselves, have come to place increasingly heavy demands upon literature, asking it to perform a redemptive function once reserved for religion alone.[73]

But in none of this can we overlook the inherently modern form (and degree) of the 'return to the self'. Deborah Haynes, then, writes of Albrecht Dürer's self-portrait (which she places at the beginnings of modernity in art): 'Here the artist no longer imitates God; the artist replaces God as the original creator and inventor.'[74] The process (of 'returning to the self') reaches some sort of ultimate degree, one imagines, in the claim: '"Making art is . . . practicing a religion . . . There is definitely something mystical about my work. *It's my own religion, my own iconography.*"'[75]

Different, but still suggestive of a 'religious sublime', is what has come to be called, following Robert Bellah, 'civil religion'.[76] Such matters doubtless vary from country to country, dependent as they are on particular national and social histories. Still, the Australian circumstance may be reasonably representative. In the past two decades this society has seen a remarkable recuperation of the public honour given to those who died in war, and of the place of the Anzac legend (Australian and New Zealand Army Corps) in national sentiment. In the 1960s these ideas had so far faded from popular consciousness that it was supposed that the ceremonies honouring the war dead (Anzac Day, 25 April; the anniversary of the landing of the Anzac troops at Gallipoli in Turkey, 1915) would disappear.[77] Quite contrarily, attendance at the parades has subsequently leapt, and young people are increasingly finding powerful symbolic meaning in the legend and the rituals.[78] The notion, 'They died for us', clearly

73. Giles Gunn, *The Interpretation of Otherness: literature, religion, and the American imagination* (New York: Oxford University Press, 1979), 70–1.
74. Haynes, *The Vocation of the Artist*, 93; see similarly, *ibid.*, 113: 'By the end of the nineteenth century . . . the artist had become an anthropocentric inventor, imitating God and creating the new world.'
75. Haynes, *ibid.*, 146, citing the artist Joan Snyder (my emphases).
76. See Robert Bellah, 'Civil Religion in America' in (Russell E. Richey and Donald G. Jones, eds.) *American Civil Religion* (New York: Harper and Row, 1974), 21–44.
77. See, e.g., Inglis, *Sacred Places*, 9.
78. The gap between the generations means that the significance now being found in the sacrifice of servicemen and women is to be distinguished from the simple or raw grief felt by relatives at the time of their death.

carries religious – at the very least religious-like – connotations for those participating.[79]

One is further tempted to wonder whether the effusion of grief for 'iconic' figures such as John Lennon, Princess Diana or the cricket player Sir Donald Bradman is perhaps not another form of modern 'sublime religion'.[80] Or yet again, Susan White asks whether technological achievement itself has not acquired a 'quasi-religious status'.[81]

My subject is: 'degrees of alterity'. The stories of the man and of the woman swept into circumstances over which they had virtually no control, illustrate, I hope, an uttermost degree of alienation (removal from the self, exposure to that which is other, alien). By contrast, when we hear an artist describing her work as her 'own religion', her 'own iconography', it is impossible not to hear the clearest echoes of Levinas' judgement. The thrill-seeker who knows in advance that her or his 'buzz' has met government regulations is another indicator of a trip to the 'edge' that was never really out of control. Even of an unquestionably sincere honouring of war dead, one must say that participation in a parade once a year, or even making a pilgrimage to Anzac Cove itself (in modern Turkey), is entirely voluntaristic. As K. S. Inglis notes, 'the plain tomb and its guardian soldier and sailor [can] bear whatever reading the Anzac marcher, the wreathlayer, the passer-by, [is] moved to make'; or again, 'People can pick and choose among the messages.'[82] This does not deny that such actions might be deeply altruistic; it is to say that there is a vast range of degrees by which people are exposed, or permit their exposure, to the margins of the manageable.

The 'vocative dimension'

The continuity running from self-possession to being possessed, with its consequent ambiguity about 'religion' – wherein this consists and what shall be its defining marks – means that we need a *much sharper criterion*

---

79. See Inglis, *Sacred Places*, 458–71, on 'the Anzac Cult', notably 470–1 (citing a Jesuit priest): 'Anzac Day . . . "deals with the ultimate questions about the value of a life posed inescapably by those who are sent to die young on a community's behalf."' Analogies between war heroes and Christ or Christian faith abound in Inglis' text; for example, pp. 453, 456.
80. Though known only in cricket-playing countries, Sir Donald Bradman is regarded as the greatest batsman in the history of the game; in Australia his exploits are legendary. On the occasion of his funeral (March, 2001) in response to popular sentiment, his son was moved to remark that his father would not have wished to have been regarded as a religious hero.
81. E.g., Susan White, *Christian Worship and Technological Change*, 110.
82. Inglis, *Sacred Places*, 462 and 471; see the longer section on 'Meanings', *ibid.*, 471–4.

of authentically religious experience than is often afforded. Over against modernity's strident advocacy of the 'return to the self', and in view of the near mesmeric power of immanentism for late modern theology, it is *otherness* or *difference* – notably the alterity inherent in any Christian confession of God as Creator, Redeemer and life-giving Spirit – which is, or becomes, this urgently necessary criteriological principle. God can never be simply another in a series.

Hence the contextual importance of Levinas' ideas. As is widely known, Levinas finds that it is *the face* which chiefly epitomizes otherness, the reference point from beyond consciousness which stubbornly announces a presence not my own:

> the epiphany of the other involves a signifyingness of its own, independently of this signification received from the world. The other does not only come to us out of a context, but comes without mediation; he [*sic*] signifies by himself . . . According to the phenomenological expression, it [his cultural signification] reveals the horizons of this world. But this mundane signification is found to be disturbed and shaken by another presence, abstract, not integrated into the world . . . [T]he phenomenon which is the apparition of the other is also a *face* . . .
>
> The presence of a face thus signifies an irrecusable order, a command, which calls a halt to the availability of consciousness. Consciousness is put into question by a face . . .
>
> The I before another is infinitely responsible.[83]

The signification of alterity in a face is, on the one hand, not *reducible* to someone's mere physical lineaments ('this mundane signification is . . . disturbed and shaken by another presence'),[84] nor, on the other hand, is it *exhausted* in personal relationships: it opens into infinity. God's alterity, for Levinas, is by no means dissociated from the alterity of persons;[85] yet God's alterity is such that Levinas will only speak of it as 'the trace' of the

---

83. Levinas, 'The Trace of the Other', 351, 352 and 353; almost identical passages are contained in the essay 'Meaning and Sense' in (Adrian T. Peperzak, Simon Critchley and Robert Bernasconi, eds.) *Emmanuel Levinas: basic philosophical writings* (Bloomington: Indiana University Press, 1996), 53–4.
84. Cf. 'The best way of encountering the Other is not even to notice the colour of his eyes! When one observes the colour of the eyes one is not in social relationship with the Other'; cited by Davis, *Levinas*, 133.
85. See for example his *Nine Talmudic Readings* (Bloomington: Indiana University Press, 1990), 27 and 66: 'The respect for the stranger and the sanctification of the name of the Eternal are strangely equivalent'; 'To sacralize the earth is to found a just community on it.'

other, or perhaps better (borrowing a phrase from Kevin Hart), 'only a trace of a trace'.[86]

The importance for liturgy of Levinas' far-reaching, often arcane, deliberations is perhaps made more accessible in an idea I borrowed much earlier from the philosopher of religion, Ninian Smart, namely, 'the vocative dimension': '[T]he language of worship begins with the vocative. In worship one *addresses* the focus of worship.'[87] 'Face', then, is transposed into 'address'; both are ways of securing the inalienable alterity of the other. It is *worship's vocative dimension*, the fact that it is constructed on the basis of an *address* to the other encountered in worship, I asseverate, which gives it (worship) its necessary critical (criteriological) clarity.

In the liturgy, 'Our dear Lord himself speaks with us in his holy Word and in reply we speak with him through prayer and praise.'[88] The fact that the language of worship consists primarily in the vocative case[89] is that characteristic which immediately distinguishes it (worship) from the multitude of variously similar 'edge' experiences. Earlier, I wanted to draw an identification between worship and Otto's generalized account of 'the numinous', but we saw, too, that just this broad recognizability creates its own problems of definition: how to *distinguish* worship among such experiences? The vocative principle is that defining force. Martin Buber, in his account of I–Thou relationships, asks (rhetorically of course): 'Can the servant of Mammon say Thou to his money?'[90] And by exactly this token we may ask: to *whom* or to *what* does the crowd address its wild elation at a last-minute winning goal? Or, can we imagine someone *praying* to a *painting*? Does it make any sense to address one's wonder to a splendid *landscape*?[91] All of them are awe-inspiring. One does not *address* them. And that,

---

86. See esp. pp. 354–9 of 'The Trace of the Other'; Hart's phrase, not directly related to Levinas, is from *The Trespass of the Sign*, 181. See further Davis, *Levinas*, 99: 'God is not simply "the first other" or the "other par excellence" or the "absolutely other".'
87. Smart, *The Concept of Worship*, 10 (my emphasis; see above, ch. 1, n. 115). Strictly speaking, Smart does not himself use the term 'vocative dimension'; I am extrapolating that from another of his works, *Dimensions of the Sacred* and applying it to the sentences I have cited in my text. On pp. 10–11 of *Dimensions of the Sacred*, Smart assembles a list of seven 'dimensions' which he thinks appertain to all religions, but the 'vocative' dimension is not among them.
88. See above, ch. 5, n. 45.
89. See again in this connection, Zimmerman, *Liturgy as Language of Faith*, 3ff., on what she calls 'first order discourse': 'the language of prayer, doxology, worship . . . is formed in encounter, confrontation, recognition, and it is full of the awed sense of the other: the "you"' (*ibid.*, 4, citing D. B. Stevick). See further, Zimmerman, *ibid.*, 119, on 'limit-language' as connected with 'limit-experience'.
90. Buber, *I and Thou*, 106.
91. See my remarks (above, ch. 7, n. 94) on Sallie McFague's obfuscation of worship's vocative dimension, including her use of Simone Weil's expression, 'absolute attention is prayer'.

in its ultimate specification of alterity, is what distinguishes worship of God from other religious and near religious experiences.[92]

The point can be sharpened still further. Luther's limpid sentence speaks not of address simply, but of dialogue, of *inter*locution. That the address in view is not unidirectional, but dialogical, points us towards the *claim* made upon the self in its encounters with another, the question that is put to it, that is, by the sheer structure of communicative discourse:[93] 'Consciousness is *put into question* by a face'; and, 'The I before another is *infinitely responsible.*' In close accordance, then, with the multiple 'degrees of alterity' I attempted to sketch, so are there infinitely variable degrees whereby the self will be open to the claim upon it, the challenge addressed to it, by the other. In a media-saturated west, for example, we are familiar with 'compassion exhaustion', in which our exposure to the victims of famine, war or disaster (their claim on us for assistance) leaves us dully unmoved. Many people's advertent adventures to the 'edge' *are* doubtless highly motivated, highly intentional, in their openness before the claim of the other. Others, one must say, are the efforts of rich, bored people trying to break out of their tedium; some are a desperate attempt to escape (through drugs) adamantine pain or despair; and some are religious or quasi-religious experimentations undertaken in variously serious intent. Wherever people find themselves, or place themselves, in relation to the challenge of alterity – the claim of the other, eventually of God's otherness – none of these will be more stringent than the claim upon the self felt and answered by subjects of an explicit religious conversion. In comparison, that is, with the exigency of biblical imperatives – 'You will have no other gods before me' (Exodus 20:3), 'If any want to be my followers, let them deny themselves,

And see there the reference to Daniel Hardy's critical rejoinder. The 'vocative dimension' of worship is attested in such sentences of Hardy as '[F]ashioning . . . a song [of praise to God] is actually the task of theology' (*God's Ways with the World*, 69); and (of 'the dynamic of praise'), 'There is reference to an addressee, the Lord, whose identity and position are established, not only by who he is but by what he has done and will do' (*ibid.*, 264).

92. I think it must, or may, be possible to speak *through* such vehicles of ultimacy to some sort of Thou lying within or behind them. Buber was already reaching for this in his recognition of the eternal Thou mediately present in all personal encounter (e.g., *I and Thou*, 75). But that, I think, is distinguishable from an address *to* the adorable (or terrifying) thing in itself which would be much harder to conceptualize (or perhaps it is what we mean by 'idolatry'). I further imagine it as possible that by a kind of extrapolation one might find oneself addressed by, and thus responding to, a work of art or literature, or a natural phenomenon. But this, too, is distinguishable from prayer; indeed, precisely the vagueness of a 'response' to an art-work (in comparison with the 'Thou' of worship's vocative dimension) very closely catches the criteriological aspect I am here reaching for. Once more, that is, one is not likely to *pray* to a *painting*.

93. See my reference above, ch. 2, n. 23, to Habermas' 'theory of communicative action'.

take up their cross and follow me' (Mark 8:34), or 'You are not your own; you were bought with a price' (1 Corinthians 6:19f.), for example – the negotiable self-determination inherent in most encounters with alterity in our society still has about it a good deal of 'the return to the self'. It is in its simple 'Yes' to the claim or call of the Other[94] that worship's vocative dimension is brought to completion; and it is here that its sharp differentiation from nearly every other boundary experience in our time is declared.

Two important footnotes to this account of worship's vocative dimension are called for. First, for reasons which I hope have been sufficiently clear, I have made much of alterity's *claim*. In all this, however, the fact may never be lost sight of that it is the *fascinans* of the mystery – that which we heard described as 'beatitude beyond compare' (above, page 267) – which effects all true religious conversion and conviction. Alterity's claim may be ineluctable; yet one does not ordinarily think of the religious convert being cowed or beaten into submission. Admittedly, some sort of final self-negation is arrived at wherein the subject confesses, 'Whatever gains I had, these I have come to count as loss' (Philippians 3:7), or, 'It is no longer I who live, but it is Christ who lives within me' (Galatians 2:20), but this is *always because of the surpassing worth* of what the convert sees before him or her. According to Origen of Alexandria: 'The soul is moved by heavenly love and longing when, having already beheld the beauty and the fairness of the Word of God, it falls deeply in love with his loveliness.'[95] The benefaction attested by the religious convert is affirmed by the philosophers of alterity. Thus is Levinas' entire, prodigious output predicated on the conviction that 'the return to the self' is self-defeating:

> Need opens upon a world that is for-me; it returns to the self. Even
> when sublime, as the need for salvation, it is still nostalgia,
> homesickness. Need is the return itself, the anxiety of an ego for itself,
> the original form of identification which we have called egoism. It is an
> assimilation of the world in view of coincidence with oneself, or
> happiness.[96]

For his part, too, Buber speaks of the acceptance of the 'Thou' as alone giving us meaning and wellbeing:

94. See again Zimmerman's sentence, n. 89 above.
95. Origen, *Commentary on the Song of Songs* as cited by William Johnston, *Mystical Theology: the science of love* (London: HarperCollins, 1995), 264; I am indebted to Judith Nelson-Clegg for this reference.
96. Levinas, 'The Trace of the Other', 350.

Man [*sic*] receives, and he receives not a specific 'content' but a Presence, a presence as power. This Presence and this power include three things, undivided, yet in such a way that we may consider them separately. First, there is the whole fulness of real mutual action, of the being raised and bound up in relation . . . Secondly, there is the inexpressible confirmation of meaning. Meaning is assured. Nothing can any longer be meaningless. The question about the meaning of life is no longer there . . . Thirdly, this meaning is not that of 'another life', but that of this life of ours, not one of a world 'yonder' but that of this world of ours.[97]

All this comes directly to expression in the liturgy: 'Our dear Lord himself speaks with us through his holy Word and in response we speak with him through praise and prayer.' The dialogical structure of the liturgy does make its claim upon our autonomy; but precisely this is the possibility for its *gift* of blessing, absolution, reconciliation and wholeness. The one is not possible without the other; claim and benediction come hand in hand.

Second, it would be the rashest of judgements to suppose of Christians gathered in worship, that – in contrast to the various religious aspirations we have surveyed – they alone turn wholly away from self-interest, self-consciousness, to embrace God's alterity without remainder. Both within and between its members, every Christian congregation is a 'mixed multitude' (Exodus 12:38, cf. Matthew 13:30). The reality, then, is one thing, by no means to be discounted, but the *gesture* is another, also deserving attention: the liturgical forms do seek, do purport, to bring people before the Face of God, and to give them language wherewith to express their adoration, their regrets, their utmost hopes and deepest fears. Just occasionally for whole congregations, more regularly for particular members thereof, hearts and minds actually follow the gesture: there is an unrestrained turn towards the unbounded otherness which Christians and religious people generally name as God. It is this – partial as it must often be, entwined with all manner of doubtful motives, and never free of cultural presuppositions, but often seriously intentional too – which, with the reciprocal greeting from God's side, I am calling worship's 'vocative dimension'.

The naming of alterity
But if worshippers are to be envisaged as standing at the edge of the known, resolutely, joyfully facing otherness, how can worship be *vocative*?

97. Buber, *I and Thou*, 110; see similarly, *ibid.*, e.g., 28, 82, on the reciprocal gift of the 'I' and the 'Thou'.

Otherwise said, how may the unknown, the unknowable be *addressed*? How shall the indescribable be *named*?[98] This is the final and most inexorable question for worship. It is the point at which the oxymoron 'an assumed naiveté' (to recall the heading of this section) must be invoked.

The question presses acutely on a theorization of worship. At the same time, neither is it absent from theology more generally. It is the question lying at the heart of iconoclastic controversies in their various manifestations: iconoclasts insist on the fundamental unknowability of otherness: *finitum non est capax infiniti* (the finite cannot contain the infinite);[99] iconodules argue oppositely that the only forms we have in which to bring to expression our sense of ultimacy are human ones: 'God has determined to give the inward [i.e., spiritual insight] to no one except through the outward [material forms].'[100] Limit experience – just in so far as it *is* limit – encompasses both points of view: it is where contingency is met by ultimacy, where likeness and difference are held in tensive dialectic, where we know that we can know no more. The limit or boundary is 'both–and', it is 'is-and-is-not', it is the point 'at which the spade is turned'.[101] On the one side, then, that which outruns human knowledge is clearly *mysterious*;[102] this is the ground of worship's in-built iconoclasm.[103] But equally, the virtual universality of what I called 'the phenomenon of limit experience' attests that this liminal place – notwithstanding modern 'forgetfulness', nor overlooking the multidimensional quality of limit experience – is indubitably *real*. In its weekly journey to the limits of the manageable, a worshipping congregation holds within itself this finally irresolvable tension: at the boundary of the knowable, it knows that *all its images of God*

---

98. See particularly Mary Collins, 'Naming God in Public Prayer' in *Worship: renewal to practice* (Washington DC: The Pastoral Press, 1987), 215–29.

99. Said to be the central motif of Calvin's theology; so Eire, *War Against the Idols*, 197. See similarly the insistence of eighth-century iconoclasts that 'Christ is uncircumscribed and incomprehensible and impassible and immeasurable' in Jaroslav Pelikan, *Imago Dei: the Byzantine apologia for icons* (Princeton University Press, 1990), 78.

100. Luther, as cited by Carlos Eire, *War Against the Idols*, 72; for the arguments derived from the inseparability of Christ's 'two natures' by the Greek iconodules, see Pelikan, *Imago Dei*, 78–98.

101. Pailin, *Anthropological Character*, 69, characterizes the dialectic quality of limit as follows: 'The ultimacy of God not only provides the limits for understanding but is itself understood in terms of what we regard as those limits.' And Gadamer says: 'What makes a limit a limit always also includes knowledge of what is on both sides of it' (*Truth and Method*, 307).

102. See, e.g., Kaufman's extended meditation on the essential mysteriousness of human existence which gives to 'God' its meaning as 'the central symbol' by which 'the reality and significance of our own finitude comes into view'; Kaufman, *In Face of Mystery*, e.g., 6–9.

103. See, e.g., Pailin, *God and the Processes of Reality*, 96: 'One implication of the recognition of this defining characteristic of the divine [i.e., perfection] is that pure worship has to be seen as inescapably iconoclastic . . . True worship is directed towards a reality which criticizes our images of the divine as inadequate.'

are constructed, and are therefore fungible before an iconoclastic critique. In its knowledge, oppositely, of its own indubitable limits, it attests *what it knows as certain fact*. In setting up this final attempt on the meaning of worship, both elements have their part to play. Between them they produce the contradiction in terms: 'assumed naiveté'.

Paul Ricoeur will be recognized as the thinker responsible for introducing to theology the notion of naiveté. It is chiefly known to us through his study of the ancient symbolic systems for naming and dealing with evil.[104] With every other thinker in the west, Ricoeur sees that pre-modern people had access to a religious universe – through mythic, symbolic and cultic forms – from which, as products of modernity, we are now debarred. This ancient confidence in a religiously coherent world Ricoeur calls a 'first' or 'primitive' naiveté.[105] Ricoeur has no wish simply to repristinate the past.[106] Neither does he doubt that, 'In every way, something has been lost, irremediably lost: immediacy of belief.'[107] His objective, then, in undertaking his work (at a time we now identify as the beginnings of postmodernity)[108] was twofold: first, to destabilize the then still regnant confidence in itself of modern, rational inquiry (which, in its 'false clarity',[109] nonchalantly relegated to a 'mythological' antiquity whatever meaning the symbols might have) and, second, in thus moving beyond such critical disdain, to reopen the possibility of learning what meaning these ancient systems of symbols might yet have for us – precisely as inhabitants of the modern or late modern era: 'Beyond the wastelands of critical thought, we seek to be challenged anew.'[110] He thus formulates his well-known proposal for 'a second naiveté'; *viz.*, a process of thought[111] in which

104. This work is usually referred to by way of the book-length study, *The Symbolism of Evil*, but is also to be found in the essays: '"Original Sin": a study in meaning', in *Conflict of Interpretations*, 269–86; 'The Hermeneutics of Symbols and Philosophical Reflection, I & II', *ibid.*, 287–334; and in 'Evil: a challenge to philosophy and theology', *Journal of the American Academy of Religion* 53 (1985), 635–48.

105. For example, *Symbolism of Evil*, 19, 351, 352.

106. 'Hermeneutics of Symbols I', 287, 296.   107. *Symbolism of Evil*, 351.

108. *Symbolism of Evil* was published in French in 1960.

109. Ricoeur applies this term to all rationalising systems, ancient and modern; see 'Original Sin' in *Conflict of Interpretations*, 282.

110. 'Hermeneutics of Symbols I', 288; similarly, *Symbolism of Evil*, 349: 'Beyond the desert of criticism, we wish to be called again.'

111. 'Thought' for Ricoeur has an especial connotation; it is explicitly *not* the rationalism, of either ancient or modern kind, which presumes a mastery of its subject matter (see, for example, the reference to 'false clarity' at n. 109 above). 'Thought' is rather that process of human reflection which understands that its own origins lie in the capacity for imagination, for making analogical connections, the capacity for language, for the poetic (see particularly, 'A Response [to the Editor's Introduction] by Paul Ricoeur' in *Hermeneutics and the Human Sciences*, 39).

a modern person first critically examines the effects of her or his own cultural conditioning *as* modern (a kind of phenomenological *epoché*), so as then to be free to ponder the ancient symbolic formulations:

> [I]f we can no longer live the great symbolisms of the sacred in accordance with the original belief in them, we can, we modern men [*sic*], aim at a second naiveté in and through criticism. In short it is by *interpreting* that we can *hear* again. Thus it is in hermeneutics that the symbol's gift of meaning and the endeavour to understand by deciphering are knotted together.[112]

Wherefore,

> the task of the philosopher guided by symbols [is] to break out of the enchanted enclosure of consciousness of oneself, to end the prerogative of self-reflection. The symbol gives reason to think that the *Cogito* is within being, and not vice versa. Thus the second naiveté [is] a second Copernican revolution: the being which posits itself in the *Cogito* has still to discover that the very act by which it abstracts itself from the whole does not cease to share in the being that challenges it in every symbol.[113]

The idea of worship's naiveté (either of a first or second order; whether assumed as in the pre-modern world, or deliberately adopted as it must now be) offers a number of important perspectives. First, it alerts us to the fact that in every act of worship – and every aspect of every act – there inheres a fundamental unsophistication. This is the product of worship's in-built iconoclasm. Quite simply, since no one ever transcends the limit so as to say definitely what otherness, the Other, is really like, no one is a master. The most elegant prayer, the most learned sermon, the most brilliant ceremony is thus shot through and through with childlike ingenuousness; nothing is exempted from this rule. Accordingly is it deeply inscribed within the tradition that it is *children* who enter the Kingdom (Mark 10:15), that it is the *modest* who go down to their house justified (Luke 18:14), and that it is the *foolish*, the *weak* and the *despised* who are called (1 Corinthians 1:27). Worship's essential simplicity dictates, second, that its most basic response is an acclamation: 'The first or central act of religion is *adoration*, sense of God, His otherness through nearness, His distinctness for all finite beings, though not separateness – aloofness – from them.'[114] So, the Apostle, having exhausted his considerable mind over the

---

112. *Symbolism of Evil*, p. 351 (his emphases).   113. *Ibid.*, 356.

114. F. von Hügel, as cited by Evelyn Underhill, *Worship* (London: Nisbet & Co., 1939), 5 (von Hügel's emphasis). Cf. also LaCugna, *God for Us*, 321: 'Ultimately, the only appropriate response to the mystery of God revealed in the economy is adoration.' And see *passim* Daniel W. Hardy and David Ford, *Jubilate: theology in praise* (London: Darton, Longman & Todd, 1984).

mystery of God's 'election', knows that only doxology will do: 'O the depth of the riches and wisdom and knowledge of God! How unsearchable are his judgements and how inscrutable his ways!' (Romans 11:33). Third, worship's iconoclastic insistence on God's ultimate unknowability teaches us that all our images are constructed. Here one must move with care, for, of course, the images do not come out of the air: the dialectic of making *and finding* means that images of God will – must! – *be congruent* with the phenomenon of edge experiences whence they arise. Still, worship's iconoclastic naiveté contests any tendency to reification; insists, that is, that our images *are* imaginative constructions.[115] Worship knows that it does *not* know whereof it speaks; thus it *confesses* its faith.[116]

So much then for the naiveté of all religious profession; what now of the deliberately *assumed* naiveté required of the modern or postmodern person of faith?

A person shaped in and by the modern paradigm cannot shed that cultural inheritance without disowning some essential aspect of her or his identity: modern is what we are! Even where, by some sort of cultural bifurcation, people of modern times desire to appropriate the forms of faith of earlier generations, this *can* never now be with the simplicity in which those people believed. Modernity has entered in. Irrevocably. 'In every way, something has been lost, irremediably lost: immediacy of belief.' In Langdon Gilkey's form of it:

> Thus religious symbols are not transferable directly into the context of the language systems of the physical or the social sciences, or even of anthropological or historical inquiry, which legitimately for their own purposes presuppose the sufficiency of explanations dependent on finite factors alone. For this reason, most of contemporary theology is correct in requiring that all religious myths and symbols be understood as 'broken', that is to say, as recognizing that, while religious discourse may be significant of our situation *vis-à-vis* the ultimate reality with which we have to do, its symbols and myths cannot be taken 'literally', as direct statements explanatory of facts or events observable in the space–time continuum.[117]

115. The constructed nature of religious symbols is already apparent in Ricoeur's treatment of the ancient formulations: in describing evil as 'stain' or 'deviation' or 'burden' there never was an *actual* stain which could be expunged or a *literal* point in the road where a turning had been missed, and so on. The pictures or metaphors (symbols) are rather the means by which the reality (that is to say, the *discovered* dimension of the symbol: the unmistakable but inarticulable sense of malaise) is enabled to come to expression. See esp. *The Symbolism of Evil*, 9, 35.
116. It is noteworthy that Ricoeur's introductory chapter to *Symbolism of Evil* is called 'Phenomenology of "Confession"'.
117. Gilkey, *Naming the Whirlwind*, 422–3.

These are the reasons which led me to say, of 'church' forms of liturgical theology and of some aspects of evangelical theology, that these show insufficient cognizance of the actual world from within which modern believers must supply interpretants for the signs of worship and thus bring the significations to their completion. This – needless now to say – is also the setting wherein, or for which, Ricoeur proposes his 'second naiveté'. The mythic representations of ultimacy can now only be appropriated in the experimental stance of 'as if'.[118]

Products of modernity cannot escape that circumstance; what they *are* free to do, however, is to subject this, their own cultural formation, to critical inspection (perhaps 'postmodernity' means just this capacity for critical review of our own cultural paradigm). In any case, it is easier to see now that the forces which shaped us are (have been) anything but benign, or – as modernity was so fond of representing itself – 'objective'. We have learned more recently that modernity is (was) an aggressively self-justifying, self-serving energy, dismissive of alternative possibilities, falsely laying claim to a cognitive mastery (at any rate potentially) of the human condition, and disseminating the illusion of security by directing attention away from its own limits and towards its technological accomplishments.[119] A late modern religious naiveté belongs within this revisionist gambit. I noted in passing that 'an assumed naiveté' is a double negation (naiveté is ordinarily *un*assuming). The religious naiveté of a late modern person thus negates the negativity of modernist dogma; it calls in question the absolutist dimensions of those forms of thought and thus holds open a space for the exploration of our limits, for the encounter with alterity. It does not disown its own cultural matrix; but it does hold it in suspension, brings to bear on it the same critical stance which modernity itself so forthrightly advocated. It is not (of course) an argument for God's existence; it does create a conceptual space in which the ancient attestations to that existence may be entertained.

---

118. Kaufman, *In Face of Mystery*, 53–5, accepts the idea, but not the terminology, of the 'second naiveté'. He fully agrees that a new, or third, 'reflective moment of consciousness' is necessary, given the aporias now attending both the primitive forms of naiveté and the critical stance. He thinks, however, that the 'third moment' is 'anything but naive: it involves a consciousness even more critical . . . than . . . the moment of criticism' (*ibid.*, 54). For a more sympathetic appropriation of Ricoeur's term, see Mark I. Wallace, *The Second Naiveté: Barth, Ricoeur and the New Yale Theology* (Macon GA: Mercer University Press, 1990), esp. pp. 111–25.
119. These judgements have been documented in my earlier reviews of twentieth-century thought. See, e.g., ch. 1, nn. 85, 86; ch. 2, nn. 63, 64; or Ricoeur's comments on 'forgetfulness' and 'the wastelands of critical thought' in nn. 28 and 110 above; on the abandonment of 'the great dream' (of a description of physical reality as it is apart from observers) see, e.g., p. 65.

Does the assumed naiveté of late modern religious profession differ in a material way from the more intuitive naiveté which, I alleged, marks some forms of liturgical theology? The answer, I think, is affirmative. In the first place, it is undertaken by someone who knows himself or herself unambiguously to *be* a modern (now, late modern) person. This must offer itself as an immense advantage over what I described as the 'cultural bifurcation' and 'conceptual brittleness' of other religious professions in our time.[120] Second, however, it means that the credal specifications of the confession will be made a great deal more lightly and experimentally than in the case of a 'first' naiveté. I said – of the naiveté inherent in faith *as such* – that this functions iconoclastically: it tells us that *none* of our images will coincide with the reality. An *assumed* naiveté brings to this (not, I think, contradictorily) an iconodulistic conviction: namely, that the only images we *have* with which to 'clothe' the invisibility of the Other are those of human devising (and particularly those of one's tradition); as noted, these will be held tentatively, experimentally. Needless to say, this will be seen as a crippling disadvantage by the exponents of a more 'direct' apprehension of the symbols, whose overriding desire is to know assuredly 'who holds the future'[121] (*how* they may know this, of course, remains the unanswerable question). Third, a religious profession made in full awareness of modern tenets will represent a much sharper confrontation of 'similarity' and 'difference'. That is, a person committing to an intentional naiveté simultaneously owns *and* criticizes the modernity of which he or she is a part. (In comparison, the more 'intuitive' forms of religious response, we saw, tend to write modernity out of the account.) If it is true that meaning comes from the interplay of identity and difference, it might follow that such a person's faith is more meaningful than that of the conservative or evangelical, though it is admittedly hard to say how that could be measured. Fourth, however, the more profound conjunction of likeness and difference held within the believing response of a person fully aware of her or his (late) modernity is likely to make that faith more daring, more experimental, more nearly a 'wager'. This is, in fact, how Ricoeur conceives it (itself an interesting appropriation of 'edge' language):

> I wager that I shall have a better understanding of man [*sic*] and of the bond between the being of man and the being of all beings if I follow the *indication* of symbolic thought. That wager then becomes the task of *verifying* my wager and saturating it, so to speak, with intelligibility. In

---

120. Above, pp. 58, 240–1, 243.   121. Ammerman, p. 239, above.

return, the task transforms my wager: in betting *on* the significance of the symbolic world, I bet at the same time *that* my wager will be restored to me in the power of reflection, in the element of coherent discourse.[122]

It is, of course, understandable that doubts will quickly be entertained as to whether a 'wager', an 'as if', can turn the trick for theistic meanings in our time. I bring the section to a close, then, in three apologetic points. First, it must absolutely be insisted upon that the option for religious belief is not a choice for 'myth' as opposed to 'reality' (or 'reason', or 'science' or whichever other dismissive aspersion high modernity called to its aid). On the contrary, in their most profound transactions *all* people – wittingly or not – make appeal to some sort of mythic 'Best Account'.[123] Because, that is, meaning is an imperative and yet our limits are ineluctable, an underdetermined theory, or picture, or account of reality informs the modern sophisticate no less than it did the so-called 'primitive' peoples. This, too, is easier to see now than it was during modernity's hegemony. The now near-ubiquitous acceptation of paradigms, as the 'fiduciary frameworks'[124] within which all our ratiocination takes place, brought about the abandonment of modernity's 'great dream' [of a description of physical reality as it is apart from observers].[125] Thus Michael Polanyi, one of the trail-blazers for the newer perspectives, says: '[T]he admission of doubt proves ... to be *as clearly an act of belief* as does the non-admission of doubt';[126] and again, 'We cannot look *at* [the grounds ... upon which we hold that our knowledge is true] since we are looking *with* them.'[127] But this which we now take for granted in intellectual discipline applies no less to the popular – though mostly unnoticed – 'myths' according to which people order their lives: consumerism, the prerogative of personal choice, the supreme desirability of sexual satisfaction, or whatever.[128] The greatest irony attending the

---

122. Ricoeur, *Symbolism of Evil*, 355 (his emphases). The notion of 'wager' is characteristic of Ricoeur's entire *œuvre*. See, e.g., his concluding remarks to his extended meditations on ideology and utopia (*Ideology and Utopia*, 312): 'We cannot eliminate from a social ethics the element of risk. We wager on a certain set of values and then try to be consistent with them; verification is therefore a question of our whole life. No one can escape this.'
123. For the term 'Best Account', see above, e.g., pp. 34, 71–2, 195–6.
124. Polanyi, *Personal Knowledge*, 264–8; see also Polanyi and Prosch, *Meaning*, e.g., 63.
125. See Putnam, p. 65 above.   126. Polanyi, *Personal Knowledge*, 294 (my emphases).
127. Polanyi and Prosch, *Meaning*, 61 (their emphases).
128. The point is made repeatedly in Kaufman's *In Face of Mystery*; see, e.g., p. 29: 'Although the human spirit has no way of overcoming the mystery of life, it is also true that we are not able simply to live with a blank, empty Void. So humans create *pictures*, pictures of what they think the world is like, pictures of what they imagine are the ultimate powers or realities

modern disdain of 'myth' is that, all the while modernity extolled itself as 'enlightened' and 'objective' and castigated alternative readings
of the world as 'imaginative' or 'superstitious', it was, as we now realize, itself operating as a colossal ideological enterprise: 'Enlightenment
is as totalitarian as any system,' cried Adorno and Horkheimer in their
disillusion.[129]

Second, though the mythic or confessional 'clothing' which people
bring to their encounters with alterity is unquestionably constructed (either from a traditional religious heritage, or, as just now claimed, from one
of the contemporary myths), it will not be conceded that the *sense of limit
itself* is anything less than real. Don Cupitt, for example, has criticized the
'as if' style of religious meaning-making as being too transparently an act
of self-deception:

> One may say of . . . ritual . . . as of religious belief generally nowadays,
> that it is performed not because our life does make sense, but precisely
> because it does not make sense. Ritual is not a response to meaning,
> but a way of creating meaning to fill the Void.
>
> There is, however, a difficulty. In periods of enlightenment such as
> our own, people become very highly reflective. We become vividly and
> ironically aware of the machinery by which we sustain the fictions we
> need in order to live, and this ironical awareness of our own
> self-manipulation imposes a certain strain on us . . . Are we quite happy
> to suggest that God, reality itself, the intelligibility of our life, the
> possibility of effective action and the difference between good and evil
> are all of them necessary cultural fictions, ritually produced and only as
> strong as our own belief in them?[130]

But meaning, we learned, is making *and finding*. The entire point about our
myths, of whichever kind, is that they are elicited by an absolutely tangible
and virtually universal discovery about ourselves: *that we are finite* in all the
ways I tried to catalogue in an earlier section. It is this found dimension to
our existence which secures the reasonableness of the 'assumed naiveté' of
religious conviction. It is thus this dimension which rebuts the accusation

with which they must deal' (his emphasis); see similarly, *ibid.*, e.g., pp. 51, 53–4, 114, 245, 256.
See also and notably Wes Howard-Brook and Anthony Gwyther, *Unveiling Empire: reading
Revelation then and now* (Maryknoll: Orbis Books, 1999), 113–15 and ch. 9 *passim*, on the
legitimating ideologies of every age which 'bind [the] visible aspects of society together' and
are 'conveyed through *myth*' (113; their emphasis).

129. Theodor Adorno and Max Horkheimer, *Dialectic of Enlightenment* (London: Verso,
1979), 24.

130. Don Cupitt, 'Unsystematic Ethics and Politics' in (Philippa Berry and Andrew Wernick,
eds.) *Shadow of Spirit: postmodernism and religion* (London: Routledge, 1992), 151.

of 'projection'.[131] It is this dimension which places firm restraint on the constructive aspects of theology. And it is this dimension which permits, in the name of ancient credal formulations, the critique of modern pretensions. The worshipper who turns away from the phenomenal world to address the Other whom Christians name as the God and Father of our Lord Jesus Christ is not indulging in sheer speculation. To repeat: there is an objective (discovered) dimension to belief fused in and with the constructed one.

Finally (to some extent following on from Cupitt's charges), it may be wondered whether the words and actions of worship offered in an 'as if' mode – and similarly received – can have the requisite believability. Can a blessing, an absolution, the proclamation of the promissory Word, *be* a Word of the Lord, if it is hedged or qualified in the manner of the 'assumed naiveté'? In some degree, an answer hinges on the 'iconic' and 'indexical' dimensions of the significations which I treated earlier in terms of liturgical semiosis. Since that could equally be to beg the question, simply to draw yet further back into the 'as if' mentality, the question demands and deserves in this place a theological response. The point must be: wherein could, or would, a 'real' blessing consist (i.e., one *not* on an 'as if' basis)? Was it ever so in the structure of things, can it ever be, that there can be an exact referential correlation between the words of worship and the things to which they refer? When and how could it ever be possible *not* to offer the significations of worship in an experimental, an 'as if', modality? If all that I have tried to say about 'coming to the perimeter' of our human competencies has any truth, we must apprehend that all the words and actions of worship are in an optative mood. They are proposals, invitations, mythic constructions; their topic is 'the landscape of the heart'.[132] They form what Ricoeur would want to call 'the world before the liturgy': 'a *proposed world* which I could inhabit and wherein I could project one of my ownmost possibilities'.[133]

131. So Kaufman, *In Face of Mystery*, 320: '[T]he word "God" stands for something *objectively there*, a reality over against us that exists whether we are aware of it or not: we did not make ourselves; we were created by cosmic evolutionary and historical processes on which we depend absolutely for our being' (his emphases); see also Pailin, *Anthropological Character*, ch. 3, on the charges against theism of 'projection'.

132. Thomas H. Troeger, 'The Social Power of Myth as a Key to Preaching on Social Issues' in (Arthur van Seters, ed.) *Preaching as a Social Act: theology and practice* (Nashville, TN: Abingdon Press, 1988), 205–34.

133. Ricoeur, *Hermeneutics and the Human Sciences*, 142 (his emphases); (see above, pp. 196–7).

Synthesis: naming God at the edge of the known

In setting out upon this account of liturgical meaning I noted (page 258 above) that in any successful service of worship the two dimensions of it which I called its recognizability and its difference are fused seamlessly: when it all 'works', worshippers will neither wish nor (usually) be able to analyse its parts. So it is that the signs of worship which, through strategies of intensification, enable or elicit for worshippers their sense of having been brought to 'the edge of chaos' (and of being safely returned), are simultaneously carrying interpretants which configure this not just as *any* adventure of limit, but as the particular interlocution which approaches, addresses and lays itself open before the Other whom we name as God.

What remains, then, is to give concrete demonstration of how the three characteristics (as I supposed) of boundary experience – its intensification of ordinariness (either as effect or cause), its religious potential and its sharpening of alterity – are, in worship, interwoven with such markers (interpretants) as to make clear what kind of event this is.

First, then, worship's intensifications: liturgical writers are wont to observe that there is not one thing in a worship service which is not commonplace in 'ordinary' life: we walk, we sit, we stand, we speak, we read, we sing, we eat and drink.[134] But liturgy does not *leave* these things as we encounter them in their ordinariness. In many and various ways we subject them to what have been called 'ritualizing strategies':[135] the ministerial party does not exactly *walk*, it processes; baptism is a form of *washing* but unlike any other lustration the candidate will undergo; the Eucharist is a *meal*, but one in which the bread is broken and given with a prayer and wine is consumed from a handsome cup; and so on, at pretty well every point. Whatever else it is, worship may be described as a richly complex series of intensifications of ordinariness.[136]

---

134. See Lathrop, for example, on the 'ordinariness' of the things of worship, *Holy Things*, e.g., 10, 87.

135. For the term and the concept 'ritualizing strategies' see Catherine Bell, *Ritual Theory, Ritual Practice* (New York: Oxford University Press, 1992), e.g., 74, 90, 140–1, 205. See also her essay 'Ritual, Change and Changing Rituals', 35: 'The basic dynamics of ritual . . . can be seen to involve two processes. First, ritualization is itself a matter of drawing strategic contrasts between the acts being performed and those being contrasted or mimed. Second, the schemes established by ritualization are impressed upon participants as deriving from a reality beyond the activities of the group.' And for a survey of typical kinds of 'ritualizing strategies', see her *Ritual: perspectives and dimensions* (New York: Oxford University Press, 1997), ch. 5.

136. So Collins, *More Than Meets the Eye*, 79: 'Like art, liturgy takes the ordinariness of life and expresses it in forms that heighten and intensify ordinary experience.'

The music of worship lends itself as exemplary of what we may call an *expansive* intensification of ordinariness. A song or a hymn consists in ordinary (in our case, English) words. There is, admittedly, a certain stock of cultic vocabulary – part of the 'confessional' or 'symbolic' heritage on which I must speak in a moment – but overwhelmingly most of the words will be found in daily newspapers. The point, of course, is that the language is not left to its ordinary prosaic potential. The first thing that happens is that the lexical items are removed from the haphazard patterns of prose. They are versified: patterned according to rhythm and sound.[137] Sometimes this patterned structure will take the form of verses and refrain; which is to say, a theme and sub-themes are linked into a progressive or cohesive whole. But the patterning of language is barely the beginning. Now the augmentation will be greatly more dramatic: I mean the shift from verse to *song*. So the tonal *range* of the voice will be vastly expanded; and this, too, will be *patterned* so as to give a recognizable melody. Under or around this basic melody other melodies will be woven to give *harmony*. Then, the pattern of sounds and words will be sung by the *whole assembly*, thus giving another dramatic degree of elaboration or intensification. Finally, not infrequently, the voices will be joined by one or more *instruments*. By this stage the ordinary words with which we began have become an occasion or the vehicle for something like Otto's *mysterium tremendum et fascinans*. The affectivity (sense of religious awe or celebration) achieved by this cumulative intensification of what started as relatively 'ordinary' language is perhaps gauged by the comparative energies released in speaking the creed and, alternatively, singing one of the great hymns of the faith or even a modern liturgical song.[138] To be part of even quite a small company singing as an act of worship is a stirring moment, but, when a concourse of, say, a thousand or more Welsh or Methodist worshippers lifts in song, the impression is nearly impossible to resist that 'God's self is present'.[139]

---

137. Cf. Northrop Frye, 'The Expanding World Of Metaphor', *Journal of the American Academy of Religion* 53 (1985), 586: 'In poetry, accidental resemblances among words create sound patterns of rhyme, alliteration, assonance and metre, and these have a function in poetry that they rarely have outside it. The function of these sound-patterns is to minimize the sense of arbitrariness in the relation of word and meaning, to suggest a quasi-magical connection between the verbal arrangement and the things it evokes.'

138. Similar comparisons are apparent when the eucharistic responses are sung rather than spoken.

139. That music has the power to 'transport' the human spirit is widely attested in the literature. Cf. this from someone called James Russell Lowell recorded by William James (the actual experience, for which music is here a metaphor, is that of a starry sky): 'The ordinary sense of things around me faded. For the moment nothing but an ineffable joy and exultation remained. It is impossible fully to describe the experience. It was like the effect of

Equally, the intensifications of worship can be *contractive* as well as expansive. Robert Hovda, for example, describes the moment in which a communicant stands before the person administering the bread or cup in eucharistic celebration:

> in the act of administering communion, the communicant stands before the minister of the plate and then before the minister of the cup only for a moment. That moment offers an opportunity for a locking of the eyes and a touching of the hands in respectful attention and mutual encouragement – i.e., in recognition of the meaning of this sacrament of peace and unity. The presider looks at the communicant and the communicant looks at the presider. One does not expect a grin or a grimace. One does expect, and one has a right to expect, a look of respect and reverence, of care and communion.[140]

In this case too, of course, we are speaking of something as essentially commonplace as was the language of the previous example. As a shared meal, the sacrament of Holy Communion incorporates the most elementary features of table fellowship, such as are present in friends taking coffee in the student common room or in more elaborate dinner parties.[141] For the meal which is the Eucharist, however, a number of 'ritualizing strategies' (note 135 above) are deliberately placed around the moment Hovda describes: people gather at a more than ordinary time and place;[142] they are assembled by an authorized leader; particular songs are sung and prayers offered; of critical importance, the story of the meal's origins will be related. In this complex of layered signification, the meal which is a Eucharist is differentiated from the commonality whence it arose. Yet in its metamorphosis of elaboration, the originating 'communion' is not at all discarded; on the contrary, it is only sharpened and enhanced. In the contraction of focus which at last leaves one person sharing a fragment of bread with another and a proffered cup of wine (surrounded as these are with the prayers

some great orchestra when all the separate notes have melted into one swelling harmony that leaves the listener conscious of nothing save that his [*sic*] soul is being wafted upwards, and almost bursting with its own emotion' (William James, *The Varieties of Religious Experience: a study in human nature* (London: Collins (The Fontana Press), 1960), 81). Hardy and Ford (e.g., *Jubilate*, 15) also connect this musical affectivity directly with an 'intensification of ordinariness' and thence to transcendent experience.

140. Hovda, *Strong, Loving and Wise*, 71.

141. See particularly Philippe Rouillard, 'From Human Meal to Christian Eucharist' in (R. Kevin Seasoltz, ed.) *Living Bread, Saving Cup: readings on the Eucharist* (Collegeville: The Liturgical Press, 1982), 126–57.

142. See, e.g., Laurence Hull Stookey, *Calendar: Christ's time for the church* (Nashville, TN: Abingdon Press, 1996), 40–1, on 'the eighth day' of Christian consciousness; or Lathrop, *Holy Things*, 36–43.

offered and the story having been told), the deep mutual respect which Hovda describes becomes precisely a *sacrament* of communion, such that we do not hesitate to call it a 'holy' communion.

The examples here offered of deliberate intensification of ordinary things so as to become vehicles of the holy are, of course, just two (though central) examples. In fact, the entire assemblage of things, words and actions which is a service of worship partakes of this meaning-giving strategy:

> These things are common, even domestic objects, so they are recognizable to us, drawing in our ordinary experience. Here, however, these common things are set out in strength, made the center of focused attention, used as symbols. A pool of water, powerful words, a shared loaf and cup, an intentional assembly at a set time in a defined space, singing – these things are proposed to us as sacred, pointing to transcendent meanings.[143]

In my earlier survey, I suggested that intensifications of ordinariness as either accompanying or effecting boundary experiences were either inadvertent or advertent. Now it must be said, of the intensifications in which liturgy consists, that both perspectives are in evidence. On the one hand, obviously, all the strategies adopted are here intentional: worship is an advertent journey to the edge. On the other hand, the effects achieved are (when the means are successful) much closer to those of *in*advertent limit experiences: in contrast to the measured degrees of exposure of most wilful limit experiences, there is here (again, when the signs 'work') the sense of being wholly overwhelmed, of powerlessness and awe, of wonder and joy, of thankful self-giving and rich benefaction.[144]

---

143. Lathrop, *ibid.*, 116.
144. The conception of worship as an 'intensification' of ordinariness holds far-reaching implications for liturgical theology, both of the 'church' variety and also for the more unselfconscious 'mainline Protestant' and 'evangelical' styles. Each in its own way seems to me to fail properly to estimate the role of the ordinary in liturgical experience. For their part, their belief in the 'sacramentality' of the world makes exponents of 'church' theology somehow blind to the actuality and power of 'disenchantment' embedded precisely in the everyday experience of modern or late modern worshippers. Thus, for Schmemann, the world is – quite simply – 'the sacrament of God' (so, e.g., *The World as Sacrament* (London: Darton, Longman and Todd, 1966)). Or David Fagerberg supposes that 'within the ecclesia . . . the distinction between the sacred and the profane has been abolished' (*What is Liturgical Theology?*, 154; see similarly Schmemann, 'Theology and Liturgical Tradition', 172–4). Though coming from an opposite point of view (the 'affirmation of ordinariness' as the realm of God's self-manifestation), Protestants, both 'mainline' and 'evangelical', also come to ordinariness too uncritically. In distinction from both approaches, then, a theology of the *intensification* of ordinariness holds that ordinariness is *capable* of disclosing the divine; but not, as it were, in and of itself, not naturally, not by wishing it so, but through deliberate strategies of ritualization, elaboration, intensification.

Second, limit experiences are inherently religious. Thus do the liturgical intensifications of ordinariness work for, or towards, the quality of religious experience without which a liturgical event will scarcely be *worship*! But I have also tried to show that not every experience of the uncanny or the ecstatic can be claimed forthwith as 'worship'. In my opening remarks to the chapter (pages 257–8) I said that worship will consist in *both* religious experience *and* doctrinal conviction. The latter element we can now elaborate as worship's 'assumed naiveté' and its 'vocative dimension'. Overtly or implicitly (this is the seamless fusion) the 'Thou' of worship's vocative utterance is *already embedded* in every gesture. In speaking a moment ago of the songs of worship as a multilayered intensification of ordinariness, I said that, although most of the language will be found in newspapers, there is a necessary quotient of – in Peirce's sense – 'symbolic' references which anchor the enunciation within the particular confessional tradition. So it is with all the linguistic, gestural, kinetic and other references of worship: people are gathered in God's name;[145] prayers are, in content and their forms of utterance, spoken 'to God, through Christ, in the power of the Spirit'; the sermon is reckoned to be God's Word; people are absolved and blessed not as a human transaction, but 'as a reality deriving from beyond . . . the group' (note 135 above); and so on *in toto*. The strategies of intensification lend the forms their evocative or emotive power; the semantic or semiotic markers (interpretants) they are carrying leave no doubt as to the degree of alterity intended or desired, nor its believed content.

Boundary experiences disclose the otherness which is so regularly obscured precisely by the familiarity of the ordinary. This, I thought, was or is a third characteristic. When the signs of worship are effective, people will know certainly that here has been proposed a radical alternative to the mundanity of competing world views. They will have been offered the 'freedom to pray and to contemplate, [not just to] speculate and invent',[146] they are here offered 'a sanctuary of meaning', they are invited to stand 'on the threshold of the Kingdom', it is 'a proposed world which [they might] inhabit', a world in which to realize their 'ownmost possibilities'.[147] All this because for a brief moment the tenacious snares of 'the return to the self' were loosened and they, as a worshipping people, have glimpsed the 'bright mystery' by which our lives are surrounded.[148]

---

145. See Krosnicki, ch. 5, n. 72, above.   146. See Turner, above, p. 59.
147. See above, p. 197, for all these references.   148. See Hardy, above, ch. 7, n. 9.

Epilogue

From this long peregrination I return to my subject entering a church unfamiliar to her, hoping and expecting that what transpires in the next hour or so will be a meaningful event. I said that the challenge she sets us is to offer an account of the meanings (meaningfulness) to which she aspires: what sort of meaning is this which we call a liturgical event? What would a theory of meaning look like which could guide or facilitate the achievement of this kind of meaning? Is it possible to give some sort of account of the ways in which such meanings are constructed and transmitted on the part of liturgical leaders and are appropriated by those who participate in a worship service (above, page 11)?

Since leaving her, we have seen that in late modernity we reckon meaning not to be some sort of monolithic abstraction, dependent on external sanction such as verification, truth condition, phenomenological constitution, structure, or deconstructive artifice. We think now it is more likely to be something 'fastened together' in a collaborative work between those who propose meanings and those who appropriate them and – to this extent – bring them to completion. Just in so far as this is a collaborative responsibility, we think it quite unlikely that there will be finally definitive meanings – some sort of God's-eye view of the world. But, equally, *because* it is a collaborative venture, neither do we see a need to resile in despair from the project as a whole; we think that such meanings as we are able to fasten together between us will be enough – a 'Best Account' – for us to get along on a day-to-day basis.

Most, if not all, our meanings, we saw, will be transacted in signs which, according to the foremost exponent, are of three orders: iconic (dependent on shared similarities), indexical (dependent on contiguity) and symbolic (arrived at by convention). The significations of worship, we saw, seemed amenable to this configuration.

As part of the abandonment of a God's-eye quest for understanding, we have learned to be reconciled to pictures of reality; not final, definitive ones, but pictures which allow us to grasp into some sort of whole the 'making' and the 'discovery' aspects of our project of meaning. One such picture which seems both to be true of common experience and to be fruitful in comprehending liturgical events envisages us as constantly constructing a great raft of meaning or meanings, a platform which at its centre is relatively stable and safe but, at its edges, is simultaneously frightening yet exhilarating, hence fascinating. Worship, we think, belongs with the sorts of daunting-but-thrilling adventures which turn outward from the safe centre towards the scary perimeter. For that is where worship (or perhaps better, the faith which issues in worship) has long learned to find its health, its sources of strength and its wisdom. In gospel idiom, it is in coming to the end of itself that it finds itself. For, in coming to its end, it meets its Other. And only in *relationship*, it has found, in *this* relationship, lies true health, 'whole-being'.

In a summary way, then, what should we expect from the various actors if my subject is to go on her way with the sense that this was a meaningful event?

Perhaps a first requirement is that those who have had general and specific responsibilities for the planning and execution of the event (those who devised the liturgy originally, those responsible for the worship space, the priest or minister, other leaders, the musicians) will have absorbed deeply into themselves an awareness that the work in which they are engaged *is* a 'boundary' or 'liminal' (threshold) event; that it takes place at a kind of virtual 'edge' of what we can manage conceptually and emotionally; that the event is nullified if it is permitted (as it threatens constantly to do) to fall back into domesticity or 'routinization'.

Second, those who lead – the presiding minister in the first place, and then all the assistant ministers – need to allow the three dimensions of liturgical signification to be present and effective in their work. The *iconicity* of the signs, for example, needs clearly to signal the 'boundary' nature of the entire event (even, in some sense, that it transcends our human limits, even while we know that such transcendence can only be an act of wonder-filled imagination). Similarly, the *indexicality* of the leaders' words and actions needs to signify something more than a 'performance';

rather, actions and words which are truly (truthfully) 'meant' (as acts of worship). Finally, the *symbolic* or traditionalizing dimension of the significations needs to declare that here is something not made up on the spur of the moment, but forged from millennia-deep sources of wisdom and knowledge.

Third, in and with all this, ministers and priests need to know that our own modernity has entered deeply – if silently – into our consciousness; that even as we attend to ancient ministrations we cannot slough off who we are. This is to say: convictions need to be held on an open palm rather than in clenched grip; our work must be undertaken in a seriously experimental way, as a wager for meaning rather than senselessness, and for the *particular* wager suggested by the liturgical signs themselves.

And for the subject herself, together with those with whom she forms a worshipping body? They, too, must allow the wager of the signs' meaning. They are invited to the work of meaning completion from within their familiar world, to bring to the signs of worship such interpretants as will allow them, the signs, to do their work. In some respects this is a task of cognition: they, the worshippers, have to *reach* for the meanings being suggested to see where, how, or perhaps whether, these can 'make sense' in terms of a recognizable world. But it is a question, too, for the heart, for affectivity, for the courage to *believe* the signs' significations. It is to recognize, that is, that the human heart, the human will, is the site of contestation for *all* myths of contemporary life; to understand that the claims of modernity itself, and then its panoply of subordinates such as the consumerist guarantee of satisfaction or of entertainment's soporific promise, are as mythic in their claims as anything that recognizable religion has to offer, though on infinitely slighter grounds. It is to *yield* to the promise and the invitation proposed in the liturgy.

But of course – since this was always a collaborative work – for someone to *hear* or *feel* the seductive power of the proposal, it had already to *be* there in the signs themselves. In proposal and in acceptance, then, is the meaning of worship constructed and transacted.

Bibliography

Adams, Doug, *Congregational Dancing in Christian Worship* (Austin, TX: Sharing Company, 1971).

Adorno, Theodor and Max Horkheimer, *Dialectic of Enlightenment* (London: Verso, 1979).

Alston, William P., *Philosophy of Language* (Englewood Cliffs, NJ: Prentice-Hall Inc., 1964).

Ammerman, Nancy T., 'North American Protestant Fundamentalism' in (Martin E. Marty and R. Scott Appleby, eds.) *Fundamentalisms Observed* (University of Chicago Press, 1991), 1–65.

Arbib, Michael A. and Mary B. Hesse, *The Construction of Reality* (Cambridge University Press, 1986).

Ashbourne, M. Susan, 'Laetatus sum in his quae dicta sunt mihi: in domum Domini ibimus', *Semiotica* 123 3/4 (1999), 299–325.

Austin, J. L., *How to Do Things with Words* (Oxford University Press, 1962).

Ayer, A. J., *Language, Truth and Logic* (London: Penguin Books, 1990).

Baer, Eugen S., 'Some Elementary Topics of a General Semiotic Theory', *Semiotica* 29 1/2 (1980), 347–64.

'Tom Sebeok's Thomism', *Semiotica* 28 3/4 (1979), 349–70.

Balasuriya, Tissa, *The Eucharist and Human Liberation* (Maryknoll: Orbis Books, 1979).

Baldovin, John F., *The Urban Character of Christian Worship: the origins, development and meaning of stational liturgy* (Rome: Pontificum Institutum Studiorum Orientalium, 1987).

Baptism, Eucharist, Ministry (Geneva: World Council of Churches, 1982).

Barfield, Owen, *Poetic Diction* (London: Faber & Faber, 1952).

Barr, James, *Fundamentalism* (London: SCM Press Ltd., 1977).

The Semantics of Biblical Language (London: Oxford University Press, 1961).

Barth, Karl, *From Rousseau to Ritschl* (London: SCM Press Ltd., 1959).

How I Changed My Mind (John D. Godsey, ed.) (Richmond: John Knox Press, 1966).

Barthes, Roland, *Elements of Semiology* (New York: Hill and Wang, 1967).

'The Death of the Author' in *Image Music Text* (London: Fontana Paperbacks, 1984).

'The Grain of the Voice' in *Image Music Text* (London: Fontana Press, 1977).

Bauckham, Richard, *The Theology of The Book of Revelation* (Cambridge University Press, 1993).

Beattie, Geoffrey and Heather Shovelton, 'Do Iconic Hand Gestures Really Contribute Anything to the Semantic Information Conveyed by Speech? an experimental investigation', *Semiotica* 123 1/2 (1999), 1–30.

Bell, Catherine, *Ritual: perspectives and dimensions* (New York: Oxford University Press, 1997).

    Ritual Theory, Ritual Practice (New York: Oxford University Press, 1992).

    'Ritual, Change and Changing Rituals', *Worship* 63 (1989), 31–41.

Bellah, Robert, 'Civil Religion in America' in (Russell E. Richey and Donald G. Jones, eds.) *American Civil Religion* (New York: Harper and Row, 1974), 21–44.

Berger, Peter L., *A Rumour of Angels: modern society and the rediscovery of the supernatural* (Harmondsworth: Penguin Books, 1970).

Berger, Teresa, 'Liturgy – a forgotten subject-matter of theology?' *Studia Liturgica* 17 (1987), 10–18.

Berthoff, Ann E., 'I. A. Richards: critic, instructional engineer, semioticist', *Semiotica* 90 3/4 (1992), 357–69.

Bevan, Edwyn, *Symbolism and Belief* (London: Collins [The Fontana Library], 1962).

Bieritz, Karl Heinrich, 'Das Wort im Gottesdienst' in (H. B. Meyer, et al., eds.) *Gottesdienst der Kirche: Gestalt des Gottesdienst* (Regensburg: Verlag Friedrich Pustet, second edition, 1990), vol. III, 47–76.

Birdwhistell, Ray L., *Introduction to Kinesics: an annotation system for analysis of body motion and gesture* (Louisville KY: University of Louisville, 1952).

Bondanella, Peter, 'Interpretation, Overinterpretation, Paranoid Interpretation and *Foucault's Pendulum*' in (Rocco Capozzi, ed.) *Reading Eco: an anthology* (Bloomington: Indiana University Press, 1997), 285–99.

Bonhoeffer, Dietrich, *Letters and Papers from Prison* (London: Collins Fontana, 1959).

    Life Together (London: SCM Press, 1954).

Bradshaw, Paul, *The Search for the Origins of Christian Worship* (London: SPCK, 1992).

    'Difficulties in Doing Liturgical Theology', *Pacifica* 11 (1998), 186–8.

Brady, Veronica, *A Crucible of Prophets: Australians and the question of God* (Sydney: Theological Explorations, 1981).

    Caught in the Draught (Sydney: Angus and Robertson, 1994).

Braga, Lúcia Santaella, 'Difficulties and Strategies in Applying Peirce's Semiotics', *Semiotica* 97 3/4 (1993), 401–10.

Brueggemann, Walter, *Finally Comes the Poet: daring speech for proclamation* (Minneapolis: Fortress Press, 1989).

Buber, Martin, *I and Thou* (Edinburgh: T. & T. Clark, 1937).

Buchanan, Colin O., *The End of the Offertory: an Anglican study* (Bramcote: Grove Books Ltd., 1978).

Buczynska-Garewicz, Hanna, 'Semiotics and Deconstruction' in (Rocco Capozzi, ed.) *Reading Eco: an anthology* (Bloomington: Indiana University Press, 1997), 163–72.

Burke, Patrick, 'The Flesh as *Urpräsentierbarkeit* in the Interrogative: the absence of a question in Derrida' in (M. C. Dillon, ed.) *Écart & Différence: Merleau-Ponty and Derrida on seeing and writing* (New Jersey: Humanities Press, 1997).

Calvin, John, *Institutes of the Christian Religion* (Ford Lewis Battles, translator) (Philadelphia: The Westminster Press, 1960).

Capozzi, Rocco, '*Interpretation and Overinterpretation*: the rights of texts, readers and implied authors' in (Rocco Capozzi, ed.) *Reading Eco: an anthology* (Bloomington: Indiana University Press, 1997), 217–34.

Caputo, John, *Radical Hermeneutics: repetition, deconstruction and the hermeneutic project* (Bloomington: Indiana University Press, 1987).

Cassirer, Ernst, *An Essay on Man* (New Haven: Yale University Press, 1944).

    The Philosophy of Symbolic Forms, 3 volumes (New Haven: Yale University Press, 1955–1957).

Chauvet, Louis-Marie, *Symbol and Sacrament: a sacramental reinterpretation of christian existence* (Collegeville: Liturgical Press, 1995).

Cohen, L. Jonathon, *The Diversity of Meaning* (London: Methuen and Co., Ltd., 1962).

Cohen, Ted, 'Metaphor and the Cultivation of Intimacy' in (Sheldon Sacks, ed.) *On Metaphor* (University of Chicago Press, 1978).

Collins, Mary, 'Critical Questions for Liturgical Theology' in *Worship: renewal to practice* (Washington DC: The Pastoral Press, 1987), 115–32.

    'Naming God in Public Prayer' in *Worship: renewal to practice* (Washington DC: The Pastoral Press, 1987), 215–29.

Collins, Patrick W., *More Than Meets the Eye: ritual and parish liturgy* (New York: Paulist Press, 1983).

    'Constitution on the Sacred Liturgy' in *The Documents of Vatican II* (Walter M. Abbott, ed.) (London and Dublin: Geoffrey Chapman, 1966).

Cooke, Bernard J., *The Distancing of God: the ambiguity of symbol in history and theology* (Minneapolis: Fortress Press, 1990).

Corrington, Robert S., 'Regnant Signs: the semiosis of liturgy', *Semiotica* 117 1 (1997), 19–42.

Cox, Harvey, *The Secular City: secularization and urbanization in theological perspective* (London: SCM Press, 1965).

Crites, Stephen, 'The Narrative Quality of Experience' in (Stanley Hauerwas and L. Gregory Jones, eds.) *Why Narrative? readings in narrative theology* (Grand Rapids: Eerdmans, 1989), 65–88 (originally in *Journal of the American Academy of Religion* 39 (1971), 291–311).

Culler, Jonathan, *On Deconstruction: theory and criticism after structuralism* (London: Routledge, 1983).

    Saussure (London: Fontana Press, 1976).

Cupitt, Don, 'Unsystematic Ethics and Politics' in (Philippa Berry and Andrew Wernick, eds.) *Shadow of Spirit: postmodernism and religion* (London: Routledge, 1992), 149–55.

Dalmais, I. H., 'Theology of the Liturgical Celebration' in (A. G. Martimort, ed.) *The Church at Prayer: principles of the liturgy* (Collegeville: The Liturgical Press, 1987), 227–80.

Danto, Arthur C., *Analytical Philosophy of History* (Cambridge University Press, 1965).

Davidson, Donald, 'Truth and Meaning', *Synthese* 17 (1967), 304–23.

Davies, J. G., *Every Day God: encountering the holy in the world and worship* (London: SCM Press. 1973).

    Liturgical Dance (London: SCM Press, 1984).

Davies, J. G. (ed.), *A New Dictionary of Liturgy and Worship* (London: SCM Press, 1986).

Davis, Colin, *Levinas: an introduction* (Cambridge: Polity Press, 1996).

De Lauretis, Teresa, 'Gaudy Rose: Eco and Narcissism' in (Rocco Capozzi, ed.) *Reading Eco: an anthology* (Bloomington: Indiana University Press, 1997), 239–55.

    'Semiotics in Italy' in (R. W. Bailey, L. Matejka and P. Steiner, eds.) *The Sign: semiotics around the world* (Ann Arbor: Michigan Slavic Publications, 1978), 248–57.

de Man, Paul, *Allegories of Reading: figural language in Rousseau, Nietzsche, Rilke and Proust* (New Haven: Yale University Press, 1979).

de Saussure, F., *Course in General Linguistics* (London: Duckworth, 1983).

Deely, John, *Basics of Semiotics* (Bloomington: Indiana University Press, 1990).

    New Beginnings: early modern philosophy and postmodern thought (University of Toronto Press, 1994).

    The Human Use of Signs (Totowa, NJ: Rowman and Littlefield, 1993).

    'Looking Back on *A Theory of Semiotics*: one small step for philosophy, one giant leap for the Doctrine of Signs' in (Rocco Capozzi, ed.) *Reading Eco: an anthology* (Bloomington: Indiana University Press, 1997), 82–110.

Dennett, Daniel C., *Consciousness Explained* (London: Allen Lane/Penguin Books, 1991).

Derrida, Jacques, *Margins of Philosophy* (New York: Harvester Wheatsheaf, 1982).

    Positions (The University of Chicago Press, 1981).

    Of Grammatology (Baltimore: Johns Hopkins University Press, 1974).

    Speech and Phenomena and other Essays on Husserl's Theory of Signs (Evanston: Northwestern University Press, 1973).

Deuser, Hermann, 'Christliche Religion: Zeichen unter Zeichen?' in (Wilfried Engemann and Rainer Volp, eds.) *Gib mir ein Zeichen: zur Bedeutung der Semiotik für theologische Praxis- und Denkmodelle* (Berlin: Walter de Gruyter, 1992), 31–43.

Dews, Peter, *The Limits of Disenchantment: essays on contemporary European philosophy* (London: Verso, 1995).

Dillon, M. C. (ed.), *Écart & Différence: Merleau-Ponty and Derrida on seeing and writing* (Atlantic Highlands, NJ: Humanities Press International, 1997).

Dix, Gregory, *The Shape of the Liturgy* (London: Adam and Charles Black, 1945).

Dougherty, William P., 'The Quest for Interpretants: toward a Peircean paradigm for musical semiotics', *Semiotica* 99 1/2 (1994), 163–84.

DuBois, James, 'The Empty Promises of Speech Act Theory', *Semiotica* 103 3/4 (1995), 369–84.

Duffy, Regis A., 'American Time and God's Time', *Worship* 62 (1988), 515–32.

Dummett, Michael, 'What is a Theory of Meaning?' in (Gareth Evans and John McDowell, eds.) *Truth and Meaning: essays in semantics* (Oxford: Clarendon Press, 1976).

Eagleton, Terry, *Literary Theory: an introduction* (Oxford: Basil Blackwell, 1983).

    'An Author and his Interpreters' in (Rocco Capozzi, ed.) *Reading Eco: an anthology* (Bloomington: Indiana University Press, 1997), 59–70.

Eco, Umberto, *The Limits of Interpretation* (Bloomington: Indiana University Press, 1994).

    The Open Work (Cambridge MA: Harvard University Press, 1989).

    A Theory of Semiotics (Bloomington: Indiana University Press, 1976).

    'Interpretation and Overinterpretation' (the Tanner Lectures, Cambridge University) in (Stefan Collini, ed.) *Interpretation and Overinterpretation* (Cambridge University Press, 1992), 23–88.

    'Semiotics and the Philosophy of Language' in (Rocco Capozzi, ed.) *Reading Eco: an anthology* (Bloomington: Indiana University Press, 1997), 1–13.

Edie, James, Introduction to Maurice Merleau-Ponty, *The Primacy of Perception: and other essays on phenomenological psychology, the philosophy of art, history and politics* (Evanston: Northwestern University Press, 1964).

Eire, Carlos M. N., *War Against the Idols: the reformation of worship from Erasmus to Calvin* (Cambridge University Press, 1986).

Ekman, Paul, 'Methods for Measuring Facial Action' in (Klaus R. Scherer and Paul Ekman, eds.) *Handbook of Methods in Nonverbal Behavior Research* (Cambridge University Press, 1982), 45–90.

Ekman, Paul and Wallace V. Friesen, 'The Repertoire of Nonverbal Behavior: categories, origins, usage and coding', *Semiotica* 1 (1969), 49–89.

Eliade, Mircea, *The Sacred and the Profane: the nature of religion* (New York: Harper Torchbooks, 1961).

Empereur, James, *Models of Liturgical Theology* (Bramcote: Grove Liturgical Publications, 1987).

  Worship: exploring the sacred (Washington, DC: The Pastoral Press, 1987).

Empereur, James L. and Kiesling, Christopher G., *The Liturgy that Does Justice* (Collegeville: The Liturgical Press, 1990).

Environment and Art in Catholic Worship (The Bishops' Committee on the Liturgy, ed.) (Washington: The United States Catholic Conference, 1978).

Evans, Alice F. and Robert A. Evans, *Introduction to Christianity: a case method approach* (Atlanta, GA: John Knox Press, 1980).

Evans, C. F., 'The New Testament in the Making' in (P. R. Ackroyd and C. F. Evans, eds.) *The Cambridge History of the Bible* (Cambridge University Press, 1970), vol. I.

Fagerberg, David H., *What is Liturgical Theology: a study in methodology* (Collegeville: The Liturgical Press, 1992).

Fann, K. T., *Peirce's Theory of Abduction* (The Hague: Martinus Nijhoff, 1970).

Fenwick, John R. K. and Bryan D. Spinks, *Worship in Transition: the twentieth century liturgical movement* (Edinburgh: T. & T. Clark, 1995).

Ferré, Frederick, *Logic, Language and God* (London: Eyre and Spottiswoode, 1962).

Feyereisen, Pierre and Jacques-Dominique de Lannoy, *Gestures and Speech: psychological investigations* (Cambridge University Press, 1991).

Flanagan, Kieran, *Sociology and Liturgy: re-presentations of the holy* (Houndmills, Basingstoke: The Macmillan Press, 1991).

Fleischer, Rudi, 'Einführung in die semiotische Gottesdienstanalyse' in (Peter Düsterfeld, ed.) *Neue Wege der Verkündigung* (Düsseldorf: Patmos Verlag, 1983), 99–122.

  'Verständnisbedingungen religiöser Symbole am Beispiel von Taufritualen: ein semiotischer Versuch' (Mainz: Dr. Theol. Inaugural-Dissertation, Mainz University, 1984).

Foucault, Michel, *The History of Sexuality* (London: Penguin Books, 1990).

  Power/Knowledge: selected interviews and other writings 1972–1977 (New York: Pantheon Books, 1980).

Francis, Mark R., 'Liturgical Inculturation in the United States and the Call to Justice' in (Kathleen Hughes and Mark R. Francis, eds.) *Living No Longer for Ourselves: liturgy and justice in the nineties* (Collegeville: The Liturgical Press, 1991), 85–92.

Frege, G., 'On Sense and Reference', in *Philosophical Studies* (P. T. Geach and M. Black, eds.) (Oxford: Basil Blackwell, 1960), 56–78 (originally published as 'Über Sinn und Bedeutung', *Zeitschrift für Philosophie und philosophische Kritik* 100 (1892), 25–50).

Frei, Hans, *The Eclipse of Biblical Narrative: a study in eighteenth and nineteenth century hermeneutics* (New Haven: Yale University Press, 1974).

Freire, Paulo, *Pedagogy of the Oppressed* (Harmondsworth: Penguin Books, 1972).

Freud, Sigmund, *Jokes and Their Relation to the Unconscious* (New York: Newton, 1960).

Frye, Northrop, 'The Expanding World Of Metaphor', *Journal of the American Academy of Religion* 53 (1985), 585–98.

Gadamer, Hans-Georg, *Truth and Method* (London: Sheed and Ward, 1975).

Gallie, W. B., *Philosophy and the Historical Understanding* (New York: Schocken Books, 1968).

Gardner, W. H., Introduction to *Gerard Manley Hopkins: a selection of his poems and prose* (Harmondsworth: Penguin Books Limited, 1953).

Garver, Newton, Preface to Jacques Derrida's *Speech and Phenomena and other Essays on Husserl's Theory of Signs* (Evanston: Northwestern University Press, 1973).

Garza-Cuarón, Beatriz, *Connotation and Meaning* (Berlin and New York: Mouton de Gruyter, 1991).

Geertz, Clifford, *The Interpretation of Cultures* (New York: Basic Books, 1973).

Gerth, H. H. and C. W. Mills (eds.) *From Max Weber: essays in sociology* (London: Routledge and Kegan Paul, 1974).

Giffen, Michael, *Arthur's Dream: the religious imagination in the fiction of Patrick White* (Paddington NSW: Spaniel Books, 1996).

Gilhus, Ingvild Sælid, *Laughing Gods, Weeping Virgins: laughter in the history of religions* (London: Routledge, 1997).

Gilkey, Langdon, *Naming the Whirlwind: the renewal of God-language* (Indianapolis: The Bobbs-Merrill Company, 1969).

Through the Tempest: theological voyages in a pluralistic culture (Minneapolis: Fortress Press, 1991).

Godkewitsch, Michael, 'Physiological and Verbal Indices of Arousal in Related Humour' in (Antony J. Chapman and Hugh C. Foot, eds.) *Humour and Laughter: theory, research and applications* (London: John Wiley and Sons, 1976).

Goodman, Nelson, *Ways of Worldmaking* (Indianapolis: Hackett Publishing Company, 1978).

Gouge, Thomas A., 'Peirce's Index', *Transactions of the Charles S. Peirce Society* 1 (1965), 52–70.

Greenlee, Douglas, *Peirce's Concept of Sign* (The Hague: Mouton, 1973).

Grenz, Stanley J., *Theology for the Community of God* (Grand Rapids: Eerdmans, 1994).

Grice, H. P., 'Utterer's Meaning and Intentions', *Philosophical Review* 78 (1969), 147–77.

'Utterer's Meaning, Sentence Meaning, and Word Meaning', *Foundations of Language* 4 (1968), 225–42.

Grisbrooke, W. Jardine, 'Oblation at the Eucharist', *Studia Liturgica* 3 (1964), 227–39, and 4 (1965), 37–55.

Grodzinski, Eugeniusz, 'Some Remarks on Joan Weiner's *Frege in Perspective*', *Semiotica* 99 3/4 (1993), 347–63.

'The Defectiveness of Gottlob Frege's Basic Logical–Semantic Terminology', *Semiotica* 103 3/4 (1995), 291–308.

Gruner, Charles E., *Understanding Laughter: the workings of wit and humor* (Chicago: Nelson-Hall, 1978).

Gunn, Giles, *The Culture of Criticism and the Criticism of Culture* (New York: Oxford University Press, 1987).

The Interpretation of Otherness: literature, religion, and the American imagination (New York: Oxford University Press, 1979).

Habermas, Jürgen, *The Philosophical Discourse of Modernity* (Cambridge, MA: The MIT Press, 1995).

Postmetaphysical Thinking: philosophical essays (Cambridge: Polity Press, 1992).

Theory of Communicative Action, 2 volumes (Boston: Beacon Press, 1984, and Cambridge: Polity Press, 1987).

'Comments on John Searle: "Meaning, Communication and Representation"' in (Ernest Lepore and Robert van Gulick, eds.) *John Searle and his Critics* (Oxford: Basil Blackwell, 1991), 17–29.

'Modernity: an unfinished project' in (Maurizio Passerin D'Entrèves and Seyla Benhabib, eds.) *Habermas and the Unfinished Project of Modernity* (Cambridge: Polity Press, 1996).

Hadar, Uri and Brian Butterworth, 'Iconic Gestures, Imagery, and Word Retrieval in Speech', *Semiotica* 115 1/2 (1997), 147–8.

Hall, Edward T., *The Silent Language* (Garden City, NY: Doubleday, 1959).

Hammarskjold, Dag, *Markings* (London: Faber & Faber, 1964).

Hanna, Barbara E., 'Defining the Emblem', *Semiotica* 112 3/4 (1996), 289–358.

Hardwick, Charles (ed.), *Semiotic and Significs: the correspondence between Charles S. Peirce and Victoria Lady Welby* (Bloomington: Indiana University Press, 1977).

Hardy, Daniel W., *God's Ways with the World: thinking and practicing Christian faith* (Edinburgh: T. & T. Clark, 1996).

'Worship as the Orientation of Life to God', *Ex Auditu* 8 (1992), 55–71.

Hardy, Daniel W. and David Ford, *Jubilate: theology in praise* (London: Darton, Longman & Todd, 1984).

Harrison, Bernard, 'Signs and the Self', *Semiotica* 104 3/4 (1995), 287–310.

Hart, Kevin, *The Trespass of the Sign: deconstruction, theology and philosophy* (Cambridge University Press, 1989).

'Ricoeur's Distinctions', *Scripsi* 5 (August 1989), 103–25.

Hawkes, Terence, *Structuralism and Semiotics* (London: Routledge, 1977).

Haynes, Deborah J., *The Vocation of the Artist* (Cambridge University Press, 1997).

Hempel, Carl G., 'Explanations and Laws' in (Patrick Gardiner, ed.) *Theories of History* (New York: The Free Press, 1959), 344–356.

Hendricks, William O., 'On Circling the Square: on Greimas' semiotics', *Semiotica* 75 1/2 (1989), 95–122.

Hertzer, Joyce O., *Laughter: a socio-scientific analysis* (New York: Exposition Press, 1970).

Hintikka, Jaako, 'What is Abduction? The fundamental problem of contemporary epistemology', *Transactions of the Charles S. Peirce Society* 34 (1998), 503–33.

Hirsch, E. D., *Validity in Interpretation* (New Haven: Yale University Press, 1967).

Høeg, Peter, *Miss Smilla's Feeling for Snow* (London: Flamingo/Harper Collins, 1993).

Hoffman, Lawrence A., *The Art of Public Prayer: not for clergy only* (Washington DC: Pastoral Press, 1988).

'How Ritual Means: ritual circumcision in rabbinic culture and today', *Studia Liturgica* 23 (1993), 78–97.

Hollenweger, Walter J., 'Intercultural Theology', *Theological Renewal* 10 (1978), 2–14.

Hookway, Christopher (ed.), *The Cambridge Companion to Peirce* (Cambridge University Press, forthcoming).

Hovda, Robert W., *Strong, Loving and Wise: presiding in liturgy* (Collegeville: The Liturgical Press, 1976).

Howard-Brook, Wes and Anthony Gwyther, *Unveiling Empire: reading Revelation then and now* (Maryknoll: Orbis Books, 1999).

Hughes, Kathleen and Mark R. Francis (eds.), *Living No Longer for Ourselves: liturgy and justice in the nineties* (Collegeville: The Liturgical Press, 1991).

Hughes, Philip J. and 'Tricia Blombery, *Patterns of Faith in Australian Churches* (Hawthorn, Melbourne: The Christian Research Association, 1990).

Hull, William E., 'Response to Robert Preus' in *The Proceedings of the Conference on Biblical Inerrancy* (Nashville: Broadman Press, 1987), 60–9.

Hurd, Robert, 'A More Organic Opening: ritual music and the new gathering rite', *Worship* 72 (1998), 290–315.

Husserl, Edmund, *Cartesian Meditations: an introduction to phenomenology* (Dordrecht: Kluwer Academic Publishers, 1993).

Ideas Pertaining to a Pure Phenomenology: first book (Dordrecht: Kluwer Academic Publishers, 1982).

Logical Investigations (New York: Humanities Press, 1970).

The Crisis of European Sciences and Transcendental Phenomenology (Evanston: Northwestern University Press, 1970).

'Philosophy as Rigorous Science' in (Quentin Laura, ed.) *Phenomenology and the Crisis of Philosophy* (New York: Harper Torchbooks, 1965), 71–147.

Hutchison, William R., *The Modernist Impulse in American Protestantism* (Oxford University Press, second edition, 1982; (first edition, Harvard University Press, 1976)).

Ingarden, Roman, *The Cognition of the Literary Work of Art* (Evanston, IL: Northwestern University Press, 1973).

The Literary Work of Art: an investigation on the borderlines of ontology, logic and theory of literature (Evanston, IL: Northwestern University Press, 1973).

Inglis, K. S., *Sacred Places: war memorials in the Australian landscape* (Melbourne: The Miegunyah Press, 1998).

Interpreter's Bible, The (twelve volumes) (Nashville, TN: Abingdon Press, 1952–7).

Irwin, Kevin W., *Context and Text: method in liturgical theology* (Collegeville: The Liturgical Press, 1994).

Iser, Wolfgang, *The Act of Reading: a theory of aesthetic response* (London: Routledge and Kegan Paul, 1978).

James, William, *The Varieties of Religious Experience: a study in human nature* (London: Collins (The Fontana Press), 1960).

Jameson, Fredric, *Postmodernism: or the cultural logic of late capitalism* (London: Verso, 1991).

The Prison-House of Language: a critical account of structuralism and Russian formalism (Princeton University Press, 1972).

Johansen, Jørgen Dines, 'Iconicity in Literature', *Semiotica* 110 1/2 (1996), 37–55.

'Let Sleeping Signs Lie: on signs, objects and communication', *Semiotica* 97 3/4 (1993), 271–95.

Johnson, Mark, *The Body in the Mind: the bodily basis of meaning, imagination and reason* (University of Chicago Press, 1987).

Johnston, William, *Mystical Theology: the science of love* (London: HarperCollins, 1995).

Kalaga, Wojciech H., 'Interpretation and Sign: semiotics versus hermeneutics', *S: European Journal for Semiotic Studies* 7 (1995), 559–586.

Kaldor, Peter, *Winds of Change: the experience of church in a changing Australia* (Homebush West, Sydney: Anzea Publishers, 1994).

Kaldor, Peter, John Bellamy, Ruth Powell, Keith Castle and Bronwyn Hughes, *Build My Church: trends and possibilities for Australian churches* (Adelaide: Openbook Publishers, 1999).

Shaping a Future: characteristics of vital congregations (Adelaide: Openbook Publishers, 1997).

Kaldor, Peter, Robert Dixon and Ruth Powell et al., *Taking Stock: a profile of Australian church attenders* (Adelaide: Openbook Publishers, 1999).

Kaldor, Peter, Ruth Powell, John Bellamy, Merilyn Correy, Keith Castle and Sandra Moore, *Views from the Pews: Australian church attenders speak out* (Adelaide: Openbook Publishers, 1995).

Kant, Immanuel, *Critique of Pure Reason* (Norman Kemp Smith, ed.) (London: Macmillan, 1992).

Kaufman, Gordon, *In Face of Mystery: a constructive theology* (Cambridge MA.: Harvard University Press, 1993).

Kavanagh, Aidan, *On Liturgical Theology* (New York: Pueblo Publishing Company, 1984).

'Primary Theology and Liturgical Act', *Worship* 57 (1983), 323–4.

'Thoughts on the New Eucharistic Prayers' in (R. Kevin Seasoltz, ed.) *Living Bread, Saving Cup: readings on the eucharist* (Collegeville, The Liturgical Press, 1982).

Kelliher, Margaret Mary, 'Hermeneutics in the Study of Liturgical Performance', *Worship* 67 (1993), 292–318.

'Liturgical Theology: a task and a method', *Worship* 62 (1988), 2–24.

'Liturgy: an ecclesial act of meaning', *Worship* 59 (1985), 482–497.

Kendon, Adam, *Conducting Interaction: patterns of behavior in focused encounters* (Cambridge University Press, 1990).

Kendon, Adam (ed.), *Nonverbal Communication, Interaction and Gesture: selections from Semiotica* (The Hague: Mouton Publishers, 1981).

Kittel, Gerhard and Gerhard Friedrich (eds.), *Theological Dictionary of the New Testament* (ten volumes) (Grand Rapids: Eerdmans, 1964–1976).

Kockelmans, Joseph J. (ed.), *Phenomenology: the philosophy of Edmund Husserl and its interpreters* (Garden City: Doubleday and Company, Inc., 1967).

Kristeva, Julia, *Revolution in Poetic Language* (New York: Columbia University Press, 1984).

'Semiotics: A Critical Science and/or a Critique of Science' in (Toril Moi, ed.), *The Kristeva Reader* (Oxford: Basil Blackwell, 1986), 74–88.

'The System and the Speaking Subject' in (Toril Moi, ed.), *The Kristeva Reader* (Oxford: Basil Blackwell, 1986), 24–33.

Krosnicki, Thomas A., 'Grace and Peace: greeting the assembly' in (Peter C. Finn and James M. Schellman, eds.) *Shaping English Liturgy: studies in honor of Archbishop Denis Hurley* (Washington, DC: The Pastoral Press, 1990).

Kuhn, Thomas, *The Structure of Scientific Revolutions* (University of Chicago Press, first edition 1962, second edition 1970).

LaCugna, Catherine Mowry, *God for Us: the Trinity and Christian life* (San Francisco: HarperCollins, 1991).

'Can Liturgy Ever Again Become a Source for Theology?', *Studia Liturgica* 19 (1989), 1–13.

Lakoff, George and Mark Johnson, *Metaphors We Live By* (University of Chicago Press, 1980).

Langer, Suzanne K., *Feeling and Form: a theory of art* (New York: Charles Scribner's Sons, 1953).

Lardner, Gerald V., 'Communication Theory and Liturgical Research' *Worship* 51 (1977), 299–307.

Larsen, Svend Erik, 'Greimas or Grimace?', *Semiotica* 75 1/2 (1989), 123–30.

Lathrop, Gordon W., *Holy People: a liturgical ecclesiology* (Minneapolis: Fortress Press, 1999).

Holy Things: a liturgical theology (Minneapolis: Fortress Press, 1993).

'New Pentecost or Joseph's Britches? reflections on the history and meaning of the worship *ordo* in the megachurches', *Worship* 72 (1998), 521–538.

Lawlor, Leonard, *Imagination and Chance: the difference between the thought of Ricoeur and Derrida* (Albany: State University of New York Press, 1992).

Lechte, John, *Julia Kristeva* (London: Routledge, 1990).

Levinas, Emmanuel, *Nine Talmudic Readings* (Bloomington: Indiana University Press, 1990).

    Totality and Infinity: an essay on exteriority (Pittsburgh: Duquesne University Press, 1969).

    'Meaning and Sense' in (Adrian T. Peperzak, Simon Critchley and Robert Bernasconi, eds.) *Emmanuel Levinas: basic philosophical writings* (Bloomington: Indiana University Press, 1996), 33–64.

    'The Trace of the Other' in (Mark C. Taylor, ed.) *Deconstruction in Context: literature and philosophy* (University of Chicago Press, 1969), 345–59.

Lindbeck, George A., *The Nature of Doctrine: religion and theology in a postliberal age* (Philadelphia: The Westminster Press, 1984).

Lonergan, Ray, *A Well Trained Tongue: a workbook for lectors* (Chicago: Liturgy Training Publications, 1982).

Longoni, Anna, 'Esoteric Conspiracies and the Interpretative Strategy' in (Rocco Capozzi, ed.) *Reading Eco: an anthology* (Bloomington: Indiana University Press, 1997), 210–216.

Lukken, Gerard, *Per Visibilia ad Invisibilia* (Kampen: Kok Pharos, 1994).

    'Die Bedeutung der Semiotik Greimas' und der Pariser Schule für die Liturgiewissenschaft', in (Wilfried Engemann and Rainer Volp, eds.) *Gib mir ein Zeichen: zur Bedeutung der Semiotik für theologische Praxis- und Denkmodelle* (Berlin: Walter de Gruyter, 1992), 187–206.

    'Semiotics and the Study of Liturgy', *Studia Liturgica* 17 (1987), 108–17.

Lukken, Gerard and Mark Searle, *Semiotics and Church Architecture* (Kampen: Kok Pharos, 1993).

Lyons, John, *Semantics*, 2 volumes (Cambridge University Press, 1977).

Lyotard, Jean-François, *The Postmodern Condition: a report on knowledge* (Minneapolis: University of Minnesota Press, 1984).

MacCannell, Juliet Flower, 'Kristeva's Horror', *Semiotica* 62 3/4 (1986), 325–55.

MacCormac, Earl R., *A Cognitive Theory of Metaphor* (Cambridge, MA: The MIT Press, 1985).

MacIntyre, Alasdair, 'God and the Theologians' in (John A. T. Robinson and David L. Edwards, eds.) *The Honest to God Debate* (London: SCM Press, 1963), 215–31.

    'The Virtues, the Unity of a Human Life, and the Concept of a Tradition' in (Stanley Hauerwas and L. Gregory Jones, eds.) *Why Narrative? Readings in narrative theology* (Grand Rapids: Eerdmans, 1989), 89–110.

Madison, G. B., 'Merleau-Ponty and Derrida: *la différEnce*' in (M. C. Dillon, ed.) *Écart & Différence: Merleau-Ponty and Derrida on seeing and writing* (New Jersey: Humanities Press, 1997), 94–111.

Mannion, M. Francis, 'Liturgy and the Present Crisis of Culture', *Worship* 62 (1988), 98–123.

Marr, David, *Patrick White: a life* (Sydney: Random House Australia, 1991).

Martimort, A. G., 'Structure and Laws of the Liturgical Celebration' in (A. G. Martimort, ed.) *The Church at Prayer: principles of the liturgy* (Collegeville: The Liturgical Press, 1987).

Martos, Joseph, *Doors to the Sacred: a historical introduction to the sacraments in the Christian church* (London: SCM Press, 1981).

Marty, Martin E., *Modern American Religion, volume 1: the irony of it all, 1893–1919* (University of Chicago Press, 1986).

Marty, Martin E. and R. Scott Appleby, 'Conclusion: an interim report on a hypothetical family' in (Martin E. Marty and R. Scott Appleby, eds.) *Fundamentalisms Observed* (University of Chicago Press, 1991), 814–42.

'The Fundamentalist Project: a user's guide' in (Martin E. Marty and R. Scott Appleby, eds.) *Fundamentalisms Observed* (University of Chicago Press, 1991), vii–xiii.

McCarthy, Thomas, Introduction to Jürgen Habermas, *The Philosophical Discourse of Modernity* (Cambridge, MA: The MIT Press, 1995).

McFague, Sallie, *Super, Natural Christians: how we should love nature* (Minneapolis: Fortress Press, 1997).

The Body of God: an ecological theology (London: SCM Press, 1993).

McGowan, John, *Postmodernism and its Critics* (Ithaca, NY: Cornell University Press, 1991).

McLuhan, Marshall, *Understanding Media: the extensions of man* (New York: McGraw-Hill Book Company, 1964).

McNeill, David, *Hand and Mind: what gestures reveal about thought* (University of Chicago Press, 1992).

Merleau-Ponty, Maurice, *Phenomenology of Perception* (London: Routledge, 1962).

Signs (Evanston, IL: Northwestern University Press, 1964).

The Primacy of Perception: and other essays on phenomenological psychology, the philosophy of art, history and politics (Evanston, IL: Northwestern University Press, 1964).

The Visible and the Invisible (Evanston, IL: Northwestern University Press, 1969).

Merz, Michael B., 'Gebetsformen der Liturgie' in (H. B. Meyer, et al., eds.) *Gottesdienst der Kirche: Gestalt des Gottesdienst* (Regensburg: Verlag Friedrich Pustet; second edition, 1990), vol. III, 97–130.

Mink, Louis O., 'History and Fiction as Modes of Comprehension', *New Literary History* 1 (1970), 541–58.

Miskotte, Kornelius H., *When the Gods are Silent* (London: Collins, 1967).

Morris, Charles, *Writings on the General Theory of Signs* (The Hague: Mouton, 1971).

Morris, Desmond, Peter Collett, Peter Marsh and Marie O'Shaughnessey, *Gestures, their Origins and Distribution* (New York: Stein and Day, 1979).

Muck, Herbert, 'Die Rezeption einer Dorfliturgie' in (Rainer Volp, ed.) *Zeichen: Semiotik in Theologie und Gottesdienst* (Munich and Mainz: Chr. Kaiser and Matthias Grünewald, 1982).

Neely, Alan, 'James Orr and the Question of Inerrancy' in *The Proceedings of the Conference on Biblical Inerrancy, 1987* (Nashville, TN: Broadman Press, 1987), 261–72.

Nerhardt, Göran, 'Incongruity and Funniness: toward a new descriptive model', in (Antony J. Chapman and Hugh C. Foot, eds.) *Humour and Laughter: theory, research and applications* (London: John Wiley and Sons, 1976), 55–62.

Nichols, Bridget, *Liturgical Hermeneutics: interpreting liturgical rites in performance* (Frankfurt: Peter Lang, 1994).

Niebuhr, H. Richard, *Christ and Culture* (London: Faber & Faber Limited, 1952).

Noll, Mark A., *The Scandal of the Evangelical Mind* (Grand Rapids: Eerdmans, 1994).

Norris, Christopher, *Deconstruction: theory and practice* (London: Routledge, 1991).

Ogden, C. K. and I. A. Richards, *The Meaning of Meaning: a study of the influence of language upon thought and the science of symbolism* (London: Routledge and Kegan Paul, 1923; second edition, Ark Paperbacks, 1985).

Ormiston, Gayle L., 'Peirce's Categories: structure of semiotic', *Semiotica* 19 3/4 (1977), 209–31.

Orr, James, *Revelation and Inspiration* (New York: Charles Scribner's Sons, 1910).

Otto, Rudolf, *The Idea of the Holy: an inquiry into the non-rational factor in the idea of the divine and its relation to the rational* (Oxford: Geoffrey Cumberledge, 1923).

Pailin, David, *God and the Processes of Reality: foundations of a credible theism* (London: Routledge, 1989).

The Anthropological Character of Theology: conditioning theological understanding (Cambridge University Press, 1990).

Passerin D'Entrèves, Maurizio and Seyla Benhabib (eds.), *Habermas and the Unfinished Project of Modernity* (Cambridge: Polity Press, 1996).

Paton, H. J., *The Modern Predicament* (London: George Allen and Unwin, 1955).

Patte, Daniel, 'Religion and Semiotics' in (Walter A. Koch, ed.) *Semiotics in the Individual Sciences* (Bochum: Universitätsverlag Dr Norbert Brockmeyer, 1990), 1–24.

Pearson, Clive, 'Christ and Context Down Under: mapping transTasman Christologies' in (Susan Emilsen and William W. Emilsen, eds.) *Mapping the Landscape: essays in Australian and New Zealand Christianity* (New York: Peter Lang, 2000), 296–317.

Peirce, Charles Sanders, *Collected Papers*, 8 volumes (Charles Hartshorne and Paul Weiss volumes 1–6, eds.) (Cambridge, MA: Harvard University Press 1931–5) (Arthur W. Burks, volumes 7, 8, ed.) (Cambridge, MA: Harvard University Press, 1958).

Pelikan, Jaroslav, *Imago Dei: the Byzantine apologia for icons* (Princeton University Press, 1990).

Petrilli, Susan, 'About and Beyond Peirce', *Semiotica* 124 3/4 (1999), 299–376.

'Dialogism and Interpretation in the Study of Signs', *Semiotica* 97 1/2 (1993), 103–18.

'The Problem of Signifying in Welby, Peirce, Vailati, Bakhtin'; Appendix 1 to Augusto Ponzio, *Man as a Sign*, 313–63.

'Toward Interpretation Semiotics' in (Rocco Capozzi, ed.) *Reading Eco: an anthology* (Bloomington: Indiana University Press, 1997), 121–36.

Pickstock, Catherine, *After Writing: on the liturgical consummation of philosophy* (Oxford: Blackwell Publishers Ltd., 1998).

Platts, Mark, *Ways of Meaning: an introduction to a philosophy of language* (London, Routledge and Kegan Paul, 1979).

Polanyi, Michael, *Personal Knowledge: toward a post critical philosophy* (University of Chicago Press, 1958).

Polanyi, Michael and Harry Prosch, *Meaning* (University of Chicago Press, 1975).

Ponzio, Augusto, *Man as a Sign: essays on the philosophy of language* (Berlin and New York: Mouton de Gruyter, 1990).

'Treating and Mistreating Semiotics: Eco's treatise on semiotics', *S: European Journal for Semiotic Studies* 9 (1997), 641–60.

Potok, Chaim, *My Name is Asher Lev* (Harmondsworth: Penguin Books, 1972).

Power, David N., *Unsearchable Riches: the symbolic nature of liturgy* (New York: Pueblo Publishing Company, 1984).

'People at Liturgy' in (Paul Brand, Edward Schillebeeckx and Anto Weiler, eds.) *Twenty Years of Concilium – retrospect and prospect* (*Concilium* 170) (New York and Edinburgh: The Seabury Press and T. & T. Clark Ltd., 1983), 8–14.

Preus, Robert, 'The Inerrancy of Scripture' in *The Proceedings of the Conference on Biblical Inerrancy, 1987* (Nashville, TN: Broadman Press, 1987), 47–60.

Pruyser, Paul, 'The Master Hand: psychological notes on pastoral blessing' in (William B. Oglesby Jr., ed.) *The New Shape of Pastoral Theology: essays in honour of Seward Hiltner* (Nashville, TN: Abingdon Press, 1969), 352–65.

Putnam, Hilary, *Exploring the Concept of Mind* (Iowa City: University of Iowa Press, 1986).

    Realism with a Human Face (Cambridge, MA: Harvard University Press, 1990).

    Reason, Truth and History (Cambridge University Press, 1981).

Quine, W. V. O., *Word and Object* (Cambridge, MA: MIT Press, 1960).

Ramsey, Ian T., 'The Logical Structure of Religious Language: models and disclosures' in (Ian T. Ramsey, ed.) *Words About God* (London: SCM Press, Ltd., 1971), 202–23.

Ransdell, Joseph, 'On Peirce's Conception of the Iconic Sign' in (Paul Bouissac, Michael Herzfeld and Roland Posner, eds.) *Iconicity: essays on the nature of culture* (Festschrift, Thomas A. Sebeok) (Tübingen: Stauffenburg Verlag, 1986), 51–74.

    'Some Leading Ideas of Peirce's Semiotic', *Semiotica* 19 3/4 (1977), 157–78.

Rappaport, Roy A., *Ritual and Religion in the Making of Humanity* (Cambridge University Press, 1999).

Raschke, Carl, 'Fire and Roses, or the Problem of Postmodern Religious Thinking' in (Phillipa Berry and Andrew Wernick, eds.) *Shadow of Spirit: postmodernism and religion* (London: Routledge, 1992).

Rauch, Irmengard, 'Openness, Eco and the End of Another Millennium' in (Rocco Capozzi, ed.) *Reading Eco: an anthology* (Bloomington: Indiana University Press, 1997), 130–46.

Reagan, Charles E., *Paul Ricoeur: his life and his work* (University of Chicago Press, 1996).

Ricoeur, Paul, *Essays on Biblical Interpretation* (London: SPCK, 1981).

    Hermeneutics and the Human Sciences (Cambridge University Press, 1981).

    Husserl: an analysis of his phenomenology (Evanston, IL: Northwestern University Press, 1967).

    Interpretation Theory: discourse and the surplus of meaning (Fort Worth, TX: The Texas Christian University Press, 1976).

    Lectures on Ideology and Utopia (New York: Columbia University Press, 1986).

    Oneself as Another (University of Chicago Press, 1992).

    Rule of Metaphor: multidisciplinary studies of the creation of meaning in language (University of Toronto Press, 1977).

    The Conflict of Interpretations (Evanston, IL: Northwestern University Press, 1974).

    The Symbolism of Evil (Boston: The Beacon Press, 1967).

    Time and Narrative, 3 volumes (Chicago University Press, 1984–8).

    'Evil: a challenge to philosophy and theology', *Journal of the American Academy of Religion* 53 (1985), 635–48.

    'Narrative Time', *Critical Inquiry* 7 (1980), 169–90.

Riemer, Andrew, *Sandstone Gothic: confessions of an accidental academic* (Sydney: Allen & Unwin, 1998).

Robinson, John A. T., *Honest to God* (London: SCM Press, 1963).

Rose, Gillian, 'Diremption of Spirit' in (Phillipa Berry and Andrew Wernick, eds.) *Shadow of Spirit: postmodernism and religion* (London: Routledge, 1992), 45–56.

Rose, Margaret A., *The Post-modern and the Post-industrial: a critical analysis* (Cambridge University Press, 1991).

Rothbarth, Mary K., 'Incongruity, Problem-Solving and Laughter', in (Antony J. Chapman and Hugh C. Foot, eds.) *Humour and Laughter: theory, research and applications* (London: John Wiley and Sons, 1976), 37–54.

Roudiez, Leon S., Introduction to Julia Kristeva's *Revolution in Poetic Language* (New York: Columbia University Press, 1984), 1–10.

Rouillard, Philippe, 'From Human Meal to Christian Eucharist' in (R. Kevin Seasoltz, ed.) *Living Bread, Saving Cup: readings on the eucharist* (Collegeville: The Liturgical Press, 1982), 126–57.

Rucker, Margaret, 'On the Principle of Disorder in Civilization: a socio-physical analysis of fashion change', *Semiotica* 91 1/2 (1992), 57–66.

Ruesch, J., 'Synopsis of the Theory of Human Communication', *Psychiatry* 16 (1953), 215–43.

Ruesch, J. and W. Kees, *Nonverbal Communication: notes on the visual perception of human relations* (Berkeley: University of California Press, 1956).

Ryle, Gilbert, 'The Theory of Meaning' in (C. A. Mace, ed.) *British Philosophy in the Mid-Century: a Cambridge symposium* (London: Allen and Unwin, 1957; second edition 1966).

Saliers, Don E., *Worship as Theology: foretaste of divine glory* (Nashville, TN: Abingdon Press, 1994).

'On the "Crisis" of Liturgical Language', *Worship* 44 (1970), 399–411.

Sandeen, Ernest R., *The Roots of Fundamentalism: British and American millenarianism 1800–1930* (University of Chicago Press, 1970).

Sauter, Gerhard, *The Question of Meaning: a theological and philosophical orientation* (Grand Rapids: Eerdmanns, 1995).

Sawyer, R. Keith, 'The Semiotics of Improvisation: the pragmatics of musical and verbal performance', *Semiotica* 108 3/4 (1995), 269–306.

Scharlemann, Robert P., (ed.), *Theology at the End of the Century: a dialogue on the postmodern with Thomas J. J. Altizer, Mark C. Taylor, Charles E. Winquist, Robert P. Scharlemann* (Charlottesville: University Press of Virginia, 1990).

Scherer, Klaus R. and Paul Ekman (eds.), *Handbook of Methods in Nonverbal Behavior Research* (Cambridge University Press, 1982).

Schermann, Josef, *Die Sprache im Gottesdienst* (Innsbruck/Vienna: Tyrolia Verlag, 1987).

Schillemans, Sandra, 'Umberto Eco and William of Baskerville', *Semiotica* 92 3/4 (1992), 259–85.

Schiwy, Günther, *Zeichen im Gottesdienst* (Munich: Chr. Kaiser Verlag and Kösel Verlag, 1976).

Schleifer, Ronald, *A. J. Greimas and the Nature of Meaning: linguistics, semiotics and discourse theory* (London: Croom Helm, 1987).

Schlick, Moritz, 'Meaning and Verification' in (Herbert Feigle and Wilfred Sellars, eds.) *Readings in Philosophical Analysis* (New York: Appleton-Century-Crofts, 1949), 146–70.

Schmemann, Alexander, *Introduction to Liturgical Theology* (Leighton Buzzard: The Faith Press, 1966).

The World as Sacrament (London: Darton, Longman and Todd, 1966).

'Theology and Liturgical Tradition' in (Massey H. Shepherd, ed.) *Worship in Scripture and Tradition* (New York: Oxford University Press, 1963), 165–78.

Schultz, Thomas R., 'A Cognitive–Developmental Analysis of Humour' in (Antony J. Chapman and Hugh C. Foot, eds.) *Humour and Laughter: theory, research and applications* (London: John Wiley and Sons, 1976).

Schutz, Alfred, *On Phenomenology and Social Relations: selected writings* (Helmut R. Wagner, ed.) (University of Chicago Press, 1970).

Schweizer, Eduard, 'Scripture–Tradition–Modern Interpretation' in *Neotestamentica* (Zurich: Zwingli Verlag, 1963), 203–35.

Searle, John R., *Expression and Meaning: studies in the theory of speech acts* (Cambridge University Press, 1979).

Speech Acts: an essay in the philosophy of language (Cambridge University Press, 1969).

'Meaning, Communication and Representation' in (Richard E. Grandy and Richard Warner, eds.) *Philosophical Grounds of Rationality: intentions, categories, ends* (Oxford: Clarendon Press, 1986), 209–26.

'What is a Speech Event?' in (J. R. Searle, ed.) *The Philosophy of Language* (Oxford University Press, 1986).

Searle, Mark, 'Liturgy as Metaphor', *Worship* 55 (1981), 98–120.

'New Tasks, New Methods: the emergence of pastoral liturgical studies', *Worship* 57 (1983), 291–308.

'Semper Reformanda: the opening and closing rites of the mass' in (Peter C. Finn and James M. Schellman, eds.) *Shaping English Liturgy: studies in honor of Archbishop Denis Hurley* (Washington, DC: The Pastoral Press, 1990), 53–92.

Searle, Mark (ed.), *Liturgy and Social Justice* (Collegeville: The Liturgical Press, 1980).

Sebeok, Thomas A., *The Sign and its Masters* (Lanham MD: University Press of America, second edition, 1989).

'Semiotics in the United States', in *The Semiotic Web, 1989* (Berlin and New York: Mouton de Gruyter, 1990).

Senn, Frank C., 'The Relation Between Theology and Liturgy', *Worship* 57 (1983), 329–32.

Sequeira, A. Ronald, *Klassische indische Tanzkunst und christliche Verkundigung: eine vergleichende religionsgeschichtlich-religionsphilosophische Studie* (Freiburg: Herder, 1978).

'Gottesdienst als menschliche Ausdruckshandlung' in (H. B. Meyer, et al., eds.) *Gottesdienst der Kirche: Gestalt des Gottesdienst* (Regensburg: Verlag Friedrich Pustet, second edition 1990), vol. III, 7–39.

'Liturgische Körper- und Gebärdensprache als Thema der Semiotik: Möglichkeiten und Grenzen' in (Wilfried Engemann and Rainer Volp, eds.) *Gib mir ein Zeichen: zur Bedeutung der Semiotik für theologische Praxis- und Denkmodelle* (Berlin: Walter de Gruyter, 1992).

'Liturgy and Dance: on the need for an adequate terminology', *Studia Liturgica* 17 (1987), 157–65.

'The Rediscovery of the Role of Movement in the Liturgy', in (Luis Maldonado and David Power, eds.) 'Symbol and Art in Worship' (*Concilium*, February 1980) (New York and Edinburgh: Seabury Press and T. & T. Clark, 1980), 112–19.

Seubert, Xavier John, 'The Trivialization of Matter: development of ritual incapacity', *Worship* 67 (1993), 38–53.

Shea, John, 'Storytelling and Religious Identity', *Chicago Studies* 21 (1982), 23–43.

Sheriff, John K., *The Fate of Meaning: Charles Peirce, structuralism and literature* (Princeton University Press, 1989).

Short, T. L., 'David Savan's Defense of Semiotic Realism', *Semiotica* 98 3/4 (1994), 243–63.

'Interpreting Peirce's Interpretant: a response to Lalor, Liszka, and Meyers', *Transactions of the Charles S. Peirce Society* 32 (1996), 488–541.

'Life Among the Legisigns', *Transactions of the Charles S. Peirce Society* 18 (1982), 285–310.

'Peirce's Semiotic Theory of the Self', *Semiotica* 91 1/2 (1992), 109–31.

'Semeiosis and Intentionality', *Transactions of the Charles S. Peirce Society* 17 (1981), 197–223.

'What They Said in Amsterdam: Peirce's semiotic today', *Semiotica* 60 1/2 (1986), 103–28.

'What's the Use?', *Semiotica* 122 1/2 (1998), 1–68.

Simmons, John K., 'Pilgrimage to the Wall', *Christian Century* 102 (1985), 998–1002.

Skagestad, Peter, 'The Mind's Machines: the Turing machine, the Memex and the personal computer', *Semiotica* 111 3/4 (1996), 217–43.

Smart, Ninian, *Dimensions of the Sacred: an anatomy of the world's beliefs* (London: HarperCollins, 1996).

The Concept of Worship (London: Macmillan Press Ltd., 1972).

Smith, Norman Kemp, *A Commentary to Kant's 'Critique of Pure Reason'* (New York: The Humanities Press, 1950, first edition 1918).

Soskice, Janet Martin, *Metaphor and Religious Language* (Oxford: Clarendon Press, 1985).

Spinks, Bryan, *The Sanctus in the Eucharistic Prayer* (Cambridge University Press, 1991).

'Christian Worship or Cultural Incantations', *Studia Liturgica* 12 (1977), 1–19.

'Two Seventeenth Century Examples of *Lex Credendi, Lex Orandi*: the baptismal and eucharistic theologies and liturgies of Jeremy Taylor and Richard Baxter', *Studia Liturgica* 21 (1991), 155–69.

Spivak, Gayatri Chakravorty, 'Translator's Preface' to Jacques Derrida's *Of Grammatology* (Baltimore: Johns Hopkins University Press, 1974).

Steiner, George, *Real Presences* (University of Chicago Press, 1989).

Stevick, Daniel B., 'Culture: the beloved antagonist', *Worship* 69 (1995), 290–305.

Stookey, Laurence Hull, *Calendar: Christ's time for the church* (Nashville, TN: Abingdon Press, 1996).

Strawson, P. F., 'On Referring' in (G. H. R. Parkinson, ed.) *The Theory of Meaning* (London: Oxford University Press, 1968), 61–85.

Stringer, Martin D., *On the Perception of Worship: the ethnography of worship in four Christian congregations in Manchester* (Birmingham University Press, 1999).

Sunday Missal, The: texts approved for use in Australia and New Zealand (Sydney: Wm Collins Pty Ltd., 1982).

'Situating Meaning in the Liturgical Text', *Bulletin of the John Rylands University Library of Manchester* 73 (1991), 181–94.

'Text, Context and Performance: hermeneutics and the study of worship', *Scottish Journal of Theology* 53 (2000), 365–79.

Taft, Robert, 'Liturgy as Theology', *Worship* 56 (1982), 113–17.

'The Response to the Berakah Award: anamnesis', *Worship* 59 (1985), 305–25.

'The Structural Analysis of Liturgical Units: an essay in methodology', *Worship* 52 (1978), 314–29.

Tarski, Alfred, 'The Semantic Conception of Truth and the Foundations of Semantics' in (Herbert Feigle and Wilfred Sellars, eds.) *Readings in Philosophical Analysis* (New York: Appleton-Century-Crofts, 1949), 52–84.

Taylor, Charles, *Human Agency and Language: philosophical papers 1* (Cambridge University Press, 1985).

Philosophy and the Human Sciences: philosophical papers 2 (Cambridge University Press, 1985).

Sources of the Self: the making of the modern identity (Cambridge University Press, 1989).

Taylor, Mark C., 'Discrediting God', *Journal of the American Academy of Religion* 62 (1994), 603–23.

'Postmodern Times' in (Michael Griffith and James Tulip, eds.) *Proceedings of the Religion, Literature and Arts Conference, 1995* (Sydney: The RLA Project, 1995), 75–96.

'Reframing Postmodernisms' in (Philippa Berry and Andrew Wernick, eds.) *Shadow of Spirit: postmodernism and religion* (London: Routledge, 1992), 11–29.

Thurian, Max and Geoffrey Wainwright (eds.), *Baptism and Eucharist: ecumenical convergence in celebration* (Geneva and Grand Rapids: World Council of Churches and William B. Eerdmans, 1983).

Tolstoy, Leo, *A Confession, The Gospel in Brief, and What I Believe* (translated Aylmer Maude, London, 1940).

Toulmin, Stephen, *Cosmopolis: the hidden agenda of modernity* (University of Chicago Press, 1990).

The Uses of Argument (Cambridge University Press, 1964).

Tracy, David, *Blessed Rage for Order: the new pluralism in theology* (Minneapolis: The Seabury Press, 1975).

The Analogical Imagination: Christian theology and the culture of pluralism (London: SCM Press, 1981).

Troeger, Thomas H., 'The Social Power of Myth as a Key to Preaching on Social Issues' in (Arthur van Seters, ed.) *Preaching as a Social Act: theology and practice* (Nashville, TN: Abingdon Press, 1988), 205–34.

Turbayne, Colin Murray, *The Myth of Metaphor* (Columbia, SC: University of South Carolina Press, 1970).

Turner, Victor, 'Passages, Margins and Poverty: religious symbols of *communitas*', *Worship*, 46 (1972), 390–412, 482–94.

Underhill, Evelyn, *Worship* (London: Nisbet & Co., 1939).

Uniting in Worship: Leaders' Book (Melbourne: The Joint Board of Christian Education, 1988).

Updike, John, *A Month of Sundays* (London: Penguin Books, 1975).

Vagaggini, Cyprian, *Theological Dimensions of the Liturgy: a general treatise on the theology of the liturgy* (Collegeville: The Liturgical Press, 1976).

van Buren, Paul M., *The Secular Meaning of the Gospel Based on an Analysis of its Languages* (London: SCM Press, 1963).

Vincie, Catherine, 'The Liturgical Assembly: review and assessment', *Worship* 67 (1993), 123–44.

Volp, Rainer, *Liturgik: die Kunst Gott zu feiern*, 2 volumes (Gütersloh: Verlagshaus Mohn, 1991–3).

'Grenzmarkierung und Grenzüberschreitung: der Gottesdienst als semiotische Aufgabe' in (Wilfried Engemann and Rainer Volp, eds.) *Gib mir ein Zeichen: zur Bedeutung der Semiotik für theologische Praxis- und Denkmodelle* (Berlin: Walter de Gruyter, 1992).

Volp, Rainer (ed.), *Zeichen: Semiotik in Theologie und Gottesdienst* (Munich and Mainz: Chr. Kaiser and Matthias Grünewald, 1982).

Wainwright, Geoffrey, *Doxology: the praise of God in worship, doctrine and life* (London: Epworth Press, 1980).

'A Language in Which we Speak to God', *Worship* 57 (1983), 309–21.

'Christian Worship and Western Culture', *Studia Liturgica* 12 (1977), 20–36.

Waismann, Friedrich, 'Verifiability' in (G. H. R. Parkinson, ed.) *The Theory of Meaning* (London: Oxford University Press, 1968), 35–60.

Wallace, Mark I., *The Second Naiveté: Barth, Ricoeur and the New Yale Theology* (Macon GA: Mercer University Press, 1990).

Walton, Janet, *Art and Worship* (Wilmington: Michael Glazier, 1988).

Warren, Michael, 'The Worshiping Assembly: possible zone of cultural contestation', *Worship* 63 (1989), 2–16.

Watt, W. C., 'Transient Ambiguity', *Semiotica* 101 1/2 (1994), 5–39.

Webber, Robert, (ed.), *The Complete Library of Christian Worship* (Nashville, TN: The Star Song Publishing Company, 1993–4).

Weber, Max, *Economy and Society: an outline of interpretive sociology* (Berkeley: University of California Press, 1978).

   The Protestant Ethic and the Spirit of Capitalism (London: Routledge, 1992).

   'Science as Vocation' in (H. H. Gerth and C. W. Mills, eds.) *From Max Weber: essays in sociology* (Routledge and Kegan Paul, 1974).

Wheelwright, Philip, *The Burning Fountain: a study in the language of symbolism* (Bloomington: Indiana University Press, 1968).

White, Hayden, *Metahistory: the historical imagination in nineteenth-century Europe* (Baltimore: The Johns Hopkins University Press, 1973).

White, James F., *Documents of Christian Worship: descriptive and interpretive sources* (Edinburgh: T. & T. Clark, 1992).

   Introduction to Christian Worship (Nashville, TN: Abingdon Press, revised edition 1990).

White, James and Susan White, *Church Architecture: building and renovating for christian worship* (Nashville, TN: Abingdon Press, 1988).

White, Patrick, *The Vivisector* (Harmondsworth: Penguin Books, 1973).

White, Susan J., *Christian Worship and Technological Change* (Nashville, TN: Abingdon Press, 1994).

Willey, Basil, *Nineteenth-Century Studies: Coleridge to Matthew Arnold* (Harmondsworth: Penguin Books, 1964).

   The Seventeenth Century Background (Harmondsworth: Penguin Books, 1962).

Williams, Rowan, 'Hegel and the Gods of Postmodernity' in (Philippa Berry and Andrew Wernick, eds.) *Shadow of Spirit: postmodernism and religion* (London: Routledge, 1992), 72–80.

Willimon, William, *Worship as Pastoral Care* (Nashville, TN: Abingdon Press, 1979).

Wimsatt, W. K. and M. Beardsley, 'The Intentional Fallacy' in (W. K. Wimsatt Jr., ed.) *The Verbal Icon: studies in the meaning of poetry* (Lexington: University of Kentucky Press, 1970).

Winquist, Charles E., 'The Silence of the Real: theology at the end of the century' in (Robert P. Scharlemann, ed.) *Theology at the End of the Century: a dialogue on the postmodern with Thomas J. J. Altizer, Mark C. Taylor, Charles E. Winquist, Robert P. Scharlemann* (Charlottesville: University Press of Virginia, 1990).

Witten, Marsha G., 'Accommodation to Secular Norms in Preaching: findings of a study of sermons from the Presbyterian Church (USA) and the Southern Baptist Convention', *Homiletic* 19 2 (1994), 1–3.

Wren, Brian, *What Language Shall I Borrow: God-talk in worship, a male response to feminist theology* (London: SCM Press, 1989).

Young, H. Edwin, 'Response to J. I. Packer' in *The Proceedings of the Conference on Biblical Inerrancy, 1987* (Nashville, TN: Broadman Press, 1987), 146–51.

Zimmerman, Joyce Ann, *Liturgy as Language of Faith: a liturgical methodology in the mode of Paul Ricoeur's textual hermeneutics* (Lanham: University Press of America, 1988).

Index